Employee Resourcing

Stephen Taylor is a senior lecturer in HRM at Manchester Metropolitan University. Formerly he taught personnel management and industrial relations at the Manchester School of Management (UMIST). Prior to these appointments he held a number of personnel management posts in the hotel industry and the National Health Service. He has been an associate examiner for the CIPD graduateship qualification since 1992 (Employee Resourcing and Core Personnel and Development). His research focuses principally on the objectives and effectiveness of remuneration policies, with particular reference to occupational pension schemes.

Other titles in the series:

Core Personnel and Development
Mick Marchington and Adrian Wilkinson

Employee Development
2nd edition
Rosemary Harrison

Employee Relations
2nd edition
John Gennard and Graham Judge

Employee Reward
2nd edition
Michael Armstrong

Essentials of Employment Law
6th edition
David Lewis and Malcolm Sargeant

Managing Activities
Michael Armstrong

Managing Financial Information
David Davies

Managing in a Business Context
David Farnham

Managing Information and Statistics
Roland and Frances Bee

Managing People
Jane Weightman

Personnel Practice
2nd edition
Malcolm Martin and Tricia Jackson

The Chartered Institute of Personnel and Development is the leading publisher of books and reports for personnel and training professionals, students, and all those concerned with the effective management and development of people at work. For details of all our titles, please contact the Publishing Department:

tel 020–8263 3387
fax 020–8263 3850
e-mail publish@cipd.co.uk

The catalogue of all CIPD titles can be viewed on the CIPD website:

www.cipd.co.uk/publications

PEOPLE AND ORGANISATIONS

Employee Resourcing

STEPHEN TAYLOR

Chartered Institute of Personnel and Development

First published in 1998

Reprinted 1998, 1999, 2000, 2001

Design by Curve

Typeset by Fakenham Photosetting Ltd, Fakenham, Norfolk

Printed in Great Britain by
The Cromwell Press, Wiltshire

British Library Cataloguing in Publication Data

A catalogue record for this book is available from the British Library

ISBN 0-85292-624-3

The views expressed in this book are the author's own and may not necessarily reflect those of the CIPD.

Chartered Institute of Personnel and Development, CIPD House, Camp Road, London SW19 4UX
Tel: 020 8971 9000 Fax: 020 8263 3333
E-mail: cipd@cipd.co.uk
Website: www.cipd.co.uk
Incorporated by Royal Charter. Registered Charity No. 1079797

Contents

Editors' foreword

People hold the key to more productive and efficient organisations. The way in which people are managed and developed at work has major effects upon quality, customer service, organisational flexibility and costs. Personnel and development practitioners can play a major role in creating the framework for this to happen, but ultimately they are dependent upon line managers and other employees for its delivery. It is important that personnel and development specialists gain the commitment of others and pursue professional and ethical practices that will bring about competitive success. There is also a need to evaluate the contribution that personnel and development approaches and processes make for organisational success, and to consider ways of making these more effective. Such an approach is relevant for all types of practitioner – personnel and development generalists and specialists, line managers, consultants and academics.

This is one of a series of books under the title *People and Organisations*. The series provides essential guidance and points of reference for all those involved with people in organisations. It aims to provide the main body of knowledge and pointers to the required level of skills for personnel and development practitioners operating at a professional level in all types and sizes of organisation.

The series has been specially written to satisfy the professional standards defined by the Chartered Institute of Personnel and Development (CIPD) in the United Kingdom and the Republic of Ireland. It includes a volume designed for those seeking the Certificate in Personnel Practice (CPP), which often provides an access route into the professional scheme. The series also responds to a special need in the United Kingdom for texts structured to cover the knowledge aspects of new and revised National and Scottish Vocational Qualifications (N/SVQs) in personnel and training development.

Three 'fields' of standards have to be satisfied in order to gain graduate membership of the CIPD: (i) core management (ii) core personnel and development and (iii) any four from a range of more than 20 generalist and specialist electives. The three fields can be tackled in any order, or indeed all at the same time. A range of learning routes is available: full or part time educational course, flexible learning methods or direct experience. The standards may be assessed by educational and competence-based methods. The books in the series are suitable for supporting all methods of learning.

The series starts by addressing *core personnel and development* and four generalist electives: employee reward, employee resourcing, employee relations and employee development. Together, these cover the personnel and development knowledge requirements for graduateship of the CIPD. These also cover the knowledge aspects of training and development and personnel N/SVQs at Level 4.

Core Personnel and Development, by chief examiner Professor Mick Marchington and his colleague Adrian Wilkinson, addresses the essential knowledge and understanding required of all personnel and development professionals, whether generalists or specialists. Practitioners need to be aware of the wide range of circumstances in which personnel and development processes take place and consequently the degree to which particular approaches and practices may be appropriate in specific circumstances. In addressing these matters the book covers the core personnel and development standards of the CIPD, as well as providing an essential grounding for human resource management options within business and management studies degrees. The authors are both extremely well-known researchers in the field, working at one of the UK's leading management schools.

Employee Reward (2nd edn), by chief examiner Michael Armstrong, has been written specially to provide extensive subject coverage for practitioners required by both the CIPD's new generalist standards for employee reward and the personnel N/SVQ Level 4 unit covering employee reward. It is the first book on employee reward to be produced specifically for the purposes of aiding practitioners to gain accredited UK qualifications.

Employee Relations (2nd edn), by chief examiner Professor John Gennard and associate examiner Graham Judge, explores the link between the corporate environment and the interests of buyers and sellers of labour. It also demonstrates how employers (whether or not they recognise unions) can handle the core issues of bargaining, group problem-solving, redundancy, participation, discipline and grievances, and examines how to evaluate the latest management trends.

Employee Development (2nd edn), by chief examiner Rosemary Harrison, is a major new text which extends the scope of her immensely popular earlier book of the same name to establish the role of human resource development (HRD) and its direction into the next century. After reviewing the historical roots of HRD, she considers its links with business imperatives, its national and international context, the management of the HRD function, and ways of aligning HRD with the organisation's performance management system. Finally, she provides a framework that sets HRD in the context of organisational learning, the key capabilities of an enterprise and the generation of the new knowledge it needs.

Employee Resourcing, by Stephen Taylor, has also been designed specifically to address the IPD and N/SVQ standards in the area. The author draws upon his wide academic and personnel background to produce a book that examines practical issues but takes into account material from an extensive literature review. He presents readers with a series of options, encouraging them to consider those that are most appropriate in the specific circumstances of their own workplace. This results in a book that is both very readable and extremely comprehensive in its coverage.

Although each of these books is carefully tailored to the CIPD and N/SVQ standards, Malcolm Martin and Tricia Jackson's *Personnel Practice* (2nd edn) is focused on the needs of those studying for the Certificate in Personnel Practice. This also gives a thorough grounding in the basics of personnel activities. The authors are experienced practitioners and lead tutors for one of the UK's main providers of CIPD flexible learning programmes.

In drawing upon a team of distinguished and experienced writers and practitioners, the *People and Organisations* series aims to provide a range of up-to-date, practical texts indispensable to those pursuing CIPD and N/SVQ qualifications in personnel and development. The books will also prove valuable to those who are taking other human resource management and employment relations courses, or who are simply seeking greater understanding in their work.

Mick Marchington   *Mike Oram*

Preface

I have been a chief examiner to the Institute of Personnel Management (IPM), its successor the Institute of Personnel and Development (IPD), and its successor again, the Chartered Institute of Personnel and Development, for over 15 years. Throughout that time, I have made every effort to promote a single key message: that human resource (HR) people need a *business* focus in everything they do. Effective personnel management is not an altruistic vehicle for doing good. Nor should professional practitioners be so people-focused in their values that they distrust – or even actively oppose – some of the competitive strategies that organisations today typically need to adopt in order to survive and prosper. The whole mission and rationale of the CIPD rightly stress the central importance of people as contributors to strategic goals, not as ends in themselves. Such an emphasis is also central to the Professional Standards, such as Employee Resourcing – and to the way that I perceive and perform my work as chief examiner.

The argument is worth emphasising. Many new recruits to HR appear reluctant to see, or to accept, that the role of the function is to enhance organisational performance through the effective mobilisation of employee capabilities. Far too often they take the 'side' of the staff against the organisation, as it were, and may even appear to undermine some of the (admittedly, unpleasant) initiatives that organisations have had to take in recent years in order to secure a competitive advantage.

Of course, I acknowledge that such initiatives can be taken too far; at one time it seemed that downsizing was almost the only 'solution' to the corporate chaos of the early 1990s. On the other hand, it cannot be legitimately argued that downsizing is inherently wicked or foolish, especially as much of it was a necessary adjustment to the overstaffing and corporate slack of the 1980s. In an environment in which organisations do not have to compete, or in which the competition is sluggish and half-hearted, then the incentive to maximise people performance is much reduced: jobs are created without any thought that the job-holders might genuinely add value strategically; structures become tall and multi-layered; adherence to procedures takes priority over empowerment and delegation; customers are ignored or denigrated; people are underutilised and complacency rules.

Downsizing, de-layering, empowerment, customer-facing values and business process re-engineering all help to remove and prevent these tendencies. Sometimes they work and sometimes they do not. Much depends on top-management consistency and leadership, or whether the organisation acknowledges its crisis (or reverts to denial), and on whether self-interest is allowed to take precedence over corporate purposes. The role of personnel – I say again – is to make a strategic contribution to survival and growth, not to remain indifferent or to subvert from the sidelines.

These views, though passionately held, are not unique. According to CEOs interviewed on behalf of the Personnel Standards Lead Body in 1993, too many personnel professionals 'emphasise specialist skills to the detriment of both business understanding and the ability to act as an accepted consultant'. They show

- an overconscious concern with rules and procedures, amounting sometimes to inappropriate policing and blocking actions

- a tendency to introduce systems and procedures that fail because they do not fit the business or are not owned by management

- an indiscriminate approach to being a 'good employer'.

Another source of support is the one-page article written for *People Management* by Rob Kuijpers, CEO of DHL Worldwide Express (published 18 May 1995). Kuijpers advances three uncomfortable perceptions:

- HR does not contribute to the business – some HR people have more allegiance to the HR function than to the organisations they are supposed to work for.

- HR does not know what is going on at the battle front – they are seen as support people who do not support, especially when they are needed most.

- Many HR people do not think strategically – and do not link their activities closely with the furtherance of strategic business objectives.

These strictures do not apply to all HR practitioners, but they do often have substance, and they do reflect *customer perceptions* about HR. If this is what customers think, then it is no good complaining that customers are 'wrong' or (at best) 'misguided': we must do something to justify a change of view.

For a change of customer perception to be achieved, and for the status, influence and power of the HR function to be correspondingly enhanced, then the whole of HR activity must actively demonstrate a business orientation, a results-driven philosophy, a customer-focused set of priorities, and a creatively restless search for continuous improvement in the advancement of corporate goals. HR must not act as if the search for some professional paradigm of 'best practice' is its principal obsession, irrespective of the resources available. *HR people must create, support, promote and reinforce mechanisms that will help the organisation achieve its mission, vision, strategic goals and objectives*: it is not HR's place to undermine, oppose or sabotage these mechanisms simply because they do not 'fit' the values of the people in the HR department.

What is particularly impressive about Stephen Taylor's book is that it entirely reflects this philosophy about HR in general and employee resourcing in particular. In preparing the book, we took particular comfort from the following passage in the (then) IPD's own 1995 position paper, *People Make the Difference*:

> Personnel and development professionals face a complex challenge. They need to administer employment systems effectively in compliance with the law and recognised standards of fairness and good practice. However, that isn't enough. *While systems are very important to the smooth running of organisations, they don't make the difference between success and failure in the market place* [my emphasis]. To add value, practitioners need to:
>
> • understand and share the objectives and business methodology of their managerial colleagues
>
> • import best practice from outside the organisation
>
> • build and measure strategic capability through the development of the capacity of people
>
> • define and promote the values of the organisation.

The realisation that organisations must engage the commitment of their employees in order to meet customer needs is a key emergent dimension of the resourcing and people-management policies in today's successful organisations. In a major DTI-funded study (reported in *People Management*, 25 September 1997), it was found that the common threads running through the HR systems for these organisations are:

• *shared goals*: understanding the business

• *shared culture*: agreed values binding people together

• *shared learning*: a commitment by employees to continuous improvement

• *shared effort*: one business driven by flexible teams

• *shared information*: effective communication throughout the company.

These threads have helped to bind together the approaches discussed by Stephen Taylor, and their reflection throughout the book is one of the major reasons why *Employee Resourcing* is so welcome. Apart from a solid conceptual foundation, *Employee Resourcing* manages effectively to integrate theory with practice to an extent that is elsewhere often promised but seldom fulfilled. It is, in short, the sort of book that I wish I had written myself.

Ted Johns

CIPD chief examiner, employee resourcing

Acknowledgements

The writing of this book has been made possible through the help and support of many friends and colleagues. Particular thanks are due to Ted Johns, Mick Marchington, Mike Oram and Matthew Reisz, who read through the first drafts of each chapter, suggesting improvements and generally giving encouragement. In the case of Ted Johns, assistance went further, with the contribution of material on interviewing which has been included in Chapter 6. Thanks must also be given to the following, whose provision of ideas and information has been of great assistance: Catherine Allen, Oonagh Barry, Louise Bartlett, Margaret Bird, Carol Brookes, Noel Burton, John Berridge, Liz Callejon, Jill Earnshaw, John Goodman, Irena Grugulis, Cecilia Hartley, Craig Lanham, Helen Look, Pamela Nichol, Ivan Robertson, Jill Rubery, Nigel Singleton, Bob Smethurst, Claire Sweeney, Susan Waller, Adrian Wilkinson and Marcus Young.

Part 1
CONTEXT

1 Introduction

Effective hiring and firing, attracting the best candidates, reducing staff turnover and improving employee performance are fundamental management functions. They are as relevant for a small family business as they are for a major international PLC. They are, however, carried out in a variety of different ways, and people have differing views about which approach is best used in different circumstances. These functions have come to form the backbone of generalist personnel and development (P&D) work. The ability to make sure that they are done well has thus become a basic requirement for any successful P&D career. Together they form the body of managerial skill and knowledge described by the Chartered Institute of Personnel and Development (CIPD) as 'the employee resourcing function'.

The principal aim of this book is to act as a general, comprehensive introduction to the learning material contained in the current CIPD professional standards for employee resourcing. However, it is designed not only for the use of students studying for CIPD qualifications. It has also been written to meet the needs of personnel and development practitioners, general managers and consultants who are interested in refreshing and updating their knowledge or in thinking about different approaches to familiar resourcing problems. It will also be of interest to those studying for other qualifications which cover employee resourcing issues.

The primary purpose of this introductory chapter is to define the term 'employee resourcing' and to explain both how it relates to other areas of P&D activity and how it supports the achievement of wider organisational objectives. In the process, the major themes that run through the book are introduced, as well as some of the most significant environmental trends that employee resourcing specialists need to understand and relate to the circumstances of their own organisations. These, like many of the issues covered in the book, are matters about which people have different views. Inevitably, it is thus impossible to write about them neutrally or in a manner that takes into account the many distinctive perspectives underpinning the thoughts and deeds of practitioners, commentators and other authors working in the employee resourcing field. This book is no exception. In its treatment of specific issues, in the significance given to some topics in comparison with others and in its general frame of reference, it reflects the background, prejudices and experiences of the author formed during several years as a P&D researcher, teacher and practitioner. These are matters on which all readers, but particularly CIPD students, are invited and encouraged to form their own views. To facilitate this process, the author's key assumptions and perspectives are therefore also briefly outlined in this chapter.

THE EMPLOYEE RESOURCING CONTRIBUTION

Employee resourcing is the broadest of the four generalist modules that those studying for the CIPD graduateship qualification can choose to study. Because, as a whole, it is less specialised than employee reward, employee relations and employee development, it is also harder to define meaningfully. Indeed, in some ways it is probably best defined simply as the range of activities undertaken by P&D professionals that do not readily fit into the other three main generalist areas. At base, however, it covers the range of methods and approaches used by employers in resourcing their organisations in such a way as to enable them to meet their key goals. The employee resourcing function is thus probably best defined as a set of management activities that facilitate the achievement of three fundamental groups of P&D objectives: staffing, performance and administration

Staffing
Staffing objectives are concerned with ensuring that an organisation is able to call on the services of sufficient numbers of staff to meet its objectives. These people may be employed in a variety of different ways, but one way or another they must be able to carry out the tasks and duties needed for the organisation to function effectively. This is often summed up in the phrase 'Securing the services of the right people, in the right place, at the right time'. To achieve this, there is a need to recruit new employees, to retain existing employees and, on occasions, to dismiss others.

Performance
Performance objectives pick up from the point at which the staffing objectives have been achieved. The aim here is to ensure that, once assembled, the workforce is absent as little as possible, and is well motivated and willing to perform to the best of its ability. To achieve this, there is a need first to monitor individual and group performance and then to develop means by which it can be improved.

Administration
Administration objectives are concerned with ensuring that the employment relationships formed are managed in accordance with the law, professional ethics and natural justice. In order to achieve these

aims consistently, it is necessary to write P&D policies, to develop accepted procedures and to draw up other documents relating to the employment of individuals (eg job descriptions, offer letters, contracts, and disciplinary warnings).

All the major components that make up the employee resourcing function are each thus concerned with meeting one or more of these three objectives. The major activities are as follows:

- forecasting the demand for employees
- forecasting the supply of employees
- drawing up job descriptions and person specifications
- recruiting new employees
- selecting new employees
- issuing offer letters and contracts of employment
- the induction and socialisation of new employees
- monitoring employee performance
- improving employee performance
- reducing absence
- reducing employee turnover
- managing redundancies
- managing retirements
- carrying out dismissals.

If employee resourcing activity is to make a real, long-term contribution to the success of an organisation, it is insufficient simply to set out to achieve the above tasks and objectives. Because the environment is continually changing and developing, and because there are always other organisations with which it is necessary to compete, there is always a need to look for ways of improving the methods used to achieve fundamental resourcing objectives. In other words, there is a need regularly to review the policies and practices used in order to maximise the contribution of the employee resourcing function to organisational success. Where the environment has changed, or looks likely to change in the future, it is thus necessary to adjust or rethink the approaches used from time to time, with a view to meeting the requirements of new business circumstances. The objectives do not change, but over time the tools used to achieve them may do so, and to a considerable degree.

Employee resourcing specialists must therefore evaluate their activities, periodically if not continually, in order to establish whether or not improvements could or should be made to their policies and practices. Key skills thus include the development of a capacity for constructive criticism, as well as a knowledge and understanding of the various possible courses of action that could be taken in any given situation.

It is helpful, when formally evaluating specific resourcing policies and practices, to think about them with three basic questions in mind:

- Are we achieving our objectives as effectively as we could?

- Are we achieving them as efficiently as we could?

- Are we achieving them as fairly as we could?

These three broad criteria (effectiveness, efficiency and fairness) underpin much of the evaluative material included in this book. Where the literature indicates that a variety of different approaches is or can be used to tackle a particular set of resourcing objectives or problems, each of the major options is assessed and its merits considered against the backdrop of different environmental circumstances and with these three basic considerations in mind. Courses of action are thus evaluated not in isolation but in comparison with other possible approaches. This reflects what has to happen in practice. Perfection is rarely possible: what is important is that the best approach is taken when compared with other options. It is also often necessary to compare taking action in a particular field with the results of not taking action, or with the approaches used by competitor organisations.

> Which employee resourcing activities does your organisation formally evaluate on a regular basis? What are the main criteria used?

ENVIRONMENTAL TRENDS

The major causes of the need to re-evaluate and alter employee resourcing practices are developments in the business environment. These are difficult to summarise succinctly because they always affect different organisations in different ways; some have to respond swiftly and radically, while others remain untouched. In the following chapter, two of the major trends (internationalisation and the increase in non-standard working) and their implications are examined in some detail. Elsewhere in the book others are referred to in the context of specific issues. The aim here is thus simply to flag some of the trends of which employee resourcing specialists need to be aware because of their long-term implications for the carrying out of the management activities described above.

Technology

There can be few organisations that have not changed their operations considerably over the past generation in response to technological developments. The impact has been, and continues to be, particularly pronounced in manufacturing, where the manner in which components are designed and made, and products assembled, has often been revolutionised and then revolutionised again in the space of a few years. Furthermore, of course, the nature of the products themselves has frequently also had to change in response to technological innovation and development. The effect in other sectors has been profound, too, and can be expected to continue to be so, and even to accelerate as the twenty-first century unfolds. Gennard (1992) identifies developments in the fields of computers, lasers and telecommunications as of prime importance in reshaping industrial activity. To these could be added linked developments in the fields of transport and, more recently, biotechnology, both of which also continue to have a dramatic impact.

The specific effects on employee resourcing practice, like the changes themselves, vary greatly from organisation to organisation. However, there are a number of common threads running across several industrial sectors. First and foremost there are the fundamental changes that technological developments impose on the way work is organised. New machinery requires new skills, and the inability of an existing workforce to adapt can mean bringing in new people and dispensing with the services of others. This may be the case where relatively minor changes are brought in, such as new software for use in an administration or distribution operation, as well as where major new production processes are being introduced. Secondly, the make-up of specific jobs or the terms and conditions on which people are employed may change. One person may be able to carry out the tasks formerly looked after by three. Alternatively, it may be possible or necessary to subcontract work previously undertaken in-house, or to bring people in on temporary contracts during the period in which major changes are occurring. Technology brings with it the need to resource the organisation with new skills, and has often created whole new occupations and career paths. Established labour markets may thus alter, with some groups who were once hard to recruit now in plentiful supply, and vice versa. This will affect recruitment and selection practices while also altering the extent to which the retention of particular staff groups is significant.

Demography
A long-term trend which is yet to have the impact that many have predicted is the changing structure of the population. Birth rates in the UK have fluctuated over time, reaching a peak in the mid-1960s, falling in the 1970s and then rising again in the 1980s. However, current projections suggest a long period of slow decline in the foreseeable future. This trend, combined with a falling death rate, means that the population as a whole will age steadily over the next 50 years. Predictions vary as to how great an impact these trends will have on the total number of people available for work, for this depends not just on raw demographic statistics but also on immigration and participation and retirement rates, as well as the numbers in full-time education. Nevertheless, it is generally agreed that we shall see a change in the age profile of the working population, with fewer younger people available for employment than is currently the case (Farnham 1995: 62–3).

The general social implications are very significant, as the trends will lead to a substantial decline in the ratio of working people to retired people, which creates problems for the long-term financing of retirement income. However, there are also potential implications for employers seeking to resource their organisations. Of these the most significant is the likelihood that demand for certain types of labour will increasingly outstrip supply. The problem will probably be most severe for employers who require people with specialised technical skills. In addition there is likely to be a more general 'shortage' of younger workers, making it harder than it is at present to secure the services of bright, keen, flexible and mobile graduates with the long-term potential to develop into senior roles.

Employers could simply respond to this by bidding up pay rates and by offering fast-track career development to these groups. To do so, however, would be to take the path that is most expensive – and hence potentially uncompetitive – over the long term. There are other possible courses of action, including a number that are described later in this book. There is the possibility of recruiting more effectively, training existing staff rather than simply buying in new skills, developing a more flexible workforce, and a whole raft of measures that are aimed at retaining employees once they have developed precious organisation-specific skills. Another much-mooted approach involves trying to tap in to parts of the labour market as yet underrepresented, by which is usually meant women with children who do not work, retired people and younger people in higher education. To accommodate these groups there is clearly a need to consider developing new and flexible working arrangements and to provide some form of childcare facilities. In general terms, therefore, demographic shortfalls require employers to give more attention than is often the case now to how the organisation competes in key labour markets and to the way in which work is organised.

Trade unions

Another underlying, long-term trend that affects some industrial sectors more than others is the reduction in the number of employees joining trade unions, and hence a reduction in the collective negotiation of terms and conditions of employment. The proportion covered by collective agreements is always higher than the number who join unions, but both figures have now been in steady decline since 1980. Whereas 20 years ago over half the workforce were members of unions, the figure is now under 30 per cent and continues to fall each year. The result has been the disappearance of union representation from some workplaces and a more general marginalisation in others. Explanations for the trend take many forms, ranging from the combination of relatively high unemployment with low inflation, the shift in employment from manufacturing and the public sector to services and the private sector, and the effect of anti-trade-union legislation, to the development of better management techniques. The truth probably lies with each to an extent, and with other factors too. What is certain is that the trend has profound effects for employee resourcing practice in many organisations, and that these will become more pronounced the longer the decline continues.

From a management perspective, weakened or absent trade unions mean that more terms and conditions can be established without the need to negotiate. This gives greater general freedom of action, as well as the opportunity to introduce individual contractual terms with new members of staff. Whereas previously, new performance management arrangements, flexible working patterns or disciplinary procedures would have to have been negotiated with trade union representatives, they can now be drawn up by managers alone, and more easily and speedily be put into effect. While it may often be wise to consult with staff representatives about such initiatives and to communicate any advantages that are expected to accrue for the organisation as a result, this no longer has to be done through collective bargaining processes. That said, there are also dangers for managers, in so far as their proposals are no longer subject to the same scrutiny as before, and may often turn out to be less effective than would be the case were they subjected to constructive criticism by union representatives. Similarly, the role played by trade unions in communicating the attitudes and feelings of staff to managers is also a potential loss, and one that has to be compensated for with new employee communication and involvement methods.

Employment law

Running in parallel with the loss of protection through trade union activity, employees have simultaneously gained a degree of protection through developments in the field of individual employment law. Increasingly, P&D managers need to have a good working knowledge of the law, and to update it regularly, if they are to carry out their function without finding themselves defending their actions in court. Three areas of employment law are directly relevant to employee resourcing work: contract law, discrimination law and dismissal law – all of which are introduced in this book. Discrimination provisions in particular have become more stringent in recent years, often in response to rulings of the European Court of Justice, but the volume of relevant case-law generally has increased as aggrieved employees have sought redress across a broader range of circumstances. The result over the past 20 years has been an increase in the number of important legal precedents of which P&D practitioners need to take account when carrying out employee resourcing activities.

The trend towards greater protection shows no signs of slowing down. Active campaigns are being pursued for the extension of discrimination rights to cover cases involving unfair treatment on the basis of age and sexual orientation, and there is also pressure on the government to reduce the two-year qualifying period for unfair dismissal rights. In addition, with the signing of the EU Social Chapter, the UK is likely to see more protection for disabled workers and additional requirements for employers to inform and consult employees directly as well as through works councils.

Which of these four trends has had the greatest impact on your organisation and on your own professional activities? Which are most likely to further affect you over the next two years?

THE QUESTION OF ETHICS

CIPD graduateship is a professional qualification, and therefore carries with it not only proof of an ability to carry out the P&D function effectively but also an obligation to uphold a high standard of professional ethics. However, defining what that means in practice is difficult, most attention in the literature focusing either on rather vague general statements or exclusively on equal opportunities issues. Like most professional bodies, the CIPD has a disciplinary procedure to which complaints of unprofessional conduct can be made. Under its terms, a disciplinary panel can be set up to consider complaints against members who are accused of actions that 'appear likely to bring discredit to the Institute or the profession'. Where a complaint is substantiated by the panel, a number of possible disciplinary actions can be taken, ranging from formal warnings through suspension to expulsion. Nevertheless, the standards of professional conduct to which CIPD members are expected to adhere, and which form the basis of decisions under the disciplinary procedure, are general rather than specific. They are concerned with ensuring that members practise P&D work with a high standard of honesty, intelligence and diligence, that they act within the law at all times, that they respect confidentiality, that they recognise their own limitations and that they continually update their skills and knowledge. In addition, members are expected to promote the removal of employment practices that unfairly discriminate against people on any grounds (ie not simply on those that are currently outlawed).

The CIPD code of professional conduct provides a sound basis for the development of ethical practices, but is not intended to give detailed guidance on how to handle day-to-day P&D decision-making. It sets a general standard, but does not specify what courses of action are considered ethical and unethical. In particular, it gives no guidance on what approach should be taken when conflicts arise between the legitimate needs of the organisation and the duty to maintain high standards of people management. These matters are either touched on or dealt with head-on at various points throughout this book. It is thus necessary at this stage only to raise the topic with a view to generating thought about what is after all a complex matter.

First and foremost it is necessary to recognise that P&D professionals are regularly faced with ethical dilemmas and have to make decisions and take actions that do not always sit easily with individual consciences. At base, these arise because the employment relationship, while technically an agreement freely entered into by two parties, is in fact very unequal. Except in the case of individuals who could be said to be members of a 'headhunted class', the employer always has some degree of power over the employee – and often a great deal. In many situations, where the law does not effectively intervene, it is very easy for employers to abuse this power. Indeed, because much employment law is inadequately policed, abuse often extends into these areas too, so that unfairness and discrimination of one sort or another continue to occur in spite of legislation.

Dealing with abuses of power is no easy matter for most P&D professionals for a number of reasons, not least because decisions in these areas are very often made by others. P&D specialists rarely become chief executives. Thus they nearly always report ultimately to managers whose career path has been based on the capacity to deliver wider organisational objectives. While it would clearly be very unfair generally to characterise such people as being capable of unethical actions, in practice many situations that occur which are potentially questionable in ethical terms arise as a result of pressure from the 'I'm going to show him who's boss – I want her out now' brigade. Organisational politics play an important part in this, people who wish to advance themselves putting their own careers and financial interests before notions of ethicality (see Badaracco and Webb 1995).

The second reason that it is difficult to define the ethical path in P&D arises because there is often a genuine conflict between the interests of employees and the interests of the organisation. It may be ethically justifiable to make substantial alterations to a set of premises to accommodate disabled workers, and it may also be ethically wrong to put pressure on someone with family responsibilities to remain at work until 8.00 at night, but in both cases the business needs of the organisation may demand that 'unethical' courses are taken. Thirdly, as has already been indicated, there is no clear statement of what *is* ethical, aside from what has been stated by Parliament and the courts. So even where a P&D specialist wishes to pursue an ethical path, it is not always easy to gain acceptance for the view that it is an ethical question at all.

In an ideal world, these issues would be resolved by each organisation's adopting a firm and agreed statement of business ethics covering the treatment of employees and potential employees, as well as customers and local communities. The statement would not only be endorsed from the top of the organisation, but would also be well enforced, with career progression and performance appraisal ratings determined in part by the presence of a good 'ethical record'. Furthermore, the statement would be well publicised and employees given the opportunity to make reference to its terms in grievance procedures that they were not fearful of invoking. Some organisations are moving in this direction, but it is difficult to avoid suspecting that, in some cases at least, their reasons have more to do with public relations (internal and external) than with practical decision-making.

For most P&D professionals, therefore, a less ambitious view has to be taken. Where ideals cannot be attained, the best that can realistically be achieved is to push decision-making and policy-making in an ethical direction. To achieve this, however, two issues have to be considered. First, it is necessary to establish a general ethical standard so that it is possible to determine what can and what cannot be regarded as an ethical issue. Secondly, there is a need to develop methods for influencing decision-making, given the restricting factors described above. As has already been indicated, the first of these is a matter for debate. What follows, therefore, is a suggested set of general principles that could be used in formulating a notion of P&D ethics. Readers might like to consider how far it accords with their own views on this subject.

• A balance has to be found between ethical considerations and the long-term survival and financial success of an organisation. This reflects a pragmatic view of organisational decision-making, based on the notion that there is no point in taking a strong ethical stand over an issue if the result is poor corporate performance and the consequent need to lay people off. It also accepts that ethical decision-making is often about choosing 'least of all evils' options in situations where all paths are unpalatable to some degree. However, it also recognises that a distinction must be made between actions that harm the interests of the organisation and those that damage the political interests of specific individuals, and that where an ethical stance does not damage the organisation, it should be pursued.

- Ethical P&D practice requires that all employees are treated consistently. Double-standards should not be applied. All employees, whatever their status, length of service, sex, race, age or experience, should thus be accorded equal respect and be subject to the same rules and expectations.

- Basic principles of natural justice should apply. Aside from consistency, employees should be treated by managers in the way that managers themselves would wish to be treated – that is, with honesty and fairness. All sides of a case should thus be aired prior to decisions' being taken about an employee's future, and issues should be looked at from a variety of perspectives. By and large this involves extending the principles (if not the procedures) set out in the Advice, Conciliation and Arbitration Service (ACAS) codes of conduct on the handling of dismissal across the whole raft of P&D decisions with an ethical dimension.

- Wherever possible, argument and not power should be used to determine actions. While it is inevitable that power will be distributed unequally in organisations, it should also be recognised that there is no need for the employment relationship to take on a feudal character. Power should be used sparingly, with implied or explicit threats made only when it is absolutely necessary, and after careful consideration. It follows that it is unprofessional and unethical to treat employees other than as adults with whom the organisation has an economic relationship. There should thus be no justification for playing games with employees or for unfairly manipulating expectations through hints, half-truths or misleading statements.

Once the principles have been established, it is possible to address possible ways of influencing the actions and approaches of senior managers and line managers with whom decision-making responsibility is shared. Where general agreement to enforceable organisation-wide standards cannot be secured, it is necessary to deploy other arguments on a case-by-case, situation-by-situation basis. Broadly, these fall into three categories: a moral, a business, or a legal case.

A moral case
It is possible to appeal purely on moral or ethical grounds, putting across principles such as those outlined above, with eloquence and a degree of passion. In other words, an ethical dilemma can be treated purely on its own terms and resolved by appealing to a

decision-maker's sense of reasonableness, of right and wrong, or of duty.

A business case

Secondly, an argument based on the long-term needs of the organisation can be formulated. Decision-makers can be urged to consider the possibility of adverse publicity or potentially damaging effects of particular actions on the ability of the organisation to attract and retain the best employees. Such arguments are most commonly associated with issues of consistency, and particularly with the case for positive action in the equal opportunities field. In some situations it should be possible to present plausible evidence from published research or from the experience of other organisations to back up these kinds of argument.

A legal case

The third kind of argument is often the most effective, because it raises the prospect not only of financial loss but also of the need to appear in court and be subjected to cross-questioning about one's actions. Clearly it can be deployed only where the decision in question has potential legal consequences and where the deployer has a good knowledge of legal principles.

Where pure argument fails, it is necessary either to accept the situation or to deploy other tactics. These would involve first of all seeking to negotiate an ethical outcome by conceding other points or ultimately, if the situation became intolerable, a threat of resignation. Professional P&D managers should clearly not take the decision to resign lightly, but where professional and ethical standards are clearly being breached and cannot be changed, this course of action is necessary. It particularly occurs in situations where the P&D professional is being required to break the law in a fundamental way (for example, by pursuing recruitment policies that unfairly discriminate or by dismissing people without first following the accepted procedural steps). In such cases, of course, the resigner may well have a very good case for pursuing a claim of constructive dismissal – another potential weapon to deploy where the most basic ethical standards are being compromised.

> What types of argument have you used in seeking to persuade someone that an ethical course of action should be taken? Which approach have you found to be most successful?

PERSPECTIVES AND ASSUMPTIONS

The final section of this introductory chapter aims to draw the reader's attention to the fundamental perspectives that the author has accepted in writing the book and the general frames of reference that have been adopted. The reasons for incorporating these are to help and encourage readers to question critically not only the views expressed and the conclusions reached in the book but also the assumptions that form their basis. The CIPD qualification, for which purposes this book has primarily been written, is intended to be equivalent to graduate level. This means that, in order to perform well and to achieve high marks, it is necessary for students to demonstrate not only that they have developed a solid understanding of employee-resourcing issues and the skills included in the published standards, but also that they have formed a view about the key issues and debates. Moreover, they should be able to justify their views with reference to forms of evidence, and show that they have evaluated their own perspectives and assumptions. The following points, like a number made elsewhere in the book, are therefore intended to provoke thought and debate.

A practitioner perspective

The book has been written entirely from the perspective of the employee-resourcing practitioner. Unlike many textbooks in the field, no attempt has been made to broaden this to take account of wider social perspectives or to strive for a degree of objectivity in the coverage of the interests of different stakeholders. The academic literature and debates are therefore reviewed and introduced from the viewpoint of the P&D function. Attention has also been given to literature that does not emanate from academic research, with references included from the writings of consultants, so-called 'management gurus', journalists working in the P&D field and experienced practitioners.

An acceptance of capitalistic work organisation

The book does not attempt to question the legitimacy of the employment relationship as it has developed in modern Western society. With one or two exceptions, literature that takes a critical perspective of this and related issues has thus not been included. Underlying this is an acceptance of the moral justification for capitalist forms of economic management. The case inevitably appeals more to pragmatists than idealists, and is simply based on the notion that, for all its faults, capitalism supplemented by redistributive taxation is the most effective system humanity has yet devised for the sustained creation of wealth.

An acceptance of contingency assumptions

Throughout the book what is generally described as 'a contingency perspective' has been adopted. It has thus been accepted that the methods and general approaches that managers take in dealing with employee resourcing questions vary – and usually should vary – depending on the specific circumstances and environment of the organisation. The main alternative view, referred to at various points, is the 'best-practice perspective', which tends by contrast to search out and focus on the single approach to dealing with each of the major issues that can be shown to have the best record. Hence, it is claimed that it is possible to identify the most valid method of selecting employees, the best way to compete in labour markets, or the most effective approach to performance management. Except in the case of legally defined best practice, this book avoids making such judgements. Instead, the approach has been to present readers with a series of distinct options under each main heading in order to encourage consideration of which ones might be more appropriate than others, given particular environmental circumstances.

A mistrust of big ideas

This book reflects the author's general suspicion of grand theories, sweeping new propositions, evangelical rhetoric and apparently simplistic answers to deeply rooted problems. There is thus a tendency to question and to downplay the significance of general theories of explanation (mostly derived from academic research) and general theories of prescription (mostly devised by HR consultants). Instead, the complexities of day-to-day employee-resourcing practice are stressed, along with the practical problems that tend to get in the way when the introduction of big new ideas is considered.

2 Brave new world?

Forty years ago, describing the typical British employee would not have been a particularly contentious exercise, because a majority of the workforce had a great deal in common. The typical employee would have been a white man who had left school at the age of 16 and who was employed to undertake unskilled or semi-skilled work. The products or services he helped to manufacture or provide would have been designed for mass consumption and thus produced at the lowest possible cost. His main terms and conditions of employment would in all likelihood have been determined at industry level through national negotiations with recognised trade unions, while his job duties would have been closely defined, allowing his easy allocation to one of a dozen or so job-based grades. The contract of employment would have covered 40 hours a week, any further work being carried out at premium overtime rates. Moreover, the employer would have primarily operated in the UK market, limiting international contacts to the purchase of raw materials or to the production of a small portion of products intended for export.

Forty years on we observe a world of employment that is far more diverse. Women now make up almost half of a workforce that is substantially better-skilled and that has experienced a higher level of formal education. A wider variety of skills is required to allow the 1990s' economy to function competitively, and with the development of specialist labour markets have come a decline in trade union membership and a strong move towards decentralised bargaining and individual pay determination. For many, internationalisation of the markets in which their organisations operate has brought increased competition and a pressure to intensify work. In turn this has led to greater flexibility in terms of hours worked and duties performed, to the need for adaptation to ongoing technological change and to an end to expectations of long-term job security. A continuation of these trends is predicted for the future, although the extent of any acceleration remains open to debate.

Long-term developments such as those illustrated above form the backdrop against which P&D specialists now operate. Like it or not, this is the environment with which we have to interact – a task that cannot be undertaken effectively without a firm understanding both of the general trends and the manner in which they affect the circumstances of individual organisations. In Chapter 1, a number of the more significant trends were introduced. This chapter focuses on internationalisation and the extension of atypical forms of employment. In both cases the underlying reasons for current trends are assessed, and their implications for employee resourcing activities discussed. At this stage the analysis is necessarily of a general nature, with specific issues raised again as the book proceeds.

By the end of this chapter readers should be able to:

• provide advice on the management of staff based overseas

• provide advice on the structuring of international organisations

• distinguish between different kinds of expatriate employment

• distinguish between functional and numerical flexibility

• assess the advantages and disadvantages of employing part-timers, temporary staff, subcontractors and homeworkers

• assess the advantages and disadvantages of employing people on flexible hours contracts.

In addition, readers should be able to understand and explain:

• the extent of and reasons for internationalisation

• the extent of and reasons for the growth in atypical working

• likely future trends in both these fields

• the major cultural differences between approaches to work and employment in different countries

• the theory of the 'flexible firm'.

INTERNATIONALISATION

A major theme of management writers in recent years has been the contention that national economies are fast being subsumed into a single global economy in which huge companies operate across national boundaries, serving world-wide markets and locating production wherever it is most cost-effective to do so. As with so much that is written about the major economic trends, there is some truth in the picture drawn, but also a great deal of exaggeration. It is true that international trade is growing faster than world output, and it is also true that the amount of direct foreign investment undertaken by companies is growing faster still. However, these are not new phenomena. The volume of economic activity carried out internationally has been growing steadily since the 1950s by a few percentage points each year (Dicken 1992: 16–17). Moreover, the volume of UK gross domestic product (GDP) accounted for by foreign trade (around 25 per cent) is still less than was the case before the First World War – so there is nothing inevitable about its continued growth (Wes 1996: 5). There is also little evidence, as yet, to show that companies are becoming 'stateless' operators. Instead, the current picture is overwhelmingly one in which nationally based organisations undertake international trade.

Nevertheless, while it is important not to be taken in by the wilder predictions, it remains the case that current trends point to a continued, if steady, growth in international trade and that its net effect over the next 40 or 50 years will be an increase in the number of businesses that operate internationally or compete with others who do so. This has several implications for employee resourcing activities, and there is thus a need for specialists in the field to develop an awareness of how exactly it will affect their industries and organisations.

There is also a need to develop an understanding of the reasons for increases in international economic activity in different industries. In many cases these are primarily technological, with the development of faster and cheaper international transport and communication links. Not only is it now economically viable to travel across the world in search of markets, it is also far easier to communicate with representatives, subsidiaries or licensees based in foreign locations. The recent extensions of e-mail and Internet services to new areas of the world, along with developments in mobile telecommunications technology, serve to speed up the communication process further. Developments in freight transport also underlie the continued increase in the volume of international trade. Container ships now transport vast quantities of goods between continents more cheaply, securely and conveniently than ever before, and at greater speed. The biggest ships now travel at the equivalent of 20 to 30 miles an hour round the clock, meaning that goods can be shipped from China to the UK and vice versa in less than three weeks. Air freight services also continue to develop. The result is a world that is far smaller, with the capability of transporting people and goods from one end to the other in little more than a single day at an affordable cost. To these technological developments are added the many measures taken in recent years to liberalise trade between countries through the removal or reduction of tariff barriers. There is thus both an increasing ability as well as an enhanced willingness to extend global economic exchanges.

It is difficult to make meaningful generalisations about the internationalisation of P&D activity, because it has a variety of different outcomes depending on individual business circumstances. Furthermore, because it does not accelerate at a uniform pace, we currently have a situation in which some industries (notably manufacturing and finance) are having to adapt far more dramatically and swiftly than others. Indeed, there are some sectors that have yet to be internationalised at all to any great degree, remaining nationally based in terms of both their product and labour markets (eg the public services, newspapers, many small businesses and much of the retailing sector). In short, the effects come in a number of different shapes and forms, and thus have rather different implications in terms of evolving employee resourcing policy. It is helpful to view the internationalisation process in terms of a continuum. At one end is a situation in which organisations take on what commentators describe as a 'global' or 'transnational' character, while at the other organisations remain entirely nationally based and may (or may not) be faced with the need to compete with commercial rivals based overseas. Inbetween is a range of other states encompassing the development of sizeable export markets, the purchasing or setting up of overseas subsidiaries and the building of strategic alliances with foreign organisations. The picture is often made more complex by the fact that different divisions within the same organisation can operate at different points along the continuum.

Increased competition

By far the most generally applicable result of these trends is the increased competition it brings. Few commercial organisations are not now touched by the presence of more overseas competitors for their products in home markets, even if they themselves do not export goods to any great degree. In some respects the rest of this book is concerned with the various choices open to P&D specialists faced with the need to assist their organisations to compete more effectively. For most, this means helping to create a workforce capable of enhancing the quality of the goods and services produced and with the capacity both to adapt to change and to generate innovative approaches. In employee resourcing terms this means finding and then retaining the best-qualified and most able individuals available. Once that part of the equation has been 'solved' there is then a need to address individuals' performance so as to ensure that the organisation gets the best return possible on its investment over the long term.

Globalisation

At the other end of the spectrum are organisations that have developed a transnational structure. Not only are their products sold all over the world, but they are also conceived, designed, manufactured, marketed, distributed and serviced in different locations. In some cases a number of stages in the manufacturing process are carried out in separate countries. Such organisations are still relatively uncommon, because most international corporations retain the preponderance of activities in a single country, but their number is growing. The implications for the P&D specialist are profound. Not only is there a need to compete internationally, as described above, but there is also a need to create, manage and develop workforces in a variety of different places. It may be, for example, that a company designs products at a head office in the UK, manufactures them in Eastern Europe, and then markets and distributes them from a further dozen locations around the world. The need to exercise control over such an organisation while ensuring that it retains a common identity and sense of purpose requires the acquisition and development of a sizeable expatriate workforce to live and work for periods overseas. Others will need to travel a great deal from location to location, commuting from country to country while being based in another location. In addition, there is a compelling need to communicate effectively with all of the international arms and to put in place, as far as is either practical or possible, common standards of P&D practice.

The international auditor

An example of the way that international companies now employ people to work around the globe is provided by the internal audit department of Sunrise Medical Inc., a US-based firm that manufactures medical equipment, principally for the use of disabled people. The company employs people in several locations around the world to work in its manufacturing units and to operate its distribution network. The company's finance department employs a small team of accountants to carry out routine internal auditing and to work on special projects in the financial field.

Each member of the team is based in a different location and is of a different nationality. In many cases members have no permanent office but are set up to work from home with computer equipment, modems, fax machines and international mobile phones. Typically an auditor spends 60–70 per cent of his or her time working abroad, meeting up with other members of the team in different locations.

Currently there is only one UK-based team member. For much of the year he spends his working week in European countries, rarely spending more than three or four weeks in one place. Moreover, because his diary is planned only a few weeks in advance, he has little idea at any one time where he will be working more than a month or two in advance. From time to time he travels further afield to Australia and the USA (where his boss is based), but when he is in Europe he commutes back and forth each week. Monday morning usually involves taking a flight to a European city and booking into a hotel. He then returns on a Friday afternoon and spends his weekends at home.

Inbetween states

Many organisations have moved beyond national boundaries in some respects but do not or cannot aspire to develop into full-blown global operators such as those described above. For some, this will involve developing durable export markets in different countries. Others go further by taking over foreign-based companies, setting up overseas subsidiaries or merging with organisations that are based abroad but operate in similar product markets. A third group enters into strategic alliances with overseas competitors with a view to enhancing shared competitive advantage. A fourth group operates internationally but not globally, restricting their activities to the European market or to one or two EU countries. In each case there is a need in P&D terms to move some of the way down the globalisation road. While there will be less of a requirement for expatriate employees, there will be much more need for key players to travel and to spend substantial periods of time in foreign locations. There is also an important communication job to do, preparing employees for change, involving them in the process, appraising them of new individual opportunities and reassuring them about their own futures.

At which point on the internationalisation continuum would you say your organisation is placed? How far do you believe this will change in the foreseeable future?

EMPLOYEE-RESOURCING IMPLICATIONS

Internationalisation brings a wide range of considerations to employee-resourcing work which are not present, or present only to a lesser degree, in nationally oriented organisations. Throughout this book these are revisited in the context of specific topics. The aim here is to introduce the subject by drawing the reader's attention to some of the general factors that come into play when an organisation makes the decision to operate internationally. While these are interlinked, for ease of description and comprehension each will be described and briefly assessed in turn.

Employing staff to work overseas

Torrington (1994: 6), in his study of international HRM, divides overseas employees into a number of distinct categories. The most important are as follows:

- expatriates (staff who live and work in an overseas location for a year or more)

- occasional parachutists (staff who spend shorter periods overseas, often working on specific projects such as setting up new production processes)

- cosmopolitans (mostly management staff who travel from location to location throughout their working year, spending little more than a week or two in each country before moving on).

Each has different requirements from the employee-resourcing function in terms of recruitment, selection and performance management in particular.

To survive and succeed professionally in any one of these three situations is difficult. It is not something that will naturally occur when someone is posted overseas. There is thus a necessity to select people carefully and to make sure that they have the support they need during the period that they are abroad. In an ideal world the nature and extent of overseas working in a job will be identified at the HR planning stage. It will then form an integral part of written job descriptions and person specifications, feature in recruitment advertisements, form a major criterion at the selection stage, and then be explicitly incorporated into individual contracts of employment. This will ensure that only people with relevant language skills and whose personal circumstances are conducive to overseas working are considered for employment in such roles. Remuneration packages designed to attract and retain such staff can then be developed along with appropriate performance management systems. However, in a volatile business environment situations often arise that do not permit such a well-planned resourcing exercise to take place. There is often a need to act speedily and opportunistically to secure business and a requirement for existing nationally based staff to be involved. As a result, the time available for preparation is brief, and any training given has to be intensive. Where such opportunities involve staff who have not specifically been selected for overseas work there will thus often be a need to provide more structured and extensive support once the individual concerned has taken up his or her post.

That said, it is clearly not usually in the interests of an organisation to encourage people to spend time travelling or to take up a position abroad against their wishes. Wherever possible, therefore, those who are likely to be asked to do so need to be recruited, at the very least, with that possibility in mind. The following factors thus need to be included in the recruitment and selection process:

- existing language skills

- capacity to learn new languages

- awareness of relevant overseas cultures

- ability to adapt to specific overseas values and norms

- preparedness for living conditions in particular foreign counties (ie rented accommodation or hotels)

- domestic circumstances.

This last point has to be handled very carefully to avoid breaching sex discrimination legislation. However, in most cases of overseas working it will inevitably arise and have to be dealt with at the selection stage. Of course, employers can do a great deal to help individuals to juggle international employment and family life by providing regular flights home or by making funds available for spouses and families to join employees while they are abroad. Help can also be given by granting such employees additional holidays or the opportunity to take sabbatical leave.

> How keen would you be to work abroad for a year or two? What would have to be included in the package before you would consider taking up any offer?

Cultural variations

A second topic of general importance for the development of employee-resourcing policy in international organisations is the need to manage within the grain of different national cultures. While some have claimed that culturally the world is becoming more homogeneous, for the foreseeable future very substantial differences between different national cultures will clearly continue. Getting to grips with these and developing an effective understanding of different norms, values and assumptions are therefore prerequisites for successfully doing business in different places. For transnational organisations, where people based in one country are managed by people based elsewhere, there is an even greater need to appreciate cultural differences and to understand how they affect employee-resourcing practice.

In recent years a number of studies have been carried out among employees and managers in different countries in an effort to 'map' or categorise in some way the cultural variations between them. The best known are the two studies by Hofstede (1980, 1991) and the more recently published research of Lewis (1996). These are all fascinating but inevitably tend to oversimplify the picture by categorising whole nations into particular cultural groups. Hence, according to Hofstede, the UK is characterised as a 'village market', in which organisations tend to have less formal hierarchical structures than elsewhere, with much decentralisation of authority, a relatively relaxed view of change and a preference for keeping emotions hidden. Clearly there is some truth in this, especially when these characteristics are compared with those that appear prevalent elsewhere. However, there are also plenty of organisations, communities and individuals who do not share these cultural norms – so care has to be taken in simply 'reading off' a set of national characteristics from such typologies.

Lewis's studies classified national cultures into three broad categories, each of which consists of a long list of characteristics covering human relationships, work style, perception of time and preferred approaches to the collection and communication of data. The three were labelled respectively as 'linear-active', 'multi-active' and 'reactive'. Linear-active cultures, according to Lewis, include the English-speaking nations and much of Northern Europe. People originating from these areas are respectful of authority, unemotional, relatively patient and keen to keep their private lives to themselves. They also tend to be analytical, making decisions based on firm data rather than hunches or personal recommendations. In terms of work organisation, the preference is for order and planning, each task carried out separately and in accordance with agreed schedules. As a result time is seen as scarce, and great emphasis is placed on punctuality.

By contrast, multi-active cultures are shared by people originating from Southern Europe, Africa, the Middle East and Latin America. Here the social norms include a greater willingness to display emotion and to appeal to a sense of emotion rather than logic when seeking to persuade. Family relationships are closer and less likely to be kept separate from work than in linear-active cultures. Body language is far more expressive, and punctuality regarded as less important. At work there is relatively little delegation of authority, the most senior figure taking decisions according to personal perceptions. Agreed plans or procedures are thus readily altered without the need to consult others.

The third culture is labelled 'reactive', and incorporates the Eastern countries, along with Russia, Finland and Turkey. Here there is great emphasis on listening and the avoidance of confrontation in relationships with others. People are often inscrutable and will go to more extreme lengths than elsewhere to avoid losing face. Decision-making tends to take a long time but, by the same token, will be made to last for the long term. Great emphasis is placed on integrity and reliability, but it takes time to build up the trust required. Discussion and negotiation tend thus to take time, each party avoiding direct answers or even eye contact but preferring instead to listen and react after careful consideration.

Hofstede (1980) focused more directly on work organisation, and has identified four dimensions that allow different national characteristics to be classified or mapped. These are:

- power distance (the extent to which members of a society accept that power in institutions is distributed unequally)

- uncertainty avoidance (the extent to which people feel threatened by ambiguous situations and have created beliefs and institutions that try to avoid these)

- individualism (the extent to which people believe that they have responsibility for looking after themselves and their own families, as opposed to institutions)

- masculinity (the extent to which the dominant values in society are success, money and material acquisitions).

More recently, Hofstede (1991) has refined his uncertainty avoidance dimension somewhat to take account of the long-term orientation of Eastern cultures compared with those prevalent in the West. In this, like Lewis, he is recognising the important differences that exist in the field of time perception, with its implications for reactive decision-making, perseverance and face-saving. Hofstede has also produced a typology of cultures based on his first two dimensions (uncertainty avoidance and power distance), which has led him to identify four basic organisational categories associated with particular countries. These are the 'pyramid of people', the 'well-oiled machine', the 'village market' and the 'family', and are best illustrated graphically (see Figure 1).

Necessarily, it has been possible here only to outline some of the main contours of research findings in the field of cultural variations. Readers are referred to more specialist texts, such as those referenced above, for more detailed material on specific countries. However, it is clear even from the briefest of surveys that assumptions about work relationships and organisations vary considerably around the globe. In employee resourcing terms this means that the approaches prevalent in the UK, or even defined here as constituting 'best practice', will often be seen as foreign and ill-judged if imposed elsewhere. In managing international organisations there is thus a need to study, and gain an

Figure 1 Typology of cultures (adapted from Hofstede 1980)

UNCERTAINTY AVOIDANCE

Pyramid of people	HIGH	Well–oiled machine
Japan		Germany
France		Finland
Pakistan		Austria
South America		Israel
Arabic-speaking		Switzerland
Southern Europe		Costa Rica

POWER DISTANCE

HIGH — LOW

Family		Village market
India		UK
Malaysia		USA
Singapore		Canada
Indonesia		Sweden
East and West Africa		The Netherlands
Hong Kong	LOW	Australia

understanding of, the key differences in work cultures, and then to develop policies that take the variations into account.

Cultural differences are reflected in the approach of different legal systems towards the rights of employees. As will be described in Chapter 5, even the basic approach to a contract of employment varies from one legal system to another. Similarly, there are widely differing approaches to trade unions, to the rights of women and ethnic minorities and to an employer's freedom to dismiss employees. Only by being aware of cultural and legal distinctions is it possible to compete in the labour market, to motivate staff and to administer the employment relationship successfully in different locations around the world.

Transnational organisational structures

A third issue of underlying significance for employee-resourcing practices in international organisations concerns the internal structures and reporting lines. While these are complex issues at the best of times for large organisations, they are made a great deal more involved when geographically diverse workforces are included. The problem is best illustrated with a fictional example – a catering conglomerate that operates only within the UK and runs a chain of restaurants and a chain of hotels. How should it structure itself? One option is for the two product groups to be managed separately, with two managerial hierarchies, each with its own maintenance, marketing, finance and personnel functions, and both reporting at the very senior level to corporate directors. Alternatively, the whole group could be managed functionally, all the chefs (from both hotels and restaurants) reporting to regional food and beverage managers, and the housekeepers, accountants, maintenance, finance, marketing and personnel people doing likewise. The third option is to organise the whole company into separate regional divisions so that there are managers with responsibility for both restaurants and hotels operating in the South-East, Midlands, Scotland etc. All three are plausible approaches. Because one language is spoken and one broad organisation culture shared, and because operations are confined to a reasonably small geographic area, any inherent tensions can be resolved relatively easily. Hence, if the organisation is structured regionally, it is still very easy for maintenance staff based in different locations to communicate, share their expertise and equipment, and come together to take part in project work. The same goes for general managers of hotels in different regions and wine-buyers within the restaurant chain. In other words, it is possible for each member of staff to have a single line manager who appoints and appraises them, but it is also possible to work to or with others on a regional or functional basis.

The larger and more complex an organisation becomes, the harder it is to resolve the tensions described in the example given above. Once international divisions are established, a further tension emerges in the form of the need for the organisation to have a common strategic focus while simultaneously taking account of local cultural norms and organisational traditions. Hence, to take the catering example further, there is a need in an international hotel chain for all units to adhere to the same basic standards, so that they can be marketed as a group, while at the same time they will be managed very differently depending on the country in which they are based. So to whom should the sales manager at the Hong Kong unit report? Should it be the hotel's general manager, a worldwide director of sales or a manager with responsibility for sales and marketing activity within South-East Asia? In practice, the answer will vary, depending on the established traditions in the company, the political strength of particular managers and the costs and benefits associated with each option.

A further option is for organisations to develop matrix structures, whereby there is no single reporting line, so that employees may be accountable to a number of different individuals at the same time. In the above example, that might mean that an aspiring sales manager for the Hong Kong hotel would be interviewed by all three potential bosses but would report to each about different areas of work. Day-to-day supervision might come from the local general manager, but this would not prevent the regional sales and marketing managers overseeing much of the individual's work. In addition, he or she might be involved in some international project work, which would require work to be undertaken for the international director. Ideally this would maximise the individual's contribution while ensuring that responsibilities at organisational, regional and unit level were all met. Such matrix structures are becoming increasingly common in international companies, because they permit cost-effective achievement of organisational objectives, but in different ways depending on local conditions. Further information on different approaches to such forms, together with a number of examples in the international field, are provided in Sparrow and Hiltrop (1994: 288–298).

Linked to the question of the overall structure is the issue of who should manage plants or other units located in countries other than that of the corporate HQ. In a truly global organisation, where the original location of the corporate HQ is irrelevant to staffing policy, and perhaps where ownership is no longer concentrated in one country, the nationality of each unit manager is less of an issue. The corporate culture supersedes separate national cultures, and it becomes possible simply to promote people to new positions across different countries on the basis of individual merit. Hence a Dutch person can be appointed to manage a Polish factory owned by a US-based corporation. It is also more common for people based in subsidiaries to spend time working at the corporate HQ as much as the other way round. However, as has already been pointed out, this kind of global organisation remains relatively rare at present, with most multinationals dominated by a strong nationally based HQ which keeps a tight rein on its overseas subsidiary units. In such situations, the choice in the above example would more typically be between a local Polish manager and an expatriate American one. The advantage of the former is local knowledge and language skills. By contrast the advantage of the latter is a knowledge of organisational culture and strategy, together with expertise in the international aspects of the operation. Again, as in the case of matrix organisation structures, the usual solution is to try to achieve the best of both worlds by employing local and home country nationals to work together – perhaps one acting as deputy to the other. The approach taken by the Shell Group is illustrated in the boxed text on this page.

HRM at Shell

The Shell group is one of the largest companies in the world. It employs over 130,000 people in 100 countries, of whom over 5,000 are working as expatriates at any one time. Its corporate HQs are in London and The Hague, which together oversee different parts of the organisation. Apart from oil, it also has well-established interests in the gas, coal and chemicals industries. Shell is well known for its decentralised structure, whereby the managers of local operating companies have overall responsibility for their units and a very wide degree of autonomy. The corporate HQ staff have two main functions: developing global strategy and providing advisory services to the decentralised units.

In human resource (HR) terms, this means that local managers have complete responsibility for the management of P&D policy and practice. Corporate HQ has no right to interfere. It therefore restricts its activities in the P&D field to assisting local units when asked for advice and to providing consultancy services. In practice, because these services are called upon, the central function is able to identify best practice and disseminate this throughout the group. HQ staff also carry out HR audits to assess the performance of one operating company in comparison with others. While HQ provides advice on expatriate terms and conditions, it is not involved in co-ordinating the movement of international staff from one part of the group to another. This too, like other employee resourcing aspects, is the responsibility of local managers.

The net result is a regional structure, but one that achieves a strong degree of international cohesion by having access to central expertise and a pool of experienced expatriate staff.

Source: Haddock and South (1994: 218–230)

ATYPICAL WORK

The second major underlying trend tackled in this chapter concerns developments in the way in which employment is organised. There is a degree of agreement among writers that the Western world is witnessing important changes in this field in response to new technologies, intensified international competition and market volatility. The result is a move on the part of employers to slim down or become 'lean' by employing fewer people on standard, full-time permanent contracts while hiring more on a part-time, temporary or subcontracted basis. However, there are substantial differences of opinion on some of the questions that follow from this basic statement, such as the following:

• Can the trend be viewed as permanent?

• Is it really new?

• How much further can the slimming process go?

• Who stands to benefit most and who will lose out?

It is beyond the scope of this book to look in detail at the evidence presented by the main protagonists in this debate. This work will therefore be summarised briefly before our focus shifts to the practical consequences of the trends for employee resourcing specialists. In later chapters attention is given to the impact of growth in atypical working in specific fields such as human resource planning and the management of performance. Here, two rather more general issues are considered. The first concerns the notion that there are now opportunities that were less evident in the past to employ a workforce on a more flexible basis. It thus concerns the advantages and disadvantages of employing individuals to undertake specific roles on non-standard or atypical terms and conditions. The second relates to the issue of the likely future impact of continued growth in atypical working for the operation of labour markets and an organisation's capacity to compete for the services of the best talent in a particular field.

Any survey of non-standard working must start with a description of the work of John Atkinson and, in particular, his proposed model of the 'flexible firm'. Published in 1984, Atkinson's model has been very influential and has led to the development of a vigorous academic debate about its merits as a tool of description, prescription and prediction. Its main feature is the suggestion that a flexible firm (by which Atkinson means one that is competitive in the modern business environment) is composed of three basic groups of employees: core workers, peripheral workers and a third group who are employed only on some kind of subcontracted basis. The basic model (adapted by the source authors) is illustrated in Figure 2.

Central to the model are two distinct types of flexibility: functional and numerical. The former is applied specifically to the core workers – that is, people who are employed on standard, permanent, full-time contracts and who undertake the tasks that are central to the success of the organisation. They are functionally flexible, in that they do not work to rigid job descriptions but carry out a broad range of duties. Moreover, they do not restrict their activities to work of a particular level. Instead, they carry out complex tasks associated with managerial or professional jobs as well as more mundane activities, depending on the day-to-day needs of the organisation.

The peripheral group can also be functionally flexible, but in the model is more strongly associated with the term 'numerical flexibility'. Atkinson divided peripheral workers into primary and secondary categories, the first forming part of the firm's internal labour market. These people are mainly full-time and have a certain degree of permanence, but tend to have lower skills than colleagues who enjoy the status of core employees. As individuals they are less central to the organisation's success because their skills are more widely available in the labour market. They therefore enjoy lower job security than the core workers and will be among the first to have their hours cut or to be laid off when business downturns are experienced. The secondary peripheral group are in an even more precarious position, because they are brought in mainly to help cover peaks in business or short-term

Figure 2 The flexible firm

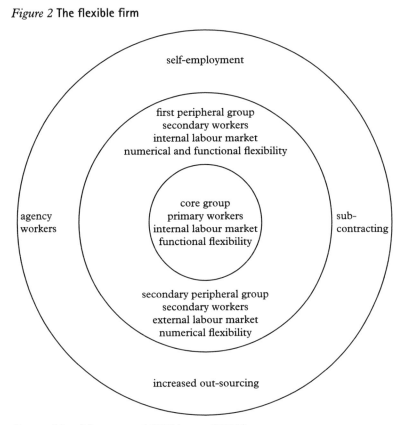

Source: Marchington and Wilkinson (1997)

needs resulting from the absence of other staff. They are employed either on a part-time or temporary basis.

The final group, located beyond the periphery, consists of people who are not employees of the firm but who are hired on a subcontracted basis to undertake a particular task or set of tasks. In the vast majority of cases this will be temporary, and hence insecure, although it is possible for a series of fixed-term contracts to follow one after another. Some may be professionally qualified people working on a self-employed basis; others may work for an agency or some other service provider. In both cases they are perceived by the other groups as being external to the organisation and thus readily replaceable by a competitor should their work prove to be unsatisfactory or more cheaply provided elsewhere.

Over recent years others have proposed similar models (eg Loveridge and Mok 1979, Handy 1989), but none has entered managerial language or generated as much debate as that proposed by Atkinson. Some, however, have gone further in suggesting that technological and competitive pressures will grow to such an extent over the coming years that the number of people employed in what Atkinson describes as core jobs will decline very rapidly, leaving most skilled people with no choice but to operate as peripheral employees. This will involve working part-time for a number of employers on a series of fixed-term contracts or on a self-employed basis. For those seen by Atkinson as currently belonging to the peripheral groups, the future is bleaker still, writers predicting substantial reductions in demand for their services over the next few decades.

In *The Empty Raincoat* Charles Handy (1994) suggests that employers will increasingly wish to buy a specific *service* from a worker rather than that person's time. The result will be a situation in which, for most people, there will be little opportunity to enjoy the security of a long-term, full-time job. Instead, Handy believes, people will have to develop portfolio careers in which they earn money by 'looking for customers, not bosses'. Employers will be both far less willing and able to employ people (especially professionals or 'knowledge workers') to come to their premises for a fixed number of hours each week. Rather, they will say, 'Do this by this date; how you do it is up to you, but get it done on time and up to standard.' The term 'job' will thus revert to its original meaning of a specific task or project rather than an occupation or profession, while individual ambitions will focus more on the achievement of employability than the status of being an employee. The same kind of analysis also underlies other influential publications concerned with the future of work, some writers going further than Handy in respect of the speed with which and the extent to which they believe these developments will occur (eg Bridges 1995, Rifkin 1995, Davison and Rees Mogg 1997).

A number of others have come out in opposition to some of these ideas, and particularly to Atkinson's model. The most noted critic is Anna Pollert, who has argued in a series of books and articles that there is nothing particularly new about flexibility as it is described by Atkinson. Firms have always had to slim down their workforces when faced with difficult business circumstances, and they have always shed subcontractors and peripheral workers first. What is new, according to Pollert (1987, 1988), is the propagation of flexibility in the form of a model intended to guide management actions. In other words, it is the idea that organisations should deliberately develop core and peripheral structures as part of a considered strategy that represents a departure from past practice. However, she goes on to argue that there is little evidence that managers are in fact adopting such strategies. Her point of view appears to be backed up by the survey evidence, which has persistently shown that while the extent of self-employment, temporary and part-time work has increased in recent years, this results from managers' reacting on an *ad hoc* basis to specific needs (Hakim 1990, McGregor and Sproull 1992). There is little evidence that flexibility of the kind described by Atkinson arises as a result of deliberate, organisation-level planning. Moreover, an alternative explanation can be put forward to explain the rise in part-time working over the past 15 years. This, it is said, arises not from changes in management policy, but simply because the proportion of jobs in the service sector has risen, reflecting a continued demand for part-timers in retailing, catering and publishing. There is also little evidence that the number of permanent positions is declining; indeed, if recruitment industry statistics are taken into account, it would appear that the period since 1994 has in fact seen the creation of substantially more permanent jobs than temporary ones (Donkin 1997).

> How have these trends been reflected in your organisation? Is there more atypical working? What are the reasons for any increase or decrease?

EFFECTS ON EMPLOYEE RESOURCING

While this debate is interesting and has profound and potentially long-term implications, the extent to which trends are occurring nationally, and the reasons for them, are of little practical day-to-day interest to employee-resourcing managers. What does matter is the extent to which such developments are occurring or could occur in specific industrial sectors or regions. Here the picture is considerably more varied, trends in different kinds of non-standard working affecting different industries unevenly. For example, there is relatively little part-time working in manufacturing, but there is a good deal of subcontracting. By contrast, the use of fixed-term contracts has grown most in the public services, where funding to undertake specific projects is limited in terms of time. Such contracts are also used extensively by employers whose workload increases and decreases on a seasonal basis (eg in tourism and agriculture), and have necessarily become highly significant in sectors where most employees are female, as a result of the greater take-up of the right to maternity leave in recent years (IDS 1995c: 4).

For the practitioner, therefore, the most important questions to ask are the following:

- In respect of the particular industry and labour markets in which my organisation operates, what opportunities exist to increase the proportion of employees on non-standard contracts?

- What are the potential short- and long-term advantages and disadvantages of doing so?

Clearly the answer to these questions will vary from situation to situation. What follows, therefore, is a brief survey of some of the factors that might need to be taken into account for each of the major categories of atypical work.

Part-time contracts

Part-time working is by far the most common form of atypical working. In the UK around a quarter of the workforce are part-timers, 85 per cent of these being women. Within certain sectors the figures are far higher. According to Marsh (1991), 41 per cent of all hotel and catering employees are women who work part-time; the figures for the health and education sectors are 51 per cent and 47 per cent respectively. By contrast, the numbers employed outside the service sector are considerably smaller, with a heavy concentration in clerical and secretarial roles. The biggest period of growth in part-time work was during the 1960s, when the proportion of the total workforce that worked part-time increased from 9 per cent to 16 per cent. Since then it has continued to rise steadily, along with the overall female participation rate (IDS 1995c: 4).

In past decades there were clear incentives for organisations to employ two part-timers instead of one full-timer. This resulted from an inequality of treatment in legal terms, whereby part-timers could be denied pension scheme membership and other fringe benefits and had to wait five years before they were entitled to bring cases of unfair dismissal. The courts have now ruled such practices to be indirectly discriminatory towards women, leading to several legislative amendments in recent years. Treating part-timers less favorably than full-timers is thus now a risky approach to take. However, it remains the case that at the lowest pay levels, part-timers often earn less than the lower National Insurance threshold, meaning that employers do not have to pay contributions when these workers are appointed.

There are two main reasons for the creation of a part-time post. The first, and most common, is to enable an organisation to respond more efficiently to peaks and troughs in demands for its services. Hence shopworkers are hired to work part-time on busy days or to cover the busiest hours of the day. The second reason is in response to a demand from employees or potential employees for part-time jobs to be created. The most common situation in which this occurs is when a woman who has previously worked on a full-time basis wishes to return as a part-timer following her maternity leave. In many cases, organisations find ways of accommodating such requests, either by re-organising job duties or by advertising for another part-timer to share the job. However, generally speaking, the inflexibility of such arrangements makes them less easy to organise for managerial employees who need to be present throughout the week in order to supervise their departments effectively. Often a difficult choice has thus to be made between accommodating employee wishes in this regard or losing a valued member of staff. The presence of reputable childcare services can reduce the likelihood of this issue's arising. Indeed there is evidence from the continent that suggests part-time working on the part of women with children is less common in countries where there is good and widely available childcare provision (Brewster *et al* 1993: 17).

Creating part-time jobs can thus bring considerable advantages to an organisation. It can reduce costs dramatically by making sure that people are present only when required and can also attract well-qualified people who, because of childcare or other commitments, are looking for less than 40 hours' work each week. Other parts of the labour market to which employers can look include retired people and students in full-time education. Another possible advantage in some situations is the apparent lack of interest among part-timers for trade union activity.

There are of course potential disadvantages too. First, there is the possibility that part-timers, because of other obligations and the fact that theirs is often not the main family income, will show less commitment to their work than their full-time colleagues. The problem is potentially compounded by the lack of promotion opportunities open to them. Part-timers can also be inflexible in terms of the hours they work because of the need to honour their other commitments. They are often attracted to the job in the first place because they need to be guaranteed fixed weekly hours (eg 12.00–2.00, or Wednesdays and Thursdays) and will thus be either unwilling or unable to change these too much. There is also the more general issue of training investment. Where two or three part-timers are employed in place of one full-timer to undertake the same role, the training time and cost will be two or three times higher. A well-rooted myth about part-time workers is the notion that they are harder to retain than full-timers, a belief that presumably arises from more general perceptions of a lack of commitment. In fact, there is little evidence to support this perception, 40 per cent staying with their employers for five years or more (IDS 1995c: 4).

Term-time working

A variation on traditional part-time working which has many attractions in principle is the employment of staff to work only during school terms. Such arrangements allow employees with childcare obligations to maximise their earnings over the course of a year while being free for their children during school holidays. Such approaches have long been used in the education sector itself, where the need for teaching and support staff is of course lower outside term time. There is, however, no reason why other sectors should not also adopt such arrangements, especially when troughs in business coincide with school holidays. The approach is particularly applicable where long-term project work is being undertaken with no particular requirement for work to proceed at the same pace all the year round.

In any case, where there remains a demand for employees in particular jobs to work throughout the year, it is still possible to offer term-time contracts, because there are always plenty of university students on the labour market looking for temporary work during the school holiday periods. The number and standard of applications returned to advertisements offering both term and holiday working should therefore be high, giving employers the opportunity to employ more highly skilled individuals and to earn a better return on their investment.

Temporary contracts

The term 'temporary worker' covers a variety of situations. On the one hand there are staff who are employed for a fixed term or on a seasonal basis to carry out a specific job or task. This category includes well-paid or senior people such as football players or public officials, as well as individuals brought in to undertake more ordinary work on a fixed-term basis. A second group are people who are employed temporarily but for an indefinite period. Their contracts thus state that they will be employed until such time as a particular project or body of work is completed. Again, this category can encompass well-paid individuals such as TV presenters and actors, in addition to those occupying less glamorous positions. A third category includes temporary agency staff who are employed via a third party to cover short-term needs.

Currently in the UK around 7 per cent of all employees are contracted to work on a temporary or fixed-term basis, but the figure rises to 8 per cent during the summer months as a result of seasonal work in the tourism and agricultural sectors (IRS 1997b: 7). The number of temporary workers tends to fluctuate with economic conditions, so we saw a rise in the early 1980s, followed by a slight reduction, before the figure rose steeply again in the early 1990s. Indeed, between 1992 and 1996 temporary work, which increased by 30 per cent, accounted for a large proportion of the 2.4 per cent increase in overall employment. Of particular significance was the very substantial growth in the number of agency workers, which rose by 148 per cent between 1992 and 1996 (IRS 1997b: 7). As with part-time working, there is very great variation between the different industrial sectors, the service and agricultural sectors accounting for a high proportion of the total. As many as 10 per cent of public sector staff are now employed on a fixed-term basis, with some positions, such as those of researchers in higher education, now usually paid for through one-off grants or single allocations of funds.

While somewhat dated, the Department of Employment's *Employer's Labour Use Survey* (ELUS), carried out in 1987, provides a good summary of the great variety of reasons employers have for employing temporary staff:

- to give short-term cover for absent staff (55 per cent)
- to match staffing levels to peaks in demand (35 per cent)
- to deal with one-off tasks (29 per cent)
- to help adjust staffing levels (26 per cent)
- to provide specialist skills (22 per cent)
- to provide cover while staffing levels are changed (19 per cent)
- because applicants request temporary work (8 per cent)
- to screen for permanent jobs (4 per cent)
- because temporary workers are easier to recruit (4 per cent)
- to reduce wage costs (1 per cent)
- to reduce non-wage costs (1 per cent).

(*Source*: McGregor and Sproull 1992: 227)

The figures in parentheses represent the percentage of employers responding to the survey who cited the reason as one they had had in appointing temporary workers. Of particular interest is the very small number who stated that cost reductions are a reason, further reflecting the apparent lack of interest in the principles of the flexible firm model. The fact that many temporary staff have no right to join occupational pension schemes, that they often have no right to redundancy payments and that those with less than two years' service are not covered by unfair dismissal legislation do not thus appear to be regarded as significant reasons for hiring temporary staff.

From the employer's perspective there is thus a number of compelling reasons to consider offering fixed-term contracts to certain groups of staff. They are particularly useful when the future is uncertain, because they avoid raising employee expectations. It is far easier, when departments close or businesses begin to fold, not to renew a fixed-term contract than it is to make permanent employees redundant. During the run-up to redundancies it is also useful to be able to draw on the services of temporary staff to cover basic tasks, freeing permanent employees who are under threat of redundancy to spend time seeking new jobs.

A note of caution is needed for those with responsibilities for the employment of staff in other EU countries, because a number have considerably greater restrictions on the employment of temps than is the case in the UK and the Irish Republic. In Italy, for example, the number of temporary workers is relatively small, despite the presence of a substantial tourism sector, because the law restricts the ability of employers to offer temporary work. Unless it can be shown that the employment has been offered to cover absence or to deal with a temporary increase in workload, it can be declared unlawful. Moreover, fixed-term contracts can stand only for three months (or six months if the work is seasonal), and temporary employment agencies are illegal. Other countries have less rigorous laws, but most have legislated in some way to discourage temporary employment (Brewster et al 1993: 20–22).

Subcontractors
Aside from the use of temporary agency workers, subcontracting comes in two basic forms. First, there is the use by employers of consultants and other self-employed people to undertake specific, specialised work. Such arrangements can be long-term in nature, but more frequently involve hiring someone on a one-off basis to work on a single project. The second form occurs when a substantial body of work, such as the provision of catering, cleaning or security services, is subcontracted to a separate company. Both varieties have become more common in recent years, leading to a rise in the number of agency employees and self-employed people. According to IRS (1994b: 7–8), 7 per cent of the total workforce now work as agency staff, and a further 13 per cent are self-employed. Self-employment is focused in the fields of technical and professional services, the majority of self-employed workers being relatively well-paid men. Most of the traditional professions provide opportunities for self-employment, but the highest concentrations are in the fields of draughting, design engineering, computing and business services.

According to the ELUS survey described above, the main reasons given for using self-employed subcontractors were as follows:

- to provide specialist skills (60 per cent)
- to match staffing levels to peaks in demand (29 per cent)
- because workers prefer to be self-employed (28 per cent)
- to reduce wage costs (9 per cent)
- because the self-employed are more productive (8 per cent)

- to reduce non-wage costs (6 per cent)

- to reduce overheads (4 per cent)

- other reasons (11 per cent).

(*Source*: McGregor and Sproull 1992: 227)

Again, the figures in parentheses represent the percentages of employers stating that the reason was one of significance in their use of subcontractors who are self-employed. As with temporary workers, it is interesting how cost-cutting opportunities appear to be so much less significant than the need to bring in specialists. This may be because, hour for hour, the employment of a self-employed contractor is often a good deal more expensive than hiring a temporary employee. Even when the lack of National Insurance and pension contributions are taken into account, along with other on-costs associated with standard employment contracts, it is usually more costly to bring someone in on a consultancy basis.

Aside from cost considerations, there are also other potential disadvantages from the employer's perspective. First, it is often suggested that self-employed people, like agency workers, inevitably have less reason to show a high level of commitment. They have no long-term interest in the organisation and are thus less likely than conventional employees to go beyond the letter of their contracts. In turn this leads to suspicions about the quality and reliability of the services they provide. Only where there is a clear possibility of an on-going relationship in the form of further work does the contractor have a serious economic incentive to overservice the client. Such a perception is of course a generalisation and is probably unfair to the majority of self-employed people, but organisations have to take such thoughts into consideration when considering whether to subcontract work and to whom. In some situations there is no choice, because all the specialists in a field have chosen to work for themselves. One such example is the computer industry, where people with expertise in particular programmes or operations know that they are in a sellers' market and that they can earn more, while keeping control of their own working lives, if they take up self-employed status.

Another possibility to consider, which is relatively common now, is the rehiring of retired employees on a self-employed basis. Both parties stand to gain from such arrangements where the retired person has a reasonable income from his or her pension. The company draws on organisation-specific expertise, but pays for it only when there is a particular demand. The retired person draws a pension and supplements it by undertaking a modest amount of work when he or she wishes to.

Large-scale subcontracting of operations has been particularly associated with the public sector over the past decade, as a result of government policy on competitive tendering. Essentially this required local authorities, health service units and other public institutions which had not been privatised to invite internal service providers to compete with external competitors for the right to continue operating.

Where external firms were successful, the services were 'contracted out', although transfer of undertakings legislation meant that existing employees received a measure of protection. Larger private-sector companies have also tended to move in this direction, as the growth of contract catering and cleaning companies testifies. The rationale behind such moves is based on the assumption that the organisation is thus best left to focus on its core businesses, bringing in specialist providers to look after peripheral or support areas. Hence, an engineering company, school or hospital no longer has to concern itself with the staffing and management of a canteen, crêche or car park. Instead, these services are provided to a higher standard at a lower cost by experts in those fields.

Flexible hours contracts

Another form of atypical working arrangement that, evidence suggests, is becoming more common involves a move away from setting specific hours of work. While such contracts come in several different forms, all help in some way to match the presence of employees with peaks and troughs in demand. They thus help ensure that people are not being paid for being at work when there is little to do, while at the same time avoiding paying premium overtime rates to help cover the busiest periods.

The most common, and least radical, departure from standard employment practices is the flexi-time scheme. Precise rules vary from organisation to organisation but they typically involve employees' clocking in and out of work or recording the hours they work each day. Typically, such schemes work on a monthly basis, requiring employees to be present for 160 hours over the month, but permitting them and their managers to vary the precise times in which they are at work in order to meet business needs and, where possible, their own wishes. Often such schemes identify core hours when everyone must be at work (eg 10–12.00 and 2–4.00 each day), but allow flexibility outside these times. It is then possible for individuals who build up a bank of hours to take a 'flexi-day' or half-day off at a quiet time.

The number of situations in which flexi-time can operate and in which it is appropriate to do so are quite limited. Clearly, it is not a good idea where the presence of a whole team throughout the working day is important. It would thus not be used for roles where there is direct contact with customers or where a manufacturing process required a large number of employees to be present at the same time. It is also inappropriate where organisational objectives and culture focus heavily on the maximisation of effort and the completion of specific tasks. In such workplaces the hours worked are often long, and there is a need to encourage employees to concentrate more on the achievement of goals and less on the actual time they are spending at work. Hence flexi-time would be inappropriate for newspaper journalists, because the hours worked are inevitably determined by the requirement to chase and write stories. In any case, the whole idea of clocking in or recording hours worked on a time sheet is seen by many organisations as undesirable in itself and representative of an approach to management from which they wish to move. According to IRS (1997b:

this was the major reason for the abandoning of flexi-time by Cable and Wireless following privatisation in 1981. Their objection was the way in which the system 'symbolised a relationship between management and employees far removed from the one to which it aspired – namely one based on trust and shared responsibility'.

However, flexi-time remains in many organisations – particularly where large numbers of clerical and secretarial workers are employed to look after a range of different bodies of work. Where deadlines are relatively unimportant, where individuals have responsibility for carrying out a prescribed range of tasks and where there is no requirement to be available to members of the public all day long, there is a good case for using flexi-time to maximise organisational efficiency. This is because it cuts out the need to pay overtime and keeps the overall headcount to a minimum. It is thus unsurprising that it is mostly used in government departments, local authorities and other public-sector organisations. In the private sector it is used mainly in larger financial services companies for clerical staff working in back-office roles.

A more radical form of flexi-time is the annual hours contract. The principle is the same, only here the amount of time worked can vary from month to month or season to season as much as from day to day. It varies from typical flexi-time systems not least because variations in hours are decided by the employer without much choice being given to the employee. Each year all employees are required to work a set number of hours (usually 1,880), but to come in for much longer periods at some times than others. Pay levels, however, remain constant throughout the year. Again, from the employer's point of view, the aim is to match the demand for labour to its supply and thus avoid employing people at slack times and paying overtime in busier periods. Variations can occur seasonally, monthly or can follow no predictable pattern at all. In tourism or agriculture, where the summer is busy and the winter quiet, this can then be reflected in the time put in by employees. In an accountancy firm, where month and year-end reports need to be produced to tight deadlines, employees can then work long weeks followed by compensation in the form of shorter ones.

According to Brewster et al (1993), the incidence of annual hours schemes has steadily increased in recent years, and they now cover around 6 per cent of the working population in the UK. However, their relative scarcity is interesting when their potential advantages from the perspective of both employers and employees is considered. In part, this is explained by the presence of similar objections as those described above in the case of flexi-time, but there are also practical difficulties. A major problem concerns what to do when an employee leaves, having worked only during a slack period, but having also drawn the full monthly salary. It can also be difficult to predict the supply of work, so that an organisation ends up either paying overtime anyway or employing more people than it actually needs to cover the work. However, where such issues can be overcome, annual hours can be attractive to employees, leading to lower levels of staff turnover and absence.

At the other end of the scale is the zero hours contract, which organisations use in the case of casual employees who work on a regular basis. They are most suitable for situations in which there are frequent and substantial surges in demand for employees on particular days or weeks of the year, but where their instance is unpredictable. An example is the employment of couriers in the travel industry. A company needs to have a body of trained courier staff it can call on to look after clients, but is unable to predict exactly how many it will need and on what dates. It therefore hires people on a casual basis, gives them training and then calls on their services as required during the holiday season. Another common example is the employment of waiting staff for banquets and Christmas parties in hotels and restaurants. Because the staff involved have no great expectation of substantial amounts of work, they usually combine casual employment with other activities. Many have other jobs too, or are in full-time education. Employers can thus not always rely on their availability at short notice and have to ensure that enough trained people are kept on their books to cover their needs at any time.

A variation on the zero-hours approach is a system that guarantees casual employees a minimum number of hours a week or days a year. IRS (1997b: 8) reports that Tesco uses such an approach in some of its stores. Tesco guarantees employees between 10 and 16 hours' work a week, but then adds to this if the workload increases or in order to cover absences among non-casual employees. The core guaranteed hours are fixed week by week, but additional hours are flexible and can be arranged as little as a day in advance.

Homeworking
The final form of atypical or non-standard working to be described in this chapter is the employment of people to work either wholly or partly from home. We are not looking here at self-employed people or casual workers, but at people whose contracts of employment are standard in other respects. The extent to which this kind of arrangement currently occurs is not easy to state with certainty because many people work from home only for a proportion of their time, but according to IRS (1994b: 7) there are around 700,000 homeworkers. However, there is clearly now considerable potential for growth with the expansion of computerised communication technology and improvements in telecommunications. At present, according to Brewster et al (1993: 46–50), full-time homeworkers fall into two camps: the up-market teleworker and the more traditional manual variety. The latter are heavily concentrated in the textile and leather goods industries, where part of the manufacturing process can be carried out by people working alone away from the shop floor. However, some routine office tasks, such as the preparation of mailshots, can also be performed at home.

For the employer, the main advantage is a reduction in the size of premises required. Savings are thus made in terms of office rents, business rates, heating and lighting. The main disadvantages relate to the low morale that homeworkers often suffer as a result of their isolation from co-workers. A different kind of supervision is thus required, along with control systems that assess performance on the basis of the quantity and quality of each batch of work undertaken. Because it is clearly not possible to oversee each individual's work, there is no opportunity either to encourage or correct when mistakes are made or when the pace of work slackens. As yet there is little specific employment law concerned with protecting the rights of homeworkers. However, campaigns are launched from time to time by trade unions and other bodies concerned about low pay and lack of employment protection, so it is reasonable to expect that legislation may soon be introduced along Continental lines. This will ensure that homeworkers enjoy the same terms and conditions as other employees and the same access to training, and that they are offered the full range of fringe benefits. There is also a strong case for bringing homework stations within the ambit of organisations' health and safety responsibilities.

The biggest problem in managing a home-based workforce is the maintenance of effective communication – a particularly important issue where members of the 'core' workforce are employed on a teleworking basis. If such arrangements are to work, more is needed than simple electronic communication. There is also a need to hold regular team meetings, as well as face-to-face sessions between supervisors and staff. In practice, as has been pointed out, most homeworking of this kind is carried out part time, the employee performing some work at the office and some at home. When managed well, this can be the best of both worlds, in that effective communication is retained while savings in terms of office space and energy use are also achieved. Of course, this can occur only if employees forgo the privilege of having their own office or desk at work and accept 'hot-desking' arrangements, whereby they occupy whichever workstation or computer terminal is free when they are not working at home.

> Which of these forms of atypical working most appeal to you? Which would be appropriate for P&D specialists in your organisation?

LONGER-TERM CONSIDERATIONS

Finally, it is necessary briefly to consider what the effects will be if the management gurus who have predicted sweeping changes in work organisation turn out to be right. What will the effects be in employee-resourcing terms if non-standard working becomes the norm and people do seriously cease to expect, or even to seek, long-term, full-time employment with a single employer, preferring instead to work on a self-employed consultancy basis for a number of clients? The straightforward answer is that there will be a need for employee-resourcing specialists to find ways of managing through or round some of the disadvantages associated with atypical working described above. However, there are other potential consequences too – some of which can already be observed in industries where there are lucrative freelancing opportunities for people with particular skills. Examples include computer programming, some branches of engineering and the provision of some specialised business services.

The most obvious result is increasing difficulty in finding people to undertake work at the rates of pay currently being offered. The organisation is thus faced with three options:

• to accept that it is necessary to employ freelancers at whatever cost

• to hire untrained staff and then to invest substantial amounts in training them

• to compete more effectively in a tighter labour market, giving particular attention to the retention of valued staff.

For many organisations this will require fundamental changes in the approach taken towards employee resourcing. It will no longer be possible simply to assume that, if someone leaves, he or she can readily be replaced by another person with similar skills. In other words, it will be necessary for managers to accept, to a far greater extent than is often the case today, that competitive labour markets exist, and that they need to develop effective strategies for competing in those that are vital to the success and survival of their organisations. Secondly, there is a need to redefine the psychological contract that is developed with employees by fostering relationships that facilitate high trust but that are not expected by either side to last for a long period of time. This involves acknowledging that employees will have different expectations from employers. Instead of seeking furtherance of a career inside an organisation, they will be looking instead for opportunities to increase their employability. To attract and then to motivate the best, more attention will thus have to be given to skills acquisition and to finding opportunities for employees to deepen their experience.

A third possibility that arises if key labour markets become much tighter than they are at present, could be a need to alter the perspective from which strategic business planning currently takes place. Instead of looking for product market opportunities and then devising employee-resourcing policies to permit their realisation, there will increasingly be a need to start the process by assessing the organisation's labour market position. Strategic planning would thus commence with questions being asked about the pool of staff and skills on which the organisation can draw. Product market strategies would then be based on the results of this analysis, rather than the other way round.

> What other consequences do you think follow from this analysis? Which groups of employees with which you are familiar is such a scenario likely to affect first?

FURTHER READING

• Both the topics covered in this chapter are covered briefly but effectively in *The Witch Doctors* by John Micklethwaite and Adrian

Woodridge (1996). A number of the themes, and their consequences for P&D in general, are also dealt with from a US perspective in articles included in *Tomorrow's HR Management*, edited by Dave Ulrich, Michael Losey and Gerry Lake (1997).

- One of the best general introductions to the process of internationalisation, which also touches on employee resourcing issues, is *Global Shift: The internationalisation of economic activity* by Peter Dicken (1992). More detailed treatment of P&D issues is found in Derek Torrington's *International Human Resource Management* (1994) and Charles Hendry's *Human Resources Strategies for International Growth* (1994).

- The debate about the flexible firm and the reasons for changing patterns of atypical working has been covered in a variety of books and articles. In addition to research work cited in the chapter, general summaries are found in *The Jobs Mythology*, an IDS Focus publication (1995), and in the article by Alan McGregor and Alan Sproull entitled 'Employers and the flexible workforce', in *Employment Gazette* (May 1992).

- The practical advantages and disadvantages of employing people on particular types of atypical contract are covered thoroughly by Chris Brewster and his colleagues in *Flexible Working Patterns in Europe* (IPD, 1994) and by the IRS in special articles featured in Issues 565 and 635 of *Employment Trends* (August 1994 and July 1997).

Part 2

PLANNING

3 Navigating the high seas of the labour market

The techniques of human resource (HR) planning are some of the most involved and complex activities carried out by employee-resourcing professionals. By contrast, the basic principles on which they are founded are straightforward, with a potential significance that is readily understood. HR planning is also an area of P&D work that has often been denigrated in recent years, with the result that it has received relatively little attention in the literature and has become less widely used in organisations. Criticism of the HR planning function has tended to come from two directions. On the one hand, it has been seen as overly mathematical and so scientifically sophisticated as to render it remote and irrelevant from day-to-day management concerns; on the other, it has been branded oversimplistic, critics challenging the very notion that it is possible to plan the staffing of an organisation with such confidence in a fundamentally unpredictable business environment.

In this and the following chapter the practice of HR planning is examined and its relevance to organisations today discussed. In this chapter, the focus is on the practicalities. The term 'human resource planning' is defined, followed by a description of the various activities that have traditionally been undertaken by HR planners. In the next chapter, the wider debate about the usefulness of HR planning in the current environment is examined, and the purposes to which HR plans can be put are discussed.

By the end of this chapter readers should be able to:

• design and implement a system for human resource planning

• estimate the future demand for labour

- measure current levels of employee utilisation, productivity and performance

- forecast the extent to which human resource needs can be met internally

- assess how far and by what means the demand for human resources can be met by external labour markets

- provide advice concerning the use of information technology in undertaking the above activities.

In addition, readers should be able to understand and explain:

- the terminology used in the practice of human resource planning

- the principles underlying effective human resource planning.

A NOTE ON TERMINOLOGY

As in so many areas of personnel management, there is some confusion about the precise meanings of the terms used to describe the human resource planning function. Here, as elsewhere, developments in terminology have moved on at different speeds and in different directions than developments in the activities themselves, leading to something of a mismatch between the concepts and the labels used to describe them. As with the term 'human resource management', there are in the field of human resource planning different uses of key terms by different authors. The main distinction is between those who see the term 'human resource planning' as having broadly the same meaning as the longer established terms 'workforce planning' and 'manpower planning', and those who believe 'human resource planning' to represent something rather different.

Foremost in the second group is John Bramham (1987, 1988, 1994), one of the most prolific writers on the subject. He makes a big distinction between 'manpower planning', which he sees as essentially quantitative in nature and concerned with forecasting the demand and supply of labour, and 'human resource planning', to which he gives a far wider meaning, encompassing plans made across the whole range of P&D activity (including soft issues such as motivation, employee attitudes and organisational culture). His book *Human Resource Planning*, published in 1994, is thus very different in terms of its content from the earlier *Practical Manpower Planning* (1988), the best established book covering the field. For others, the term 'human resource planning' is simply a more modern and gender-neutral term with essentially the same meaning as 'manpower planning'. Both are concerned with looking ahead and using systematic techniques to assess the extent to which an organisation will be able to meet its requirements for labour in the future. They are thus undertaken in order to assess whether an organisation is likely to have 'the right people, with the right skills, in the right places at the right time'. According to this definition, human resource planning is a relatively specialised subdiscipline within the general activity undertaken by personnel managers.

It is the latter definition that is used by the CIPD in its Professional

Standards, and it is the one that is accepted for the purposes of this text. While the term 'human resource planning' will be used throughout, it can thus be taken by readers to refer to the same disciplines and activities traditionally encompassed by the terms 'manpower' and 'workforce' planning.

STAGES IN HUMAN RESOURCE PLANNING

Human resource planning is principally concerned with assessing an organisation's position in relation to its labour markets and forecasting its likely situation in years to come. It is thus mostly used to formulate the data on which plans of action can be based rather than in the actual drawing up those plans. If, for example, a supermarket chain is planning to open a large new store for which it believes there is a market, the human resource planning function would be responsible for identifying how easily – given previous experience of opening superstores of a similar size – the organisation will be able to recruit the staff it needs from internal and external sources to launch its new venture. It is thus concerned with identifying potential or likely problems with staffing the store and not with the development of specific plans to recruit and develop the employees needed. John Bramham, in defining manpower planning, has developed the metaphor of a ship at sea to illustrate the distinction between planning in general terms and the devising of specific plans of action (Bramham 1988: 5–6). Seen in this way, human resource planning has more in common with navigation than piloting. It is about assessing the environment and bringing together the data required to plan the direction the organisation needs to take if it is to achieve its goals.

The forecasting function has three general stages, which will be dealt with one by one in this chapter. First, there is the need to assess what demand the organisation will have for people and for what skills as its business plans unfold. This stage is therefore about distilling the human resource implications from overall organisational strategies. If the business aim is expansion to new product markets or regions, then calculations need to be made about how many people, with what training, will be required at what stage. If the business strategy emphasises consolidation and innovation rather than growth, there is still a need to assess what new skills or competencies will be required if the plan is to be met. Having determined the likely demand for labour, the next two stages involve assessing the potential supply of human resources. First, there is a need to look at internal supply – at the likelihood that those already employed by the organisation will be able, or indeed willing, to remain in their employment and develop sufficient skills and gain enough experience to be capable of meeting the demand identified in the first stage. The final stage considers any gap between likely demand and likely supply identified in stages one and two. Here the planner is concerned with forecasting how far skills and experience not available internally will be obtainable externally through the recruitment of new employees.

FORECASTING FUTURE DEMAND FOR HUMAN RESOURCES

The process of assessing demand is defined by Smith (1976: 20) as follows:

> Analysing, reviewing and attempting to predict the numbers, by kind, of the manpower needed by the organisation to achieve its objectives.

The ability of human resource managers to predict accurately how many people will be required and with what skills depends on a number of factors. First, there is the timescale that the forecast is intended to cover. Except in the most turbulent of environments, it is possible to look forward one or two years and make reasonable assumptions about what staffing requirements will be. It gets far harder when timescales of three, five or ten years are contemplated. This is because relevant technological or economic developments that will have a profound effect on the level and kind of activity carried out by the organisation may not yet even have been contemplated.

The other major variable is the nature of the activities carried out by the organisation. Those in relatively stable environments are able to forecast their needs with far greater confidence than those operating in inherently unstable conditions. An example of the former might be a government department such as the Foreign Office or a local authority social services department. Here, relatively little is likely to change, except at the margins, over the foreseeable future. Such change as there is likely to be will be gradual and brought in steadily over a manageable period. It is therefore quite possible to make reasonable estimations of how many diplomats, administrators or social workers will be needed in five or ten years' time. While there may be increases in productivity brought about through re-organisation and new working methods, such matters are predictable to a considerable degree. By contrast, a company with a relatively small market share of an international market can make such forecasts with far less confidence. Even looking forward one year, it is difficult to say for certain how many will be employed, or what roles they will be undertaking.

The timescale and the nature of the business will influence which of the various available techniques are used to forecast the demand for human resources. We divide these into four basic categories: systematic techniques, managerial judgement, combining systematic and subjective approaches, and working back from costs.

Systematic techniques

At root, most mathematical and statistical techniques used in demand forecasting are concerned with estimating future requirements from an analysis of past and current experience. A number of distinct approaches are identified in the literature, including time series analysis, work study and productivity trend analysis.

Time series or ratio-trend analyses look at past business patterns and the numbers of people employed in different roles to make judgements about how many will be required to meet business targets in the future. Such an approach is straightforward and appropriate only in relatively stable business environments. Common examples are found in the public services, where the number of school children or elderly patients that require education or treatment is predicted some years in advance on the basis of population trends. In such circumstances it is possible to project how many teachers, nurses, doctors and support staff will be needed, given the staff–student or staff–patient ratios of the past.

The method is also helpful in businesses subject to cyclical fluctuations over time. Where it is known, on the basis of past experience, that the number of customers is likely to increase and decrease seasonally or in tandem with economic cycles, it is possible to plan future staffing requirements accordingly. The principle is best illustrated graphically. In Figure 3 past occupancy and staffing rates in a large seaside hotel employing 250 full-timers are shown. The thin line represents occupancy rates and the thick line the number of whole-time equivalent staff employed. Future projections are shown as broken lines. Here there is a clear pattern of full or near-full occupancy in the summer and very low occupancy in the spring with an intermediate position at Christmas. The projections of future occupancy are based on the average figures for past years. The number of seasonal, temporary staff needed in the future at particular times of the year can be estimated using the scale marked on the y axis. Thus, for December 1999 the hotel will need to hire and train around 40 temporary staff to assist its 250 full-timers.

This is, of course, a very simple example used to illustrate a planning technique that is potentially far more complex. In practice, most organisations would have to analyse separate time series for different departments or grades of staff to obtain useful information. It is also likely that, for many, the fluctuations are less predictable, requiring predicted levels of business to be adjusted as the date in question approaches. The more complex the organisation and the variations in staffing levels, the more useful computer programmes designed to assist in this kind of analysis are.

The work study approach has a different basis. Here, instead of assuming that the ratio of business to staff will remain broadly constant, special studies are undertaken of individual tasks or processes carried out by the organisation in order to establish the numbers required to complete them most effectively and efficiently. The method is thus suitable in situations where there are no clear past trends to examine, or where wholly new production or service methods are being planned. Work study is most commonly associated with manufacturing industries where the work is readily divisible into discrete production-line tasks (for example, when a new plant is being brought into service using hitherto untried production methods). The work study specialist then observes employees undertaking each task involved in the manufacturing process during the development stage. Once the most productive systems have been observed, it is possible to compute the number of staff required and the type of skills they will require.

According to Silver (1983: 49–60) a further approach involves

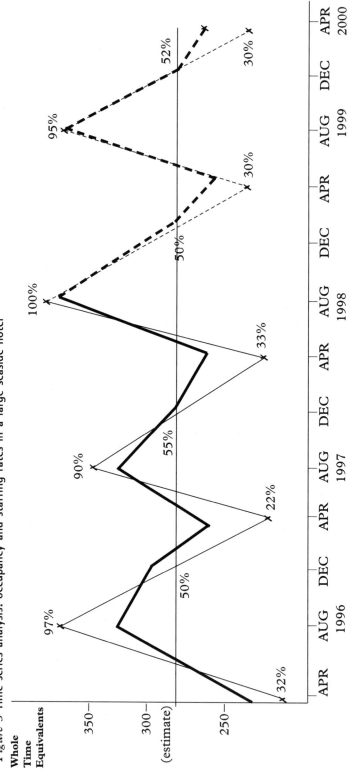

Figure 3 Time series analysis: occupancy and staffing rates in a large seaside hotel

incorporating productivity trends into the time series calculation. This method removes from the time-series analysis described above the assumption that the ratio of staff to work (labour to capital) will remain constant over time. Instead, improvements in productivity over past years are calculated and extrapolated forward when calculating future human resource requirements. The approach is best suited to long-term forecasting, perhaps when major capital investment is being contemplated which has a long lead time. An industry for which such an approach might be feasible today would be banking, where large organisations employing skilled employees have seen very considerable productivity improvements in recent years. Given this experience, it would be appropriate to take account of that productivity trend, as well as the likely volume of work in the future, when forecasting the numbers to be hired and trained over future years.

Managerial judgement
A very different approach to forecasting demand dispenses to some degree with systematic approaches. Instead, it bases forecasts on the subjective views of managers about likely future human resource needs. Clearly, in situations where the business environment is highly volatile and where future staffing patterns may well bear little resemblance to past experience, there is no alternative, if planning is to occur, to using informed opinion as a basis for estimates. According to Stainer (1971: 98) there are three principle advantages arising from this approach:

• It is quick and requires little or no data collection.

• Basically intangible factors, such as changes in fashion, social opinion and taste, can be brought into account.

• The opinion of managers from different organisations as well as that of other experts can be used, as far as they are available.

This last point is probably less relevant in the current environment, where competition between employing organisations has replaced central planning, even in much of the public sector. Nevertheless, it is possible to envisage situations in which managers from other organisations who have experienced a particular set of changes might be able to offer valuable assistance in planning for similar developments elsewhere. An example is the NHS Unit Labour Costs scheme, which puts managers from hospitals in one part of the country in touch with others elsewhere to exchange such information. Another approach commonly used is the recruitment of new managers from organisations that have a similar pattern of development. Thus a British car manufacturer wishing to adopt certain Japanese production techniques might well hire senior figures with direct experience of managing such plants. Their judgement as to the number and type of staff required in the future will clearly be invaluable. Management consultants with similar experience can also be brought in to assist in demand forecasting.

A method that has received considerable attention in the literature on human resource planning is known as the 'delphi technique'. It is a systematic approach to decision-making that aims to introduce a measure of objectivity into the process by which forecasts are made on the basis of managerial judgement. According to Jackson and Schuler (1990: 163), its principal aim is to 'maximise the benefits and minimise the dysfunctional aspects of group decision-making' – achieved by removing group dynamics and political considerations from the process. In human resource planning the delphi technique requires several managers and experts to submit their own forecast in writing (often anonymously) to a central contact, who then circulates the estimates among the other members of the group. Each then revises his or her own forecasts, taking account of the factors suggested in colleagues' submissions. Sometimes several rounds of adjustments are undertaken before a consensus forecast emerges. A form of delphi technique is currently used in parts of the NHS. An example is given below in the boxed text on pages 49–50.

Combining systematic and subjective approaches

In Stainer's view, there are great disadvantages to relying on managerial judgement alone when conducting demand forecasting exercises (Stainer 1971: 98–99). He believes that the complexity of the process and the number of factors at work are often too great for a single brain or group of brains to cope with. Furthermore, he expresses the view that organisational politics and 'emotional attachments' almost inevitably get in the way of objective decision-making when making forecasts of this kind. There is therefore a good case for incorporating both statistical analysis and managerial judgement into the demand forecasting process. Computer modelling greatly enhances the possibility of merging the two approaches successfully, because it permits many more variables to be included in the statistical formulae used than is practicable when calculations are done manually. Such approaches involve statistical analysis, but the assumptions made in the calculations are based on managerial or expert judgement.

Leap and Crino (1993: 179–181) give an example of a formula which fits this description:

$$E = \frac{(L + G) \ 1/X}{Y}$$

Here E represents the number of staff required at a particular date in the future, L the current level of business expressed in terms of turnover, G the expected growth in business level, X the productivity improvement expected during the planning period, and Y the amount of business activity divided by the number of staff (ie the staff:business ratio). In the following example it is assumed that a health authority currently employing 1,385 GPs is considering how many will be needed in the year 2005.

L (current budget for GPs):	£69.25 m
G (expected growth in budget due to increased patient numbers and inflation):	£4.6 m
X (expected productivity growth):	1.02 (indicating an expected productivity improvement of 2 per cent)

Y (current budget per doctor): £50,000

$$E = \frac{(69.2m2 + 4.6m) \times 1/1.02}{50,000}$$

$$E = \frac{72,324000}{50,000} = 1446.48$$

The conclusion is that a total of 1,446.48 GPs will be needed in the year 2005.

Working back from costs

Bramham (1987, 1988) outlines an alternative approach to demand forecasting which removes past experience from the equation altogether. Here the process begins with the future budget – the amount of money the finance department expect to be available for staff costs in coming years. The human resource planner then works out, given that constraint, how many people at what salary level will be affordable. Current methods, ratios and productivity levels are thus ignored, the focus being on designing organisational structures and methods of working that will permit the budget to be met.

In recent years such approaches have been adopted far more frequently in the public services than in the past. With governments continually pressing for greater productivity, the emphasis in planning terms has been less on how many people are required to deliver a particular service given past experience, and more on what the taxpayer is prepared to spend or the government happy to allocate, given its public-spending targets. In the jargon of politicians, resource-based provision has replaced that based on need. The future budget has thus been the starting-point in HR planning rather than the cost of providing the service in question in the past.

Forecasting the demand for nurses

Since April 1997, responsibility for forecasting how many trained nurses will be needed in the future has been transferred from the regional health authorities to education consortia set up in different areas of the country. They are charged with developing five-year rolling plans, on which decisions are based about how much nurse-training must be purchased in the future. There is a need to look five years ahead because it takes three years for a state registered nurse to graduate. Expected shortfalls have thus to be pointed out well in advance. Each of the education consortia consists of representatives from NHS trusts in the area, health authorities, social services, the private healthcare sector and voluntary organisations. The aim is to include in the planning process all bodies that employ nurses. Each year, between March and May, consortium members develop five-year forecasts.

In the hospitals, the plans are drawn up by workforce planners in consultation with nurse managers. At present, the demand forecasts rely very heavily on managerial judgement, few statistical techniques being used. In addition to stating the numbers required, the plans submitted to the consortia also highlight important supply issues, such as problems in recruiting certain grades and in retaining existing staff. Any expected changes in demand resulting from skill-mix reviews are also included. Once all the forecasts are received, consortia employees develop an overall plan covering all grades of trained staff which is submitted to the regional health authority. The document then forms the basis of decisions concerning the amount of nurse training commissioned over the coming five years.

How far does your organisation go in forecasting future demand? To what extent is it possible to do so, given your business environment?

FORECASTING INTERNAL SUPPLY

There is a variety of techniques used to assess the extent to which the demand for human resources can be met by the existing staff employed by an organisation. However, all share the same basic characteristic: they involve analysing the current workforce department by department or grade by grade before estimating the numbers likely to remain employed and the skills they are likely to possess. As in the case of demand forecasting described above, most of the tools used rely on a mixture of statistical analysis and managerial judgement in assisting planners to make informed forecasts. The key here is detailed analysis. In forecasting internal supply, overall figures about staff turnover rates are of little help. What is important is the likely turnover rate among specific groups of staff, such as those of a particular age, those with a defined length of service or those employed at different levels to do different jobs.

Predicting likely staff turnover (better described from the perspective of P&D managers as 'wastage') with any degree of accuracy is a complex activity, because people leave their current jobs for a variety of reasons. The following list covers many of these, but is by no means exhaustive:

• internal promotion

• internal transfer

• internal demotion

• to take up a different job offer elsewhere

• to retire

• to enter full-time education

• through illness

• redundancy or end of temporary contract

• dismissal for misconduct or incapability

• to take a career break

• to set up a new business

• as a result of a spouse or partner's relocating.

While the instance of some of these can either be increased or reduced by actions taken in the employing organisation, many are linked to factors in the wider environment – social, political, economic and technological. Others are linked to the age of the employee concerned. All these factors need therefore to be considered when developing meaningful forecasts of turnover rates in the future. Edwards (1983: 62) makes the following general observations, which still hold true in the 1990s:

• wastage rates decrease with increasing age

• wastage rates decrease with increasing length of service

• wastage rates decrease with increasing skill and responsibility

• wastage rates are higher for female than for male staff

• wastage rates decrease when the general level of unemployment rises.

However, the experience of particular organisations or individual departments may well not correlate with these general observations, or may do so only to a limited extent. Meaningful forecasts of turnover must thus incorporate consideration of the organisation's experience while building in assumptions about the probable future effects of environmental and demographic factors. Past figures are primarily analysed using the wastage and stability indices, together with analysis of specific employee cohorts and internal promotion patterns.

Wastage analysis
The wastage index is one of the basic formulae used by human resource planners in calculating likely future turnover rates. It is calculated thus:

$$\frac{\text{Number leavers in a specified period}}{\text{Average number employed in the same period}} \times 100$$

The raw calculation is multiplied by 100 to allow the result to be expressed as a percentage. As has previously been stated, general organisation-wide turnover statistics are of limited use. While they may be helpful in making broad year-on-year comparisons or for general target-setting, they are misleading if used as the basis of forecasting future internal supply. This is because the overall figure may mask very great differences between separate departments in the organisation and different groups of employees. In particular, raw figures do not take into account the tendency, identified above, for wastage to decrease with tenure and age. It is quite possible to envisage circumstances in which an organisation with a very low wastage rate might see it increase several times over when it embarks on a programme of expansion – particularly if it brings in large numbers of younger people in the process. Moreover, the overall wastage figure may mask big differences in turnover rates between different posts in the organisation. Hence an organisation with 60 per cent turnover may actually have quite low wastage in most posts, but a very high rate in others.

Stability analysis

The method used to give more meaning to wastage rates is the stability index, also expressed in percentage terms:

$$\frac{\text{Number of employees with } x \text{ years' service at a given date}}{\text{Number employed } x \text{ years ago}} \times 100$$

Thus, if an organisation employs 1,000 people at the start of 1998, and calculates at the end of the year that 800 remain in their jobs, it would have a stability rate of 80 per cent. It thus looks at staff turnover from the opposite angle, focusing on the proportion of human capital that is retained, and not on the numbers lost.

Cohort analysis

A method used to make forecasts in an effort to further improve the accuracy of wastage predictions is cohort analysis. Here, instead of focusing on the stability and turnover for the staff generally, separate figures are calculated for each cohort of staff – usually the group hired in a particular year. The stability index is therefore adjusted somewhat to calculate a 'survival rate' for each cohort. In effect this involves simply calculating, on an annual basis, a different stability index for each year's intake of new employees. An example is shown in Table 1, focusing on stability rates among a cohort of a company's 150 graduate trainees starting in January 1990.

Again, as with the other approaches, the purpose of cohort analysis for human resource planners is to enable them to focus on past trends and use them as the basis for forecasting the extent to which an organisation is likely to be able to meet its future demand for labour internally. With cohort analyses it is common to calculate 'half-lives' for each group under examination. This is the length of time, expressed in years or months, that it takes for each cohort to halve in size. In the example below, 50 per cent is reached between two and three years – after 32 months or so. The half-life figure can then be readily used to compare one group of jobs in an organisation with another, allowing meaningful predictions to be made about likely future internal supply.

Table 1 Cohort analysis for graduate trainees starting in 1990

Year index	Number employed at year end	Survival rate %
1990	120	80
1991	90	60
1992	67	45
1993	48	32
1994	41	27
1995	36	24
1996	30	20
1997	24	16

Internal promotion analysis

In larger organisations with well-defined hierarchies there is a need, when forecasting internal supply, to take account of movement up the ranks or grades, in addition to general wastage rates. It is important to know not only how many trainees remain employed but also how many are likely to achieve promotion to different levels in the organisation. In a department store, for example, knowledge of the stability and wastage indices for shop supervisors is meaningless if account is not also taken of the fact that 90 per cent of supervisor vacancies are filled through internal promotion.

A variety of statistical models has been developed to assist in predicting human resource flows into, out of and up graded hierarchies. The best known is the Markov model, in which past data is used to work out the statistical probability that vacancies at each level will be filled internally. A straightforward example might be a traditional restaurant, where waiting staff are graded as follows:

a) junior waiter

b) chef de rang

c) restaurant supervisor

d) restaurant manager.

Past patterns of promotion can then be used to work out how often, in practice, vacancies at each level are filled through internal promotion from the grade below. In most large hotel and restaurant chains the majority of those in grades b and c will have been promoted through the ranks. An understanding of such processes and their frequency is essential if employee resourcing specialists are to forecast accurately how far future demand for chefs de rang and supervisors will be met internally, and thus how many vacancies will have to be filled externally.

As was indicated in the section on demand forecasting, in most situations there is a need to combine the statistical forecasts based on past activity with the judgement of managers and other informed observers as to what factors are likely to change the patterns in the future. The result will be a forecast based on analysis of past wastage that also takes into account some of the factors listed above, such as unemployment rates, anticipated retirements, likely promotions and any other actions taken by managers or planned for the future that might alter the prevailing trends.

> Which of the above techniques have you observed being used? Which do you think is most appropriate for your organisation?

FORECASTING EXTERNAL SUPPLY

Having established the future demand for different kinds of employee, and how far these needs will or will not be met internally, it is necessary to give attention to filling the gap and reconciling supply and demand using the external labour market. While internal data can help planners make judgements about trends in different labour markets (eg response rates to advertisements, the proportion of turnover explained by individuals leaving to join competitors, the performance of new starters), for the most part relevant information is found outside the organisation.

Most labour markets are local. That is to say, applications for vacancies will come only from people already living within commuting distance of the principal place of work. The trends that are important in such circumstances, from an employer's point of view, are thus those occurring within the relevant 'travel to work area'. For other jobs, usually those requiring greater levels of skill or commanding higher salary rates, the relevant labour markets will be national or even international. In either situation there is a need for human resource planners to gain an understanding of the dynamics of these labour markets and to update their plans as trends change and develop. As far as the immediate travel to work area is concerned, the following statistics are the most helpful:

- general population density
- population movements in and out of the area
- age distribution
- social class
- unemployment rates
- school leavers
- the proportion with higher education
- skill levels.

Statistics of this nature for each local authority area are collected by the government and published in the monthly journal now known as *Labour Market Trends*, until recently entitled *Employment Gazette*. Other useful publications include *Labour Market Quarterly*, the annual *Social Trends* survey and the reports that are published following each national census (undertaken every 10 years). In addition there are commercial organisations, often specialising in particular groups of employees or industries, that collate information from other sources and undertake research themselves. An example is a consultancy set up to provide information to NHS units in the North of England, which produces a quarterly journal as well as providing specific advice to individual trusts. Other sources of local information are Chambers of Commerce and (in England and Wales) the Training and Enterprise Councils (TECs). In addition to the basic statistics, there is a need to apply judgement and experience to assess the potential impact of other local factors. Those that might be relevant include any developments in the local transport network that might effectively expand or contract the travel to work area, the opening or closure of other units and the construction of new housing developments.

Where employers operate in national labour markets there is far less meaningful information available, because only very major trends are likely to have a substantial impact on future recruitment and retention exercises. The fact that unemployment increases or decreases nationally may well have little or no impact on specific labour markets – as was shown in the recessions of the 1980s and 1990s, when skill shortages remained in some areas despite the large number of people seeking work. That said, there are national statistics that may be of relevance in specific circumstances, particularly for larger employers. These would include statistics on the number of individuals leaving higher education with specific qualifications and the number of employers competing for their services.

As was the case with local labour markets, there is also a need to keep an eye on any other major developments that might have an impact on the organisation's ability to recruit sufficient numbers in the future. Examples would include new government initiatives in the field of education and training, and the manner in which particular jobs or professions are portrayed by the media.

HRP at a high-street chemist

A good illustration of the application of the human resource planning principles and techniques described in this chapter is the plan drawn up by a chain of high-street chemists to cope with an expected shortfall in the number of pharmacists early in the twenty-first century.

Here, the starting-point was a change in the external environment: the expansion of the UK pharmacy degree course from three to four years from 1997. The company has always hired substantial numbers of qualified pharmacists to work in their stores straight from university, so they are faced with a significant problem in 2001, when no new pharmacists will be graduating.

In order to address the problem the company has undertaken a human resource planning exercise involving forecasts of the likely demand for and internal supply of staff in 2001. The demand analysis included consideration of the following factors:

- the number of new stores the company plans to have in operation by 2001

- the staffing implications of Sunday trading and extended weekday opening hours

- the changing job roles undertaken by pharmacists.

Having worked out how many pharmacists they will require, they then undertook an analysis of how many they would be likely to have, were they to continue operating established recruitment practices. This exercise involved consideration of likely staff turnover figures for pharmacists between 1996 and 2001, but also took account of expected maternity leave and secondments out of high-street stores.

The final stage involved determining how great the shortfall was likely to be and formulating plans to match the gap **with additional** recruitment in the years prior to 2001. In addition, P&D policies are being developed aimed at reducing turnover among pharmacists so as to reduce as far as possible the magnitude of the skill shortage.

COMPUTER APPLICATIONS

There are many different ways in which information technology can be used to support and undertake human resource planning. However, these can be divided into three broad categories: information provision, modelling and presentation. An important role played by computer databases is storing the information required to undertake meaningful forecasts of demand for staff and internal supply. Not only do computerised personnel information systems (CPISs) allow more data to be stored about jobs, employees and past applicants, they also permit far swifter generation of reports summarising the data than is ever possible using manual information storage systems. The larger and more complex the organisation, the more added value is gained by the presence of a CPIS with such capabilities.

Much information held in CPISs can be used in human resource planning, and forms the basis for the calculations and judgements referred to above. The following list is indicative but by no means comprehensive:

- sex

- age

- start date

- pay levels

- test scores at selection

- internal career history

- career history prior to joining

- educational qualifications

- skills/training completed

- performance/productivity ratings

- sickness/absence records

- promotion record

- turnover record.

Data such as this, analysed for hundreds or thousands of present and past employees, provides raw data for the calculation of formulae such as the wastage and stability indices, and for the analysis of cohorts and promotion patterns. It also permits HR planners to calculate correlations between wastage and variables such as age, sex, type of job and pay rate. In addition it facilitates analysis of the organisation's bank of skills when calculations are being made about its ability to meet future demand internally. Furthermore, the reporting facilities built into personnel databases readily permit comparative analysis between one department and another so as to make forecasts more accurate.

The second major application of information technology in human resource planning is in the field of modelling. The ability of a computer to handle vast quantities of data permits highly complex formulae containing numerous variables to be built up and results to be calculated in seconds. While specialist modelling programmes are available on the market, most human resource forecasting can be undertaken using basic spreadsheet programmes – best illustrated with an example. Table 2 shows a fictional spreadsheet application for a computer software company. The columns each represent a different variable.

Table 2 **Spreadsheet application**

Job title	A	B	C	D	E	F
Manager	6	5%	20%	60%	7.5	3.0
Administrator	28	15%	20%	3%	37.8	36.6
Accountant	12	3%	20%	10%	14.8	13.3
Sales executive	40	60%	30%	5%	76.0	72.2
Software developer	35	12%	30%	20%	14.7	11.8
Software support	30	23%	30%	7%	15.9	14.8

Key
A   Total number of whole time equivalents in post at 1 January
B   Turnover rate based on past trends
C   Increased demand expected during the coming year
D   Number of vacancies typically filled by internal promotion
E   Number of vacancies expected in the coming year
F   Number of posts to be filled externally in the coming year

Columns A, B, C and D are calculated using analysis of past data, adjusted as is seen fit, given expected environmental changes. Columns E and F are calculated using statistical formulae that include the variables A, B, C and D. In this case E is calculated using the formula $[(A \times C) + A] + (A \times B)$. The number of vacancies is therefore calculated with reference to current numbers, likely growth and expected turnover rates. By contrast, F is calculated using the formula $E - (E \times D)$. It thus takes into account both the number of vacancies and the number of internal promotions.

Even with a small-scale exercise of this kind looking at forecasts for one year in a relatively small company, the assistance of a computer makes the planning process far quicker than would be the case if the calculations were undertaken using a calculator. The advantage becomes far greater when more rows and columns are added, looking at incorporating additional variables, forecasts for a number of years ahead and the building-in of cost assumptions. In the above example it would be very straightforward to add further columns representing forecasts for 1999, 2000 and beyond, and others calculating the costs of training and recruiting new staff members in the various categories. Spreadsheets also permit the development of far more complicated formulae involving averages, fractions, logarathims, standard devia-tions, variances and many other statistical tools. It is also possible to build IF ... THEN ... ELSE commands into the formulae used (eg: IF (a $\times$ c) > b THEN e ELSE a $\times$ b).

Perhaps the greatest advantage of the computer in human resource planning, examined in more detail in the next chapter, is the ability it gives the planner to undertake 'What if?' analyses, altering figures or formulae to calculate what the implications would be, were key trends to change. In the example given here, the effect of increased or reduced turnover on the future supply of and demand for labour could be calculated with very great ease: it would simply be necessary to alter the figures in column B and to watch while the computer recalculated the figures in columns E and F.

The third major contribution of computer technology in the human resource planning field is in the capacity of proprietary systems to generate attractive and user-friendly reports and summaries. The advantage of innovations in this area is the relative ease with which data is interpreted. It is possible to present senior managers with well laid-out graphics that summarise forecasts without the need to spend time drawing up such documents separately. The credibility and efficiency of the P&D function in general, as well as the HRP function in particular, is thus increased.

> In what ways could human resource planning in your organisation be improved with greater use of computer applications? Could such activities be justified in cost terms?

FURTHER READING

- The best general introduction to the practice of human resource planning is John Bramham (1988)'s well-established text *Practical Manpower Planning*. There are other books that cover the topics but they are now for the most part quite dated and available only in libraries. These include a booklet produced by the Department of Employment, entitled *Company Manpower Planning* (1971) and *Manpower Planning* by Gareth Stainer (1971).

- There is also a number of edited texts containing short articles about different aspects of human resource planning and the various statistical techniques used. The most recent is *Manpower Planning: Strategy and techniques in an organizational context* by John Edwards *et al* (1983). Other, rather older, books include *Manpower Planning: Selected readings*, edited by D.J. Bartholomew (1971), and *Corporate Manpower Planning*, edited by A.R. Smith (1980).

- The specific topic of the use of computers in human resource planning is covered by Bramham (1988) and in *Human Resource Management Systems: Strategies, tactics and techniques* by Vincent Ceriello (1991).

4 Human resource planning is dead, long live human resource planning

In the previous chapter, the various forecasting techniques developed by human resource (HR) planners were described and their objectives discussed. In this chapter we turn our attention to broader issues in the field of HR planning, and in particular to the question of its relevance to employing organisations operating in turbulent and unpredictable environments. Our focus therefore switches from the tools used to undertake HR planning to the utility of formulated plans and the fundamental problems associated with this area of P&D work. In addition, three other specific issues are explored: the extent to which HR planning is undertaken in practice, methods used in its evaluation, and approaches to planning human resources in international organisations.

By the end of this chapter readers should be able to:

- evaluate HR planning activity

- assess the extent to which forms of HR planning can benefit organisational effectiveness

- give advice concerning the application of HR planning in international organisations.

In addition, readers should be able to understand and explain:

- the main arguments against comprehensive HR planning

- the potential benefits of HR planning

- the relationship between HR plans and key environmental trends.

THE PURPOSE OF HR PLANNING

Any fundamental review of the relevance of HR planning must start by asking the most basic question of all: what exactly is it for? It is easier to sing the praises of strategic approaches to the management of people in general terms than it is to make a convincing business case for actively undertaking the processes involved. The clearest summary of the reasoning behind HR planning is given in a discussion paper published by the Labour Government in 1968 (Department of Employment, 1971: 5–7). Bramham (1987: 56–57) also discusses the key objectives. Between them, six basic objectives of HR planning are identified. We shall discuss each in turn.

Recruitment

HR planning provides the information on which recruiters base their activities. It reveals what gaps there are between the demand for and supply of people with particular skills and can thus underpin decisions about whom to recruit and what methods to use in doing so. HR planning aims to ensure that there are neither too many nor too few recruits to meet the organisation's future needs.

Training and development

In forecasting the type of jobs that will need to be filled in the future, as well as the number, HR planning aims to reveal what skills training and development activity need to be undertaken to ensure that existing staff and new recruits possess the required skills at the right time. The longer and more specialised the training, the more significant accurate HR planning is to the organisation's effective operation.

Manpower costing

The accurate forecasting of future staff costs is an important activity in its own right. HR planning assists in cost reduction by aiming to work out in advance how organisational operations can be staffed most efficiently. It is also significant when new ventures or projects are being considered, because it provides information on which to base vital decisions. Too high a labour cost, and the project will not go ahead; too low an estimate, and profit levels will be lower than expected.

Redundancy

HR planning is an important tool in the anticipation of future redundancies. It therefore allows remedial action to be taken (recruitment freezes, retraining, early retirements etc) so as to reduce the numbers involved. As a result, considerable savings in the form of avoided redundancy payments can be made. While redundancies may not be avoided altogether, adequate warning will be given, thus reducing the adverse impact on employee relations associated with sudden announcements of dismissals and restructuring.

Collective bargaining

In organisations with a strong trade union presence, HR planning provides important information for use in the bargaining process. It is particularly significant when long-term deals are being negotiated to improve productivity and efficiency. In such situations, the information provided by HR forecasts enables calculations to be made concerning how great an increase in pay or how great a reduction in hours might be conceded in exchange for more productive working methods and processes.

Accommodation

A final practical advantage associated with HR planning is the information it provides concerning the future need for office space, car parking and other workplace facilities. Such considerations are of most importance when organisations expect fast expansion or contraction of key operations. As with the other objectives described above, the basic rationale is that planning enhances cost control over the long term because it helps avoid the need to respond suddenly to unforeseen circumstances.

THE CASE AGAINST HR PLANNING

The above objectives of HR planning seem at first sight to be universally applicable to any employing organisation. As a result, it is easy to jump to the conclusion that the use of the tools and policies outlined in the previous chapter must be a prerequisite of effective competition over the long term in all product and labour markets. While many have argued that such is the case, a number of other authors have developed alternative arguments, putting a case against HR planning that seems to have more and more resonance as the business environment becomes increasingly turbulent.

The essence of the argument against the HR planning function is based on the simple proposition that it is impossible to forecast the demand for and supply of labour with any accuracy – a classic case of a brilliant theory being undermined by insurmountable problems when put into practice. In recent years, the most celebrated critic of business planning processes in general (ie not just those in the HR field) has been Henry Mintzberg. In a series of books and articles he has advanced the view that, in practice, most forecasts turn out to be wrong and that, as a result, the planning process tends to impede the achievement of competitive advantage (eg Mintzberg 1976, 1994). His points have been further developed and applied specifically to the P&D field by Flood *et al* (1996).

The main problem with forecasting, so the argument goes, is its reliance on past experience to predict future developments. The main techniques involve the extrapolation of past trends and predictions based on assumptions about the way organisations interact with their environments. In practice, according to Mintzberg, this means that one-off events that fundamentally alter the environment cannot be included in the forecasts:

> When it comes to one-time events – changes that never occurred before, so-called discontinuities, such as technological innovations, price increases, shifts in consumer attitudes, government legislation – Makridakis argued that forecasting becomes 'practically impossible'. In his opinion, 'very little, or nothing can be done, other than to be prepared in a general way to react quickly once a discontinuity has occurred.
>
> Mintzberg (1994: 231)

The point about discontinuities is that not only is the event or trend difficult to predict itself, but there is also a whole set of problems associated with assessing its likely impact on the organisation over time. As a result, except in situations where the organisation itself is able to exert control over future developments, all forecasts are inevitably based on questionable assumptions. It therefore follows that preparations undertaken to meet inaccurate predictions may well cause the long-term interests of the organisation greater harm than would have been the case had a less definite view been taken of unfolding developments.

The time-bomb that failed to explode

A classic example of mis-forecasting is described by Sisson and Timperley (1994: 169–171) in their discussion of the response of UK firms in the late 1980s to predictions concerning the impending explosion of a 'demographic time-bomb'. Declining birthrates after 1960 combined with a steep growth in the number of young people remaining in full-time education after the age of 16 led many commentators and government agencies to warn employers that there would be a severe drop in the number of 16–20-year-olds entering the labour market in the 1990s. Organisations were therefore advised to develop plans to enable them to cope with the labour shortage when it occurred. Among the measures suggested were reorganisation of working methods, the recruitment of older workers, retraining programmes for unemployed people and the development of long-term plans to compete more effectively for the services of the limited number of younger workers looking for employment.

In the event, of course, the time-bomb failed to explode at the expected time. Instead, the early 1990s saw the onset of a deep economic recession and very high levels of unemployment. Instead of difficulties in recruiting young people, employers were faced with a glut – many with qualifications for which there was no market. In effect, therefore, the exact opposite of what was predicted occurred, owing to circumstances that few in government or industry had foreseen. Those employers who failed to draw up plans to cope with demographic down-turns were thus left no worse off and, in many cases, better off than their counterparts who had developed elaborate strategies.

Planners in the NHS, praised by Sisson and Timperley for their 'considerable imagination' in anticipating change, were actually left to cope with the aftermath of the implementation of inaccurate plans. In fact, two planning mistakes were made. In the late 1980s too much new-nurse training was commissioned, at considerable cost to the tax-payer. When it became clear, some years later, that an error had been made and that there would be too many trained nurses looking for work, the NHS overcompensated by reducing the number of training places being offered. The result in the late 1990s is a shortage of trained nurses coming onto the labour market.

The general case against HR planning was acknowledged to have some relevance in the 1960s and 1970s in the context of a relatively stable business environment, when organisations were being urged to 'take the plunge' despite understandable reservations about 'taking a long-term view on assumptions that are decidedly shaky' (Department of Employment 1971: 8). It is therefore unsurprising that it should be more widely accepted in the increasingly unpredictable world of the late 1990s. What was appropriate for large organisations with a dominant or complete share of national markets in 1970 is no longer of any use to organisations with a relatively small share of an international market. The problems are summed up in the following quotation from the Institute of Employment Studies:

> Firms at the moment are very uncertain about what to expect in the future in terms of their size, structure and the design of jobs. Some

companies may know what business they will be in in a few years time, but they don't know how they will be doing it.

Speechly (1994: 45)

Competitive advantage today, according to critics of strategic planning, comes from generating responses to fast-changing circumstances that are swifter, more creative, more innovative and more flexible than those of key competitors – qualities that are stifled by the bureaucratic characteristics of planning processes (Smith 1996: 31). In other words, it is claimed that because the world is increasingly complex and unpredictable it is not worth trying to predict what will happen more than a year ahead. Any plans that are made will, in all likelihood, have to be revised several times in the light of changing environmental developments. Using Mintzberg's terminology, the number of obstacles to effective planning, in the form of discontinuities, are now so legion as to render the long-term planning process effectively redundant.

Consider what discontinuities have occurred in your organisation's business environment over the past two or three years. How far were these predicted? Would it have been possible to predict them?

THE USE OF HR PLANNING IN PRACTICE

The research evidence on the issue of how many employers currently carry out systematic HR planning is unclear but tends to indicate that the majority of employers do not give the function a high profile. In recent years few surveys have looked directly at the use or lack of use of specific HR planning techniques, preferring instead to look at wider issues. It is thus necessary to make inferences about the extent to which they are in fact used from surveys on computer usage and the introduction of 'strategic HRM'.

A study for the (then) Institute of Personnel Management (IPM – now the Chartered Institute of Personnel and Development) by Cowling and Walters (1990) asked a range of questions to establish whether or not particular activities associated with systematic HR planning were carried out. In each case respondents were asked to state whether the operation was undertaken 'on a formal and regular basis', 'as an *ad hoc* activity' or 'not at all'. The results indicated that only three activities were undertaken formally and regularly by a majority of respondents (the identification of future training needs, analysis of labour costs and productivity, and an assessment of the need for structural change resulting from business plans). Fewer than half, therefore, carried out formal forecasts of supply and demand of labour, and less than 20 per cent formally monitored HR planning practices. However, the figures rose considerably when the number of respondents claiming to carry out these activities on an *ad hoc* basis was added. When it is considered that the response rate for this survey was only 2.45 per cent, it is difficult not to conclude that a large majority of UK employers see HR planning activities of the kind described in the previous chapter as a low priority for their organisations. Only in a minority of cases could a fully fledged HR planning function be said to have been established.

Further evidence for informal and unsystematic approaches comes from surveys of computer use in P&D departments. According to a survey undertaken in 1993, 75 per cent of UK P&D departments used computers, but only a third of these (25 per cent of the total) used them for purposes related to HR planning (Kinnie and Arthurs 1993). A more recent survey barely registered any use of planning at all, although respondents did suggest that they believed such applications would become important in the future (*Personnel Today* 1995: 33). The overall picture painted by these and other research projects as reported by Rothwell (1995: 175–178) strongly suggests that systematic HR planning carried out in the manner advocated by writers in the 1960s and 1970s is now rarely found in UK industry. Its use is thus mainly restricted to large public-sector organisations and firms operating in reasonably stable, capital-intensive industries. Others, if they use it at all, do so in a more casual and irregular way – perhaps relying more on managerial judgement and intuition than on established statistical approaches.

A variety of reasons have been put forward to explain the apparent abandonment of HR planning techniques – as far as they were ever well established – by employers in the UK (see Rothwell 1995: 178–180, Marchington and Wilkinson 1996: 104–105). These include the following:

• a hostility to the use of statistical techniques in place of managerial judgement

• the belief that HR planning, while desirable, is not essential to organisational effectiveness; funding therefore tends to be funnelled elsewhere

• the prevalence of a short-termist outlook in UK industry, the result being a belief that individual managerial careers are unlikely to be enhanced by long-term activities such as HR planning

• practical problems associated with inadequate historical data on which to base forecasts

• ignorance of the existence of HR planning techniques and their potential advantages for organisations

• a more general ignorance or fear of mathematical methods.

Undoubtedly one or more of these may be a valid explanation for each organisation, but it is difficult to avoid making the observation that many others fail to carry out HR planning because they concur with the points made by its critics (outlined above). It would seem that employers, quite simply, prefer to wait until their view of the future environment clears sufficiently for them to see the whole picture before committing resources to preparing for its arrival. The perception is that the more complex and turbulent the environment, the more important it is to wait and see before acting.

THE CASE FOR HR PLANNING

A number of writers working in the P&D field have taken issue with the arguments put forward by critics of business planning. In addition to generally restating the potential advantages of HR plans they also reject the assertion that because accurate forecasting is complex, difficult and subject to error it follows that organisations should abandon long-term planning altogether. Two main arguments are put forward: the need to view plans as adaptable, and the greater attention to planning required by a more turbulent environment.

The need to view plans as adaptable

The point is made that HR planning has never been intended to produce blue-prints that determine the direction that recruitment and development policy should take years in advance. Instead, it is viewed as a less deterministic activity, in which plans are continually updated in the light of environmental developments:

> Pin-point accuracy in forecasting is rarely essential; the real purpose of looking ahead is to do as much as possible to reduce the area of uncertainty, to minimise the unknown factor ... Few major changes in a company's operations take place over night and cannot be anticipated in some measure. If there is some agreed procedure for examining closely the manpower implications at an early stage, both the company and its employees will reap substantial benefits from the longer period they will have to prepare for change.

Department of Employment (1971: 8)

Mintzberg's central point about discontinuities rendering plans redundant is thus disputed. In practice, it is said, changes in the environment rarely occur as suddenly as he suggests. As a result, when unforeseen developments do occur, there is time for plans to be adapted and updated to enable the implications to be met.

In fairness to Mintzberg, it must be stressed that his arguments concern business planning in general and are not related only to the management of people. When making long-term plans for major capital investment projects (building new plants, research and development into new technologies etc), discontinuities potentially interfere far more dramatically. The time-horizons for P&D practitioners are not so long, except in the case of the development of highly skilled employees. A great deal more can be adapted and changed in six months in the P&D field than is the case for capital investment in new plant and machinery. It thus follows that Mintzberg's arguments, while valid from a general management perspective, may have less relevance to P&D.

Turbulence requires more attention to planning

Linked to the first argument is the idea that because the business environment is becoming increasingly turbulent and unpredictable on account of the threat from potential discontinuities there is an even greater need for organisations to develop the capacity to plan accurately. Bramham (1988: 7) puts the case as follows:

It is of course a paradox that as it becomes more difficult to predict and select, so it becomes more necessary to do so. The 19th-century businessman would have found his 20th-century counterpart's obsession with planning strange. But, of course, the environment is now changing more rapidly and the conflicting pressures are greater. The modern manager must develop the systems and controls which increase the likelihood of the environment being controlled to a reasonable extent. Without an accurate awareness of his position, a manager will quickly lose his way in this rapidly changing environment.

In effect, what is being argued for is that it is both possible and desirable to plan for uncertainty. When faced with an unpredictable environment, employers have two basic choices: they can abandon formal planning activity and rely on intuition – reacting swiftly and decisively at the point at which a clear picture of the future comes into view – or they can plan their HR policies so as to enable them to meet the future with a variety of different responses. If the second course is taken, the emphasis in HR planning will be on maximum future flexibility. In theory, the organisation will then have the capability to respond even more quickly than rivals who pursue the first approach.

The point is perhaps best illustrated with an example. One group of manufacturers currently facing considerable uncertainty, even turbulence, are the makers of 'alcopops' – soft drinks with a moderate alcoholic content. These were launched in 1997 and have quickly developed a reasonable market. At the time of writing (late 1997) they are widely available in pubs and in licensed retail outlets. However, they have attracted a great deal of criticism on account of their potential attractiveness to children and young teenagers, and the fact that they are priced within pocket-money range. As a result a campaign has developed for them to be banned. The manufacturers can therefore have no idea what the future holds for their new product. On the one hand, the market may grow very rapidly, alcopops becoming fashionable drinks for consumers across a range of countries. On the other, governments may be tempted to ban them or to impose punitive sales taxes to deter their purchase by underage drinkers. Were that to happen, circumstances could quickly occur in which the drinks became unfashionable, or even unobtainable. Inbetween the two extremes lies a range of other possibilities, including the development of strong competition within an expanded alcopops market. The P&D practitioners responsible for staffing the manufacturing and sales operations therefore have a difficult judgement to make. Is it worth their while to undertake detailed HR forecasting or not? Does the uncertainty they face mean that HR planning is so hazardous as to be a waste of resources, or should they take the view that in order to maximise their future profits they need to plan for all possible contingencies?

Supporters of HR planning would advise the latter course of action. The aim of doing so would not be to follow any plan to the letter, but to create a flexible plan covering different possibilities which can later be updated as knowledge of the future environment becomes clearer. To achieve maximum potential competitive advantage, HR planners need to ensure that they have committed people with the right skills to exploit whatever opportunities arise. It is therefore the uncertainty that provides the rationale for increased attention to thinking ahead.

> What are the main uncertainties faced by your organisation at present? To what extent could plans be put in place to enable these to be met more effectively by you than by your competitors?

ADAPTING TRADITIONAL HR PLANNING

It can be argued that in this debate, as in so many featured in the management literature, there is no clear right or wrong answer. It is not a question of whether or not HR planning *per se* is a good or a bad thing, but of the extent to which it is appropriate in different circumstances. This is not a field in which general theories or sweeping judgements can be applied at all usefully. As was shown in the examples given in Chapter 3, there remain employers for whom traditional approaches to HR planning (ie the use of systematic techniques to forecast supply and demand three to five years ahead) are very appropriate – at least for certain staff groups. These share the following characteristics:

- organisations that are large enough to be able to dedicate resources to the establishment and maintenance of an HR planning function

- organisations operating in reasonably stable product and labour markets

- organisations for which key staff groups require lengthy or expensive training

- organisations competing in industries in which decisions concerning future investment in plant and equipment are made a number of years ahead and are essential to effective product market competition (ie capital-intensive industries).

In the UK, large numbers of organisations share most or all of these distinguishing features. In addition to the major public services (health, education, social services, defence, local and central government), many larger companies would also be included (utilities, oil producers, major banks and building societies, large retailers etc). In all of these cases, while change may be occurring quickly, it is relatively predictable over the short term. The closure of departments or plants, expansion into new markets and changes in organisation do not take place overnight. Typically there will be at least six months' warning of likely changes, allowing time for established HR forecasts to be adapted and revised plans established. For such organisations, the criticisms of the HR planning process described above are applicable in relatively few situations and for relatively few staff groups. It can thus be plausibly argued that the absence of an HR planning function in such employing organisations will mean that they are not maximising their long-term efficiency and effectiveness.

The traditional approach to HR planning has a great deal less relevance for other employers (ie those that are small players in their industries, operating in a fast-changing technological field, or unable to know from one quarter to the next what turnover is likely to achieved). For such organisations the case against HR planning presented above will have greater resonance. The establishment of a formal, systematic planning function making forecasts on the basis of past trends and managerial judgement is not a cost-effective proposition. The market is simply too unpredictable to enable meaningful forecasts to be made and plans to be established concerning staffing needs a year or more ahead. However, that is not to say that such employers should not plan – merely that the traditional approach to planning described in Chapter 3 has little to offer. A case for these organisations to undertake some form of HR planning can still be made, but it involves methods that have somewhat different features.

What is needed is an adaptation of the principles underlying HR planning, together with the development of newer techniques and approaches. Many of these – now well covered in the literature – are also relevant for the larger, more stable organisations, where they can be used in addition to the longer-established HR planning techniques. Here four of these adaptations are described. In two cases the HR planning process becomes less all-encompassing and instead aims to focus on specific organisational developments or groups of employees. In a further two, the nature of the forecasting operation moves away from focusing simply on 'the right people in the right jobs, at the right time'.

Contingency planning

Contingency planning is rarely given more than passing reference by authors assessing the worth of HR planning, yet it can be seen as an approach that is almost universally applicable. Instead of seeing the HR planning process as one in which a single plan is developed and then adapted as the environment changes, contingency planning involves planning possible responses to a variety of potential environmental developments. The result is that HR planning effectively switches from being a reactive process undertaken in order to assist the organisation achieve its aims, and becomes a proactive process undertaken prior to the formulation of wider organisational objectives and strategies. The purpose of contingency planning in the HR field is thus the provision of information on which decisions about the future direction the organisation takes are made.

As was argued in Chapter 3, the development of computer applications that permit 'what if' analyses greatly assists the contingency planning process. They are particularly useful in their capability to calculate very rapidly the cost implications of certain courses of action or shifts in environmental conditions, a basic spreadsheet program being all that is necessary to undertake these activities. Once developed, it is a very straightforward process to alter one or more sets of figures or assumptions to forecast what would happen in HR terms were certain scenarios to unfold or be pursued.

A straightforward example would be a retailer who decides whether to open a new store and what size it should be. A spreadsheet could be constructed in which assumptions were made about the number and type of staff that would be required, the likely turnover rate in the first year and the cost of recruiting and training the new employees required to fill the posts. Different figures could then be plugged into the program representing different scenarios in terms of costs, training times, difficulty in recruiting staff, turnover, wage rates, business levels etc. Particularly useful is the capacity such approaches have for calculating, in cost terms, potential best and worst scenarios. In the case of the retail company, such analysis would produce estimates of the highest and lowest possible costs associated with opening the new store. In addition a range of other estimates could be generated, given a variety of different potential outcomes. Senior managers, charged with making the decision about whether or not to invest in a new store, would then base this partly on information provided by the HR planner.

Contingency planning in a manufacturing company

An example known to the author of the effective use of contingency planning occurred recently in a major manufacturing organisation. The company produces two distinct household products under a well-known brand name, and until 1995 did so in three plants located respectively in Italy, Germany and the UK. At that time it was decided to rationalise the company's operations and concentrate the manufacturing of each item on one site, a decision that necessitated the closure of one of the three plants. The question was, which should close?

While many considerations were taken into account in making the decision, HR issues played their part. Plans were thus drawn up looking at the outcomes in cost terms of different contingencies: closing the UK plant and focusing production of one product in Italy and one in Germany, closing the Italian plant and producing the products in Germany and the UK, and so on. In the event the decision was taken to close the German factory and to produce one of the two principal products in the UK and the other in Italy. The cost in HR terms of each scenario was a significant factor in the final decision and was informed by the HR planning programme.

In the following year, managers at the UK plant had to retrain large numbers of employees in new production processes, made some redundant and hired others with particular skills. However, as a result of the contingency planning process, it had a very good idea of when each stage in the restructuring programme had to take place (ie what staff it needed in what jobs at what time) and a good estimate of the programme's cost in terms of recruitment, redundancy and retraining.

Succession planning

Another adaptation of the principles of traditional HR planning is the development, mostly in larger organisations, of a succession planning function. The objective here is to focus HR planning activity on the recruitment and development of individuals to fill the top few posts in an organisation. Succession planners are mainly interested in ensuring that their employer has enough individuals with the right abilities, skills and experience to promote into key senior jobs as they become vacant. While some organisations have succession plans covering several hundred top jobs, for many the focus of attention is on 'once-in-a-generation' appointments such as the chief executive, board-level directors, hospital consultants, professors, newspaper editors, ambassadors and top civil servants. These jobs typically represent the pinnacle of an individual's career, and tend to be occupied by a single employee for between five and twenty-five years. Needless to say, ensuring that the right people are available to fill these posts at the right time is particularly important to the on-going achievement of organisational success. According to Jackson and Schuler (1990: 171), succession planning differs from traditional HR planning in that 'the prediction task changes from one of estimating the percentage of a pool of employees who are likely to be with the company x years into the future, to one of estimating the probability that a few particular individuals will be with the company x years into the future'. In other words, the planning process covers a narrower group of employees but does so with a higher degree of intensity; because plans concern relatively few, they can be considerably more sophisticated. The time-horizons involved are also longer than is the case with traditional HR planning. Succession plans, by their very nature, often involve forecasting and planning the progress of individuals 20 years or more ahead.

The technique is most often associated with hierarchical organisations in which individuals develop careers by moving upwards and sideways over a number of years as they acquire the required skills and experience. The aim is to ensure that enough individuals with the potential to succeed to senior positions are available when an appoint-ment needs to be made. Rothwell (1995: 189) reports that three candidates are typically identified for each senior post:

- one who is ready now and could succeed immediately if necessary

- one who will be ready, if needed, in two to three years' time

- one who will be ready in five years' time.

In addition, succession planners have an input into decisions about the numbers and kinds of graduates that are employed on graduate training programmes each year. While it is rare for individuals to be earmarked for senior posts at this stage, a major purpose of the graduate recruitment process for many employers is the development of a pool of people with the potential to reach the highest levels.

In technical terms, succession planning involves collecting and manipulating data about individuals and tracking their performance and progress as they move from job to job over a period of time. Files therefore have to be kept containing information about training programmes, results of performance appraisals, career histories and qualifications, as well as details of any potential constraints that might hold their development back (such as a disinclination to move to a new region or country). Customised and proprietary computer systems are now available to help match people to jobs (IRS 1990: 16), although some of these appear to be too sophisticated and prescriptive to be of any great practical use (O'Reilly 1997: 4).

Skills planning

A further adaptation of traditional HR planning principles to meet new circumstances is a shift away from a focus on planning for people towards one that looks first and foremost at skills. Instead of forecasting the future supply of and demand for employees (expressed as the numbers of whole-time equivalents required or available), skills planning involves predicting what competences will be needed one to five years hence, leaving open the question of the form in which these will be obtained.

The approach is novel in so far as it acknowledges that as product markets have become increasingly turbulent, new forms of employment (such as those described in Chapter 2) have developed to meet the need for labour flexibility on the part of employers. It therefore abandons the assumption inherent in the traditional model of HR planning that organisations in the future will employ staff in the same manner as they have in the past. Skills-based plans thus incorporate the possibility that skill needs will be met either wholly or partially through the employment of short-term employees, outside contractors and consultants, as well as by permanent members of staff. Examples of the adoption of this approach are reported by Speechly (1994: 45–47).

Skills planning is particularly appropriate in situations where there is a variety of different methods by which employee resourcing needs can be met. An example might be a computer company launching a new software package for use in industry. Managers may have a rough idea of how many licences they will sell, but are unable to predict how much training customers will require or what type of servicing operation will be necessary. They need to put in place plans that focus on their ability to provide different levels of training and service, but because these services will be provided by temporary employees and subcontractors as much as by permanent members of staff, there is no point in making plans that focus on the number of new staff posts needed. Instead, the plans focus on the possible skill requirements and form the basis of strategies designed to make sure that those skills are obtainable in one form or another.

Soft human resource planning

There is a degree of disagreement in the literature about the use of the term 'soft human resource planning' and its precise meaning. Marchington and Wilkinson (1996: 89) define it broadly as being 'synonymous with the whole subject of human resource management' while others, such as Torrington and Hall (1995: 82), appear to accept a narrower definition involving planning to meet 'soft' HR goals – particularly cultural and behavioural objectives. Torrington and Hall use the label to give meaning to a distinct range of HR activities which are similar to hard HR planning in approach, but which focus on forecasting the likely supply of and demand for particular attitudes and behaviours rather than people and skills. Soft HR planning can thus be seen as a broadening of the objectives associated with the traditional approaches described above.

Like skills planning, soft HR planning accepts that for organisations to succeed in the current environment they need more than the right people in the right place at the right time: they also need to ensure that those people have an appropriate outlook and set of attitudes to contribute to the creation of a successful organisational culture. More importantly, undertaking systematic soft HR planning can alert organisations to long-term shifts in attitudes to work among the labour force in general, allowing them to build these considerations into their general planning processes. An example might be a need on the part of an employer for sales staff who are not just appropriately trained, but who also exhibit the behaviours required to interact successfully with customers. There is thus a requirement for staff with a particular set of attitudes, so that an effective customer-focused culture develops. Traditional, hard HR planning takes no account of such issues, a deficiency corrected with the addition of a soft dimension.

Techniques for assessing the internal supply or availability of people with desired attitudes and behaviours are described by Torrington and Hall (1995: 85). They include the use of staff surveys, questionnaires and focus groups to establish the nature of employee motivation, the general level of job satisfaction and commitment and the extent to which certain behaviours are exhibited. Methods for analysing external supply are discussed by Jackson and Schuler (1990: 157). The emphasis here is on making an assessment of the likely impact of general societal attitudinal change on the future needs of the organisation. Published surveys are the main source of external data. Among the changes in attitudes they report in the USA are the following:

- Employees are becoming increasingly resistant to relocation.

- There is a general reduction in loyalty towards individual employers.

- Younger workers have considerably less trust in and respect for authority than their older counterparts.

- Younger workers tend to look for work that is fun and enjoyable, whereas older workers see it as 'a duty and a vehicle for financial support'.

- Younger workers have a different conception of 'fairness' in the work context than older colleagues. They see it as involving being tolerant towards minorities and allowing people to be different, while older workers define it as 'treating people equally'.

Advocates of soft HR planning argue that such matters can and should be considered when forecasting future needs in addition to data concerning the numbers of staff and skills that are likely to be available.

An interesting example of a 'soft' trend in the UK and the response of employers is described by Wills (1997: 31–34). She observes that, in response to the decline in the number of 'jobs for life', employees are increasingly viewing their employment first and foremost as a means by which they can gain work experience and boost their own employability. As a result, less attention is given to securing promotion by impressing managers and to focusing on achieving organisational goals. The response of companies who wish to retain staff in whom they have invested a great deal of time and resources is to give greater attention to career management, developing a network of mentors and advisors who try to ensure that internal moves are available so as to retain the interest and loyalty of employees.

> Which of these adaptations of traditional HRP is most relevant for your organisation? Which is least relevant?

HR PLANNING IN AN INTERNATIONAL CONTEXT

The globalisation of organisations has a number of distinct implications for the HR planning function, raising fundamental questions about the extent to which it is useful to carry it out and about the level at which such activity should be undertaken. In practical terms, there are two major implications for international organisations: the requirement for language skills and the need to move skilled employees and managers from country to country. Both complicate the planning process and make forecasting supply and demand for key groups of employees a considerably harder task. Added to this is the inherent instability associated with much international business activity. Companies are bought, reorganised and resold regularly, production is shifted from country to country as economic conditions change, and strategic alliances are formed that can easily alter a company's HR planning needs overnight.

In forecasting the demand for and supply of language skills, the HR planning function has a potentially crucial role to play, so fundamental is the need for effective communication between employees in different countries. Forecasting demand a year or so ahead is not a major problem; nor is forecasting likely internal supply. The problem arises in estimating the external supply by accessing data on the number of people in different countries proficient in different languages at different levels. As a result, accurate forecasting of the amount of language training that needs to be provided is necessarily problematic. However, the importance of the issue and the length of time needed for most people to acquire reasonable proficiency in a new language mean that factoring such considerations into the HR planning process is an important potential source of increased organisational effectiveness.

The practice of succession and career planning also becomes more complex and more important when organisations become international. This is because to develop people in order that they are ready to take on senior roles at a later date, it is necessary for them to develop international careers, including spells working as an expatriate in one or more foreign countries. Succession planners therefore have to add to the considerable amount of data they already hold further information about language, the willingness of individuals to work abroad (together with spouses and families) and the costs associated with organising overseas postings.

However, these complexities are small fry when general HR planning in international organisations is considered. It is hard enough, as was illustrated above, to generate accurate forecasts for the supply of and demand for employees in one country; doing so across several countries renders the process a great deal more complicated. Not only do basic labour market conditions vary considerably between countries over time, there are also, as Hofstede (1980) and others have shown, substantial differences between the attitudes and expectations of different national workforces towards their jobs, their careers and their employers. When the problems associated with obtaining access to robust external labour market data in different countries are added to the equation, it becomes clear that the operation of a single HQ-based HR planning function is unlikely to be a practical option for international companies. Instead, what is required, if HR planning is to be carried out in any meaningful way, is separate regional or national HR planning functions, each focusing on developments in their own labour markets and reporting to a central co-ordinating department. This will ensure that HR planning is carried out for each key labour market and that information is provided from each in a similar format. Planning data can then be used to inform decision-making about future investment and downsizing programmes.

EVALUATING HR PLANNING PROCESSES

In 1992, the (then) IPM issued a *Statement on Human Resource Planning* which suggested three criteria for evaluating the process:

- the extent to which the outputs of HR planning programmes continue to meet changing circumstances

- the extent to which the programmes achieve their cost and productivity objectives

- the extent to which strategies and programmes are replanned to meet changing circumstances.

The last two apply to the HR planning function the same kind of evaluation criteria as might be applied to any department of an organisation. They simply ask how far the day-to-day objectives are met effectively and efficiently. By contrast, the first advocates the evaluation of the plans themselves.

Were HR planning exercises to be one-off affairs, making single sets of long-term forecasts, evaluation would be a very straightforward matter. An organisation would simply ask how far the forecasts of demand for and supply of labour in fact proved to be accurate. However, as has been made clear, HR planning is an ongoing activity in which forecasts are continually reviewed, updated and adjusted as circumstances change. What is important is how effective the whole HR planning process is in supporting the achievement of wider organisational objectives. Ultimately therefore, as argued by Rothwell (1995: 197) and Jackson and Schuler (1990: 173–174), it is the effectiveness of strategies developed on the back of the HR planning process that provides the most meaningful evaluation criteria. The planning process itself is thus less significant than the extent to which it supports the evolution of training and development programmes, recruitment policy and P&D interventions aimed at reducing turnover. In the case of planning for a reduction in the number of employees, the appropriate criteria would be the number of compulsory redundancies avoided as a result of planning activity.

In addition, as with all evaluation activity in the P&D field, there is a need to estimate the value of a particular intervention against the likely outcome of not intervening and a need to compare outcomes with those of key competitors. In the HR planning field this will involve asking the following kinds of questions:

- Does the presence of a long-term HR planning function contribute to the achievement of organisational objectives?

- What would have been the result in recent years had no such function been present?

- Does the function justify its presence in cost terms?

- How does our organisation's performance compare with that of competitors who have either a (more or less) sophisticated HR planning function, or no such function at all?

FURTHER READING

- The specific issue of the case for and against HR planning in the current environment has rarely been addressed in a balanced way in the literature. It is thus necessary to look in different places for the arguments on either side. The case against is best articulated by Henry Mintzberg (1994) in *The Rise and Fall of Strategic Planning*, but is also covered more briefly by Flood *et al* (1995) in *Managing without Traditional Methods* and by Micklethwait and Wooldridge (1996) in *The Witch Doctors*. The counter-arguments in favour of HR planning are best articulated in Bramham (1988), Torrington and Hall (1995) and Marchington and Wilkinson (1996).

- Up-to-date case-studies focusing on the aims and outcomes of HR planning are also relatively rare. However, Terry Hercus (1992) describes the approaches taken in eight organisations based in the UK, and Jackson and Schuler (1990) include good examples from the USA in their article entitled 'Human Resource Planning: Challenges for Industrial/Organisational Psychologists'.

- Evaluation issues are covered in some detail by Jackson and Schuler (1990) and by Sheila Rothwell (1995). A good summary of the international issues is found in Damian O'Doherty's (1994) chapter on HR planning in the textbook edited by Beardwell and Holden.

Part 3

RECRUITMENT

---

5 Putting flesh on the bones

Once the need for additional employees has been identified, a series of distinct steps has to be taken before the new people are both established in their jobs and performing satisfactorily. Two of these, namely recruitment and selection, each accounts for a substantial portion of the employee resourcing specialist's work, and are covered extensively in the following three chapters. Here the focus is on the other tasks and processes that need to be completed, in some shape or form, if human resource plans are to be effectively realised.

A variety of P&D responsibilities are covered, starting with the administrative tasks carried out prior to recruitment and selection: job analysis and the drawing-up of job descriptions and person specifications. Next we turn to contracts of employment, offer letters, and the statements of terms and conditions that employers of any size are now required to provide to new starters. Finally consideration is given to the formal and informal processes employed during the first days and weeks of a new employee's arrival to assist him or her to adjust to a new environment and reach a high level of performance at the earliest possible date. All three areas of activity are potentially of substantial significance, yet all seem to have been underresearched and are consequently rarely covered in great depth in standard P&D texts.

By the end of this chapter, readers should be able to:

- undertake job analysis
- write job descriptions
- draw up person specifications
- write offer letters
- prepare a standard contract of employment and associated documentation

- design, implement and evaluate induction programmes.

In addition, readers should be able to understand and explain:

- the principles underpinning job analysis
- the distinction between contracts of employment and contracts for services
- national variations in contracts of employment
- the distinction between induction, orientation and socialisation.

JOB ANALYSIS

Formal analysis of the jobs that make up an organisation should, theoretically, form the basis of much P&D activity. Apart from its role in recruitment and selection, which is our main concern here, it also has a central part to play in the determination of pay differentials, the identification of training needs, the setting of performance targets and the drawing-up of new organisational structures. Furthermore, without effective and objective job analysis as their foundation, it is difficult to justify key decisions in the fields of promotion, redundancy, disciplinary action for poor performance and changes in rates of pay. As such, while essentially being a technical administrative task, job analysis (also known as occupational analysis) can be convincingly characterised as a process that adds value to an organisation's activities:

> Occupational analysis is a business investment – it requires considerable expenditure of funds, human effort, and time. These costs, however, can be amortized over a period of time, during which the data base can be used to avoid costs, tailor programs, increase efficiency and flexibility, improve quality control, and effect operational change. The data developed during occupational analysis can serve initially to validate existing programs, to document or articulate specific program needs, and to influence almost every aspect of the personnel management program within that occupation.
>
> Legere (1985: 1327)

In the fields of recruitment and selection, job analysis is important because it provides the information on which to base two important types of document: the job description and the person specification. The first summarises the tasks that make up a job, together with statements of reporting lines, areas of responsibility and performance criteria. The second identifies those human attributes or personality traits that are considered necessary for someone holding the job in question. Of course, it is quite possible to draw up written job descriptions and person specifications without first undertaking rigorous job analysis. Indeed, it is often the case that job advertisements are compiled and interviewing processes undertaken without the assistance of these documents at all. In such cases, however, the likelihood that selection decisions will be properly objective and capable of identifying the most appropriate candidates for appointment is much reduced.

Pearn and Kandola (1993: 1) see job analysis as a form of considered research, and define it simply as 'a systematic procedure for obtaining detailed and objective information about a job, task or role that will be performed or is currently being performed'. It is therefore a process, or a means to an end, rather than an end in itself. This definition, though, is very much a general statement of what job analysis involves. In practice, a wide variety of distinct approaches has been developed which analyses jobs in different ways and at different levels.

The first question to ask when approaching a job analysis exercise is the type of information that is sought. Only then can appropriate decisions be taken on the method that will be used. If the analysis is to form the basis of personnel selection decisions, there is clearly a need to focus not just on the tasks carried out but also on the skills deployed in the job, the equipment used and the environment within which the various activities are carried out. The Position Analysis Questionnaire, one of a range commercially produced for use as job analysis tools, gathers six distinct classes of information:

i)   the source of information used to perform the job

ii) the kind of mental processes used to perform the job

iii) the output expected and methods used

iv   the types and levels of relationships with others

v)   the physical and social context in which the job is performed

vi) other job characteristics and activities not covered by the above (eg hours, payment arrangements, level of responsibility).

Job analysis is thus not merely concerned with data on the content of a job or the tasks that make it up. It also looks at how each job fits into the organisation, what its purpose is, and at the skills and personality traits required to carry it out.

A number of distinct methods of gathering job analysis data are employed – some more straightforward than others. The most basic of all simply involves observing a job-holder at work over a period of time and then recording what has been observed. In most cases the observation is supplemented with an interview carried out at the same time or later to clarify points and gather information about mental activities that are less readily observable. The main drawback concerns the length of time it takes to get a full picture of the tasks carried out by any one job-holder. Where the job varies from one day or week to the next, certain aspects only taking place occasionally, observation cannot be the main tool of analysis used. It is most appropriate in the case of straightforward jobs, which are primarily physical and which involve carrying out the same tasks in the same setting each day. One would thus expect to see observation used in the case of low-skilled manual work or in situations where the work, though more complex, is carried out cyclically, each day's routine broadly resembling that of the next (eg shop assistants, nursery school assistants, clerical workers).

The great weakness of the observation method is the strong possibility that the individuals being observed are **unlikely** to behave as they usually do, given the presence of a job analyst. Some will feel threatened, others will be out to impress; few will find themselves able to ignore the observer and continue as if no job analyst were there. Some have suggested that this kind of distorting effect can be reduced if observers are carefully trained and then introduced to the workplace tactfully. The need is to build trust with those being observed and to tell them the purpose of the exercise. Another method used to reduce the distorting effects of observation is the use of video cameras placed at a discreet distance from the place in which the observer is working. Again, this may have an effect if the individuals concerned are well prepared, but is unlikely to render an altogether accurate picture of day-to-day work, because people inevitably alter their behaviour when they know they are being watched.

The second approach is the job analysis interview. Here trained analysts ask job-holders (as well as their supervisors and colleagues) to describe the job concerned, how it fits into the organisation and what it involves. Wherever possible interviewees are invited to open up and discuss particular events or occurrences to illustrate the points they are making. Interviews also provide the opportunity to probe points made by job-holders and to clarify any areas of uncertainty. Information given can then be checked against answers given by colleagues and managers.

Here too there is always a danger that interviewees will 'talk up' their work in a bid to appear impressive. They will downplay the more routine aspects of their work and seek to focus on the more interesting and significant parts. There is also a tendency for people to believe that they have greater authority and influence than they do actually enjoy – especially in situations where a degree of decision-making authority has been delegated but is still exercised under reasonably close supervision. Interviewees with a number of years' experience in the job being analysed are thus often less suitable than colleagues who have only spent one or two years in that role. As with work observation, it is possible to train job analysts to recognise such problems and to focus the attention of interviewees on the nuts and bolts aspects of what they do. Above all, it is important to make it clear that it is the job that is being analysed and not the individual's performance in the job. Where these approaches fail, another method used to ensure that individuals do not puff themselves up too much is to conduct a group interview with several job-holders at the same time.

Aside from the group approach, a number of specific job analysis interviewing techniques have been developed in a bid to overcome the problems described above and to ensure that only the most important information is gathered. One of these is known as the 'critical incident technique' and involves focusing the attention of interviewees on only those aspects of their jobs that make the difference between success and failure. The starting-point here is a study of the key job objectives, so a critical incident interview always begins by establishing with the interviewee the central performance indicators or outcomes that are expected of any job-holder. The interview then proceeds with the interviewee's being asked to describe actual events or incidents that resulted either in key objectives' being met or not met. In addition to describing the critical incident, interviewees are also asked to describe the background and to state specifically what their own contribution to the outcome was. The advantage of this approach is that it forces people to think about specific occurrences when being interviewed and not to dwell on general points. As a result, far more detailed and specific information is gathered to help the job analyst build up a picture of what the most significant job tasks are, the environment in which they are performed and what type of behaviours determine the extent to which success is achieved.

Another method that focuses on key aspects of jobs, but which requires a greater level of training, is the repertory grid approach. It involves first compiling a list of the tasks that form part of a job and then comparing and contrasting each with the others in terms of the skills or abilities needed to carry it out effectively. Random pairs or trios of tasks are usually selected and analysed by job-holders, their supervisors and other colleagues until no new information on the skills required to perform the job is forthcoming. The lists of tasks and skills are then placed at right-angles to each other on a repertory grid so that each skill can be rated in terms of its significance to the achievement of each task (a very simple illustrative example is shown in Table 3). A seven- or five-point rating scale is usually used, a score of 1 indicating that the skill is not relevant to the accomplishment of a task and 5 or 7 signifying that the skill is crucial or essential to its successful completion.

Computer programmes can then be used to analyse the scores and to establish which skills or personality attributes are most important overall. This part of the process goes beyond job analysis to the

Table 3 **An example of a repertory grid for an office receptionist**

DUTIES (SKILLS/COMPETENCES)	Sensitivity to customer needs	Ability to plan own work	Good spoken communication skills	Reliability	Ability to analyse straightforward data	Typing skills	High level of personal presentation	Initiative
Open and close premises	1	1	1	5	1	1	1	4
Maintain filing system	1	4	1	5	4	2	1	4
Order office supplies	1	5	2	5	3	1	1	4
Deal with telephone enquiries	5	1	5	3	4	1	1	4
Welcome visitors	5	1	5	3	4	1	5	4
Type documents	1	3	1	4	5	5	1	2
Postal distribution	1	4	1	5	5	1	1	4
Arrange appointments	4	4	5	4	3	1	2	2

development of person specifications, but that does not negate the potential usefulness of the earlier stages as analytic tools. As with the critical incident approach, in breaking the job down into its constituent parts and reflecting on the detail of each the process is made more structured, thorough and objective than is the case with a straightforward interview.

The third commonly used approach is the administration of a prepared job analysis questionnaire. While it is possible for employers to develop their own, many either adapt or directly administer a proprietary scheme which they obtain a licence to use. The more reputable providers also give training in the use of the questionnaire and in its analysis. Where the jobs involved are not too unusual, this approach is probably the most efficient and straightforward to use. Because all interviewees are asked identical questions there is less opportunity for interviewer-bias to creep in, leading to a higher level of objectivity than is the case with observation or conventional job analysis interviews.

There are a number of questionnaires on the market, two of which (the Work Profiling System and the Position Analysis Questionnaire) are described and reviewed by Pearn and Kandola (1993: 51–65). All the better products contain hundreds of questions and have been developed using data gathered from a very broad cross-section of job types from a number of industries. Most are now computerised, which greatly speeds up the analysis of data collected, and permits the generation of reports summarising key tasks and the competences that are most important to perform the job successfully. They also have the advantage in that where yes and no answers are inappropriate, a series of descriptive statements is provided from which the most appropriate response can be chosen. The following examples come from the Medequate Job Analysis Questionnaire developed by KPMG for use in the NHS.

Why do people seek advice from the job-holder?

i) First point of contact (the job-holder is readily available).

ii) Recognised authority (the job-holder is the first source of advice within a particular function and can handle standard/routine requests for advice within their particular field. The job-holder would pass on detailed/difficult/out of the ordinary requests to a senior authority).

iii) Senior authority (the job-holder would handle more involved/out of the ordinary requests for advice leaving the more routine requests to subordinates).

iv) Acknowledged expert/specialist (the job-holder is a respected source within an area of expertise/specialism; only in exceptional circumstances would the job-holder need to refer to a higher source or a second opinion).

v) Ultimate authority/expert (as a result of experience and authority, the job-holder is seen as the organisation's ultimate source of information in a certain field and would be expected to provide expert advice within their own speciality; the job-holder would be consulted in all the most difficult/complex cases).

Describe the nature of the majority of the decisions taken by the job-holder.

i) Straightforward choices (little scope for decision-making, eg yes and no answers).

ii) Few and well-established (the decisions made will be few in number and will follow well-established procedures or precedents).

iii) Many and well-established (decision-making will be frequent and over a wide range of topics, but each decision will follow well-established procedures or precedents).

iv) Unprecedented (decision-making will be over a wide range of topics but will often be outside existing procedures and no precedents may exist).

Organisations also employ other methods of job analysis which do not fit into any of the three broad categories identified above. These include asking individuals to complete work diaries detailing the tasks they complete each day; the use of documentary evidence such as performance appraisal results and training manuals; and consultation with experts in particular fields. In most cases these methods will be insufficient in themselves, but may well assist in so far as they back up or contradict the results of job analysis exercises using the more conventional approaches. The use of panels of experts is particularly useful when a job that does not yet exist is to be analysed. In these circumstances, where there is no job-holder to question or observe, there is no real alternative but to ask well-informed people what the key job tasks and competences are most likely to be.

> Which of the above approaches would you consider to be most appropriate to employ when analysing complex, senior job roles?

JOB DESCRIPTIONS

A written job description or job summary is the main output from the job analysis process. As has been stated, it forms the basis of a variety of decisions and processes across the range of P&D activity, including the drawing-up of training plans and the determination of pay rates. However, it is no less important in the staffing field where, once compiled and filed, it is used in five specific ways:

* *as a tool in recruitment.* Job descriptions are used to assist in the writing of job advertisements and will be given to agents hired to undertake all or part of the recruitment process. Copies are also typically sent to people who enquire about specific jobs, along with application forms and person specifications.

* *as a tool in selection.* Decisions about who to employ from among a range of possible candidates can be taken with reference to job descriptions. This helps ensure that there is a clear match between the abilities and experience of the new employee and the requirements of the job.

* *as the basis of employment contracts.* Frequently organisations make specific reference to job descriptions in their contracts of

employment. They can thus have an important legal significance if someone is dismissed for failing to reach expected performance standards or resigns and claims constructive dismissal when he or she has been unreasonably told to undertake duties that lie outside the terms and conditions of his or her employment.

• *as part of an employer's defence in cases of unfair discrimination.* Where an individual has been refused employment or promotion and believes that this is on account of direct or indirect discrimination, he or she may threaten the employer with legal action. The presentation in court of a job description can then be used as part of a case to establish that the selection decision in question was carried out objectively and that other candidates were judged to be more suitable than the complainant. As is so often the case with employment law, the existence of evidence of this kind is most important in so far as it deters people from bringing actions in the first place.

• *as a means by which the employer's expectations, priorities and values are communicated to new members of staff.* Statements can be included in job descriptions that make clear what the employee is expected to achieve and how he or she will be rewarded for so doing.

Job descriptions are one of the best-established institutions in the P&D field. As a result, a consensus has grown up about what they should include and the level of detail that should be used. They thus vary surprisingly little from one organisation to another in terms of style and coverage. Typically the following headings are included:

• job title

• grade/rate of pay

• main location

• supervisor's name/post

• details of any subordinates

• summary of the main purpose of the job

• list of principal job duties together with very brief descriptions

• reference to other documents (such as collective agreements) that may clarify or expand on other items.

Most will also include a date at the end indicating the point at which the document was last updated. In most cases they will also include some kind of general statement indicating that other duties may be carried out by the job-holder from time to time. Where the job description is explicitly incorporated into the contract of employment, it is also wise to state that the content and reporting lines may be reviewed, and that they cannot be assumed to remain the same indefinitely.

Armstrong (1995: 312–313) includes some very useful general advice about the language that should be used in compiling job descriptions and the methods that can be used to edit them down to a manageable length. He suggests that each item in the job description should relate to the 'outputs' that the job-holder will be expected to achieve or produce, and that each should therefore state what the job-holder can be held responsible for. Where a job task is performed under supervision, such should be clearly stated. Likewise, where there are deadlines to work to, those too should be included, or at least their existence recognised, in the job description. Fine and Getkate (1995: 2–3) go further in proposing that the language used should always refer to 'what gets done' rather than 'what workers do', on the grounds that this allows far more effective description and less room for ambiguity. So, rather than state that the job involves 'consulting' (ie what is done), the job description should use terms such as 'communicates with', 'explains', 'clarifies', 'discusses' or 'informs', which give a more precise meaning to the activity being described.

> Do you have a job description? If so, which of the above items are included? How could it be improved?

PERSON SPECIFICATIONS

The second piece of documentation that is derived from the job analysis process is the person or personnel specification. Here the emphasis is not on what the job involves but on the attributes that are required of someone aspiring to fill the role. Effectively it lists the criteria the organisation proposes to use in shortlisting and selecting an individual to fill the job concerned. Typically, person specifications include information under a number of headings such as skills, knowledge, personality attributes, education, qualifications and experience. Where the hours of work deviate from standard patterns or where the work is carried out on a number of sites, the ability and willingness to meet these requirements will also be included. It is also common for items in the person specification to be divided into 'desirable' and 'essential' characteristics.

A well-known tool for drawing up person specifications is Rodger's seven-point plan, first published in 1952. This suggests that each of the following are considered:

i) physical make-up

ii) attainments

iii) general intelligence

iv) special aptitudes

v) interests

vi) disposition (personality)

vii) circumstances.

Munro-Fraser's five-fold grading system has a slightly different emphasis, but sets out to achieve the same broad objectives:

i) impact on others (appearance, manner etc)

ii) acquired qualifications

iii) innate abilities

iv) motivation

v) adjustment (stability, resilience etc)

It is unlikely that all of these points will be relevant for any one job, and some of the headings will be of significance only in the case of appointments to specialised roles. Nevertheless, the two systems taken together are useful as check-lists covering possible points to include and can also be used in preparing questions to ask at interview.

That said, care must of course be taken to include in a written person specification only items that really are 'essential' or 'desirable' in someone appointed to a particular job. The presence of a professionally compiled document will be of no help in front of an industrial tribunal when a case of unfair discrimination is brought by an aggrieved candidate who failed to be appointed or promoted to a new job. It is the responsibility of the P&D specialist to make sure that problems of this kind do not arise and that the items included can clearly be objectively justified.

The case of St Matthias Church of England School

The difficulties faced by employers in determining what is and what is not a fair criterion to include in a person specification is well illustrated in the case of *Crizzle v St Matthias Church of England School* (IRLR 1993). Here, a deputy headteacher, Ms Crizzle, was not appointed to the headteacher's job when it fell vacant on the grounds that she was not a committed Christian communicant. Over half the school's pupils were Bengali, and Ms Crizzle herself was of Asian origin.

Ms Crizzle appealed to an industrial tribunal, claiming that her failure to be shortlisted for the headteacher's job amounted to indirect racial discrimination. Her case was founded on the argument that her personal religious beliefs would not stand in the way of her managing the efficient education of the children from the local community. The industrial tribunal upheld her case.

The school's board of governors then appealed to the Employment Appeal Tribunal, and were successful in getting the industrial tribunal's judgement overturned. The judges took the view that a school's objective was more than 'efficient education', and that the board behaved quite reasonably in deciding that they wanted a head teacher who was a full member of the Anglican Church and who could lead the school in worship.

PROBLEMS WITH JOB ANALYSIS

Having put the case for detailed job analysis and the production of written job descriptions and person specifications, it is now necessary to point out some of the drawbacks. One, which has already been alluded to, concerns the problems inherent in carrying out the analysis. Some argue that any exercise of this kind, even when its sole purpose is to support fair decision-making in recruitment and selection, is so difficult to achieve objectively that it is not an appropriate way to use organisational resources. According to this point of view, all the main methods used are deficient in some shape or form: observation, because of people's suspicion and their tendency to behave differently when being watched; interviewing, because of people's tendency to puff up their own importance; and questionnaires, because they are unable to include all aspects of a job role. The result, therefore, is inaccurate job descriptions and misleading person specifications – a bureaucratic procedure which takes up time and effort that could be more usefully employed elsewhere.

The problem of inaccuracy is compounded in situations where jobs change in terms of their content, character or complexity. Where this occurs, the written job descriptions can very easily become outdated, with the result that it is of little or no use as the basis of a recruitment and selection programme (let alone the other P&D functions that draw on job descriptions). Aside from dispensing with detailed job analysis altogether, there are two methods that can be used to minimise this effect: regular updating and loose descriptions.

Regular updating
Once job descriptions for all positions have been established, each line manager can be asked formally to review their content on an annual basis. The best time to do this is when the individual job-holder is receiving his or her formal yearly appraisal. The process can then be tied in with a general review of the role, and the job description can anticipate future changes, rather than simply reflect those that have already occurred.

Loose descriptions
Where jobs are genuinely subject to substantial, ongoing change, job analysis can be undertaken on a looser basis, with the result that job descriptions are couched in less precise language than is usually the case. Instead of specifying the exact job duties and responsibilities, the focus is on the general level of the work and the degree of skill employed. So, instead of stating explicitly that the job involves supervising three administrators performing specific tasks, a more general statement is included simply making clear that the job-holder is expected to undertake supervisory duties across a more broadly defined field.

The third commonly cited drawback associated with job analysis and the development of written job descriptions relates to the fact that they may be used by employees as part of a case for refusing to undertake reasonable management instructions. In other words, it is argued that people cannot say 'I'm not doing that – it's not in my job description' if they have no documentation to refer to. Linked to this is the suggestion that, where job duties are written down, managers are liable to be required to negotiate changes with employees or their representatives and that this tends to decrease organisational effectiveness. Again, this problem can be minimised to a great extent if care is taken in drawing up job descriptions and person specifications. Not only should clear and explicit reference always be made to the possibility that other duties may be undertaken from time to time, but the job description can also contain some reference to the possibility that duties will change over time and that the job-holder will be expected to co-operate where such changes are reasonable.

CONTRACTS OF EMPLOYMENT

One of the most common fallacies that people continue to believe is that a contract of employment can exist only as a written document. This leads even those who have worked somewhere for months or years to state quite falsely that they 'do not have a contract', when a contractual relationship was in fact formed on the day they first accepted the offer of employment. As a P&D manager it is therefore often necessary continually to remind people that the contract of employment is no more or less than an agreement between two parties to create an employment relationship. It can thus quite easily exist only in an oral form or with an offer letter and acceptance forming the only written evidence of its existence.

There are in fact four simple legal tests as to whether or not a contract exists:

• Has an offer of employment been made?

• Has the offer been accepted?

• Does consideration exist (see below)?

• Is there an intention to create legal relations?

The question of consideration relates to the law of England and Wales. In the modern context it means that the employee agrees to perform the job and that the employer agrees to make payments in the form of wages. In other words, the employment relationship can be likened to a bargain in which both parties give something up (time and effort in the case of the employee, and money in the case of the employer). According to Aikin (1997: 10), under Scottish law it is insufficient simply to show that 'consideration' exists. The employment relationship is seen as something more than an economic bargain. Instead, there has to be 'causa', which also includes an acceptance of moral obligations on behalf of the two parties.

Legally this is very significant, because once a contract of employment exists, both parties are said to owe certain duties to one another that are enforceable at law. These are known as 'implied terms' because they are held by the courts to exist even though neither party has agreed to them in writing. In addition, all employees are entitled to the protection of some statutory employment legislation (ie laws passed by Parliament). While much dismissal law currently applies only to employees with over two years' continuous service, other legislation applies from day one and is relevant wherever a contract of employment has been agreed. Examples include laws relating to unfair discrimination, equal pay, health and safety at work, maternity leave and statutory sick pay.

The question of implied terms is more complex because they can vary from situation to situation - for example, where over a period of time employer and employee have both acted as if there was an agreed term or where certain obligations can be said to have emerged through custom and practice. That said, there are common-law implied terms that exist simply because a contract of employment has been agreed. For example, the employer is obliged to pay wages, to treat employees courteously, to provide support to help employees undertake their work, to reimburse expenses incurred in the performance of the job and to provide a safe working environment. In return, employees are expected to be willing to work, to be honest, to co-operate with an employer's reasonable instructions, to be loyal and to take care in performing their duties (ie not to be careless with the employer's property).

While it is important to appreciate that contracts of employment – and therefore duties and obligations – exist whether or not they are agreed in writing, it is far more satisfactory for all parties if there is evidence in writing of both the existence of the contract and its main terms. This will not make the contract any more valid, but will make it far easier to prove if challenged, and puts the relationship on an open, clear footing from the start. There are three types of written document which are most commonly used to provide evidence of the contract and its contents: an offer letter and acceptance, written particulars of the terms and conditions, and other documents expressly incorporated into the contract (eg collective agreements).

OFFER LETTERS

The style and length of offer letters clearly vary greatly from position to position. Where the terms and conditions of employment are standard across the organisation, the offer letter itself can be short and to the point. A copy of the standard terms and conditions can then be enclosed or sent a short time later. Where the contract is unusual or particularly different from the standard, there is a need to write longer and more detailed offer letters. In any case, the following should always be included:

- job title
- start date
- starting salary
- pay date (ie weekly or monthly)
- hours of work
- any probationary or fixed-term arrangements.

Some employers go further at this stage and make specific mention of bonus schemes, sick pay arrangements, holiday entitlements, pension schemes, periods of notice and other matters. By and large, unless the employee concerned is to be treated differently from others, or unless he or she has specifically asked about these matters at interview, there is no need to include them in the offer letter. What is important is that the letter is dated and that a reply is requested within so many weeks of receipt. Where this is not done, potential employees are liable to wait several weeks before replying, by which time the job has been offered to another candidate.

WRITTEN PARTICULARS OF EMPLOYMENT

In the Trade Union Reform and Employment Rights Act (TURERA) 1993, the Conservative Government incorporated the EU Written Particulars Directive into UK law. This means that new employees have to be sent a written statement summarising their terms and conditions within two months of the start of their employment. Anyone who was in employment before 30 November 1993 is also entitled to receive a statement, if one is requested. The written particulars must cover the following in a single document:

- the names of the employer and employee between whom a contractual relationship has been formed
- the date the employment commenced
- the job title or a brief description of the work concerned
- the amount of pay
- the dates on which pay will be received
- details of bonuses or commission to be paid
- the hours of work
- holiday and holiday pay entitlements
- the place of work.

Where an employee has moved to a new job with a new employer but remains in the same parent organisation, it is common for continuity of employment to be retained. In other words, the employee is not required to work for a further two years before being entitled to full employment rights. Where internal moves of this kind have occurred, and where continuity of service is not deemed to have been broken, the written statement is also required to state that such is the case.

Employees have also to receive other documentation which can be incorporated into the principal statement described above or can be sent separately. These are the following:

- sick pay arrangements and other terms and conditions relating to sickness
- notice periods for both employer and employee
- details of any occupational pension arrangements
- the anticipated duration of the contract, if it is temporary
- details of any collective agreements which govern the terms and conditions of employment.

In the case of employees working abroad, there is also a requirement to indicate the duration of the period to be spent overseas and the currency in which payments will be made. Additional allowances and benefits for overseas workers have also to be included.

Finally, the written particulars must include details of relevant disciplinary and grievance arrangements. The full procedures do not need to be sent to everyone, but everyone needs to be informed of where they can have access to these documents. As a rule, disciplinary and grievance procedures do not themselves form part of the contract of employment, which is stated clearly in the written particulars. Employees thus have a contractual right to be informed that they exist but cannot use the law either as a means of forcing an employer to apply them or to sue for breach of contract where this has not occurred.

It must again be stressed that *the written particulars do not amount to a contract of employment.* Even when signed by an employee and returned for filing, they are legally seen only as written evidence of the contract and as such representative only of the employer's view of what the contract itself contains. However, in practice, they are generally accepted by the courts as good evidence of a contract's details, and it is very difficult for employees to suggest otherwise when they have not complained of any inaccuracy previously.

INCORPORATED DOCUMENTS

Notwithstanding the minimum requirements described above, employers often do expressly incorporate other documents into contracts of employment. The most common examples are job descriptions, collective agreements and staff handbooks, but there is no reason why other material such as a disciplinary procedure or a set of health and safety rules should not also be incorporated. Whether or not this is done is a matter for the employer, and there are arguments for and against doing so.

The argument against
Once procedures are incorporated, an employee gains the right to sue the employer if those procedures are not followed. For example, if the staff handbook is incorporated and it states that all employees are entitled to a month's notice, then any employee, even if he or she has not yet completed a month's service, could sue for damages if summarily dismissed. In incorporating these documents, the employer is in effect conveying on employees more generous terms and more extensive rights than they are entitled to at law. The argument against doing so is therefore that this amounts to an unnecessary risk.

The arguments for
Where an employer wishes to be seen as being fair and applying best practice, there is a good case for incorporating such documents as a means of indicating that all employees will be treated equally well from the start of their employment. Incorporation ensures that this is the case and that exceptions are not made in the case of recent starters. The rationale, as with all commitment to best practice, is that as a result the organisation will be better able to attract, retain and motivate the best available people. Incorporation, if done conspicuously, can make a sizeable contribution to the achievement of this objective.

The second argument in favour of incorporation is the clarity that it can bring to the employment relationship. Provided the documents concerned are written unambiguously, they should act to set out exactly what is expected of each party and thus avoid disputes breaking out about interpretation. For example, where a grievance procedure exists but is not incorporated, and an employee with less than two years' service wishes to complain about his or her manager's actions, there will always be a temptation among some managers either to threaten dismissal if the allegation is not withdrawn, or actually to dismiss the employee. Such action could very easily lead to anger or less co-operation on the part of others, or to calls for collective action. Where the policy is incorporated into contracts of employment everyone should know where they stand from the start, thus avoiding such situations.

SPECIFIC CONTRACTUAL TERMS

Employers are free in principle to seek to include whatever terms they wish into a contract, and will be able to enforce these at law provided they are not superseded by implied terms or statutory employment rights. Similarly, in principle, employees are free to accept or reject any offer that is made to them. However, in practice, for the vast majority of people contracts take a pretty standard form and it is only in relatively exceptional cases that there is a need to require lengthy notice periods, unusual patterns of hours or peculiar payment arrangements. However, where such is the case, there will be a need to draw up a more substantial, individual written contract rather than relying simply on an offer letter and written particulars.

That said, there are a number of potential express terms that most P&D practitioners are likely to come across at some stage and about which it is wise to have some knowledge. In some cases they can simply be inserted into an offer letter; in others it may be felt more appropriate to include them in a separate written contract. They include the clauses discussed below.

Fixed-term clauses
Employing people on a fixed-term basis is becoming increasingly common, particularly in the public sector. Where funding is limited or where the job is clearly of fixed duration, it is necessary to include such a clause in the original contract.

Waiver clauses
Where people are employed on a fixed-term basis, they can be asked to sign a waiver clause, renouncing their right to a redundancy payment. (See Chapter 13 for more detail on this term.)

Probationary clauses
Many employers initially hire people for a probationary period of six months or a year, at which point their performance is reviewed and a decision taken on whether or not to confirm the appointment. Where this is the case it is important to gain the employee's agreement and to ensure that he or she understands the probationary arrangements together with the consequences of failure.

Restraint of trade clauses

Another common express term that is incorporated into contracts seeks to deter employees from working for rival employers in their spare time or using information gained in their employment to help business competitors (eg by leaking trade secrets).

Restrictive covenants

These are like restraint of trade clauses, but refer to the period after the employment has ended. They usually seek to prevent employees from taking up employment with competitors for a certain period of time after they leave. They are covered in greater detail in Chapter 12.

Contracts for services

As was seen in Chapter 2, it is increasingly common for people to take on 'atypical' work which does not resemble the traditional 40-hour, Monday–Friday, 9–5.00 form that has dominated for generations. In these cases it is not always easy to state with certainty that a contract of employment actually exists. It may be that even though the employees believe themselves to have contracts of employment, albeit on an atypical basis, they are in fact employed as an independent contractor through a 'contract for services', which is a very different legal beast. In this case, because the individual concerned is technically self-employed, there are fewer obligations, but far fewer rights too.

In determining whether the relationship is governed by a 'contract of employment' or a 'contract for services', industrial tribunals are required to look at the facts of each case. It is therefore difficult to identify any overriding general principles that are applied. However, according to Macdonald (1995: 2) the following questions are some of those usually asked when a case falls into the grey area between the two types of status:

- Is the person in business on his or her own account?

- Is the work performed an integral part of the company's business?

- Is the work performed under the direction and control of the company?
- Is the person obliged to do any work given or can he or she choose whether to do so?
- Is the company obliged to give the individual work to do?
- Is the individual required to do the work personally or can he or she see that it is done by someone else?
- To whom do the tools and equipment belong?
- Is a fixed wage or salary paid?
- Is work also taken from other employers?
- Is tax and national insurance deducted by the company?
- Are company benefits such as pensions or holiday pay received?

NATIONAL VARIATIONS

Organisations operating in a number of countries need to comply with local laws concerning the regulation of the employment relationship. While something similar to the contract of employment, as defined in UK law, exists in most countries, there are substantial differences in important areas. First, different countries have different rules concerning who qualifies as an 'employee', different tests being used by the courts to reach decisions. In many countries the key test is the extent to which there is dependency – a less difficult hurdle to clear than the multiple tests used in the UK courts. Secondly, countries vary to a considerable degree in the extent to which they permit freely agreed contracts to form the basis of an employment relationship. In the UK, the state has traditionally intervened very little, leaving it up to individual employees and trade unions to negotiate terms and conditions with their employers. Hence, there is no statutory right to paid holiday or any holiday at all, and no labour inspectorate employed by the government to enforce the minimum standards that are determined by Parliament.

It is beyond the scope of this book to go into any great detail about how terms and conditions are determined in other countries. The aim is to flag the fact that substantial differences do exist, especially in the treatment of such special groups as apprentices, seafarers, home-workers, professional sportsmen and agricultural workers. A major area of difference relates to employees of the state – an employment relationship that has not traditionally been governed by freely negotiated contracts in many countries.

Within the European Union there has been a tendency in recent years to harmonise the approaches of the member states, but as the relevant IDS/IPD European Management Guide (1995) shows, there are still very considerable differences. Among the most common is the tradition in several European countries for employees to be classed legally either as blue-collar, white-collar, professional or managerial staff, different contractual standards applying in each case. In others, including the Scandinavian countries, the law explicitly involves trade unions in the determination of all contracts of employment. Other examples are as follows:

- German law prescribes very strict conditions under which it is permissable to agree a fixed-term contract.

- In France everyone is entitled to a minimum of 30 working days of holiday each year.

- In Italy the law requires companies to pay their senior managers minimum rates of pay set by union negotiations.

- All Danish contracts of employment must be in writing.

- In Spain employees have a right to take unpaid leave for a period of to two to five years once they have been employed in an organisation for at least a year.

Which of these approaches would you like to see incorporated into UK law? Which would you argue against?

INDUCTION

Once the offer letter has been sent and the basic terms of contract agreed, the final stage in the recruitment and selection process can begin – namely, the induction of new employees. There is some confusion between different writers in the terminology used to describe events and procedures surrounding the arrival of new staff, so it is important to distinguish between different aspects of the subject. For the purposes of this chapter, 'induction' is used as a general term describing the whole process whereby new employees adjust or acclimatise to their jobs and working environments; 'orientation' refers to a specific course or training event which new starters attend; and the term 'socialisation' is used to describe the way in which new employees build up working relationships and find roles for themselves within their new teams.

There is nothing easier than giving new starters a poor induction, achieved simply by neglecting them and failing to consider their basic needs. On the other hand, making it work well is both difficult to achieve consistently and time-consuming. There is also a need to persuade others of the value a well-designed induction has for the organisation. The following quotation puts the nub of the case most effectively:

> Few things affect employees more than the way they are first introduced to their job, to their workplace, and to their co-workers. If new employees are treated with indifference, considered a necessary nuisance, left to wait interminably 'till people get around to you', loaded down with incomprehensible policy and procedure manuals, given sketchy introductions to the people and things they encounter, left with their questions unanswered and their curiosity unslaked, they are likely to be far less than fully productive new employees. However, if a new person's and the organisation's human resources department staff carefully plan and implement an effective programme for proper induction and orientation, they are making a wise investment in that person's growth, development and output, and in the organisation's efficiency, productivity and future success.
>
> Shea (1985: 591)

It is not just a question of creating the conditions for employees to reach their full potential as soon as is possible. Important though that is, there is also a need to minimise the other effects of 'induction crises', such as low morale and resignation. In some industries, as will be seen in Chapter 12, staff turnover is particularly high in the first months of appointment. The result for the organisation is the presence of avoidable costs, as jobs have to be readvertised and selection procedures used more often than is necessary. Of course, not all early leaving is avoidable, but there is evidence to suggest that effective initial induction has an important contribution to make in encouraging employees to stay who might otherwise have been tempted to leave (see Fowler 1996a: 1–6).

At base, it is a question of recognising, as Wanous (1992) argues, that starting a new job is a highly stressful experience for the average employee. Adjusting to a new environment, and taking in and committing to memory new procedures and terminology while building up relationships with new colleagues is an onerous, confusing and tiring process. It is made all the more difficult when the employees concerned have moved to new locations or are starting work in an industry with which they are unfamiliar. That said, it is also the case that employees have very different requirements when they join a new organisation, and there are thus dangers in making blanket assumptions about what they need to know and how much assistance they will need in adjusting. Putting everyone, regardless of rank or experience, through an extensive, identical, centrally controlled induction programme can well be counter-productive, whatever its intentions, as it will inevitably be inappropriate for some participants.

On the other hand, there are some aspects of induction which, if they are to be managed efficiently, have to be organised on a collective basis and must be provided for all new starters. Examples are fire regulations, security arrangements, canteen facilities, the distribution of organisation handbooks, the setting up of payment arrangements and the completion of forms detailing next of kin in case of emergency. There is thus a good case for running a general induction session covering these matters on a weekly basis and making sure that all new members of staff definitely attend.

In larger organisations, other matters that are traditionally dealt with at orientation sessions held in the first few weeks include a formal welcome from senior management, the setting-up of occupational pension arrangements and general tours of the premises. There is also a need to appraise new employees of current organisation-wide trends and to let them know about centralised administrative arrangements such as expense claims, welfare services and rules covering absence, discipline, holidays and the making of telephone calls. Because these activities do not have to be covered on an employee's first day, and because they are likely to lead to discussion and questioning, they are probably best organised for small groups of new employees to attend some days after their start date. This also allows flexibility in terms of who is invited to each session, so that school-leavers, graduate recruits, senior staff and junior employees are invited to separate sessions. Differentiation of this kind will, of course, not be an option for smaller employers who have relatively few new employees starting each month.

Other matters to be covered during an employee's induction are specific to each department or job. They are therefore the responsibility of line managers to organise. Aside from the basic issues of performance standards, training arrangements and introductions to colleagues, some also argue that there is a need for employers consciously to use the induction period to ensure that the organisation's values and culture is assimilated by the new employee. Achieving this is easier said than done, and there are dangers that too regular a repetition of such points can demotivate and actually increase the time it takes an employee to adjust and reach a good standard of performance.

For organisations seeking, and then trying to hold on to, the Investors in People (IiP) Award, induction is particularly important, as they need to be able to show that there are effective systems in place for introducing new employees to their jobs and organisations. The need to provide evidence inevitably leads P&D managers to develop control systems designed to ensure that the departmental orientation and socialisation processes are carried out to a sufficiently high standard. The most common mechanism for achieving this is a check-list of points that supervisors are required to cover which new employees tick off or sign when completed. Another means of making sure that induction procedures are being followed is for P&D specialists to see new staff formally a month or two after they have started work in order to ascertain how they are getting on and whether or not they have any outstanding questions about what is expected of them.

The other aspect of induction that needs to be worked at is the need for new starters to be made to feel comfortable socially. For strong extroverts this aspect of starting a new job is not a problem: they will relish the opportunity to meet new people and will quickly ensure that they fit in with the prevailing social norms. For others, being new in a department filled with old hands is daunting and can very easily hold back the speed with which they adjust and reach their full potential. More fundamentally, a lack of social ease is likely to discourage new starters from asking questions or being honest about their training needs. Again, there is no great strategy needed to deal with this issue. It is simply a question of reminding people of its existence, asking them to recall how they felt when they started jobs, and suggesting that attention is given to making new starters feel welcome. According to Skeats (1991: 56), an approach that can be successful is the identification of an established staff member to act as mentor or 'buddy' to each new employee. This person should be approximately the same age and have similar status to the new starter, and should have a good working knowledge of the job the newcomer will be doing. The buddy then makes contact before the start date to introduce him or herself and is responsible for showing the newcomer where facilities are located. Ideally they will also take meals together in the first days and discuss some of the prevailing norms and unwritten rules that govern the way the department operates.

Reflect on the induction you have received when starting new jobs. Which aspects were helpful? How could the process have been improved?

The Texas Instruments studies

A classic research exercise designed to investigate the benefits of induction was carried out in the USA in the 1960s by two occupational psychologists called Gomersall and Myers. Working among employees at an electrical assembly plant, they started by ascertaining from existing employees what aspects of the work they had found to be most stressful when they first took up their jobs. Acting on this information, they designed a six-hour orientation programme designed to reduce stress among new starters. The course covered four areas:

- New recruits were assured that failure rates were very low and that the vast majority of starters quickly learned to perform to a satisfactory level.
- They were told to expect some baiting from established employees, but to ignore it because the same treatment tended to be given to all new starters.
- It was suggested that they took the initiative in terms of communication with others, including their new supervisors.
- They were each given some specific advice about how to build up a good working relationship with their particular supervisors.

A hundred new starters, selected at random, were then put through the new orientation programme, and a further hundred given the standard two-hour course offered by the company. The result was a substantial divergence between the performance of the two groups, those who had attended the six-hour session achieving higher productivity rates. They also had better attendance records and required less training time than those who had been given the standard two-hour introduction.

Source: Wanous (1992: 178–179)

FURTHER READING

- Michael Pearn and Rajvinder Kandola's *Job Analysis: A manager's guide* (1993) provides a thorough overview of different approaches to the topic and contains a number of short case-studies outlining the methods used by four organisations. The wider issues are well covered in two American textbooks: *Human Resource Management* by Carrell, Elbert and Hatfield (1995) and *Personnel/Human Resource Management* by Leap and Crino (1993).

- *Contracts* by Olga Aikin (1997) is a good starting-point for further reading on the topic of contracts of employment. Useful information can also be found in most general texts covering employment law. *Hired or Fired, Sick and Tired* by Lynda Macdonald (1995) also provides a readable and easily understood guide to basic contract law as it applies to employment relationships.

- International comparisons are less well covered. H. Barbagelata's article in *Comparative Labour Law and industrial Relations* edited by R. Blanpain (1985) provides a general overview, while *Contracts and Terms and Conditions of Employment*, jointly published by IDS and the IPD (1995), gives more detail about particular European countries.

- Two general management guides to employee induction are *Successful Induction* by Judy Skeats (1991) and *Employee Induction: A good start* by Alan Fowler (1996). Academic research on the topic is summarised by John Parcher Wanous in *Organizational Entry* (1992).

6 Casting your net upon the waters

The recruitment of new employees is an area of work in which all personnel professionals are involved in some way. According to Fair (1992: 56), it is not unusual for a sum equal to 2 per cent of an employer's total wage bill to be spent on recruitment advertising and agency fees. For a company employing 100 people at national average earnings this would mean that over £30,000 a year was committed to recruitment before taking account of administration costs. For larger organisations employing in excess of 3,000 people, the annual cost will amount to millions of pounds. Recruitment can also take up a great deal of time. One recent survey suggested that on average this area of work accounts for 16 per cent of a typical personnel department workload (*Personnel Today* April 1996: 3). It is thus important to appreciate how recruitment arrangements can be managed as efficiently as possible while making sure, at the same time, that the approaches chosen remain effective and do not breach the law.

This chapter focuses on the key decisions that need to be taken in managing recruitment processes and on the skills needed to undertake them with maximum effectiveness, efficiency and fairness. The different kinds of recruitment methods that can be used are described and the advantages and disadvantages of each assessed. Particular attention is given to recruitment advertising, the employment of external agents to undertake all or part of the process, and liaison with educational institutions. We then examine legal and ethical issues before looking at methods used for evaluating policies and practices in this field.

By the end of this chapter readers should be able to:

- draft advertisements for filling vacancies and select appropriate media for specific cases
- evaluate advertising media and other methods of recruitment
- evaluate recruitment processes generally
- decide which recruitment techniques to use.

In addition, readers should be able to understand and explain:

- the legal and ethical framework of recruitment

• CIPD advice relating to recruitment.

DEFINING RECRUITMENT

The terms 'recruitment' and 'selection' are often considered together, but they are in fact distinct personnel management activities. While recruitment involves actively soliciting applications from potential employees, selection techniques are used to decide which of the applicants is best suited to fill the vacancy in question. We can thus characterise recruitment as a positive activity requiring employers to sell themselves in the relevant labour markets so as to maximise the pool of well-qualified candidates from which future employees can be chosen. By contrast, selection can be seen as a negative activity in so far as it involves picking out the best of the bunch and turning down the rest.

An important question to ask whenever recruitment is being considered is whether or not there really is a need to recruit outside the organisation at all. Giving thought to alternative approaches might lead to the development of effective solutions at considerably lower cost. An interesting example is the experience of the UK Air Directorate.

Having made the distinction between selection and recruitment, it is

---

Recruiting air traffic controllers

During the 1980s, the UK Air Directorate was faced with a shortage of applicants for enrolment as air traffic control cadets. The problem arose for a number of reasons. It was partly caused by increased traffic in UK airspace, but also arose because of competition for air traffic controllers from overseas operators and a substantial number of early retirements.

External recruitment was deemed necessary, but its scale was greatly reduced in two important ways. First, the training programme was shortened very considerably, allowing cadets to graduate after 18 months rather than two years. This involved forcing cadets to specialise at a far earlier stage but had the advantage of bringing them into control centres much sooner. Secondly, air traffic control assistants were actively encouraged to apply for promotion to the rank of controller – a career move that had occurred only rarely previously.

Source: G. Brown (1993)

---

important to understand that there are times when selection techniques have a recruitment role and vice versa. An employment interview, for instance, while primarily a tool of selection, is also an experience that enables applicants to evaluate the organisation and to decide whether or not they wish to take up any offer of employment that may be made. Similarly, there is a strong element of selection in many recruitment processes. For example, one aim of a good job advertisement is to enable potential applicants to self-select, so that only those who truly have the required qualifications and attributes make formal applications.

Table 4 **Recruitment Methods**

Printed media	national newspapers local newspapers trade and professional journals magazines
External agencies	job centres outplacement consultants headhunters employment agencies forces resettlement agency recruitment consultants
Education liaison	careers fairs college tutors careers advisors student societies
Other media	direct mail local radio teletext bill boards internet TV and cinema
In-house methods	in-store posters factory gate posters internal newsletters notice boards past applicant records open days
Professional contacts	conferences trade union referrals suppliers industry contacts

RECRUITMENT METHODS

There are numerous different approaches used to attract applications from prospective employees – some more conventional than others. In practice, for most jobs the formal methods can be listed under the following six headings: printed media, external agencies, education liaison, other media, professional contacts and in-house methods (see Table 4). In addition, there are informal methods that can be used whereby employees, suppliers or personal acquaintances get to hear about a vacancy via word of mouth or the 'grapevine'. All these methods are used to a greater or lesser degree. Some, like job centres or word of mouth, cost next to nothing. Others, including national newspaper advertising and the employment of headhunters, require considerable expenditure. A few methods, such as the use of cinema and TV, are only realistic propositions for the largest employing organisations seeking to recruit substantial numbers. An example would be the use of such media by Army and Navy recruiters.

When deciding which method to use, a variety of other considerations must also be taken into account. For example, it is necessary to consider how precisely the approach adopted will hit its target audience. For this reason we can safely conclude that it would be as inappropriate to advertise for a new chief executive in a job centre as it would be to place an advertisement for an engineer in a medical journal.

Recruiters also need to be mindful of the image of their organisation they are portraying in the labour market. While a small local news-paper advertisement might attract large numbers of applicants, there is a case for spending rather more on a substantial advertisement set by professionals as a means of suggesting to job seekers that the organi-sation compares favourably with others as a place to work.

Some methods are ruled out because of time constraints. Most personnel specialists will at some time have experienced pressure from line managers to fill vacancies within days rather than weeks, with the result that the range of possible recruitment methods is severely restricted. In such cases the only realistic options are employment agencies, job centres, personal contacts and those local papers that advertise positions on a daily basis.

Another important consideration is the volume of applications that each method is likely to yield and the ability of the personnel department to administer them effectively. While it would be grossly inefficient to choose a method that brought in hundreds of applications for a single unskilled job vacancy, there are situations in which it is necessary to attract very large numbers. One example would be advertisements seeking applications for very senior jobs where the widest possible pool of appropriately qualified individuals is needed to enable the organisation to screen out all but the very best candidates. Another common instance is the opening of a new plant or store leading to the creation of hundreds of new jobs.

The national lottery

A recent high-profile example of mass recruitment occurred when Camelot were successful in their bid to run the national lottery in May 1994. The lottery itself was launched only six months later – in the event, very smoothly - but prior to this the company needed to recruit over 500 people and then train them. For most, quite literally, this was a whole new ball game: few can have had experience of running a similar operation because none existed in the UK. Recruiting them was made particularly difficult by the tight timescales involved. A proportion had to be employed in planning functions prior to the announcement of which consortium had won the contract to operate the lottery. Their posts were necessarily temporary in the first instance.

In the event a variety of different recruitment sources were tapped and several recruitment methods employed. About 10 per cent of the staff were recruited from within the companies backing the Camelot bid. Others were recruited through two specialist employment agencies which focused on management and technical functions respectively. A further source of candidates was the Watford Job Centre, situated close to the company's HQ. The Employment Service then passed details of the jobs on to other centres around the country. The final source of candidates was the thousands of speculative applications Camelot received as a result of the publicity surrounding their successful bid. In total, using all four methods, over 16,000 applications were received. Turning these into 500 employees occupied 20 personnel officers for several months.

Source: G. Huddart (1995).

INFORMAL METHODS

In 1995 an NOP opinion poll suggested that just under half of employees were recruited into their present jobs either by a direct approach from the employer or as a result of hearing about the vacancy through word of mouth (Table 5). By contrast, only 4 per cent had been recruited via a private recruitment agency and only 3 per cent after seeing national newspaper advertisements. While it is clear that the use of informal methods is very widespread, opinion is divided as to how much they really have to offer employers when compared with formal approaches.

Table 5 Recruitment methods in practice

Recruitment method	Percentage
Word of mouth	35
Direct approach from employer	13
Daily local/regional newspaper	10
Weekly local/regional newspaper	9
Job centre	7
Trade/professional press	5
Recruitment agency	4
National newspaper	3
Other methods	14

Source: Recruitment Today (June 1995)

Some research findings, such as those of Kirnan *et al* (1989), strongly suggest that informal recruitment methods yield a better selection of well-qualified applicants than formal methods. The same study also found a correlation between informal recruitment and staff turnover, with fewer employees recruited via informal channels leaving the organisation soon after taking up employment. This could be because candidates recruited by word of mouth self-select to a greater degree than those finding out about the job from other sources. They therefore have more opportunity to ask questions about the employer and the job duties and are better placed to decide for themselves whether or not it is suitable for them. The relatively low turnover rates are probably best explained by the likelihood that informal recruits have more realistic perceptions of what the job will be like than those recruited through formal channels.

However, both word of mouth and direct approach methods can be criticised on the grounds that, by definition, they only reach a very limited target audience. The employer may have a good group of candidates from which to choose but it will not be a very extensive selection – nor is it likely to be representative of the wider community. It could thus be argued that a formal method, such as a recruitment advertisement, might yield an even better pool of candidates if it was designed effectively and printed in an appropriate publication. It may not be the formal methods themselves that are ineffectual, but the manner in which they are deployed. The use of some informal methods, as we shall see later in this chapter, may also cause employers to breach discrimination legislation.

RECRUITMENT ADVERTISING

Advertising space in newspapers is generally sold in units of 3cm by 1cm. An advert measuring 10cm by 6cm will thus involve purchasing 20 of these blocks of space. The cost of each unit is known as 'the single-column centimetre rate', which varies very considerably between different publications and over time. The market place is highly competitive, particular newspapers offering a range of preferable rates to employers and agents who place large volumes of business with them. Over the last 10 years the *Guardian* newspaper has managed to gain a substantial share of the national market (40 per cent in 1996) with very competitive pricing. As a result it now tends to dominate public sector and middle-range management job advertising. The market for senior management positions, by contrast, is divided between other quality papers like *The Sunday Times* and the *Daily Telegraph* – which charge considerably more per single-column centimetre than the *Guardian*. (See Table 6.)

Table 6 Market share of national newspaper recruitment advertising (1996)

Paper	Percentage of market share
Guardian	37
Sunday Times	17
Daily Telegraph	15
Times	12
Financial Times	9
Independent	7

The choice of publication will depend very much on the target audience. Opinion poll research has indicated that around 70 per cent of people buy a different newspaper when they are looking for a new job (*Recruitment Today* June 1995), so information about readership levels and profiles is only of limited use in deciding where to place a job advertisement. The first question to ask is whether or not there is a need to advertise nationally. For most jobs local newspapers are preferable, because they reach potential applicants only within the relevant travel-to-work area. It is only necessary to advertise on a national basis for relatively specialised vacancies for which there is a national labour market. An example of this distinction would be the labour markets for kitchen employees in expensive hotels and restaurants. In order to recruit a kitchen porter or junior chef it will probably only be necessary to advertise locally. A national advertisement might well not yield many responses, because these are not generally jobs that people would happily move house to take up. On the other hand, the market for top head chefs is national or even international – so a local paper would clearly be inappropriate in these cases. The higher the salary and the more specialised the job, the more geographically widespread the labour market will be.

Another consideration is the possibility of placing recruitment advertisements in trade and professional journals. These tend to cost rather less than either local or national papers (around £30 per single-column centimetre) but have a far lower readership than either. Again the decision will depend on the nature of the labour market concerned. Some industries, by nature or tradition, offer clearer career prospects to individual entrants than others. Some also tend to favour internal candidates over outsiders because of the need to recruit individuals with industry-specific skills or competences. Where this is the case and a national or international labour market exists, there is a strong case for advertising in the relevant trade journal. An example might be the *Nursing Times*, which serves the largest single professional group of staff in the UK.

> Where does your organisation advertise? What considerations are taken into account in deciding which papers or journals are most appropriate?

STYLE AND WORDING

Any cursory flick through the appointments pages of newspapers and journals reveals how different one recruitment advertisement is from another. There is clearly no one best approach, because in this field 'best' can often mean 'distinctive'. Some of the key decisions that recruiters face in drawing up effective advertising copy are examined in the following paragraphs.

Wide trawls v wide nets
A fundamental decision is the number of applications it is intended should be received. Wide trawls bring in lots of different fish, while wide nets only catch the biggest. According to De Witte (1989: 210), 30 per cent of the population of working age is actively looking for a new job at any one time, so in principle it is not difficult to attract very large numbers of applicants. The question is how useful or desirable such an approach might be.

Where a wide trawl is required the advert has to be striking in appearance. It will probably be large and make use of pictures or unusual graphics. By contrast the wide net approach requires less razzmatazz. The key aim here is to reach a relatively narrow audience and then to encourage self-selection on the part of job seekers. This often means including a substantial quantity of detailed information about the job and the kind of candidate being sought.

Realistic v positive
Another important decision in designing advertisements concerns how accurate the information contained should be. One option is to use an unashamedly positive approach. The aim is to create an image of the job as an exciting and challenging opportunity for a well-motivated person. Any drawbacks in the contract or less attractive aspects of the job are thus either downplayed or left out of the advertising copy altogether. The alternative is to design a realistic advertisement which mentions all aspects of the job (potentially attractive and unattractive). It might state that the work is complex and technically demanding or that a high degree of job security is unlikely to be given.

As was the case with informal methods, the realistic approach has the advantage of encouraging people to self-select and moves some way towards the 'realistic job preview' that is said to have such a marked effect on reducing staff turnover in the first months of employment (Hom and Griffeth, 1995: 193–203). On the other hand, it can be argued that self-selection is often not in the interests of the employer because too heavy a dose of realism can discourage excellent potential applicants from responding. There is thus a good case for adopting a positive approach at the advertising stage and keeping back some of the potential drawbacks of a job for discussion at the selection interview once the candidates' appetites have been whetted.

Corporate image v emphasis on the job

Recruitment advertisements also vary greatly in the emphasis they give on the one hand to the organisation as a potential employer and, on the other, to the nature and duties of the job. Some advertisements thus make great play out of their well-known brand names, while others put the emphasis on the job. In some cases the name of the employer is omitted altogether, with potential applicants asked to contact an agency.

In part this decision is determined by the extent to which the employer is well known in its target labour markets. People are lured towards 'big names' because they perceive that a spell of employment in such organisations will enhance their future career prospects, self-esteem or social status. However, it also important to be mindful of the potential general publicity a recruitment advertisement incorporating well-known brand names can generate. They can thus have two purposes; to attract applicants and to increase sales of well-known products.

Precise v vague information

The research carried out by De Witte (1989) showed above all else that job seekers like to have as much basic information as possible in job advertisements and that vague forms of words resulted in considerably lower response rates. So what possible justification can there be for the many advertisements that contain only imprecise information? The answer mainly lies in the frequent need to preserve confidentiality.

The absence of precise salary information is relatively common because of potential problems that can arise if other employees see the advertisement and compare their own packages unfavourably with that on offer to job applicants. There may also be a case in some circumstances for making no mention of the employer's name and using an agency to advertise the position. This would be the case if it was thought desirable for existing employees to remain ignorant of the recruitment process. An example might be a situation where an individual's contract is to be terminated with immediate effect and where a replacement is needed to take over very swiftly. In such circumstances there may be insufficient time to advertise the job and fill the vacancy after the previous job-holder has left. In extreme cases it may be deemed desirable further to disguise the organisation's identity by making only very vague references to its markets and location.

However, there is a further possible explanation for the vagueness that is characteristic of many advertisements placed by agencies on behalf of clients – namely, their wish to have on their books as many potential job applicants as possible. The aim of the vague advertisement is thus not primarily to attract candidates seeking the particular job in question, but to generate a large response from people whom the agent may be able to place in other positions at some time in the future.

There is also an argument in favour of vague approaches on the grounds that they contribute towards flexible working. According to this point of view, successful candidates are less likely to come to the job with strong preconceptions about their duties and position in the organisational hierarchy than colleagues recruited via very precise advertisements. In an age when flexible working is becoming increasingly important in many quarters, such arguments can be judged to have some validity. You could certainly use them as part of a case for omitting from advertisements details of hours of work or reporting lines. Moreover, a case can also be made for vaguer approaches on grounds of cost because imprecise wording can often take up less space than detailed information. In recruitment advertising the less wordy the advertisement, the cheaper it is to publish.

Plain-speaking v elaborate

There is an ongoing debate among recruitment specialists as to the desirability or utility of incorporating expensive artwork or colour into recruitment advertisements. An interesting selection of views on this topic was featured in *Recruitment Today* in 1996, recruiters putting forward contrasting views. At one extreme is the kind of view identified by John Courtis (1989: 34) that 'too much arty input' can reduce the effectiveness of an advertisement and that the inclusion of straightforward relevant information is all that is really necessary. The alternative view, expressed by John Ainley, the head of group personnel at W.H. Smith, is that refreshing and distinctive visual approaches are more eye-catching and thus yield more applicants. He also expresses the view that the image of the employer in the labour market is an important consideration and that stuffy or impersonal approaches are less effective than those which 'read like a conversation' (*Recruitment Today* February 1996: 7).

> How elaborate are the advertisements for jobs used by your organisation? Could they be improved either by reducing or by increasing their visual distinctiveness?

USING AGENTS IN THE RECRUITMENT PROCESS

A variety of different external agencies can be employed to undertake some part of the recruitment process on behalf of employers. In addition to government and voluntary agencies involved in finding jobs for people, there is now a well-established recruitment industry that exists to serve the needs of employers and job seekers in ever more complex and competitive labour markets. From a personnel management perspective this provides interesting opportunities for increasing the effectiveness and efficiency of recruitment activity but the use of agents also carries risks. In particular, there is a need to establish at the outset exactly what the agent can offer and precisely how much the service is going to cost. The advantages and disadvantages of agents vary considerably with the type of agency service on offer. These can broadly be categorised under four headings, each discussed below.

Government and voluntary agents

In addition to the government's employment service and its network of job centres, there also exists a number of other state-sponsored organisations which offer employers a free recruitment service. One is the Forces Resettlement Agency, which assists ex-Army personnel to find jobs in civilian life. As well as providing its regular job advertising function, the Employment Service also runs a range of training programmes for people who have been out of work for a prolonged period. Their initiatives often involve placing unemployed people in workplaces free of charge in exchange for training. The aim is to improve individuals' skills while giving them an opportunity to gain work experience. From an employer's perspective, as long as there is suitable work and training opportunities, such schemes provide additional employees at low cost. They also allow managers to preview an individual's work before deciding whether or not to offer employment on a longer-term basis.

A number of voluntary bodies undertake similar programmes either with or without government support. Two examples are *Comeback*, an agency originally set up by British Rail to find jobs for ex-offenders (Donaldson 1995: 45), and *Workable*, which finds work placements for disabled job seekers (Kent 1996: 47).

Advertising and recruitment consultants

These are private companies which, in return for a fee, will undertake a part of the recruitment process on behalf of employers. They act like any other management consultants, except that they specialise in the recruitment and selection functions. Perhaps the most useful are recruitment advertising agents who assist employers in the drawing-up and placing of job advertisements. They are often mistakenly believed only to offer a 'Rolls Royce service' involving the production of showy artwork for publication in newspapers and careers brochures. While much of their work is at this glossy end of the market, they also have a potentially useful range of services to offer regular job advertisers. This is made possible by the muscle power they have in the recruitment advertising market. Because they represent large numbers of clients and consequently do a great deal of business with newspapers and trade journals, they are able to negotiate substantial bulk discounts, a portion of which can be passed on to employers. The net result is that a large agency is able to give advice on the wording and placing of advertisements while also improving the appearance of the advertising copy and charging a lower fee than would be paid were the employer dealing with the newspaper independently.

Recruitment consultants, by contrast, take over a larger part of the recruitment process. In addition to handling the advertising they will also undertake much of the administration by sifting initial applications and providing employers with a short-list of candidates. Such arrangements are expensive, the client either being charged an hourly fee or an overall sum calculated as 10 per cent–20 per cent of the first year's annual base salary for the job in question. Sometimes both approaches are used, a retainer or advance fee being paid, followed by further payments on production of a short-list and the appointment of a candidate. The potential advantage to the employer is access to the agent's expertise and the saving in terms of time associated with outsourcing administrative activity. Such arrangements are particularly appropriate when employers are operating in unfamiliar labour markets (eg overseas) or when a major recruitment drive is being undertaken over a limited period of time. An example might be the launch of a major new tourist attraction by a company with a relatively small personnel function. In such a situation it makes more sense to buy in a one-off recruitment service than to set up a major new in-house facility.

Temporary employment agencies

As competition has become tougher and more international, the use of temporary staff to cover peaks in business has grown. There are now large numbers of agencies that retain casual employees on their books to serve the needs of employers with short-term vacancies. Traditionally these have operated in the secretarial and clerical field, but there are increasing numbers of agencies specialising in the provision of staff to fill a variety of other functions. Examples are companies that have taken over the running of nurse banks from the hospitals, and the growing number of agencies specialising in the provision of catering and computer staff. It is also possible to find work as a personnel and development specialist on a locum basis through some agencies.

Cable and Wireless

An interesting innovation introduced by Cable and Wireless Plc was the establishment, in 1995, of an in-house employment agency. It has been set up as a subsidiary company with its own managing director, but unlike most agencies it is expected only to break even and not to make a profit. It exists to provide staff for other parts of the Cable and Wireless operation to undertake project work on short-term contracts.

There are two advantages for the company. First, the agency provides specialist support staff, many of whom are ex-employees of the company. Most staff on the agency's books have undertaken a number of different assignments for the company and are thus far more familiar with its business and corporate culture than regular agency employees would be. Perhaps more importantly, the in-house agency is far cheaper. Its requirement only to cover its own costs means that it charges staff out at approximately half the charge-out rates offered by external agencies.

Source: Walker (1996).

For the employer, temping agencies potentially provide a reliable source of well-qualified staff at very short notice. They will also replace an unsatisfactory temporary worker with someone more suitable if asked. While the primary purpose of such arrangements is to undertake a short-term assignment, caused perhaps by absence or a sudden increase in workload, there are also advantages for employers with longer-term vacancies to fill. First, the agency can provide someone to undertake work during the time that the search is on for a permanent replacement. This can be indispensable if an employee undertaking important work leaves at short notice. Secondly, these agencies can provide staff on a temporary basis who can later be offered full-time positions. The great advantage of such arrangements from the employer's perspective is the opportunity they give to observe an individual's work prior to making him or her an offer of employment. The employee also gets a realistic job preview and thus accepts a job less blindly than the candidate whose only knowledge of the employer derives from perceptions gained at a selection interview.

The drawback is the cost. Hourly rates for agency workers are invariably double those paid to regular employees. In addition the agency will often incorporate charges into the contract that place a financial penalty on employers who make permanent offers of employment to their temps. Despite these barriers, a number of companies still manage to appoint permanent staff using this method.

Headhunters and permanent employment agents
The fourth group of agencies offering recruitment services to employers has a number of titles. They often call themselves 'recruitment consultants' but are also known by such terms as 'headhunters' and 'executive search consultants'. They differ from the varieties of agent described above in so far as their purpose is the identification of candidates for permanent employment – often in tight labour markets. They operate on a 'no sale, no fee' basis but charge high sums (typically 30 per cent of the first year's salary) when an offer of employment is made. Essentially they act like dating agencies, selling the job to the potential candidate and then trying to sell the candidate to the employer. Their great advantage from an employer's perspective is the opportunity they give to open up confidential channels of communication with high-flying employees working for competitor organisations. As such, they allow recruitment managers to tap into a reservoir of interesting potential applicants who are not actively seeking new jobs.

While it is possible for personnel professionals to build up effective relationships with trusted agents operating in this way, there is a fundamental conflict of interest which has to be managed if any association is to prove fruitful over the long term. The problem arises from the fact that the recruitment industry is highly competitive and makes money only by successfully filling vacancies. There are no prizes for coming second in this cut-throat business, commission making up a high proportion of an agent's remuneration. The competitive pressure derives from the low start-up costs or barriers to entry into the business. It is technically very easy to start up an agency – all that is needed are effective selling skills and sufficient contacts in a particular trade or labour market – so there are hundreds of agents competing for relatively scarce rewards. As a result, the agent's overwhelming aim has to be finding candidates for vacancies quickly and at the lowest possible cost. Ideally they want to place individuals already on their books so as to avoid undertaking time-consuming additional research.

By contrast, while employers may want to employ a new person quickly, they have to pay far more attention to the quality of the individual and the possibility that they will perform effectively over a prolonged period. Hence the possibility of a conflict of interest and, on occasions, the presence of hard-selling and sharp practice on the part of the agent. The potential problems are outlined in some detail by John Courtis (1989: 40–49), and many will be familiar to any personnel manager who has experience of recruiting in tight labour markets. A common example is an agent finding a new employee for you, charging a hefty fee, and then returning to poach them 12 months later on behalf of a rival employer. Others include the beefing up of CVs to make candidates appear more experienced than they really are, and agents' replying to advertisements placed in professional journals that serious job-seekers would in all likelihood have seen in any event.

The (then) IPD recognised the potential conflict of interest and the fact that the recruitment industry had yet to evolve enforced professional standards with the publication of a special *Code of Conduct for Career and Outplacement Consultants*. This provided a mechanism whereby employers and candidates could take formal complaints about the conduct of an agency to a disciplinary panel that could give official warnings to, or even expel, individuals from the Institute. It is thus well worth asking agents whether or not they are CIPD members before entering any arrangement with them. (The IPD became the CIPD in July 2000.) Having pointed out the potential pitfalls, it is also necessary to stress that it is possible to develop healthy and workable long-term relationships with particular headhunters. Indeed, in some labour markets, where headhunters have gained an unassailable position, employers have few practical alternatives if they wish to recruit the best people.

The key is to agree the ground rules from the start and to make sure that the charging structures are fully explained and understood. Courtis (1989: 41–42) makes a number of helpful suggestions, including the following:

- Offer the agency a degree of exclusivity.

- Ask for temps who are prepared to become permanent when you and they fit well.

- Pay promptly.

- Give the agent as much information as possible about the job and person specification.

- Explain what selection or rejection criteria you are likely to use.

- Always ask why a particular candidate is being put forward.

Over time such an arrangement should allow the negotiation of better terms than are offered by rival agencies with whom no long-term relationship has been established. The key is to gain an understanding of the labour market and the way headhunters operate. That way it is possible to avoid employing them where to do so is unnecessary, and it is also possible to save on costs.

EDUCATION LIAISON

In the 1980s there was a period when the personnel management press gave a great deal of attention to the problems associated with the 'demographic timebomb' – the anticipated decline in the number of school-leavers and graduates coming onto the job market. The predicted 25 per cent decline from 1980 to 1995 caused employers to take two distinct courses of action. On the one hand, they devoted more time, money and effort to enhancing their systems for recruiting young people while, on the other, they gave greater attention to attracting applicants from other sources. In the event, as a result of economic recession, the timebomb failed to go off in the manner predicted. Instead, the number of unemployed young people rose while the number entering higher education increased beyond expectation from one in 10 to one in three between 1984 and 1994 (*IDS Focus* August 1994).

Despite the absence of the expected recruitment crisis, links with schools and colleges, as well as graduate recruitment, remain important activities for many organisations. There are several reasons for this. First, there have been a number of government initiatives set up – often (in England and Wales) under the auspices of Training and Enterprise Councils (TECs) – that actively encourage links between industry and educational institutions. Secondly, employers have continued to appreciate how by involving themselves in activities with schools and colleges they can be seen to be supporting their local communities and so benefit from the good public relations that result. There is also some evidence of companies getting involved in order to influence curriculum development and make educational qualifications more appropriate to their needs (*IDS* 1990: 1). Collaboration with universities on research projects may also have a direct financial benefit to the sponsoring organisation.

Recruitment objectives also have a role to play in explaining the prevalence of education liaison. The demographic timebomb may not have exploded spectacularly, but there is still heavy competition among employers for the very best graduates. According to IDS, employers perceive about one in 60 graduates to be truly of 'high calibre', and view the process of recruiting them as resembling searching for a needle in an ever-growing haystack (*IDS* 1994: 13). The continued importance of graduate recruitment for many firms has led not only to the design of more attractive financial and development packages, but also to a refinement of the methods used to recruit and select graduates.

Graduate recruitment is an expensive business. According to Watson (1994: 195) the cost can easily exceed £10,000 for each graduate employed. It is also very time-consuming. Until their recent reorganisation, Courtaulds reported that 37 per cent of their personnel department's time was taken up with this activity (*Personnel Today* April 1996: 3). Much of the time and money is taken up with sending company representatives to the various universities to talk to groups of students, to man stands at careers fairs, and to brief careers advisors about the organisation and what it can offer to the right individuals. The more effectively these activities are carried out, the greater the organisation's prospects are of reaching that elusive creature – the well-qualified, well-motivated, intelligent, energetic and mobile graduate with management potential. In addition, there is a need to produce eye-catching literature setting out what is on offer and what kinds of individual the organisation is looking for. The same fundamental decisions have to be taken in designing graduate literature as with the more conventional forms of recruitment advertising discussed above.

It has been argued that the cost of graduate recruitment could be reduced in a number of ways. First, employers could focus their recruitment activity on a few specific universities including those in the localities where they have the greatest presence. They would not reach such a wide pool of potential recruits that way, but they might be more successful in stimulating interest and thus making themselves attractive to students approaching graduation (*IDS* 1994: 13–14). Secondly, employers can question the need to take on so many graduates by analysing critically their existing training programmes and by considering other sources of graduate-calibre employees. However, while there is always the option of improving career progression and training for employees who have not completed university courses, the costs associated with such strategies may well be high.

Another approach is for graduate recruiters to develop links with universities using the methods long favoured in schools liaison. According to IDS (1990: 1), these have traditionally included providing work experience opportunities for pupils and industry placements for teachers, buying or donating equipment, sponsoring school events, arranging workplace visits for school parties, providing teachers with places on in-house training courses, helping out students with project work and encouraging employees to become school governors. All these activities raise the profile of the organisation in the community and, crucially, among school pupils who will be seeking jobs in the near future. It can thus be an important means by which employers improve their position in local labour markets and hope, as a result, to attract a greater number of high-quality applications than their competitors.

Since the late 1980s, employers have had the opportunity to put such activities on a more formal footing by participating in 'compacts' organised and funded by their local TEC (*IDS* 1990). These arrangements are mainly directed at improving the job prospects of school-leavers in areas of high unemployment, and have principally been associated with the inner cities. Essentially a compact is an agreement between an employer and one or more schools to give special consideration to their pupils when recruiting school-leavers into jobs. Participating employers are also expected to provide work placements and are encouraged to take part in school life in the various other ways outlined above. In return, employers get access to so called 'compact graduates' – pupils who have met specific goals. These may include measures of punctuality, attendance, homework completion rates and accreditation in basic English and Maths. In theory, therefore, the employer, pupils and school stand to benefit. For organisations based in specific localities with an interest in recruiting school-leavers, such arrangements are worthy of serious consideration. The costs are few and the potential benefits substantial.

> How could your organisation's educational liaison activities be improved? What arguments would you employ to persuade managers to pay greater attention to relationships with schools and colleges?

ETHICAL AND LEGAL CONSIDERATIONS

Anti-discrimination and equal opportunities law covers the conduct of recruitment activity and must be adhered to if costly legal cases are to be avoided. The relevant legislation is contained in the following Acts of Parliament and subsequent amendments: the Sex Discrimination Act (1975), the Race Relations Act (1976), the Rehabilitation of Offenders Act (1974) and the Disability Discrimination Act (1996). In addition, recruitment often falls within the purview of European legislation via Article 119 of the Treaty of Rome and other social measures. As is the case in a number of other areas affecting personnel management, the law in this field is regularly added to, new rulings setting precedents that make clearer requirements in areas that were hitherto ill-defined. Recruiters are therefore advised to keep a close eye on legal developments as well as to develop a thorough grasp of the basic legal principles that have evolved. When in doubt it is best to err on the side of caution so as to deter aggrieved individuals from taking legal action.

In the case of discrimination on grounds of sex, race and disability the law operates on the same basic principles. It is, quite simply, unlawful to discriminate unfairly against people on grounds of their sex, marital status, race or disability either directly or indirectly. In the field of recruitment this clearly means that the use of gender-specific terminology in advertisements is unacceptable, as would be any recruitment practice that explicitly discouraged applications from particular racial groups or from disabled persons. For this reason we have increasingly seen new forms of gender-neutral wording developed by job advertisers in recent years. Chambermaids have been replaced with 'room attendants', waiters with 'waiting staff' and firemen with 'fire-fighters'. You also no longer see adverts asking only for manageresses or nursing sisters.

Legislation on indirect discrimination is more difficult, but no less important, to grasp. In recruitment this occurs when an advertisement

Chartered Institute of Personnel and Development

Customer Satisfaction Survey

We would be grateful if you could spend a few minutes answering these questions and return the postcard to CIPD. <u>Please use a black pen to answer.</u> If you would like to receive a free CIPD pen, please include your name and address. IPD MEMBER Y/N

....

1. Title of book ....

2. Date of purchase: month .... year ....

3. How did you acquire this book?
   ☐ Bookshop ☐ Mail order ☐ Exhibition ☐ Gift ☐ Bought from Author

4. If ordered by mail, how long did it take to arrive:
   ☐ 1 week ☐ 2 weeks ☐ more than 2 weeks

5. Name of shop .... Town.. Country............

6. Please grade the following according to their influence on your purchasing decision with 1 as least influential: (please tick)

	1	2	3	4	5
Title					
Publisher					
Author					
Price					
Subject					
Cover					

7. On a scale of 1 to 5 (with 1 as poor & 5 as excellent) please give your impressions of the book in terms of: (please tick)

	1	2	3	4	5
Cover design					
Paper/print quality					
Good value for money					
General level of service					

8. Did you find the book:
   Covers the subject in sufficient depth ☐ Yes ☐ No
   Useful for your work ☐ Yes ☐ No

9. Are you using this book to help:
   ☐ In your work ☐ Personal study ☐ Both ☐ Other (please state)

Please complete if you are using this as part of a course

10. Name of academic institution...

11. Name of course you are following? ....

12. Did you find this book relevant to the syllabus? ☐ Yes ☐ No ☐ Don't know

Thank you!

To receive regular information about CIPD books and resources call 020 8263 3387.

1795/05/00

2

Publishing Department

Chartered Institute of Personnel and Development

CIPD House

Camp Road

Wimbledon

London

SW19 4BR

or other recruitment technique favours a significantly greater proportion of one population group covered by the legislation than
another. It is unlawful, whether or not there was any intention to
discriminate on the part of the employer, and applies to recruitment
practices that in themselves do not appear to discriminate unfairly. The
most celebrated case is *Price* v *the Civil Service Commission* (1978),
which serves as an excellent illustration of the way indirect
discrimination law works in practice. In this case an employer decided
to include an age range of 17 to 28 in its criteria for promoting internal
applicants to a senior position, but was found to have discriminated
unfairly because fewer women than men in the workforce were between
those ages. Organisations might therefore be seen to be inviting claims
of unfair discrimination by relying exclusively on internal recruitment
or on advertising a post in a newspaper read mainly by members of a
specific racial group. In either case it is possible that individuals of one
race were disadvantaged when compared with others. The same kind
of actions could also be brought against employers where word-of-
mouth recruitment significantly disadvantages one racial group.

The only truly effective defence available to employers relates to the
presence of a 'genuine occupational qualification', which requires the
employer to recruit from a particular group. Examples include the
recruitment of models, actors and actresses for theatrical or promotional work, and of people to work in single-sex establishments or
situations where decency may be a factor (eg lavatory attendants and
prison officers). It is also permissible to advertise in the UK for men
to work overseas in countries where work opportunities for women are
severely limited by law or tradition. An example is the Saudi Arabian
operation run by British Aerospace.

The law relating to practices that discriminate in favour of disadvantaged groups is less clear. In general terms, the courts have
made a distinction between 'positive' or 'reverse' discrimination,
which clearly acts to the detriment of a group (in this context usually
men), and 'positive action', which assists underrepresented or disadvantaged groups while stopping short of actual discrimination. In
practice, however, this distinction is often hard to draw. Personnel
professionals are probably best advised to take legal advice from
solicitors or from ACAS advisers concerning specific cases. Legal
precedents have established that it is unlawful to have quotas for

---

All-women short-lists

The complexities of the law on positive discrimination gained an
unusual amount of publicity during 1994 and 1995 with the introduction by the Labour Party of 'all-women short-lists' in the selection
of prospective parliamentary candidates for some safe seats. The issue
here was whether or not such a post came within the legal definition of
work. Cases were brought by two men who were deprived of the
opportunity to stand for selection. To avoid further actions, and after 35
women had been selected, the Party announced that it was to end this
policy.

numbers of men and women in particular jobs, but that it is lawful to set targets for increasing the numbers of a particular underrepresented group. Similarly, while it is unlawful to request applications only from women, or members of a defined ethnic group, it is quite lawful to include equal opportunities statements in job advertisements.

The policing of these laws falls mainly on the Commission for Racial Equality (CRE) and the Equal Opportunities Commission (EOC). They bring cases themselves, and help fund aggrieved individuals who wish to take employers and prospective employers to court. They also undertake formal investigations into recruitment practices that they believe might be discriminatory. However, the limited resources available to these bodies means that their policing is often ineffective, allowing employers to get away with practices that do discriminate unlawfully. Nevertheless, it remains the case that, in doing so, employers risk inviting legal actions, and it is thus the responsibility of professional personnel managers to warn against this possibility. In serious cases, complaints can also be made to the CIPD on the grounds that a member has breached the Code of Professional Conduct. This goes beyond minimum legal standards to advocate the promotion of equal opportunities for disadvantaged groups other than those currently protected by unfair discrimination laws.

Aside from legal and ethical considerations, there is also a 'business case' that can be advanced in support of rigorous equal opportunities policies and practices which is endorsed, in some particulars, by the CIPD. The main thrust of the business case is as follows:

- A commitment to equal opportunities makes the organisation more attractive in the labour market.

- Equal opportunities practices help ensure that the organisation has the widest possible field of candidates from which to choose.

- A commitment to equal opportunities is appreciated by employees, who, as a result, respond with increased commitment to the organisation.

These arguments are controversial and may not readily be accepted. In particular, there is a fundamental question concerning the costs associated with effective equal opportunities monitoring and the low priorities such activities inevitably have in very busy workplaces. One can also ask, quite legitimately, why, if the business case is so compelling, there is a need for such a comprehensive body of anti-discrimination law?

What are your views on this debate? How convincing a business case could you make in the context of your organisation?

EVALUATING RECRUITMENT PROCESSES

There are three basic questions that need to be asked when evaluating recruitment methods, techniques and policies:

i   Do our recruitment practices yield sufficient numbers of suitable candidates to enable us to select sufficient numbers of high-calibre employees?

ii Could a sufficient pool of suitable candidates be attracted using less expensive methods?

iii Are the recruitment methods used fulfilling the organisation's equal opportunities responsibilities?

The first question focuses on the effectiveness of recruitment practices. Asking it will lead to consideration of whether too few sufficiently qualified candidates are applying for jobs. It may be the case that those of the very highest calibre are not being caught in the recruiters' net. The second question focuses on efficiency. It leads to consideration of the relative merits of different recruitment methods in terms of their cost. It is also possible that too many applications are being received, leading to unnecessary expenditure in terms of the time spent on administration. The third question considers the fairness of recruitment processes. Subsequent questions might focus on the extent to which applicant pools are, or are not, representative of all sections of the community.

Answering these questions is a good deal harder than asking them. However, it is possible to move some way to finding answers by using two basic kinds of technique: quantitative and qualitative.

Quantitative approaches usually involve comparing various recruitment methods with each other in terms of their results. We might, for example, choose to compare the effectiveness of using a recruitment advertisement designed by an advertising agency with a similar but less elaborate version set by the newspaper. Which one brought in the greater number of applications? Which one yielded the highest-quality applications? Is there a difference between them in terms of the subsequent performance or turnover rates among selected employees? The same kind of analysis can be undertaken to compare the results of national newspaper advertising with local newspapers, or simply comparing formal with informal recruitment methods. The larger the organisation, the more meaningful the analysis will be. However, it is important to be careful not to read too much into a relatively small sample of cases – plenty of other factors aside from the recruitment method might explain any differences discovered.

Quantitative evaluations of recruitment methods are routinely carried out by many large employing organisations. The main vehicle used is the job reference number, which employees are asked to quote when they respond to advertisements in newspapers, job centres, careers centres etc. Employers wishing to compare the different methods include a different reference number in each advertisement and then undertake quantitative comparisons like those described above.

By contrast, *qualitative* evaluation methods try to locate potential problems with recruitment practices in terms of the three criteria identified above, and consider possible missed opportunities. The aim is to think constructively about ways in which improvements can be made. While a number of approaches are possible, the most common involve asking both successful and unsuccessful candidates to evaluate their experiences during the recruitment process and to compare them with those they have encountered in the past. Reaching successful candidates is straightforward – it is less easy to gather meaningful information from those who have not been offered jobs. One way of doing so is to offer all candidates feedback on their performance at the selection stage. Such activity is often seen as being solely for the benefit of candidates, but this is not the case: it also provides a good opportunity for employers to gain constructive qualitative feedback on their own recruitment processes from the candidates' perspective.

Other forms of qualitative evaluation might involve investigating the length of time the organisation took to respond to enquiries and formal applications, or evaluating how effectively telephonists and receptionists respond to enquiries about actual or possible vacancies. It may be that good candidates are put off applying because of a lack of courtesy on the part of the employer. Another common form of qualitative evaluation focuses on investigating ways of reducing the number of words in an advertisement without diminishing its effectiveness.

FURTHER READING

> What forms of evaluation have you observed either as a candidate or as a recruiter? How useful do you consider them to be?

- Three books by John Courtis give an interesting perspective, from the point of view of an experienced recruiter. These are *Recruiting for Profit* (1989), *Cost Effective Recruitment* (1985) and *Recruitment Advertising: Right first time* (1994).

- The best treatment in academic textbooks is Thom Watson's chapter on recruitment and selection in *Personnel Management: Theory and practice in Britain* edited by K. Sisson (1994). Recruitment is also covered in some detail, including interesting material on international recruitment, by Mary Wright and Julie Storey in their contribution to *Human Resource Management: A contemporary perspective* edited by Ian Beardwell and Len Holden (1994).

- A good source of information on legal issues is *Employment Law* by Deborah Lockton (1997). On the wider ethical issues, the clearest statement of 'best practice' is found in the IPD Code of Conduct and *Guide on Recruitment* referred to in this chapter.

Part 4

SELECTION

7 The classic trio

The choice of appropriate employee selection techniques is a field in which there is great divergence between the recommendations of academic writers and day-to-day practice in organisations. When applying for a job, most people expect to have to fill in a standard application form, attend one or more interviews and then receive an offer of employment subject to satisfactory references being provided by the referees they have named. These three methods were labelled 'the classic trio' by Mark Cook (1993). It is the expectation because in most cases this is the approach taken by organisations. What is interesting is that this traditional approach continues to dominate in the face of apparently conclusive evidence that other tools of selection have far greater predictive power. In the present and the following chapters we discuss this conundrum in relation to the wide range of different selection methods available to employers. We also assess the advantages and disadvantages of each in different situations, and examine ways in which each might be improved against a range of criteria.

In this chapter we focus on the traditional approaches described above. We concentrate principally on the interview, since this appears to be the one approach to selection that virtually all selectors consider to be indispensable, but also look at the use of application forms and references in the screening process. In the following chapter we consider those selection methods that are less commonly used but that are said to be far more accurate as predictors of job performance.

By the end of this chapter readers should be able to:

- devise application forms
- draw up a short-list of candidates
- conduct a selection interview
- make effective use of employment references

• advise on the effectiveness of traditional selection tools.

In addition, readers should be able to understand and explain:

• the theoretical advantages and disadvantages of different selection methods

• employer objectives in the use of interviews, references and application forms.

RESEARCH IN EMPLOYEE SELECTION

There is a long tradition going back to the beginning of the century of academic research into the relative merits of different selection tools. For the most part, the field has been dominated by occupational psychologists who have worked with a shared set of assumptions concerning personality traits and their relationship to job performance. Foremost among the approaches undertaken have been validity studies, in which a selection process that results in the appointment of several individuals is observed. The scores given to candidates at the selection stage are recorded and compared with their actual performance on the job some months or years later. Different selection methods can then be compared according to how accurately they predict job performance (ie the extent to which candidates who score particularly well at selection achieve higher levels of performance than colleagues who impressed less at the selection stage).

The unit of measurement used in these studies is the correlation co-efficient – a measure of how closely scores at the selection stage correlate with those awarded for later performance. Were a selection process to be found to have resulted in a correlation co-efficient of 1, it would have predicted the relative performance of employees with perfect accuracy. Conversely, a correlation co-efficient score equal to 0 indicates the absence of any predictive accuracy at all – the employer might as well have picked candidates at random. A modest validity study looking at a small group of employees chosen using one selection tool, while interesting, is not especially helpful in allowing generalised judgements to be made about the predictive qualities of any particular selection method. However, over the years many hundreds of such studies have been carried out in many countries which can be combined and assessed together using computer programs. It is the results of such exercises, known as meta-analyses, that have apparently confirmed what many have long believed, namely that traditional methods of selection such as interviews are markedly poorer at accurately predicting job performance than more sophisticated techniques such as personality tests and assessment centres. The results of recent meta-analyses are illustrated in Table 7.

Despite the presence of this research and the accompanying bad publicity for traditional selection methods, there is plenty of evidence to show that they remain very widely used in the appointment of new employees. In 1986, Robertson and Makin reported that in their survey of 108 major UK companies, only 1 per cent of respondents claimed never to use interviews in selection decision-making and that 81.4 per cent always used them. As far as employment references were

Table 7 **Accuracy of some methods of selection**

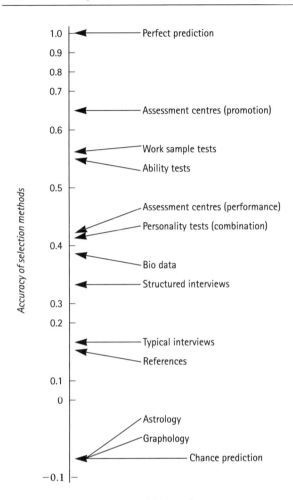

concerned, 3.7 per cent said that they were never used, while 67.3 per cent reported using them for all new appointments (Robertson and Makin 1986). Shackleton and Newell (1989), in their survey, found that interviews were used in all appointments, references in 96 per cent of cases and application forms in 93 per cent. The most recent surveys confirm the picture, with IRS (1997d: 10) finding 100 per cent coverage for selection interviews and over 90 per cent in the case of application forms. The current picture would thus appear to confirm the observation made by Robertson and Makin (1986) that in the UK 'the frequency of a method's use is inversely related to its known validity'.

However, what is particularly interesting in the IRS survey is the response of employers when asked to reflect on which selection techniques they found most useful. For all grades of staff, a very clear majority stated that the interview was the most important tool for them in making selection decisions. There is thus clearly a great gulf between the considered views of academics and practitioners about the relative usefulness and value of different selection methods. Possible reasons for this disagreement will be explored in relation to each of the selection methods described in this and the subsequent chapter. It is, however, useful to make one or two general observations at this stage.

First, it should be pointed out that the 'classic trio' are the most straightforward and least expensive of the range of selection methods available to employers. The use of reputable personality and ability tests requires costly training or the employment of trained consultants, to which is added the cost of the tests themselves. The potential expense of an assessment centre is clearly far higher and is not in any case a practical option for small organisations or for the selection of relatively low-skilled personnel. Secondly, it is important for employers to have an eye on the effect the selection methods they use have on candidates and potential candidates. Such matters have not generally concerned psychologists, who have preferred to concentrate purely on the predictive qualities of each tool.

Furthermore, because application forms, interviews and references are so commonly used, they are *expected* by job applicants. Too much innovation in the selection procedure might be disorienting and thus reduce the effectiveness of a candidate's performance. In certain situations the prospect of being judged by the selection methods with the highest validity may actually dissuade good candidates from applying.

The reluctance from the candidates' perspective springs from the lack of control they can exercise over the process when the more scientific approaches are adopted. Not only, therefore, are we more comfortable with the classic trio because we expect them and have experienced them before, we also prefer them because we think we understand how they work, and feel that they give us a greater degree of influence over the selection decision.

Mention should also be made of criticisms that have been made of the psychological research itself. Iles and Salaman (1995: 219–224) argue persuasively that the assumptions on which much validity research is based are open to question. In particular, they take issue with the notion that personality is on the one hand readily measurable, and on the other necessarily stable over time. In other words, they question the very basis on which psychometric studies of selection are based. They also draw attention to the fact that job content varies to a great extent over a period of years, or even months, and that the individual attributes candidates display when selected may be less and less relevant as time passes and the nature of the job develops and changes. It follows from this argument that what is important at selection is finding an individual who generally 'fits in' with the culture and values of the organisation and is sufficiently well qualified to undertake a range of possible tasks. The aim is thus less to 'match' a personality with a job than to screen out people perceived as likely to be dishonest, lazy, difficult to work with or unsatisfactory for a variety of other reasons.

The use of graphology

An interesting example of the use of selection methods that are neither scientific nor systematic is the use of graphology or hand-writing analysis. Despite firm evidence of its poor predictability (Smith *et al* 1989: 86–88) it appears to be used surprisingly widely. In the UK it is rare for employers to admit to its use in selection, although some have confirmed that they use it as one of a range of techniques (see North 1994: 3, Cooper and Robertson 1995: 137–140). However, on the Continent it is much more common, with over half of smaller French companies believed to use it in employee selection, and a good proportion of employers in Belgium and Germany also apparently believe it to have an effective role to play.

A possible reason for the use of graphology is its apparent 'reliability' as a selection tool. People's handwriting tends not to change to any great extent during their adult life, although it can be made neater with effort. It is also a 'reliable' method in so far as different graphologists have been found to reach similar conclusions about a candidate's personality when given the same handwriting sample to analyse – not a situation that typically occurs when several people interview the same candidate at different times.

However, *reliability* should not be confused with *validity*. There is also evidence to show that graphology is a poor diviner of important personality traits and is thus probably a poor predictor of job performance. According to Smith *et al* (1989), when tested, graphologists were unable to distinguish between real and faked suicide notes, and failed to identify which of a range of handwriting samples had been submitted by people diagnosed neurotic. Further research reported by Watson (1994: 208) supports this view, leading him to conclude that, as yet, there is insufficient evidence to support the use of graphology as part of a fair and objective selection procedure.

APPLICATION FORMS

In its sample of 157 UK employers, IRS (1997: 8–11) found that application forms were used in some shape or form by 93 per cent of respondents. In larger organisations they appear to be used for all jobs except those at the very highest level, and in many public-sector organisations are filled in by applicants for senior directorships. The alternative is to allow or encourage applicants to compose their own curriculum vitae or CV. IRS found that, outside the public sector, CVs were also very widely used. In some cases employers accepted either, while in others (mainly smaller organisations) the CV was the preferred approach.

From an employer's perspective there are advantages and disadvantages both to application forms and CVs. In principle, the CV is preferable because it gives applicants the freedom to sell themselves in their own way. They are thus able to tailor their applications to their own strengths and are not restricted to fitting relevant information into boxes of predetermined size. Some application forms, because they are so restrictive in their design, may lead to excellent candidates' being overlooked. An example might be a form that contains a set of questions and several blank spaces under the heading 'Present employment'. In putting so much emphasis in the form on this aspect, the likelihood is that otherwise good candidates who are not currently in full-time employment will be disadvantaged. A similar problem confronts an applicant who, while in work, is unhappy and is perhaps seeking a new position after just a few weeks or months in this employment. Indeed, a poorly designed application form has been shown to put many applicants off applying in the first place (Jenkins 1983).

However, CVs can be criticised for giving job applicants the opportunity to sell themselves to a potential employer by including material in their applications that is wholly irrelevant to the position being advertised. Similar 'contamination' effects can occur when a CV is particularly attractively presented or structured, leading unwary selectors, perhaps unconsciously, to favour applications from otherwise unimpressive candidates over those of their better-qualified rivals. In extreme cases, candidates engage in sophisticated 'impression management'. Having learned (from Tom Peters) that 'perception is all there is', they consequently go to great lengths to dazzle with well-bound, professionally produced CVs with career and other achievements highlighted and a judicious mix of leisure interests. A few, through individual quirkiness or a belief that their career opportunities are enhanced through making themselves memorable, produce CVs that make them unforgettable but also unemployable. It is for this reason, according to IRS, that many public-sector organisations refuse to accept CVs at all.

Perhaps the best solution is to design separate application forms for each vacancy advertised. This gets round the problem of inappropriate design and allows specific questions to be posed relevant to the job in question. With the development of more sophisticated word-processing and printing equipment, such an approach should be used more frequently, but as yet there is little evidence to suggest that employers have moved away from the standard organisation-wide form that has long been used across the whole range of jobs on offer. Individualisation would also permit the inclusion, where appropriate, of spaces for candidates to write longer descriptive answers to more involved questions.

Whether the application form used is standard or original to the job advertised, it will fill a number of distinct functions. According to Smith and Robertson (1993: 81–82) these are the following:

- to enable a short-list of candidates for interview to be drawn up

- to provide information that can be drawn on during the interview

- as a means by which information about good but unsuccessful candidates can be filed away for future reference

- as a means of analysing the effectiveness of the various alternative recruitment media used (see Chapter 6)

- as a public relations tool enhancing the employer's image as 'an efficient, fair and well-run organisation'.

It follows that the best application forms are designed so as to fulfil each of the above functions as effectively as possible. The first three factors require the presence of clear, concise language and a layout that allows candidates sufficient space to include all relevant information. The public relations function is best served by the use of good-quality paper and typesetting.

A typical application form would include questions asking for basic biographical information, previous work experience, educational background, vocational training undertaken and future career aspirations. Forms often ask about previous convictions and the applicant's state of health. Asking candidates to include a passport-size photograph is also relatively common, although in practice candidates often fail to do so. Another relatively recent development is the request for information concerning gender and ethnic background to enable organisations to undertake equal opportunities monitoring. More often than not, this is included on a separate form that is detached or removed from the original prior to short-listing. The question of nationality, by contrast, is usually included in the main body of the form to allow the employer to discuss matters relating to work permits with candidates at their interviews.

There are a number of questions commonly included in application forms that are controversial and that are often the subject of heated discussion among recruiters. Examples are those asking applicants to state their age or date of birth, and those asking them to list their hobbies and interests. The latter is a peculiar type of question because it usually has no relevance at all to the ability of candidates to fulfil the requirements of the job. It is also very likely indeed to be answered untruthfully, candidates taking care to include only mainstream or 'politically correct' interests. If candidates' main hobbies are eating fast-food, watching adult movies and smoking illegal substances, they are unlikely to include them in the response.

The question of age is more interesting. On the one hand, there is an argument for including this question on the grounds that it is not illegal to do so and that there are circumstances in which it might be a reasonable criterion for screening candidates in or out of the selection process. An example might be a vacancy for a position as a supervisor of a group of middle-aged employees. While the presence of a young supervisor might not necessarily cause problems, some employers might think it reasonable to include age as one of the criteria used in deciding who to invite for interview. It would then be possible to ensure that there were at least some older people short-listed. The opposite point of view stresses the irrelevance of age to job performance, and argues that including it encourages those undertaking the short-listing process to prejudge applications on unfair grounds. Perhaps this is another situation in which there is a case for designing different applications for different jobs. The question about age or date of birth would then be included only when judged strictly necessary.

In the next chapter we examine the use of weighted application forms and biodata. These are methods that enhance the role of application forms in the selection process and that have been found to have relatively high validities when compared with other selection methods.

> Where do you stand in this debate? Can you think of other circumstances in which it would be appropriate to request information about dates of birth?

SHORT-LISTING

The next stage in the traditional approach to selection is to boil down the applications received to a short-list of candidates to invite for interview. Here again, as so often in employee selection, there is a potential tension between the relative merits of methodical and more informal approaches. All descriptions of best practice, including that contained in the (former) IPD's *Guide on Recruitment* (1996: 5–6), advocate a systematic approach to short-listing whereby a list of criteria are drawn up from the person specification. Each application form is then judged and scored against these standards. Torrington and Hall (1995) suggest that the drawing-up of criteria is best done by a panel, but that the short-listing itself should be undertaken on an individual basis, each panel member looking at all application forms separately and drawing up his or her own list. Any candidate chosen by all the screeners is then invited to interview, while any discarded by all is rejected. Panel members then debate the merits of the remaining applicants with regard to the requirements of the person specification until a consensus is reached about who should and who should not be interviewed.

The argument in favour of such an approach is its inherent fairness. It discourages selectors, either consciously or unconsciously, from discriminating unfairly on the basis of factors unrelated to the content of the job. It thus reduces the chances of well-qualified candidates' being screened out on account of peculiar handwriting, marital status or place of birth. Research undertaken in the USA quoted by Cook (1993:16) has found evidence of unfair discrimination on grounds of sex occurring at the short-listing stage through the stereotyping of men and women as suitable or unsuitable for particular jobs. Other examples of stereotyping that have occurred in the experience of the author include making negative assumptions on the basis of:

- first names that are perceived to be unusual, old-fashioned or associated with low levels of education

- the kind of school (private, grammar or comprehensive) that some-one attended

- the fact that a candidate was an ex-Army officer.

It goes without saying that it is easier for individual managers who are racially prejudiced to screen out members of ethnic minorities if there is no panel to whom they must justify their actions.

Having put the case for a systematic approach, it also reasonable to point out the drawbacks. The main problem arises if the criteria drawn up are too exacting, leading to the screening-out of good candidates who fail to respond to questions on the application form with precisely the answers required. An example might be a situation in which the agreed criteria include a requirement for short-listed candidates to have had some years' experience in a particular role or at a specified level in an organisation. A typical case might be one in which applicants for a personnel management job are required to have worked for a minimum of three years in a senior HR role in manufacturing. While relevant and justifiable, such a parameter might lead to the rejection of the best candidate on the grounds that he or she has only two years' experience as a general manager in a service industry.

There is thus a strong case for allowing a degree of flexibility in the screening of application forms and for avoiding too narrow or bureaucratic an approach. If a candidate looks interesting, for whatever reason, it does no great harm to invite him or her to interview. To reject purely on the basis of an arbitrary set of criteria may be theoretically justifiable, but might well not be in the long-term interests of the organisation.

How systematic are the approaches to short-listing used in your experience? What examples of stereotyping have you come across?

Short-listing at Daewoo

An example of systematic short-listing occurred recently when the Korean industrial corporation Daewoo established a car company in the UK. The sales arm was set up from scratch in the year following June 1994, requiring the HR department to fill several hundred vacancies in just a few months. The jobs on offer were based at retail stores across the country and at the company's UK headquarters in Hertfordshire. Local newspapers were used for advertising, each leading to the receipt of around 800 completed application forms. The company then had to screen out 90 per cent of these so that the interview stage might become manageable. The aim was to interview four or five applicants for each available position.

This was done in two ways. First, a computer system was used to rank the applicants in each town or city according to the answers given to specific questions on the application form. For the most part, these focused on the amount of work experience applicants had completed in the motor trade or in retailing and finance functions. Other questions asked about length of experience in working with information technology, managing staff, managing budgets and dealing with the public. Experience of unconventional working patterns was also included. The computer screening identified the 'top' 25 per cent of candidates.

The numbers were then further reduced by HR officers examining how applicants had answered other questions relating to experience in previous jobs. Here the focus was on how sales were achieved, what was understood by the term 'customer service', and previous successes applicants could point to in the fields of staff supervision and teamworking.

Source: IDS (1995d: 10–11)

PROBLEMS WITH INTERVIEWS

As was stated above, there is plenty of apparently authoritative research in support of the claim that traditional selection interviews are poor predictors of future job performance. The term 'traditional' refers to typical, unstructured interviews in which different candidates may be asked quite different questions. The traditional interviewer thus gathers information in a relatively unsystematic manner, and may reach judgements about candidates on a number of different grounds. Anderson and Shackleton (1993), drawing on a wide variety of academic studies from several countries, very effectively summarise the reasons put forward to explain why such interviews have been criticised for their poor predictive validity. The following list is based on their summary:

- *The expectancy effect*: undue influence being given to positive or negative expectations of a candidate formed from his or her CV or application form.

- *The self-fulfilling prophecy effect*: interviewers asking questions designed to confirm initial impressions of candidates gained either before the interview or in its early stages.

- *The primacy effect*: interviewers putting too much emphasis on impressions gained and information assimilated early in the interview.

- *The stereotyping effect*: interviewers assuming that particular characteristics are typical of members of a particular group. In the case of sex, race, disability, marital status or ex-offenders, decisions made on this basis are often illegal. However, the effect occurs in the case of all kinds of social groups (see the boxed text of stereotyping on page 129).

- *The prototyping effect*: interviewers looking for or favouring a particular type of personality regardless of job-related factors.

- *The halo and horns effect*: interviewers rating candidates as 'good' or 'bad' across the board and thus reaching very unbalanced decisions.

- *The contrast effect*: interviewers allowing the experience of interviewing one candidate to affect the way they interview others seen later in the selection process.

- *Negative information bias effects*: interviewers giving more weight to perceived negative points about candidates than to those that are more positive.

- *The similar-to-me effect*: interviewers giving preference to candidates they perceive as having a similar background, career history, personality or attitudes to themselves.

- *The personal liking effect*: interviewers making decisions on the basis of whether or not they personally like or dislike the candidate.

- *The information overload effect*: interviewers forming judgements based on only a fraction of the data available to them about each individual candidate.

- *The fundamental attribution error effect*: interviewers incorrectly assuming that some action on the part of the candidate is or was caused by an aspect of his or her personality rather than by a simple response to events.

- *The temporal extension effect*: interviewers assuming that a candidate's behaviour at interview (eg nervousness) is typical of his or her general disposition.

What are we to conclude from this litany of criticisms? The most tempting and apparently rational conclusion would be to consign the traditional interview to the personnel management dustbin on the grounds that selection decisions reached in this manner are inevitably infused with subjectivity, prejudice and displays of cognitive dissonance. However, such action would be hasty. A different conclusion is an acceptance that the validity of some traditional interviews is probably higher than others. In other words, we might acknowledge that interviews in which the above traps are avoided are likely to have greater predictive power than those in which they feature strongly. It follows that it may not be the interview as a selection tool that is faulty so much as the interviewer. With thought, care, experience and training it should then be possible consciously to avoid making many of the basic errors that have been described.

> Where do you stand in this debate? Is it the traditional interview that is faulty or is it the typical interviewer who is responsible for giving the method such a bad press?

Stereotyping

An example of the ways in which common misconceptions can inform the selection process is the wide belief that disabled job applicants will suffer higher levels of sickness absence than non-disabled people. In practice, the data does not support such a proposition. Only recently, Barclays Bank has scrapped its system of pre-employment medical examinations because it found that there was no correlation between the absence levels of disabled employees who had been given medicals and those of non-disabled staff who had not been examined. A random survey of 400 of the bank's staff showed that, on average, disabled workers were absent for eight days over two years, while their able-bodied counterparts were away for 10 days in the same period. It was conceded that pre-employment medicals could not reliably predict high or low sickness absence, so application forms now ask applicants to state their level of absence over the previous 12 months. Only in cases where absence levels exceed 15 days are medicals required (whether the candidate is able-bodied or not).

Source: *People Management* (June 1996)

THE SURVIVAL OF THE TRADITIONAL INTERVIEW

Another reason for hesitating before abandoning traditional approaches to interviewing is their continued popularity as tools of selection among both managers and candidates. Despite the presence for a number of years of evidence that suggests they are poor predictors of performance, they continue to be the most favoured and frequently used of the available selection techniques. It is wise, therefore, at least to consider whether managers may in fact be right to continue swearing by the interview.

A number of alternative explanations can be put forward to explain the survival of traditional interviewing, some of which have already been touched on. One possibility is that managers have simply remained unaware of the research evidence amassed over the years. Another is that they are aware of the defects of traditional interviews but feel it to be counterintuitive and therefore discount its relevance. Others accept some of the research evidence but regard themselves as exceptions (ie good, intuitive interviewers who avoid making the classic errors). This last suggestion lies at the heart of the adage that individuals will not tolerate criticisms of their performance as lovers, drivers or interviewers, since all such criticisms strike deep into the core of the human ego.

Another explanation is the relatively low cost of carrying out simple one-to-one interviews and the consequent perception that their efficiency outweighs their ineffectiveness as predictive techniques. In some cases it is also true that unstructured interviews are used as one of a range of selection tools, and that their principal role is to confirm impressions or clear up points left unresolved from the other selection methods used. However, the most straightforward and significant explanation is that interviews are not only arranged for the purpose of enabling managers to make predictions about future performance on the job. According to Herriot (1987), there are in fact three key objectives for selection interviews, of which only one is their function as tools of assessment. The others are labelled 'mutual preview' and 'negotiation'.

The mutual preview function refers to the opportunity the interview gives both employer and applicant to meet face to face and exchange information unrelated to the prediction of performance, but nevertheless essential to any recruitment and selection process. In particular, it gives candidates the opportunity to ask questions about the job and the organisation as part of the process whereby they decide whether or not they wish to take the job. Interviewers also have the opportunity to inform candidates about the duties they can expect to undertake and the role they would be expected to fill, were they successful. It must be appreciated that in order to make effective choices about whether or not to accept the position on the terms offered, any candidate needs sufficient information about how the type of work and the organisational environment compare with those of existing or other employers. The negotiation function is another part of the selection process that can only realistically occur by means of an interview. Here we are concerned with the processes that have to be gone through prior to the issuing and subsequent acceptance of a contract of employment. According to Anderson and Shackleton (1993: 42), matters up for negotiation include start dates, relocation procedures and allowances, training provisions and all other terms and conditions of employment.

A further role played by an interview is that of a labour market public relations exercise. There is every advantage to be gained from sending candidates away (a) believing that they would like the job if subsequently offered it, (b) determined to seek other positions within the organisation if other opportunities present themselves, and (c) willing to speak well of the organisation because of the efficiency, effectiveness, fairness and courtesy displayed towards them. The interview provides the only real opportunity for organisations to carry out this PR function with any degree of success.

Poor selection, on the other hand, leads to damaging, negative PR. If individuals depart perceiving that they have been treated unfairly, incompetently or harshly, they are likely to share their experiences with others. As the word spreads, it almost inevitably becomes embellished and distorted with repetition, which is exactly what we find in the field of consumer affairs. In 1986, the Ford Motor Company discovered that people who are pleased about their cars tell an average of eight others, whereas dissatisfied customers boast about their experiences to at least 22 others (who in turn tell 22 others, and so on). The result is that, in the realm of products and services, organisations lose customers; in the field of selection, organisations lose potential talent. It is not even absurd to believe that individuals treated badly as candidates might withdraw their business from the offending organisation, and that they might encourage others to do so as well. It can thus be contended that giving no interview, as much as giving a bad one, is likely to lead to such occurrences. People expect to be interviewed, and will not feel that they have had a fair hearing or respectful treatment if one is denied.

It can therefore be concluded that the interview has a number of distinct objectives, and that these can be summarised as follows:

- to predict future job performance and behaviour
- to focus on aspects of behaviour and performance that cannot easily be addressed by other methods
- to supply information to the candidate
- to persuade suitable candidates to accept the job offered and join the organisation
- to create good will for the organisation.

For these reasons, whatever the potential dangers of relying too heavily on traditional interviews, there is no practical substitute for some form of informal face-to-face meeting between employer and candidate. The interview is the only way in which the range of fragmented information about candidates gathered from the use of other selection techniques can be integrated into a meaningful pattern.

VARIETIES OF INTERVIEW FORMAT

Interviews and interview questions come in diverse forms. For this reason, when one is about to be interviewed, it is very difficult to predict exactly what will be involved or the general approach to questioning that will be taken. An obvious variable is the number of interviewers – will the interview be conducted by one person, by two, or by a panel?

The one-to-one interview has the advantage of informality and thus helps reduce the artificiality of the process. The intimacy makes it relatively straightforward to gain an interviewee's trust and thus to encourage them to relax. In the view of Munro Fraser (1979: 140), this is the most important objective of any interview:

> The first requirement of a selection interview is that the interviewee should feel at ease and that he should talk freely and frankly. In practically every case, this will depend on the skill of the interviewer. If he behaves in a formal manner, asking questions and appearing to evaluate the answers, he will cease to be an interviewer and become an interrogator. There will thus be little chance that the interviewee will behave in his normal manner, and the amount of information he supplies will be minimal.

However, against this are the considerable drawbacks of cosy one-to-one interviews. First, there is the danger alluded to (page 128) of information overload. It is very difficult for one interviewer simultaneously to encourage openness by relaxing the candidate while concentrating on what he or she is saying and considering what question is best to ask next. What is gained in informality is lost in effectiveness. Secondly, having just one interviewer greatly increases the possibility of unfair bias in the final decision. Many of the problems with traditional interviews discussed above – particularly the halo and horns effect, the similar-to-me effect and the personal liking effect – are far less likely to play a part in the evaluation of candidates if multiple interviewers have to justify their thinking to one another.

While drawbacks can be ameliorated to an extent by the presence of two interviewers, it is only in the panel format that information overload and unfair bias are excluded to a satisfactory degree. However, the panel interview (when up to a dozen interviewers are present together) suffers from the very artificiality and formality that are such positive features of the one-to-one and two-to-one formats. Panel interviews are also difficult to arrange, as so many people have to make sure they are available at the same time over a day or two while a series of candidates are seen. According to Anderson and Shackleton (1993: 75), they are also frequently controlled poorly, leading to the presence of unprofessional practices.

Perhaps the best solution of all is the sequential interview, in which the candidate is interviewed by several people over a period of time, but only sees one or two at a time. In principle, such an approach is the best of both worlds. The danger here, however, is that each interviewer or duo simply ask the same questions as each other. The result is a bored candidate and less information on which to make selection decisions. Sequential interviewing thus only lives up to expectations when different interviewers agree in advance which areas of questioning each will cover.

360-degree interviewing

An intriguing form of interviewing senior managers was instigated in the London Borough of Havering in 1996, when applicants for directorships and the post of chief executive were interviewed by their future subordinates. The thinking behind the innovation was that these people, were they to be successful in their posts, would have to lead and motivate the organisation. How better to test their ability to do so than by getting the staff to interview them? In this case, trade unions were also involved in the process, which lasted three days.

Perhaps more common is the practice whereby members of a team interview future colleagues – a form that could perhaps be labelled 180-degree interviewing. It is most commonly associated with the selection of board directors, but is also used in other situations where effective team membership is crucial to success in a role.

Source: Daly (1996: 1)

VARIETIES OF INTERVIEW QUESTION

Another way that interviews vary is in the type of questions asked. While there are many approaches, three types are given particular attention in the literature: hypothetical, behavioural and stress questions.

Hypothetical questions

Also referred to as problem-solving or situational questioning, this method involves asking candidates how they would react or behave in specific situations. The problems posed will usually be examples of those that might be encountered in the job in question, but there may be situations in which examples from outside work could be used in an attempt to obtain evidence of the candidate's customary reactions to pressured or unusual circumstances. The obvious problem, of course, is the opportunity that such questions give the quick-witted candidate to think of the best answer, or that which is expected. When asked how you would react if a customer complained loudly about sloppy service, it is very easy to say that you would deal with the situation calmly and cool-headedly by taking the complainant to a private area and listening carefully to their points, before judiciously offering discounts or complimentary products. The extent to which people would really manage the situation so professionally and effectively remains open to question: it is far easier said than done.

There is also the problem of asking candidates about situations that they cannot have encountered and would not be expected to deal with anyway without relevant training. In such cases honest candidates will say, 'I don't honestly know', or 'I would ask head office what to do' – answers that are likely to do them little credit. Others will make up a plausible response without having any idea about whether they have answered correctly. To that extent, hypothetical questioning can be said to introduce an unsatisfactory element of chance into the interview. Perhaps, as Torrington and Hall (1995: 275) argue, it is best to use hypothetical questioning only in order to test basic knowledge about the tasks that make up the job in question, and not to ask about social situations or those that are particularly complex.

Behavioural questions

Less commonly used, but in the author's view more effective, are questions that focus on past events in a candidate's life. These are also referred to as Patterned Behaviour Description Interview (PBDI) questions, which seek to focus the candidate's attention on critical incidents from his or her past. In so doing, the interviewer hopes to hear of occasions when the interviewee has demonstrated those abilities or behaviours that are most relevant to the job for which he or she is applying. An example might be a job in which decisiveness was seen as a crucial attribute. A behavioural question would then involve asking candidates to describe an occasion when they took a particularly difficult decision or were forced to make an important decision without having as much information as they would have liked. In putting this question, the interviewer is looking for hard evidence that candidates have acted with sufficient decisiveness in the past. The assumption is then made that, put in a similar situation, they would display the same behaviour in the future.

When asking behavioural questions, it is often necessary to home in on the detail of a critical incident by seeking supplementary information. Once the candidate has given a broad description of a relevant occasion, the interviewer probes more deeply by asking, 'What exactly happened?', 'What was your personal contribution?' or 'Tell me more about how you reacted.' Only when hard evidence of the behaviour in question has been gained can the candidate be deemed acceptable on that count.

It is harder to make up answers to behavioural than hypothetical questions because of the need to give believable answers to the probing supplementaries. They also have the advantage, from the interviewer's point of view, of providing a good basis on which to justify an appointment or promotion. When asked why someone was unsuccessful, it can simply be pointed out that there was no hard evidence given of sensitivity, persuasiveness, creativity or whatever other attributes were deemed important for a job-holder to possess.

There are few disadvantages of this approach to interviewing recorded in the research literature. However, problems can arise when the behaviours asked about in the interview are not strictly those required to undertake the job effectively. It is actually very difficult to pick three or four key attributes or personality dimensions for any one job and, as a result, different interviewers often end up asking very different questions. There is thus clearly a need to base such

> Would you like to be interviewed using behavioural questions? What are the advantages and disadvantages from the perspective of the candidate?

questioning on the contents of agreed person specifications, or ideally on discussions with a current holder of the job in question.

Stress questions

A third type of question apparently used quite regularly is one that is disparaging or aggressive. These 'stress' questions can also involve deliberately contradicting something the interviewee has said. Often this practice has no real purpose and is carried out only because it is hugely enjoyable for a particular type of sadistic selector. However, some argue that stress interviews are necessary in some circumstances in order to observe, at first hand, reactions to stressful or uncomfortable situations. There is also no clear agreement as to what exactly is encompassed by the term 'stress' in these circumstances. Some people might find being asked to 'sell themselves' highly stressful, while others will not blink an eyelid when given a thorough interrogation.

In general this author would argue that there are precious few circumstances in which there is any case for deliberately putting a candidate under undue stress. Reactions are likely to be as artificial as the behavioural patterns of individuals in any kind of selection interview; moreover, candidates are being asked to produce spontaneous responses in unfamiliar circumstances when, in practice, they would have the opportunity to think about options in advance. There is also a grave danger that the interviewee will react badly, assume that the interviewer has acted unprofessionally and share their negative experiences with others. In this respect the stress interview can be said to generate bad labour-market PR of the kind described earlier.

Of course, not all interview questions fit neatly into one of these three categories. There is a case for asking easy-going and chatty questions to which there are obvious answers in order to put candidates at their ease and hence glean more meaningful information. Such approaches are particularly useful at the start of interviews when candidates may be less than forthcoming, because they are apprehensive.

However, at all times, there are certain basic rules to follow in posing interview questions. According to Goodworth (1979: 51–61), these include the following:

- Ask open-ended questions, ie those starting with the words 'what', 'when', 'why', 'where', 'which' and 'how'.

- Avoid direct (or 'closed') questions to which the candidate can answer simply yes, no, or 'That's right.'

- Avoid asking questions that reveal the answer you want. An example given by Goodworth is, 'We place great faith in our house magazine as a medium of communication – are you in favour of house journals?'

- Avoid engaging in arguments with interviewees. Restrict yourself to restrained and courteous discussion about issues of importance in the job.

• Ask one question at a time. Avoid the temptation to string one or two together, as this will confuse the candidate.

STRUCTURING INTERVIEWS

The one constructive and consistent message that emerges from the large body of research into selection interviewing is the finding that structured interviews have considerably higher predictive validity than their unstructured equivalents. There is also agreement that structured interviews form a very small proportion of the total number of selection interviews carried out. However, academic commentators differ in their interpretations of how substantial an improvement is made by structuring. Smith *et al* (1989: 9) suggest that structured interviews have validity co-efficients of approximately 0.3, although they also refer to studies that have found them to have greater predictive qualities. Anderson and Shackleton (1993: 49–51), on the other hand, give structured approaches a far better press. They quote meta-analyses that suggest validity co-efficients in excess of 0.6 – as effective as any selection technique can ever reasonably be expected to be.

The term 'structured' in the context of selection interviewing has a number of distinguishing features:

• Questions are planned carefully before the interview.

• All candidates are asked the same questions.

• Answers are scored according to agreed rating systems.

• Questions focus on the attributes and behaviours needed to succeed in the job.

While structuring interviews in this way may be a highly effective method of improving their predictive quality, it is not necessarily conducive to the creation of a relaxed atmosphere in which the candidate can easily open up. The artificiality of these approaches may also dissuade candidates from entering into a two-way exchange by asking their own questions. In short, the mutual exchange and negotiation functions are less well served than the assessment function. There are two compromise solutions that help ameliorate these problems: semi-structuring and multiple approaches.

Semi-structuring
The interviewer can opt for the approach referred to by Anderson and Shackleton (1993: 72) as 'focused', in which there is a degree of structuring, but also a greater degree of flexibility than a fully structured approach would allow. The interviewer thus plans a series of topics to cover in the interview but follows up what individual interviewees say with supplementary questions. A degree of spontaneity is therefore made possible which permits the candidate some control over the direction of the interview. Meaningful two-way exchange is thus retained.

Multiple approaches
The interviewer can use different questioning techniques at different

stages in the interview. Hence, at the start, in order to facilitate mutual exchange and to help the candidate relax, unstructured spontaneous questions are asked. Later, in order to maximise the effectiveness of the assessment function, a greater degree of structuring is introduced, with all candidates asked the same questions. Unstructured approaches are then returned to in the final stages when the negotiation function becomes significant.

PREPARING FOR INTERVIEWS

In this section some of the basic steps that need to be taken in preparing to interview candidates are outlined. While many of the points may seem rudimentary, in the author's experience they are frequently handled poorly or forgotten altogether. The key points are the need to ask questions that are clearly relevant to the job for which the candidate is applying, and the need, at all times, to be concerned about the image of the organisation in the potential recruit's mind.

- In writing to invite a candidate for interview, address him or her by name and not by a ritualistic mode of address like 'Dear sir or madam'.

- Specify the date, time and place of the interview. Also include a location map with details of access for cars and pedestrians, parking and public transport. Disabled access arrangements should also be mentioned.

- Indicate in the letter the purpose of the interview by distinguishing between a screening interview, speculative discussions and the final decision-making event.

- Outline the likely duration of the exercise and the format the interviewee can expect (ie panel, one-to one, sequential etc).

- Include the names and job titles of the interviewers.

- Give details of other aspects of the proceedings so that nothing takes candidates by surprise. For instance, if they are expected to undergo a medical examination, then they should be advised in advance.

- State what documents applicants need to bring with them (eg proof of qualifications, driving licence, indemnity insurance certificate). Specify the need to bring originals, not copies.

- Explain how (or whether) expenses will be paid.

- Ask candidates to confirm their intention to attend the interview at the stated time and place.

- Close the letter with optimistic or enthusiastic remarks about the forthcoming process.

- End by giving a name (not an illegible signature) and methods by which candidates can make contact (address, phone number, e-mail etc).

- Base interview questions on a comprehensive, accurate and up-to-date job description.

• Ask questions derived from a meaningful person specification that genuinely discriminates between the 'essential' and the 'desirable' in a fashion that, at least in principle, enables definitive judgements to be made.

• In framing questions for unstructured and semi-structured interviews, refer to the CV or application form so that any inconsistencies or omissions can be followed up.

• Give active consideration to the current environment and to any important business issues of relevance to the vacant job. This background material should be used in question design and can also be imparted to candidates during the interview so that they can answer questions as effectively as possible.

EMPLOYMENT REFERENCES

The reference letter of recommendation or testimonial is the third of the three selection techniques that make up the 'classic trio'. Like interviews and application forms, it is very widely used – by over 99 per cent of employers, according to the most recent survey (IRS 1997: 16) – but has been found to be of very limited value by researchers. As predictors of job performance it has low validity and has often been found to contain more information about its author than about its subject (Cook 1993: 73).

A number of reasons have been put forward to explain the limitations of references. According to Cooper and Robertson (1995: 142), they are 'highly subjective' and 'open to error and abuse' because 'the flow of information is between two people who are unlikely to meet and about an applicant who will never know what is written'. The implication is that employers, when asked, are generally disinclined to regard the giving of a fair, considered assessment of a former employee to be a high priority. The result is carelessness and a reluctance to put a great deal of time or thought into the writing of the reference. Furthermore, a number of specific problems have been identified:

• A tendency to give individuals a similar rating when asked about different aspects of their work and personality. If asked to comment separately about someone's social skills, conscientiousness, initiative and attendance records, referees tend to rate candidates as good, moderate or poor on all counts.

• A tendency to give good ratings. It is comparatively rare for employers to receive poor references. While, this could be simply because candidates name only people who, they believe, will write a positive assessment, there is also evidence to suggest that employers are generally reluctant to mark someone down in a reference report. A range of average or non-committal ratings or statements thus often indicates a weak performer.

• A tendency, when given a five-point scale, to rank individuals in the centre. Employers seem reluctant to give excellent ratings.

As was the case with interviews, given these damning research findings it is reasonable to ask why references retain their near universal appeal for employers. Here, too, the answer probably lies in the function that references fulfil. According to IRS (1997: 16), nearly half of references are taken up after the selection decision has been made. The aim is therefore less to assist in the prediction of job performance and more to do with double-checking factual information and seeking confirmation of general impressions gained during the selection process. The reference provides one more piece of information, but is rarely crucial in determining who will get a job.

There are three exceptions to this. The first is the case of internal candidates. In large organisations where people compete for in-house promotions, references are likely to play a more fundamental part of the selection process. In such situations both the selector and the referee will take the process of writing references more seriously. The same kind of influences also come into play in the case of applicants for jobs in professions occupied by relatively few people. Here, although job transfers are occurring between organisations, the chances are that referees know those responsible for the selection of candidates. As a result, references are generally more reliable than they are when the writers and recipients are anonymous to each other. Examples include academic and senior medical appointments. The other exception is the case when a reference reveals that candidates have been less than honest in statements they have made in interviews or on their application forms. Common examples include misleading information about dates of employment, salary, seniority and reasons for leaving previous jobs. Where references brings dishonesty of this kind to light, they can be crucial in determining that offers of employment are not made. Perhaps the most useful question of all is 'Would you re-employ this person?' If former employers answer negatively, there is a need to probe further and find out why.

There are three improvements to the process of reference-gathering that researchers have found increase the quality of the information gathered. The first is to contact former employers and named referees by telephone. Doing so is less anonymous and thus increases the chances of a candid and balanced assessment. Provided that the questions asked over the phone are precise and job-related, this approach can work well. It also has the advantage of making it harder for ex-employers to avoid giving references, as around half will if sent a request in writing (Cooper and Robertson, 1995: 144).

The second widely mooted improvement is to design structured assessment forms that relate specifically to the skills and experience necessary to perform well in the job under consideration (Dobson 1989). As with structured interviewing, this requires much more preparation than the placing of a pre-printed form in an envelope. It requires separate forms to be constructed for different jobs, with questions related to the criteria agreed in the job specification.

The third means by which references can be made more useful is to request more than just one or two. Asking a candidate for permission to approach half-a-dozen referees increases the chances of receiving meaningful information. It also makes it harder for the candidate to name only people who are likely to give unblemished reports. It is for this reason that applicants for positions in the security services are asked to name several referees, including employers whom they left many years previously.

Interestingly, the likelihood of eliciting frank and honest references from former employers is perceived to have become harder in recent years, with some interesting new legal judgements (IRS 1997d: 16). These have led a number of employers to review policy concerning the giving of references by agreeing to give factual information only or by insisting that references are issued only once they have been approved by personnel managers. Potentially, referees can be sued by both the ex-employee and their new employer if they knowingly make false statements. According to IDS (1992: 56):

> An employer who provides a reference owes a duty to the recipient of that reference, usually the new employer. If the recipient of the reference suffers loss as a result of relying on the inaccurate reference, he may be able to claim damages from the writer of the reference. The loss may be the expense of recruiting a replacement employee or, more seriously, the loss consequent upon the incompetence or dishonesty of the employee.

The situation with ex-employees is more complicated because of the range of different grounds on which cases can be brought. These include defamation, injurious falsehood and negligent mis-statement. The law is quite clear that employers owe a duty of care to ex-employees and are thus obliged to take care to write references based on accurate facts. As is the case with most legal issues in personnel management, the law on these matters is complex and subject to adaptation by judges over time.

Perhaps the best approach to the use of references, like so many tools and techniques in personnel management, is not to have too great expectations about them. They are not a panacea; nor are they a substitute for managerial judgement. They have very great limitations, but can nevertheless be useful and informative *provided they are treated warily*. If they are approached in the full knowledge that they are less than perfect and likely to be overgenerous towards candidates, they have a positive role to play in selection. The danger is relying too heavily on them.

FURTHER READING

- There is good coverage given to the general topic of research into employee selection in all the current personnel management text books. The most accessible books on the topic are *Selection and Assessment: A new appraisal* by Mike Smith, Mike Gregg and Dick Andrews (1989), *Personnel Selection and Productivity* by Mark Cook (1993), and *The Psychology of Personnel Selection* by Dominic Cooper and Ivan Robinson (1995).

- There has been a great deal published on the topic of selection interviewing. All the above texts discuss the topic in detail as do two specialist academic books of edited articles: *Assessment and Selection in Organisations* edited by Peter Herriot (1989), and *The Employment Interview* edited by Robert Eder and Gerald Ferris (1989).

- The best general guide to interviewing practice is *Successful Selection Interviewing* by Neil Anderson and Vivian Shackleton (1993). This is rooted in recent research but is aimed at students and practitioners, and is very accessible.

- A number of general handbooks have been published by experienced selectors that contain helpful advice and are often thought-provoking on the subjects contained in this chapter. These include *Employment Interviewing* by John Munro Fraser (1979) and *The Selection Interview* by Penny Hackett (1995).

- Comparatively little has been written on the subjects of application forms and references. However, Paul Dobson's article on references in the book of articles edited by Herriot (1989) is useful, as are the relevant sections of Mark Cook's general text on selection referred to above.

- The two most useful guides to aspects of best practice in the selection field generally are contained in *The IPD Guide on Recruitment* (1996) and in the Equal Opportunities Commission publication entitled *Fair and Efficient: Guidance on equal opportunities policies in recruitment and selection procedures* (1986).

8 Sorting the wheat from the chaff

In recent years, despite the continued prevalence of traditional methods in employee selection, there has been increased interest shown by employers in a range of other techniques. While few have dispensed altogether with interviews, references and application forms, substantial numbers now supplement information gathered from their use with a range of more sophisticated assessment techniques. Such methods cost a great deal more to operate fairly and effectively, but have all performed comparatively well when subjected to analysis by occupational psychologists. As a result, they can probably be said to be the most accurate techniques available in terms of their ability to predict job performance.

In this chapter we complete our discussion of employee selection by examining four specific 'high-validity' selection methods: biodata analysis, ability tests, personality tests and assessment centres. In addition, particular attention is paid to the issue of professionalism and ethicality in the use of selection tests. The chapter concludes with a section outlining the main legal considerations of importance in the management of employee selection.

By the end of this chapter readers should be able to:

- advise on the sources and standards for biodata, assessment centres, aptitude and personality tests

- recommend and assist in devising a variety of exercises for use in an assessment centre

- seek and evaluate sources of professional advice about psychometric testing and other 'high-validity' selection methods.

In addition readers should be able to understand and explain the:

- benefits and shortcomings of biodata, aptitude tests, personality tests and assessment centres

- different situations in which each would or would not be appropriate

- legal and ethical framework for employee selection.

BIODATA

The use of biodata (biographical data) to predict job performance has a long history. According to Cook (1993: 85), its use can be traced to the nineteenth century, and it has attracted the attention of researchers ever since. However, in the UK the method has only ever been used by a minority of employers – 5 per cent in the most recent survey (IRS 1997d: 15). This is probably because, in spite of its apparent high validity, it remains both controversial and costly to develop. In practice biodata tends to be used only in the limited number of situations to which it is most suited.

Selection using biodata takes a number of forms, but at base all involve using detailed information concerning an applicant's past to make deductions about his or her likely performance in a future job. Typically, the employer using the approach requires applicants to fill in a detailed questionnaire that contains a large number of items about their work and personal lives. These often take a multiple choice form, allowing for ease of analysis. The questionnaire is usually sent to applicants in the post with a request that it should be returned within a few days. The data collected is then fed into a computer and a score generated. Some companies now take a more direct approach and read out the questions over the telephone. The candidate's answers are then fed directly into the computer for immediate analysis.

The scoring system operates in a similar manner to those operated by insurers and actuaries, the employer screening applicants according to how closely their history or characteristics match those of the better, existing employees. Just as an insurance company determines its prices and willingness to insure property according to the age of applicant, location of house, type of property, type of employment and number of previous claims, the employer using biodata seeks to predict from a range of factual data how effective an employee each applicant is likely to be if appointed. In both cases, experience of the characteristics of previous clients or employees is being used to make predictions about whom to insure or employ in the future.

A biodata questionnaire is effective only if designed separately for each job type. Typically, it involves an employer choosing a sample of existing employees that includes the best and poorest performers. These individuals then complete very extensive questionnaires covering a whole range of issues related to their work history, hobbies and personal circumstances. The results are then analysed and conclusions drawn about which questions most effectively delineate between the good and poor performers. The process can throw up some extraordinary results, as is illustrated by the following quotation:

> Mosel (1952) compared the best and worst saleswomen in a large department store, and found the ideal saleswoman was: between 35 and 54 years old, had 13–16 years' formal education, had over five years' selling experience, weighed over 160 pounds, had worked in her next to last job for under 5 years, lived in a boarding house, had worked in her next to last job for over 5 years, had her principal previous experience as a minor executive, was between 4'11" and 5'2" high, had between 1 and 3 dependants, was widowed and had lost no time from work during the past two years (in order of predictive validity).
>
> Cook (1993: 87–88)

Having established which attributes are shared by the best, existing employees, a biodata questionnaire is drawn up containing the questions found to have elicited information about the relevant characteristics. If, for example, it is found that the best employees tend to have achieved GCSE level in Maths and English and that poor employees have not, questions would be included about educational attainment in these subjects. By contrast, if it was found that the age at which employees left school had no statistically significant bearing on whether they were good or poor performers, then no such question would be included.

Opinion among writers is divided over the extent to which biodata questionnaires should include 'hard' and 'soft' questions. Hard questions are those that ask for information of a factual nature which is, at least in theory, objectively verifiable. Examples might be 'How many children do you have?' or 'In which year did you pass your driving test?' By contrast, soft questions are more directly job-related and are closer to items commonly found in psychometric tests. Rather than asking for factual information, their aim is to allow inferences to be made concerning the personality traits shared by better-performing job-holders. The problem here is that they generally do not allow candidates to say that they would react differently according to the circumstances. Instead, there is a requirement to opt for one of a number of starker options. An example of a soft question is given by Drakeley (1989: 440):

> When people in front of you talked through the beginning of a film at a cinema did you:
>
> i) ignore them
>
> ii) get up and move
>
> iii) ask them to be quiet
>
> iv) call the manager
>
> v) none of the above.

Questions such as this have the advantage of directly tapping into personal qualities that are related to the job and are thus readily justifiable. The disadvantage is that, unlike hard questions, they are not easily verified, making it easier for applicants to choose the response they believe is likely to give them the highest score. In the above example, it is not difficult to spot that the employer is looking for evidence of assertiveness. It would thus not be a good idea to answer (i) or (ii) – whatever the truth might actually be! It is thus the hard variety of questions with which biodata is more commonly associated.

The use of biodata can be criticised from a number of perspectives. First, it can be perceived as unfair by rejected candidates and may thus have adverse effects on an organisation's image in the labour market. An example known to the author concerns a major UK company which uses biodata to screen out large numbers of applicants for its graduate trainee programme. One of the questions applicants are asked is to identify which university awarded their first degree.

The company then rejects all applicants who did not attend one of 10 specific universities. This is very rough on otherwise excellent candidates who may spend a great deal of time completing application forms and researching the company before being rejected on grounds over which they have no control at all. In one case, an applicant who had gained a post-graduate degree at one of the approved institutions was rejected because her first degree had been awarded elsewhere. Another example is quoted by Cooper and Robertson (1995: 124). Here an employer found that there was a significant correlation between an individual's work performance and their preferred holiday location. The result was a negative score for future applicants who stated that they enjoyed holidays in Spain.

It is the apparently arbitrary nature of making selection decisions on the basis of such questions that is disturbing, however effective the approach may be at predicting effective job performance. The result can very easily be strong feelings of unfairness and injustice. For these reasons, employers using biodata approaches have to take very great care to avoid using questions that might be construed as unfairly discriminating against one sex, any racial group or people with disabilities. Whatever the validity of the method in terms of its ability to predict job performance, it may easily also fall foul of discrimination law.

Biodata has also been criticised on practical grounds. In particular, detractors have pointed to its lack of portability between job types. A questionnaire that is good at predicting the performance of airline stewards will be very different from one that aims to forecast how effective pilots are likely to be. Researchers have also found that biodata questionnaires age fairly rapidly, and thus need to be revised every few years if they are to retain their predictive power (Cook 1993: 98–99). These factors, combined with the need for large numbers of existing employees to take part at the development stage, greatly limits the number of situations in which it is practicable to employ the approach. Smith *et al* (1989: 56) suggest that, in order for a questionnaire to be effective, the sample of existing employees should not generally be less than 300, 'and in any event should be at least four times the number of items in the questionnaire'. It can therefore be concluded that biodata is best used in the following circumstances:

- where large numbers of applications are received for a particular job

- where there are large numbers of existing staff employed in the same position

- where the nature of the work performed is not likely to change to any great degree over time

- where job applications are screened centrally (ie where the process has not been dissolved to separate divisions or business units).

Its use is thus effectively restricted to large organisations aiming to employ the most systematic and valid technique to screen candidates prior to inviting them to an interview or assessment centre.

> For which particular jobs or professions would you consider biodata to be an effective and efficient selection method?

ABILITY TESTING

According to IRS (1997: 13), over three-quarters of employers now use ability tests compared with half of a similar sample taken in 1991. However, results from such tests seem most often to be used as a back-up to other selection techniques rather than as the main determinant of hiring decisions. Tests of basic literacy and numeracy tend to be used to weed out the poorest candidates rather than as a means of distinguishing between those considered appointable. It should not be surprising that ability testing is becoming increasingly widely used, as it is the least controversial of the high-validity selection methods, with great potential advantages over other approaches. According to Smith *et al* (1989: 9) and Cook (1993: 119), validity co-efficients of 0.5 are achievable using such approaches.

A broad distinction can be made between tests of specific job-related abilities and the more general tests of mental or cognitive ability. The former category includes the use of typing and shorthand tests in the case of applicants for secretarial appointments and driving tests for potential drivers of heavy goods vehicles. In practice, employers who use such methods are making selection decisions on the basis of a sample of the quality of the work candidates will be able to offer if successful in their applications. However, in many cases people apply for jobs made up of tasks they have not undertaken previously. In manufacturing this is very common because of the specialised machinery that is often used. In such situations it would clearly be impractical and unfair to expect candidates to be able to demonstrate ability in the principal job duties. One means of getting round this problem is the trainability test, described at length by Downs (1989: 392–399).

Here the aim is to make deductions about future performance by observing how effectively candidates learn a job-related task when given a standard set of instructions or training from an instructor. It is particularly suited to jobs in which new recruits are required to master new and complex machinery. An example given by Downs (1989: 394) is a test designed by British Airways to assess how quickly aspiring electricians might become sufficiently well-qualified to maintain aircraft engines. Her advice is to develop tests that stretch candidates to the full and, when scoring their performance, to focus on the number and type of errors made.

Pre-employment training at Courtaulds

An interesting experiment in employee selection was reported in 1997 when Courtaulds set out to select around a hundred new process technicians to work at a new textiles plant in the north-east of England. Prior to opening the plant, the company operated an intensive evening training programme for prospective employees running over 12 weeks. The courses were held in sessions of four hours on two nights a week and took place at a local college. Participants were not paid for attending, but completed a level-3 NVQ qualification, whether or not they were taken on to work in the new plant. The course was run by managers and cost just £1,000 per candidate to provide. The topics covered included process control, safety, basic science, computing and team-building.

Participants were assessed according to their performance in a written examination but were also scored for team-working ability and leadership potential. Inferences were also made, from participants' approach to the course, about motivation levels and likely attendance records. The managers responsible were happy with the experiment (though they have stated that in future they will be cutting the length of the programme). Not only did the course successfully identify the most effective employees, it also ensured that a good part of their initial training was already completed when they took up their new posts.

Source: Burke (1997: 29–30)

A substantial amount of research has been carried out in the field of mental ability testing, with apparently encouraging results. Meta-analyses of many small-scale validity studies carried out in the 1980s seem now to have established, to the satisfaction of most researchers, that tests of intelligence or intellectual ability are among the most effective predictors of job performance available. The main controversy seems to be between those who believe it is possible to devise fairly short pencil-and-paper tests that can deliver meaningful measurements of general intelligence in less than an hour (see Toplis *et al* 1991: 17) and those who argue that a more sophisticated battery of different tests is required to achieve reliable results (Cook 1993: 122–123).

In theory, tests of mental ability are superior to other selection methods on a variety of counts. The biggest advantage is their transportability – they do not have to be designed afresh for each job, each organisation or even each country. Once a test is accepted as being a valid measurement tool, it can be used across a wide variety of job types in all manner of organisations. There is thus no need for extensive job analysis, as in the case of personality testing, or for development among a specific group of staff, as in the case of biodata. Tests can be bought from a supplier, and training in their use undertaken before they are administered to job applicants at all levels in an organisation. If designed with care, they can also be shown not to discriminate unfairly between members of different racial groups or between men and women (Cook 1993: 121).

Test questions come in a variety of forms and are forever being updated and improved by suppliers, who operate in a very competitive market. However, most share the same basic format. First, they all contain questions to which there is a right answer – in most cases requiring candidates to pick from a set of multiple choice options.

Secondly, all tests are designed to be taken under examination conditions with a set time limit and standard instructions. Typically, before applicants undertake each type of question, there are practice examples given which can be checked by the instructor to ensure that everyone fully understands what exactly they are expected to do. Another feature shared by all reputable tests is the process by which they are developed. This is a lengthy and costly operation involving hundreds of volunteers to enable the scoring system to reflect the performance of certain 'norm' groups. Norming allows the employer marking the test to know how well a particular candidate has done in comparison with a specified population such as graduates, school-leavers or senior managers.

Some of the most common types of question are illustrated below (Byron and Modha 1991, 1993).

1) Verbal Reasoning

i)   Ocean is to Pond as Deep is to
a) Shallow   b) Well   c) Sea   d) Lake

ii) Early is the Opposite of
a) Evening   b) Late   c) Postpone d) Breakfast

iii) What means the same as Portion?
a) Whole   b) Part   c) Chip   d) None

iv) Which would be the third in alphabetical order?
a) Sevene   b) Severn   c) Seveen   d) Seven

v)   Which is the odd one out?
a) Lock b) Quay   c) Bollard   d) Anchor

vi) Which is the penultimate letter in the word REST?
a) R   b) E   c) S   d) T

2) Numerical Reasoning

Which number comes next in the following series:

i)   12 10 8 6 4
a) 3   b) 2   c) 1   d) 0

ii) 1 1 2 3 5
a) 7   b) 10   c) 8   d) 9

iii) 10 25 12 30 14
a) 16   b) 50   c) 24   d) 35

iv) 81 27 9 3 1
a) 0.5   b) 1   c) 0.33   d) 0.166

v)   If a set of five screwdrivers costs £4, how much does each one cost?
a) 50p   b) 60p   c) 70p   d) 80p   e) 90p

vi) If a 90-litre tank needs to be filled up using a hose pipe that allows water to flow at 2 litres per second, how many seconds would be needed to fill up the tank?
a) 180   b) 90   c) 45   d) 22.5   e) 11.25

3) Analytical Ability

Janet, Marcus, Eric and Angela sit in this order in a row left to right. Janet changes places with Eric and then Eric changes places with Marcus.

i) Who is at the right end of the row?

ii) Who is to the left of Eric?

James is eight years old and half as old as his brother Humphrey. Jenny is two years younger than James and the same number of years older than Mark.

iii) Who is the oldest?

iv) Who is the youngest?

v) How old is Mark?

Often the questions in tests of mental ability are not in themselves particularly difficult, but become far harder when part of a long questionnaire which has to be completed in a limited period of time. There is also a tendency for the questions to get very much trickier as the test proceeds. This makes it possible for people with a wide range of mental ability to be scored after sitting the same test. A recent innovation in abilities testing is the use of computer software packages. In such situations the candidate answers using a keyboard, and the score is automatically recorded. The great advantage of these packages is the capability they have to tailor the standard of questions to the appropriate level for each individual applicant. If a candidate performs well in the early questions the computer starts generating more difficult problems. As a result, less time is taken to establish the level of mental ability demonstrated in each individual case.

An issue of significance with this kind of test is the extent to which candidates can raise their performance with practice. Opinion is divided on this issue, writers of books aimed at helping candidates to prepare claiming that practice improves performance (eg Byron and Modha 1991: 9), while psychologists and test-providers downplay the extent to which this can in fact occur. Toplis *et al* (1991: 61–2) suggest that retesting candidates with the same test a few days after their first attempt usually leads only to a marginal improvement in performance. Clearly the extent to which candidates can prepare will vary from test to test, with some forms of ability test more susceptible than others to this kind of effect. Another variable is the effectiveness of any feedback that a candidate may be given on their performance when first attempting a particular type of test.

Ultimately, it is probably wise to accept that no method can be perfect, and that some candidates may perform better than others for a variety of reasons. No predictive selection method is a panacea, and management decisions in this field are bound to contain a measure of error. It can nevertheless be said that, according to current research and against a range of criteria, ability testing is more effective than other methods. Furthermore, it would appear to be a least-worst option across a very wide range of selection situations. That said, there are of course plenty of jobs for which too high a level of intelligence would be a drawback. Where duties are purely manual or highly simplistic and repetitive, and where there is no clear upward career path to more interesting work, it can plausibly be argued that they are not best undertaken by people who score highly in tests of mental ability. The result would be boredom, low levels of commitment and high staff turnover.

> For what jobs in your organisation would mental ability tests be appropriate? For which would they be inappropriate?

PERSONALITY TESTING

The use of tests that purport to measure personality in the selection process is a field of activity that has generated a vast literature and that remains highly controversial. It is not within the scope of this book to deal with the very many issues that this long-lasting and wide-ranging debate has encompassed. The aim here is to introduce the topic in general terms and to give a general assessment of the effectiveness of using personality tests in different situations. While a number of distinct approaches to personality testing have been developed by psychologists, in most selection situations inferences are made about candidates' suitability for a particular position from responses given in answer to personality questionnaires or inventories (mostly pencil-and-paper tests produced by commercial organisations).

The validity of personality testing ultimately rests on a number of basic assumptions about which psychologists and other researchers have very different ideas, namely that:

- human personality is measurable or 'mappable'

- our underlying human personality remains stable over time and across different situations

- individual jobs can be usefully analysed in terms of the personality traits that would be most desirable for the job-holder to possess

- a personality questionnaire, completed in 30 to 60 minutes, provides sufficient information about an individual's personality to make meaningful inferences about their suitability for a job.

A large body of research into these questions and the validity of the various psychological instruments developed to map personality has been undertaken. Nevertheless, opinions among specialists in the field – let alone lay people – differ very considerably, making it difficult to come to firm conclusions about the validity of the personality test *per se*. To a great extent the jury is still out, test providers and their supporters claiming them to be effective predictors of various aspects of job performance, and others questioning their claims. For reasonably accessible introductions to these debates the following are recommended: Cook (1993: 131–163), Fletcher (1991: 38–42) and Van der Marsen de Sombrieff and Hofstede (1989: 353–367).

For the purposes of this text, and while acknowledging its controversial nature, the broad thrust of the case for personality testing is accepted. When used carefully and professionally, personality tests at least have a potentially useful role to play in the selection procedure. This position appears broadly to be shared by most occupational psychologists working in the field of employee selection. The general consensus is that well-designed tests can, if used properly, predict aspects of job performance reasonably accurately. The problem is the large number of poorly designed tests on the market and misuse by untrained assessors (Smith *et al*, 1989: 77–78).

The Barnum effect

A classic piece of research carried out in 1958 should act as a warning to those who place great faith in the power of personality testing. In Dr R. Stagner's study – written up under the heading *The Gullibility of Personnel Managers* – 68 managers completed a personality questionnaire. At the end, each was presented with a written profile summarising the main characteristics of their personalities. They then completed a further questionnaire asking how accurate they believed the profile to be. Fifty per cent ranked the profile overall as being 'amazingly accurate' and a further 40 per cent as 'rather good'. However, the researchers had tricked the managers by giving them all the same faked personality profile to assess, instead of genuine summaries of their own personalities.

The experiment shows how very easy it is for the devisers of personality tests to profit from their high face-validity by taking advantage of the fact that the results can appear a great deal more accurate and meaningful than they actually are. Personality tests of this type are said to sell as a result of the 'Barnum effect' – the belief that 'you can fool most of the people most of the time'. Prospective purchasers of tests should, therefore, be highly suspicious of tests that produce profiles similar to those written by astrologers in the tabloid newspapers!

Source: Jackson (1996: 37–38)

IRS (1997d: 13) reported that the use of personality testing has remained stable during the 1990s, approximately three-fifths of organisations stating that the method forms part of selection procedures for some positions. They are used for all appointments by fewer than 10 per cent of employers. Interestingly, this finding contrasts with the great growth in the use of ability tests over the same period, and may well reflect unease about their accuracy in terms of predicting job performance. That said, it would seem that the majority of applicants for managerial jobs are now asked to fill in personality questionnaires when short-listed. According to IRS (1997d: 10), the tests are also widely used in graduate selection and in the case of candidates for professional and technical positions. While they form a part of selection procedures in most industries to a greater or lesser extent, their use appears to be particularly heavy in the finance sector, over 85 per cent of employers stating that they employ them in the selection of some staff.

All the major personality questionnaires available on the market employ the same basic methodology: the aim being to help assessors in making inferences about an individual's psychological make-up from answers given to a standard set of questions. Underlying this is an acceptance of the idea that people differ one from the other in terms of their personality traits. According to Cooper and Robertson (1995: 22–25), it is now possible to state with some confidence that there are five basic psychological constructs or 'traits' which form the building-blocks of our personalities and explain the differences between us:

- extroversion – introversion (the extent to which we enjoy socialising with others, excitement and change)

- emotional stability (the extent to which we exhibit tension and anxiety)

- agreeableness (the extent to which we avoid conflict and exhibit good-nature, warmth and compassion)

- conscientiousness (the extent to which we are well-organised, concerned with meeting deadlines and the making and implementation of plans)

- openness to experience (the extent to which we are imaginative, flexible and view new experiences positively).

Personality questionnaires are designed to assist selectors in finding out where individuals lie on scales like these. In so doing, it is claimed, it is possible to predict the manner in which people are predisposed to react in given situations. Using this knowledge, selectors can make inferences about a number of important matters:

- how well the individual's personality matches that believed to be ideal for the job

- how well the individual will fit in with the general organisational culture

- how well an individual's personality or predisposition to behave in a particular way might complement those of existing team members

- whether an individual, otherwise well-qualified, might in fact be unsuitable for a post because he or she scores too high or too low in terms of a particular personality trait.

Even if the results of the personality questionnaire are not themselves crucial determinants of the selection decision, they can flag areas to raise and discuss at the interview stage.

Like mental ability tests, the better personality questionnaires are developed using large numbers of volunteers. Aside from testing the validity of the instrument, this also enables each individual's scores to be compared with those typical of humanity in general or a particular sector of the population. However, personality tests differ in that individuals completing them are not usually given strict time limits. Indeed, it is essential that applicants complete all questions in order to enable a full and well-balanced assessment to be made of their psychological make-up.

There is a number of different forms of question asked in personality inventories. According to Cook (1993: 134), most require applicants to agree or disagree with a statement. In some cases this simply involves choosing one of two options: true or false, yes or no. In others, a three-point scale is used, allowing candidates to state that they are uncertain about the statement or that their answer is 'inbetween' yes and no. These fictitious examples are from Jackson (1996: 154):

1) I lose my temper over minor incidents.

    a) True   b) In Between   c) False

2) I like giving practical demonstrations in front of others.

    a) True   b) Uncertain   c) False

3) I double-check for errors when I perform calculations.

    a) True   b) Sometimes   c) False

A further development of this approach is to give the applicant five options in response to each question. Such questionnaires often make use of a Likert scale, as in the following examples:

1) I like working to strict time deadlines
    a) strongly agree
    b) agree
    c) unsure
    d) disagree
    e) strongly disagree

2) On TV, drama series are more interesting than factual series
    a) strongly agree
    b) agree
    c) unsure
    d) disagree
    e) strongly disagree

A problem with these approaches is the apparent ease with which candidates can fake their responses in an attempt to make themselves appear more appropriate for the job. If applying for a position as a senior manager, no serious candidate will want to give the impression that they lack decisiveness or assertiveness. On a Likert scale it is not difficult to spot which questions are concerned with these traits and to tailor answers accordingly. In an attempt to reduce faking of this kind, some questionnaires use ipsative or forced-choice questions, in which applicants are required to choose between a number of statements or descriptive words that appear equally desirable or undesirable. The following examples are typical:

1) Would you rather work with people who are:
    a) generous   b) hard-working

2) Do you feel that it is best:
    a) to be too assertive   b) not to be sufficiently assertive

3) Which word appeals to you most in each of the following pairs?
    a) effective   b) pleasant

    a) loyal   b) ambitious

In tests such as these candidates have to choose one or other option, so they cannot say that they are 'unsure' or that their preference is 'in between'. Another ipsative format asks candidates to choose which of four descriptive words is most, and which is least, appropriate as a description of their personality:

1) a) kind   b) influential   c) respectful   d) inventive

2) a) refined b) adventurous   c) tactful   d) content

However, ipsative questions have also been criticised because they set one psychological construct against another. In such a questionnaire, a question does not, for example, simply assess how conscientious someone is: it forces the candidate to choose between a statement concerning conscientiousness and another concerning extroversion. As a result, the fact that someone is both relatively extroverted *and* relatively conscientious is not recorded. For this reason the scoring and meaningful interpretation of ipsative tests is particularly difficult to carry out, and raw results can be highly misleading. The extent to which, in practice, they deter faking is also questionable. While it is harder to spot which traits the forced-choice questions are focusing on, to do so is not an impossible task for anyone familiar with the way personality questionnaires work.

An alternative approach to the problem of faking personality questionnaires is to include a 'lie-index' – also known as a 'social desirability index'. While these do not deter candidates from faking responses, they can help indicate to the assessor that the truth has been embellished in some way by sending warning signals concerning honesty. The approach used is to include in the questionnaire a number of questions to which there is, for the vast majority of individuals, only one honest answer. An example from one of the most widely used tests is a question that invites people to agree or disagree with the following statement:

> 'I sometimes talk about people behind their backs.'

Anyone claiming to disagree – or even strongly disagree – with this statement is considered by the test devisers to be giving a socially desirable response, as opposed to a true one. If several questions of a similar kind are answered in the same manner a high social desirability score will show up when the test is analysed. There are two implications for the employer:

- There is an indication that the test in general may not have been completed accurately.

- It may be possible to infer that the candidate is not a particularly honest individual.

A significant recent development in personality testing is the use of computers. As in the case of ability testing, software is available that permits candidates to answer questions generated on the screen using the keyboard. The result is far greater speed and accuracy in the scoring of tests. For a number of years paper-and-pencil tests have made use of technology that allows computer scanners to read score sheets. However, these are often user-*un*friendly, leading to confusion on the part of candidates when answering the questions. Perhaps the greatest advance made possible by computer technology is the extensive print-outs that are now generated summarising the main features of the candidate's personality. To some extent this obviates the need for a trained psychologist to be present to interpret the results of the questionnaire. The print-out permits individuals with far less extensive training to make meaningful inferences from the results of personality tests. By way of illustration the following extract is taken from a print-out generated following the completion of the one such test:

> Temperamentally, Mr **** has quite a trusting nature and is inclined to believe that people are basically genuine and honest. An easy-going, affable group member, he may occasionally be accused of being overindulgent, and consequently may be taken advantage of. He will generally give people the benefit of the doubt (without being unduly credulous). Social demands do not play a significant part in determining his behaviour. Not being particularly concerned about how others view him, he will prefer to relate casually to others rather than be constantly alert for the need to observe social etiquette. Although his affinity with group activities is above average, he may have difficulty conforming to its rules. He is unlikely to make a popular group member in situations where individualism is strictly discouraged. Somewhat unpretentious, genuine and rather outspoken, when asked for an opinion, Mr **** may on occasions, unintentionally (or otherwise), express himself in a direct and uncalculated manner.

PROFESSIONAL ISSUES IN THE USE OF SELECTION TESTS

As has been made clear in the above paragraphs, selection using either ability or personality tests is a complex field. The theories under-pinning their use are sophisticated and subject to disagreement among occupational psychologists. Furthermore, there are a bewildering number of different tests on the market claiming to provide managers with objective methods of predicting job performance. The highly competitive nature of the business and the sizeable costs involved in developing truly robust and valid tests means that unwary personnel managers can easily find themselves spending too much on buying licenses to use questionnaires that are largely ineffective.

In the absence of any detailed statutory regulation, the (former) IPD updated its long-standing code of practice on psychological testing with a guide for its members (IPD 1997a). This in turn accepted and made explicit reference to the professional standards drawn up and validated by the specialised professional body for occupational psychologists – the British Psychological Society (BPS). The following six points summarise the most significant points set out in the IPD guide:

- Selection decisions should not be made using psychological tests alone. If used, they should always form a part of a wider selection process. Inferences made from test results should always be backed up with data from other sources.

- Anyone in the organisation who has responsibility for supervising applicants taking tests, evaluating results, or giving feedback should have gained the relevant certificate of competence from the British Psychological Society. In the case of ability tests, these people should be trained and certificated to level A, and in the case of personality tests, to level B.

- Feedback from tests should be given to all candidates – successful as well as unsuccessful – concerning their performance in tests. However, such feedback should be given only by individuals who have been professionally trained in interpreting test results and who are skilled at giving appropriate feedback.

- The only tests that should be used are those 'which have been through a rigorous development process with proper regard to psychological knowledge and processes'. It is also important to ensure that any test used does not discriminate unfairly on grounds of gender, ethnicity or disability.

- Test users should maintain the highest possible standards of confidentiality, with results made available only to those with 'a genuine need to know'.

- Test results should be used only to make decisions between candidates when they are shown to have a clear potential impact on likely performance in the job in question. Test results should not therefore be used as the basis for making decisions based on personal preference for a particular character type.

Perhaps the biggest problem for P&D practitioners is making sure that what they are being sold by the test providers does in fact conform to the above standards. It is very tempting, when being offered an apparently plausible product at a competitive price, to overlook the lack of evidence of BPS approval or the lack of professional training needed to operate the test. The best advice in such circumstances is to seek professional assistance from a chartered psychologist. The British Psychological Society can recommend appropriate professionals for this purpose. When considering introducing tests or replacing existing products, it is also a good idea to research the issues explored above thoroughly and to familiarise yourself with the alternative products on the market. Sources of further reading on this and other relevant topics chapter are given at the end of the chapter.

ASSESSMENT CENTRES

The assessment centre has been referred to as 'the Rolls Royce' of selection methods, and is the approach that has received the best press of any surveyed in this and the previous chapter. Validity studies have consistently found assessment centre techniques to have good predictive ability, and they appear to be liked by candidates too. Perhaps the only drawback, albeit an important one, is the cost associated with their preparation and administration. While the approach can also be used for developmental purposes, the aim here is simply to review its application in the selection field.

Assessment centres involve assembling in one place several candidates who are applying for the same position and putting them through a variety of different tests. Centres can be operated over one day, but usually involve an overnight stay. They will typically include a conventional interview, together with paper-and-pencil tests both of mental ability and personality. In addition, a range of other exercises are included to test a variety of specific competences. It is the presence of so many different selection tools acting together that is thought to account for the high validity that the approach has been found to possess. This permits assessors to observe candidates' behaviour in a number of distinct situations, removing the need to make inferences based on only one technique (interview, psychometric test, application form etc).

However, most centres are not exclusively concerned with the identification of underlying personality traits or constructs, as is the case with personality testing. Instead, the aim is to observe actual behaviour in a work-related situation. The concern is not therefore with identifying an underlying predisposition to be assertive, conscientious, sociable or whatever, but to assess each candidate's actual actions and reactions when they are placed in job-related situations. A particular feature of the method is its ability to focus on potential rather than on achievement. Unlike the other commonly used selection methods, assessment centres are not concerned with making inferences about the candidates' likely future performance from evidence of their past activities. Instead, the focus is on anticipating how potential employees are likely to behave, if appointed, from direct observation of their behaviour in circumstances similar to those they are likely to encounter on the job.

A number of researchers have pointed out that, in practice, assessors tend to resist scoring candidates according to specific psychological dimensions, but instead prefer to judge their general performance in each exercise (Woodruffe 1993: 199–203). In other words, managers who are supposed to be looking out for evidence of specific behaviours when observing an assessment centre activity end up giving high scores to those candidates of whom they have formed a generally good impression, whatever specific behaviours are demonstrated. The result is an apparent preference on the part of managers to see the assessment centre as an extended interview or work sample rather than as a psychometric selection technique. The high validity may thus result as much from the period of time over which candidates are observed as from the combination of selection tools being used together.

According to IRS (1997d: 14–15), assessment centres are used for the selection of some staff by almost half of organisations. However, the extent of their usage increases very steeply with the size of employer (they are used by 75 per cent of organisations employing over 5,000 people, but only by 20 per cent of those employing fewer than 200 staff). There seems to be little variation between industrial sectors, most larger private- and public-sector organisations employing the assessment centre approach in the selection of managers, professional grades and new graduates. Furthermore, the IRS survey suggests that the use of the method is generally increasing, over 40 per cent of respondents claiming to have introduced assessment centres for the first time in the previous two years.

The fact that assessment centres are mainly used by larger organisations is not surprising when the costs associated with the development and running of an effective centre are considered. At the very least, the following activities have to be undertaken and either paid for directly or accounted for in terms of management time:

- analysis of the key competences required to perform the job in question

- the development of appropriate exercises to measure or permit observation of the competences

- the purchase of psychometric tests or other proprietary products to use at the assessment centre

- short-listing of applicants to be invited to the centre

- training of assessors and other employees actively involved in conducting the exercises

- food and accommodation at the centre for candidates and assessors

- the presence of senior managers to act as observers and interviewers

- the giving of meaningful feedback to successful and unsuccessful candidates

- evaluation and validation.

When it is considered that, to run an effective assessment centre it is necessary to have a candidate–assessor ratio of around 2:1, it is easy to see how the costs can mount up – especially when a number of centres are set up for the selection of different staff groups. For this reason, the approach is only really appropriate for the selection of individuals who fall into one or more of the following categories:

- people who will be employed in the most senior positions with large staffs to supervise or sizeable budgets to manage

- people who will be employed to undertake work which is absolutely crucial to the success of the organisation (perhaps jobs in which the making of errors has unusually important consequences)

- people (like graduates) who are expected to remain employed by the organisation for a long period and in whom significant investment will be made.

An advantage of assessment centres is their flexibility. They are not purchased 'off-the-shelf' like psychometric tests, and are not as time-restricted as interviews. There is therefore plenty of scope to introduce exercises that are of specific relevance to the job and the organisation involved. For this reason, each centre is likely to differ from others to a considerable degree. That said, there are a number of exercises and types of exercise that are associated with assessment centres and which are frequently included: these are now discussed.

In-tray exercises

A common exercise used in assessment centres is the in-tray or in-basket test. Here each candidate sits at a desk and is given a pile of documents to read through. The pile consists of a mixture of memos, letters, notes, telephone messages and other documents related to the job for which candidates attending the centre are applying. Participants are then given a limited amount of time to read the documents and state what action they would take in each situation. In some tests they are explicitly required to prioritise their actions by listing what they would do, and in what order, on an answer sheet.

The more sophisticated in-tray tests take place over a two- or three-hour period and require candidates to digest fairly complex written material before recommending courses of action. It is also possible for assessors to add extra pieces of paper to the in-tray and to take away completed work (the out-tray) at set time-intervals. A further variation involves instructing candidates to demonstrate writing skills by composing a letter or report in reaction to an item in the in-tray. In some centres, candidates are interviewed after completing the test to allow assessors to explore their thinking and the reasons for the decisions they have made.

In-tray exercises have a number of very useful functions. They are relatively straightforward to develop and can be undertaken by all candidates at the same time. However, their greatest advantage is the number of different competences they require candidates to demonstrate. According to Jansen and de Jongh (1997 :36), these include intelligence, interpersonal sensitivity, planning and organising ability, delegation skills, problem analysis, problem-solving ability and decisiveness. While the test requires candidates to give an indication of their interpersonal style and approach to dealing with colleagues and customers, it clearly does not directly test social skills such as assertiveness or a candidate's ability to negotiate effectively.

Group exercises
Interpersonal competence is usually tested by means of a variety of group exercises which a group of four or five candidates carry out together. A common approach is the 'leaderless' project, in which the group is given instructions to carry out a particular task and a time limit, but are left to decide for themselves how the project is to be tackled and who is to do what. The aim here is to allow assessors to observe how each candidate behaves in relation to the others. The kind of questions they will be looking for answers to are: Does someone take the lead? Does someone hold back but contribute effectively later? Does someone negotiate between opposing views? Is one candidate more persuasive than the others?

Some assessment centres give groups fairly involved tasks to complete, some of which resemble management games more commonly used for developmental purposes. In some cases the group is presented with a problem to which there is a definite right answer. The assessors then observe which of the candidates played the greatest part in reaching it, and how this was achieved. Other group exercises are open-ended, the instruction being simply to design or build something, to draw up a strategy or action plan, or to agree among themselves a common position on some issue. Often the group is then required to present their solution to the panel of assessors. Such exercises test creativity and the ability to present ideas confidently, as well as a wide range of interpersonal skills. An interesting feature of some group exercises is the use of the outdoors to allow for greater flexibility in the type of tasks the group is required to undertake.

Other group exercises differ in that candidates are, in turn, assigned leadership roles. The content of the tests is similar but the type of behaviours being observed are different, the emphasis being on how well and using which methods the leader motivates others, exercises effective control or delegates tasks. The difficulty with such approaches arises from the unavoidable presence of competition between candidates who are, after all, applying for the same job. To discourage other group members from undermining the 'leader' it is necessary to point out that other behaviours are also being observed (eg the ability to work as an effective team member).

Presentations

Most assessment centres also contain exercises that require candidates to make some kind of presentation or put a case to other participants and assessors. Again, these come in many different forms. At one extreme is the highly unpleasant exercise in which candidates are required to speak off-the-cuff for a few minutes on a subject, without notice. In turn they are simply given a subject and asked to respond immediately. Understandably, many find this very difficult and find themselves either waffling or drying up completely. At the other end of the scale are exercises that test the candidates' ability to make a longer and more considered presentation. Typically this approach involves giving each candidate some information to read – perhaps concerning a specific organisational problem – before explaining that they have a limited period of time to prepare a presentation.

Role-playing

A variety of assessment centre exercises employ the services of staff members to play roles of one kind or another. The classic exercise involves observing how a candidate deals with an irate customer, but there is no reason why other job-related scenarios should not be included. Role-playing is a good way of observing how effectively someone deals with subordinates in need of emotional support or effective counselling. It could also be used as a means of scoring candidates in terms of their ability to handle the disciplining of subordinates or negotiations with hard-bargaining suppliers. Another test that makes use of role-playing is the fact-finding exercise, in which candidates are given incomplete written information about an organisational problem. They then each have a limited time to question a role-player with a view to discovering the missing information. In some versions, the person playing the role is under instructions to be evasive or to challenge the line of questioning. According to Jansen and de Jongh (1997: 39), when properly designed, fact-finding exercises allow assessors to evaluate candidates in terms of their intelligence, thoroughness and decisiveness, as well as their interpersonal skills.

Other tests used include exercises requiring candidates to compile an extensive piece of written work in the form of a report, and all manner of problem-solving exercises carried out alone rather than in groups. Other organisation-specific exercises include some of the work-sample and trainability selection techniques identified above. Ideally, more than one exercise will be devised to test each of the key behaviours the assessment centre is concerned with identifying. The aim here is to reduce the extent to which situational factors may obscure a candidate's abilities. It is possible, for example, that one participant might appear to have poor skills of persuasion when observed carrying out a group activity, but will subsequently show considerable persuasive skills in giving a presentation. The more tests that are included to test each key attribute, the more chance there is of seeing the whole picture.

A common method used to demonstrate which exercises are testing which competences is the assessment centre matrix. An example is shown in Table 8.

Table 8 Barclays personnel procedures manual – sample assessment centre matrix

Competencies	Exercises						Total
	GE	IT	PRES	IV	OPQ	WR	
Analysis		X	X			X	3
Business awareness		X		X			2
Competitive	X			X	X		3
Decision-making	X	X					2
Drive/enthusiasm			X	X			2
Leadership	X				X		2
Oral communication	X		X				2
Written communication		X				X	2
Planning/organising		X			X		2
Interpersonal sensitivity	X			X	X		3
Achievement/motivation			X		X		2
Total	5	5	4	4	5	2	25

Key
GE = Group Exercise   OPQ = Occupational Personality Questionnaire
IT = In-Tray   IV = Interview
PRES = Presentation   WR = Written Report   IDS 1995

Assessment centres throw up particular issues concerning fairness. Aside from the need to ensure that equal opportunities law is complied with and that tests do not unfairly discriminate on grounds of sex, race or disability, there is also a potential problem of unfair bias towards candidates with relevant work experience. A special difficulty arises when internal as well as external candidates are present at the same assessment centre. There are two alternative approaches to coping with this:

• Take care to design exercises that are job-related but do not give a particular advantage to those with extensive knowledge of the job or the organisation.

• Retain the organisation-specific exercises while taking account of the advantages to internal and experienced candidates at the scoring stage.

The Civil Service Selection Board

The selection procedures for entry into the UK Civil Service 'fast-stream' are notoriously tough and rigorous. Around 80 per cent of applicants are turned down after the first stage on the basis of biodata analysis and performance in a series of mental ability tests sat at regional testing centres. Those who successfully negotiate these first hurdles are invited to a two-day assessment centre known as the Civil Service Selection Board (CSSB).

Before they arrive at the assessment centre, candidates are informed of the key qualities the service is looking for in new recruits. These include:

*   the ability to communicate effectively at all levels
*   a strong intellect coupled with common sense
*   the ability to think quantitatively
*   drive and determination
*   readiness to accept responsibility
*   awareness of the outside world.

In order to test for these qualities, the CSSB includes two group exercises: an in-tray exercise and a series of written tests which resemble Civil Service work. Candidates are required to assimilate information from several documents, make recommendations, summarise information, draft letters and participate in the running of a committee. At the end, each candidate is given three interviews: two with senior Civil Servants and one with a psychologist. Eight hundred candidates are invited to CSSBs each year. Of these, 22 per cent go on to the final stage in the selection procedure – a panel interview lasting approximately one hour.

Source: IDS (1995)

LEGAL ISSUES IN SELECTION

The principles of current discrimination law were explored in Chapter 6 in the context of recruiting employees. The basic issues – direct, indirect and positive discrimination, genuine occupational qualifications and the role of the statutory commissions – are the same in the field of employee selection. It is thus clearly unlawful to fail to select a well-qualified candidate who has performed well in the selection procedures on the grounds of sex, race, marital status or disability. At present, legal protection does not extend to cover direct discrimination in selection on grounds of age or sexual orientation, but it is very possible that this situation will change in the future as cases working their way through the legal system are decided. The most common example of potential indirect discrimination in employee selection is the presence of unintended bias against one gender or a racial group in the selection tools used. Great care must thus be taken when undertaking job analysis and formulating person specifications to omit any item that could be construed as favouring one group over another. The same rules apply in the design of application forms, the framing of interview questions and the content of reference request documentation. In these cases removing items that could be construed as being indirectly discriminatory is a relatively straightforward matter – it is a lot harder to evaluate the 'high-validity' selection methods discussed in this chapter. The extent to which, for example, a question in an aptitude test favours candidates with English as their first language is essentially a matter of opinion rather than a matter of fact. The same is true of biodata criteria, work samples and most assessment centre exercises. It is nevertheless important actively to give consideration to these matters so that particular questions or tests can be defended if legal action is taken. If in doubt, it is wise to consult your organisation's solicitors or legal department. ACAS may also be able to give advice on these issues.

The situation with personality and ability tests bought from suppliers is different, in so far as it is possible to ask, prior to purchase, whether or not the products have been tested among different groups and found to be free of unfair bias against those protected in law. Producers of the well-established tests should also be able to provide evidence that in practice they have been found not to discriminate unfairly. If it is not explicitly stated in the sales literature, it is wise to ask what evidence there is, from the experience of their use in other organisations, that sufficient numbers of women, members of ethnic minorities and disabled applicants are in fact selected. Larger organisations can undertake monitoring of this kind themselves.

FURTHER READING

- A number of texts cover all four of the selection methods discussed in this chapter as well as the legal and ethical issues. The most comprehensive are *Personnel Selection and Productivity* by Mark Cook (1993) and the book of articles edited by Peter Herriot entitled *A Handbook of Assessment in Organisations* (1989).

- Aside from coverage in these texts, the application of biodata in selection has received relatively little attention. An exception is two articles in the first issue of *Recruitment and Development Bulletin* (IRS 1990).

- There are numerous specialist texts and a great deal of academic literature covering psychological testing. In addition to coverage in the two general texts mentioned above, two useful and accessible books are *Psychological Testing: A manager's guide* (3rd edn) by Toplis, Dulewicz and Fletcher (1997) and *Understanding Psychological Testing* by Charles Jackson (1996). In addition, there is the (former) IPD's guide setting out recommended professional standards in the field of psychological testing (IPD 1997a).

- There are also two recent books that deal specifically with the subject of assessment centres. These are *Assessment Centres: Identifying and developing competence* by Charles Woodruffe (1993) and *Assessment Centres: A practical handbook* by Paul Jansen and Ferry de Jongh (1997).

- Readers seeking information about particular psychological tests are referred to the guides produced by the British Psychological Society. These are expensive but contain detailed and authoritative reviews of all personality and ability tests recommended by the society. Another useful and unbiased review of the major tests is contained in the article by Richard Bell in *Professional Issues in Selection and Assessment* edited by Mike Smith and Valerie Sutherland (1993).

- In 1994 each issue of *Personnel Management* contained an article about a commercially available selection test. These were written mainly by the test producers and cannot therefore be expected to be unbiased. However, they do provide a useful starting-point for personnel specialists exploring the possibility of using tests.

Part 5

PERFORMANCE

---

9 Raising our game

Reducing the incidence of poor performance, and improving organisational performance generally, is one of the key priorities for any P&D function. It is a complex process with no easy solutions, which has generated a vast literature exploring all manner of approaches used to enhance both individual and collective performance. The aim of this chapter is to give an overview of the subject and to put forward a number of distinct approaches that can be used by P&D managers in seeking to improve performance. In Chapter 10 attention turns to performance appraisal systems and in Chapter 11 to the specific issue of absence management. The role of training and development, payment arrangements and employee involvement in enhancing performance levels are recognised, but are covered in less detail than is the case in other books in the series (see Marchington and Wilkinson 1996, Armstrong 1996, Harrison 1997 and Gennard and Judge 1997).

In this chapter the objective is to address in quite general terms the following question:

What options are open to an organisation seeking to improve the performance of its employees?

One answer is to take what Levinson (1973) referred to as an 'asinine' perspective of the employment relationship and to motivate members of staff as one would a donkey, using on the one hand the carrot and on the other the stick – that is to say, a mixture of incentives and disincentives. While both these approaches have a part to play, it is important also to recognise that employees are many times more sophisticated than donkeys, and that other strategies are also available for adoption. In particular, it is necessary to give consideration to the underlying causes of limited performance levels and to what might be done to address these. There is also a place for the use of effective negotiation and coaching skills.

By the end of this chapter readers should be able to:

- evaluate the principal methods for managing performance
- advise on their benefits and shortcomings in particular situations
- set up systems for measuring and obtaining data on performance.

In addition, readers should be able to understand and explain:

- different definitions of the term 'performance management'
- the potential role of job redesign, teamworking, counselling, negotiation, discipline, persuasion and reward in improving performance.

DEFINING PERFORMANCE MANAGEMENT

The term 'performance management', like a number that make up the language of P&D work, is used in a variety of different ways. Two particular definitions, however, stand out that are rather different and can thus easily cause confusion. First, the term can be used as a general description of the various management processes by which standards of performance are addressed at both the individual and organisational level. In this guise, 'performance management' would cover the wide range of techniques used to raise performance standards, including the use of disciplinary or punitive sanctions. A similar term that has appeared in recent literature and which also reflects a broad perspective on the topic is 'high-performance working'. The second definition, by contrast, is a good deal narrower and is used to describe one specific approach to the raising of performance standards. Armstrong's definition is as follows:

> Performance management is about getting better results from the organisation, teams and individuals by understanding and managing performance within an agreed framework of planned goals, standards and competence requirements. It is a process for establishing shared understanding about what is to be achieved, and an approach to managing and developing people in a way which increases the probability that it will be achieved in the short and long term.
>
> Armstrong (1995: 429)

Under the second definition, 'performance management' thus refers to the use of objective-setting and performance reviews via employee appraisal – one of a range of possible approaches that can be used in managing for improved performance. For the purposes of this book, the first definition broadly covers the material that is presented in this chapter, and the second, that covered in Chapter 10.

OBTAINING DATA ABOUT PERFORMANCE

Fundamental to any programme aimed at improving standards of performance is some form of judgement about how an individual employee or team of employees is currently performing. Inevitably this involves devising, however informally, some kind of rating system so that a conclusion can be made as to how far below the expected or optimum standard an individual or team's performance can be judged to be. Measurement then provides the means by which performance improvements are later tracked. It thus forms the cornerstone of any management process aimed at raising standards.

The great problem, of course, arises from the fact that some aspects of performance are more readily measured than others. Moreover, it may be that the most important are those that can be measured only in a subjective way. As a result, there is a danger that judgements about individual or group performance are largely made on the basis of information that is easily quantifiable and that can be collected with a degree of objectivity. Hence, there is a reliance on output measures of one kind or another to judge overall performance, with the result that employees strive to achieve only those quantifiable goals. The results are often damaging, as the following quotation suggests:

> There are countless organisations where the totality of individual performance measures serves to undermine, rather than enhance, corporate performance. We have all seen examples of organisations in which production staff are measured primarily on the basis of output (regardless of quality), sales staff are measured primarily on the basis of orders taken (regardless of whether the order can be met), managers are measured primarily on the basis of reducing costs (regardless of the long-term impact on performance) – and at the end of it all the organisation proclaims itself a 'total quality company'!
>
> Walters (1995: 18)

The opposite effect can also easily occur, whereby a level of achievement, although deemed poor when measured crudely, was actually a good performance given the environment in which it was achieved. Hence, a director who presides over a year in which corporate profit levels fell may in fact have presided over a good set of figures given the background of a general economic downturn. Similarly, a police force may actually have performed reasonably well despite the fact that crime in its area rose if that rise merely reflected an increase in the number of reported incidents.

It can thus be concluded that too simplistic an approach to the measurement of performance is generally unwise. This is not to say that measures of output or results are irrelevant, but that there is also a need to focus on how they were achieved in order to encourage employees to go about meeting their objectives in a manner that serves the long-term interests of the organisation. A mixture of measures thus needs to be considered when evaluating the level of performance. Some will be output-focused, systematic and quantifiable, while others will be more subjective, focused on processes rather than results and less easily quantified. The following are output-based measures that are characterised by varying degrees of objectivity, but that can claim to be systematic to some degree: productivity measures, quality measures, and objectives set and met.

Productivity measures
These simply involve assessing an individual's or team's ability to achieve or exceed production targets. In a normal manufacturing

operation, it is a question merely of measuring the number of products or parts that individuals produce in a given period of time. Comparisons are then made over time and between different individuals or teams to establish what level of productivity is considered acceptable and hence what level is deemed to be either excellent or poor. Where the quality of products is relatively unimportant, such as in the case of products that are very simple and are to be sold cheaply, crude measures of performance such as these may be applicable. However, in most cases there is also a need to introduce a quality-control element as well so as to ensure that efficiency is not achieved at the expense of poor workmanship and the production of unreliable goods. Hence it is the number of products manufactured of acceptable quality that is measured when productivity rates are calculated. Productivity measurement is of course not restricted only to manufacturing operations. The speed with which tasks are completed to required quality standards is a feature of many different kinds of operation – indeed, there is an element of efficiency in most. Examples from the service sector would be the number of customers that a check-out operator deals with in a busy supermarket, the number of trains that arrive at their destination on time and the number of school meals that are cooked and served in a given period of time. In all these cases, as in countless others, measurement is relatively straightforward, with the result that cost comparisons can be made between different units, teams or individuals.

Quality measures
While the measurement of quality is often more subjective than is the case with productivity, there are approaches available that increase the level of objectivity. First of all, it is possible to draw up a set of criteria that defines different levels of product quality. Examples of such approaches include the methods used to assess teaching standards in schools and colleges, the star rating for hotels or the standard of service provided in first- and standard-class trains and aeroplanes. An assessor then uses his or her judgement to determine how far the established criteria are being met and hence the relative level of performance being achieved.

A common approach to performance evaluation where some objective measure of quality is needed involves surveying customer opinion. This can be done by means of a questionnaire sent to a cross-section of customers or through the employment of telephone canvassers. Where one individual provides the main contact point between the organisation and its clients, the enquiry can focus on the individual's performance as on well as that of the organisation as a whole. Examples include many sales staff, people employed to maintain and service equipment, and a range of business-service providers. In the case of retail, garage, transport, tourism and catering services, it is common for organisations to undertake spot-checks on individual units by employing assessors to visit premises periodically in the guise of customers. Here too, while there is clearly an element of subjectivity in the judgements reached, standard training and the provision of quality check-lists can both bring some objectivity and permit comparisons to be made between individual units.

Objectives set and met

The third approach to evaluation is that which forms the basis of many performance appraisal systems and is covered in greater detail in Chapter 10. This involves judging performance according to the extent to which agreed objectives have been met over a set period of time by an individual job-holder, a team of employees or a division of the organisation. There is a strong element of objectivity, because it is usually quite clear whether or not specific objectives have been achieved. However, problems arise where environmental circumstances or the actions of others have had a role in preventing their achievement. In deciding how to rate the performance, it is thus necessary for the assessor to determine how far a failure to meet a specific performance objective was, in fact, avoidable.

The advantage of goal-setting approaches to the measurement of performance over straight productivity and quality assessments is the wide range of jobs that can be encompassed in the system. While many job roles do not specifically have measurable efficiency or quality outcomes, there are few for which some objectives cannot be set and then worked towards over the course of six months or a year.

> Which of the above approaches to measurement would be suitable as a means of evaluating your performance in your current job? How far would such methods enable a fair performance rating to be determined?

BEHAVIOUR-ORIENTED APPROACHES

Many commentators and writers have argued that the above approaches, while neatly quantifiable, do not permit a balanced assessment of an individual employee's performance. Instead, they argue that *behaviour* needs to be assessed as much as outcomes. In other words, it is argued that the processes by which achievements are reached are as important as the achievements themselves. Indeed, some go as far as to argue that the behaviours exhibited by employees should form the whole basis of performance assessments, and that outputs or results should thus be looked at only indirectly (eg Levinson 1976, Murphy and Cleveland 1995). This, it is argued, permits a more just rating of employees and more constructive approaches to be devised when considering how performance can be improved; it is fairer, because it focuses on what individuals actually do, thus removing environmental factors and the input of others from the assessment. Where only results or objectives achieved are considered, it is not always easy to take account of such distortions. Focusing on employee behaviour and how job tasks are achieved also provides a firmer basis for discussing possible approaches to improving the performance standard.

However, employee behaviour, unlike the results-oriented approaches, is less readily measured. As a result, conclusions concerning performance standards have to be reached without the aid of quantifiable data. Instead, supervisors have to use their own judgement in reaching a balanced verdict. The main methods used are thus direct observation of the employee at work and the reports of others (peers, subordinates, suppliers, customers etc) who have observed the employee at work. As with outcome-focused methods, a number of different approaches is used: rating scales, critical incidents and reactive approaches.

Rating scales

The most systematic behavioural assessments involve rating scales to judge the performance of individual employees over a set period of time. Typically, they will involve Likert scales, with aspects of behaviour that have been agreed to be significant determinants of overall performance scored on a five-point scale. The criteria vary from job to job, but often include scales such as those illustrated in Table 9.

Table 9 **A five-point rating scale**

	Excellent	Very Good	Good	Average	Poor
Timekeeping					
Appearance					
Communication skills					
Relationship with subordinates					
Relationship with senior staff					
Organisation skills					

Carrell *et al* (1995: 359–360) argue that, in the case of performance measurement, judgements can be made more valid with the use of non-graphic rating scales. Here, instead of the supervisor's rating employees as 'excellent', 'good' or 'poor' in respect of an aspect of their behaviour, a series of alternative phrases is provided. The supervisor then chooses the most applicable or appropriate. In the case of personal appearance, this might mean choosing one of the following five options:

• frequently untidy and scruffily dressed

• occasionally untidy and careless about appearance

• generally neatly dressed

• careful about personal appearance

• impeccable appearance and standard of dress.

The advantage of non-graphic scoring is its tendency to reduce the degree to which value judgements are subjective. Although two or more assessors might disagree about what constitutes 'good' appearance, when presented with descriptive phrases such as these they are more likely to agree on how to rate an individual's appearance. This occurs not least because the factors they are expected to consider in reaching a judgement are implied in the phrases themselves.

Critical incidents

An alternative approach is to focus on actual occurrences to evaluate individual performance. Here, instead of making general judgements about different aspects of an employee's work, attention is focused on incidents that have occurred during the review period that form examples of particularly good or particularly poor performance. It is best if these are recorded at the time, because some that may be significant will inevitably be forgotten or only half-remembered when a formal performance review is held some months after the event. Using this method, the effectiveness of a supervisor's relationships with subordinates, for example, would be judged not in the round or on the basis of a general impression, but with reference to specific episodes that reveal strengths or weaknesses. Occasions when subordinates complained about their supervisor's behaviour, or when someone left citing unfair treatment as a reason, would thus be considered as negative critical incidents. On the other hand, examples of inspired leadership under difficult circumstances, or of occasions when poor working relationships had been improved through the intervention of the supervisor, would be recorded as positive critical incidents.

Although the critical incident approach makes it possible to measure performance quantifiably, its real purpose is to analyse job performance so that measures to improve it can be put in place. It does this by drawing employees' attention to aspects of their performance that are especially effective or that are regarded by the organisation as poor. The employee, with the support of the organisation, can then take steps to increase the number of positive incidents and reduce the number that are recorded as negative.

Reactive approaches

While there are advantages in terms of fairness and consistency in using formal and systematic approaches to gathering data about employee performance, in many cases it is necessary to act quickly in response to particular events. Rather than waiting until a formal review to discuss and put right negative critical incidents or other unsatisfactory aspects of job performance, matters have to be dealt with more swiftly. In such cases, the information is gathered and conclusions reached about aspects of performance in a less systematic manner. Often the process starts as a result of an observation made by a supervisor, but an individual may also be investigated following a report from another member of staff, a supplier or a customer. In other cases, evidence of unsatisfactory performance is discovered by chance through overhearing a conversation or stumbling across documents that make it clear that certain performance standards have not been, or are not being, met. The result is a meeting with the person or persons whose actions have resulted in poor performance. Although in some situations this will involve holding a disciplinary hearing, there is in any case a need to check all salient facts before taking any action. Particular care must be taken when information concerning individual poor performance is obtained from fellow employees or some other source that may be questionable (see the boxed text on 'Information gathered through surveillance').

Which of the above methods of collecting data about employee performance is used in your organisation? In your experience, what are their advantages and disadvantages?

Information gathered through surveillance

An interesting and potentially disturbing issue that arises from the installation of new technologies in workplaces is their potential use in monitoring employee performance. For some time now, closed-circuit TV cameras have been installed in premises for security purposes. It is not difficult to see how they could also be employed to survey staff at work and then used as a source of evidence against an employee whose performance is alleged to be inadequate. Indeed, it is likely that the installation of security cameras pointed at reception desks or other workplaces will result in slackness or unprofessional conduct being spotted by supervisors. New telecommunications technology also permits employers to eavesdrop on employee telephone calls, thus catching employees who are using telephones for private purposes or who are spending too long dealing with routine matters.

It can be argued that such means of gathering information about performance standards amount to an invasion of privacy, particularly when carried out without telling employees that they may be subject to surveillance of this kind. To avoid such accusations there is a need to draw up guidelines or formal policy statements setting out exactly how and when new technologies will be used for performance surveillance purposes. It is also probably unwise to rely solely on data gathered in this way when taking formal action against any employee – even where poor performance is discovered by chance and not as a result of systematic attempts to check on staff in their places of work.

IMPROVING PERFORMANCE THROUGH NEGOTIATION

Having established where and how far performance falls below desirable and achievable levels, the next step is to consider what can be done to raise it. A number of different strategies are available, some of which require greater effort and expense than others. One of the most common in situations where collective employee performance needs to be improved is the negotiation of improvements with workforce representatives. Such approaches are most commonly associated with collective bargaining and trade unions, but are equally applicable wherever the desired performance improvement requires the consent and co-operation of a team of employees. Negotiation is also the approach used where people are employed on a sub-contracted basis.

In a unionised setting the most common manifestation of negotiation as a means of enhancing performance is productivity bargaining. This occurs when the management side wishes to reorganise working systems or organisational structures in order to facilitate efficiency improvements. In order to achieve this, formal negotiating meetings are then held in order to secure staff-side agreement. Provided negotiations do not break down, the result is a settlement that brings satisfactory benefit to both sides. The union agrees to some or all of the proposed changes in return for concessions in other areas or some form of compensation. A common example would be a negotiation that resulted in base-pay rises in return for greater flexibility in the way that work is organised and carried out. However, increased remuneration is not necessarily an outcome. It is possible that employee representatives will see advantages in the proposals and that they will agree to the changes on the understanding, for example, that additional training is given or that aspects of work organisation or workplace rules of which they disapprove are replaced.

Negotiated solutions can also operate in less formal ways. For example, where a small team of clerical workers is employed to manage a body of work, it is often the case that the most fruitful means of introducing efficiency savings is to negotiate some form of gain-sharing deal. Suggestions as to how work could be organised more productively or the quality of service improved are then brought forward, team members themselves often being the main source of ideas. A new remuneration package is then developed and offered to the team. If it is accepted as a fair deal, the changes are introduced. If it is rejected, managers will consider whether or not to offer an improved package. The same kind of process is equally applicable in the case of individual employees whose performance could be improved were established forms of working to be altered.

Where collective bargaining is not the established mechanism for introducing change into a workplace, negotiated performance improvements are most suited to situations in which there are difficulties in recruiting and retaining good people. Seen purely in cost terms, it will usually be less expensive to impose changes on employees, management determining any compensation changes unilaterally. Where such approaches are likely to lead to high turnover, and particularly to the resignation of individuals with valuable organisation-specific skills, bargaining in some shape or form is necessary. By giving employees a degree of control over changes in working arrangements and involving them in determining any compensatory settlement, the likelihood of resistance, demotivation and significant resignations is greatly reduced.

IMPROVING PERFORMANCE THROUGH PERSUASION

A very different approach, also relevant in the case both of individuals and groups of employees, involves seeking to persuade or encourage employees to raise performance standards without directly compensating them for their efforts – at least in the short term. The term 'persuasion' in this context is used in an entirely positive way, and is associated with the techniques and skills of effective leadership and coaching. At root, the approach is based on an acceptance of the assumptions concerning human motivation at work described by Douglas Macgregor (1960) as 'Theory Y', whose proponents hold that people are naturally drawn to hard work and responsibility. It thus follows that, if encouraged and given opportunities, people will seek to contribute to the achievement of organisational goals. Macgregor contrasted this with another philosophy of motivation, Theory X, which assumes the average employee to be lazy and liable to avoid work or responsibility. The implication is that staff will not perform to a higher standard without coercion or compensation.

Effective coaching is often explained with reference to the motivation of sportsmen and -women. For many, it is primarily defined as a training and development activity through which skills and knowledge are imparted. However, it can also be seen simply as a form of communication or as a set of diverse activities which all aim to bring out the best in people. According to Kalinauckas and King (1994), the key features of effective coaching include the following:

- active listening

- questioning

- giving praise and recognition

- building rapport

- creating trust

- being non-judgemental

- being candid and challenging

- giving encouragement and support

- focusing on future opportunities.

A good coach thus avoids subjective judgements and criticism. Instead, individual work performance is reviewed constructively and enthusiastically, with a focus on future activities.

Effective leadership often encompasses coaching skills but is generally accepted as having other characteristics too. Writers tend to have different conceptions of what exactly constitutes good leadership, some stressing the significance of qualities acquired (eg Makin *et al* 1989) and others putting the emphasis on innate personality traits (Atwater *et al* 1991). This debate serves to illustrate that successful leadership can come in a variety of shapes and sizes, and that what may be highly appropriate in one situation may actually be ineffective in another. This is recognised by Bernard Bass (1990), who distinguishes between 'transactional leadership' and 'transformational leadership', and argues that the latter is becoming increasingly relevant in the current business environment. Whereas transactional leaders set objectives and administer a mixture of rewards and penalties to ensure that performance standards are reached, transformational leaders 'broaden and elevate the interests of their employees, generate awareness and acceptance of the purposes and mission of the group and stir their employees to look beyond their own self-interest for the good of the group'. Research carried out by Bass suggests that it is possible to identify four key characteristics shared by transformational leaders:

- charisma (provides vision and a sense of mission, instils pride, gains respect and trust)

- inspiration (communicates high expectations, uses symbols to focus efforts, expresses important purposes in simple ways)

- intellectual stimulation (promotes intelligence, rationality and careful problem-solving)

- individualised consideration (gives personal attention, treats each employee individually, coaches, advises).

As a practical proposition for raising performance standards, the use of persuasive approaches has many attractions. Where carried out effectively, the result is a highly motivated and committed staff capable of sustaining over a prolonged period standards of performance superior to those of competitors. It is thus unsurprising that much recent management literature contains many examples of business success stories brought about through the efforts of charismatic leaders and the development of 'coaching cultures'. However, that does not mean that a strategy of persuasion is universally applicable or that it will always succeed in raising levels of performance. For a start, it is necessary to recognise that truly effective leaders and coaches are a relatively rare breed. Even if it is accepted that theirs are acquirable skills, they are not the kind that can be picked up in a short time or simply by attending training courses. Organisations may thus be unable to adopt persuasive approaches because existing managers and supervisors do not have the ability or the inclination to manage people in that way. Over a period, cultures can be changed and new management techniques introduced, but these inevitably take a good deal of time to bed down and start producing results.

In addition, as Makin, Cooper and Cox (1989: 74–75) point out, there are very real difficulties in introducing approaches to management that derive from Macgregor's Theory Y when the assumptions that underlie Theory X have governed management and employee expectations for a long time. In their view, a shift away from a situation in which people expect to be told what to do to one in which they are encouraged to take their own decisions and solve their own problems can easily lead to a 'period of considerable confusion and a resulting drop in levels of performance'. Consequently, the organisation finds itself with no alternative but to re-introduce methods based on the administration of rewards and penalties. It is probably wise to conclude that, as a means of improving standards, persuasion is attractive in principle and in theory, but may not be achievable in practice for many organisations. Where over a period of time, employees develop the capacity to lead and coach effectively (and to be led and coached), such a strategy can be relied on to drive standards upwards. In other situations there will be a need to adopt other approaches too.

IMPROVING PERFORMANCE THROUGH DISCIPLINE

The use of punitive measures to improve standards of performance is

> What other problems can you think of which might act as barriers to the use of persuasive approaches to performance management? How might they be overcome?

unfashionable at present and thus tends to be covered in management literature in mainly critical terms. It is seen nowadays as a necessary evil, used where low-trust relationships persist or where other approaches have failed. It is thus portrayed as symbolic of poor or ineffective management. Criticisms go beyond a condemnation of arbitrary punishment or of disciplinary measures applied indiscriminately without proper procedures being followed. It is, for example, pointed out that discipline often has little effect on individual standards of performance, because it fails to address the root causes of the problem. Hence, where the poor performance arises because of a personality clash or problems in the employee's personal life, any number of disciplinary sanctions will not lead to improvements. The other main criticism relates to the de-motivating effects of disciplinary action, both on the individual employee who is disciplined and on other employees who may perceive such treatment as iniquitous. While it is agreed that punitive sanctions can effectively deter slackness or carelessness on the part of employees, it is also argued that their overall effect is more damaging in the long term. Applying disciplinary measures, it is said, lowers trust and demotivates employees, leading to less commitment and higher staff turnover.

Although it is correct to argue that a performance management system based entirely on the threat of disciplinary action would be inappropriate for any organisation seeking to succeed in the late-twentieth-century business environment, it is also reasonable to assert that discipline still has an important role to play. It is for this reason that an IRS survey carried out in 1995 found that every one of its respondents had a written disciplinary procedure and that, on average, 5 per cent of employees faced some form of disciplinary action each year. Furthermore, the survey found that the most common 'offences' that led to the application of disciplinary sanctions were poor records in absence, performance and timekeeping. In other words, basic performance issues were more frequently dealt with through the use of disciplinary measures than conduct issues such as fighting, alcohol and drug abuse, swearing, theft or infringements of health and safety regulations (IRS 1995a: 4–5).

A number of arguments can be advanced in favour of the use of discipline as a remedy for poor performance. The first is very practical and relates to the significance that UK industrial tribunals now give to procedural questions when judging cases of unfair dismissal. The requirement that employees who are dismissed either on grounds of ordinary misconduct or poor performance have received two or three formal warnings before dismissal has created a situation in which employers feel it necessary to discipline any employee who might ultimately be dismissed on account of poor work performance. As a result, the prudent P&D manager who wishes to avoid having to appear before a tribunal and possibly lose a case tends to ensure that disciplinary action is taken whenever a serious individual performance problem materialises. Even when there is no clear expectation of a dismissal and when other approaches are considered more appropriate as potential remedies, formal oral or written warnings are thus issued.

The second argument in favour of disciplinary approaches is based on the notion that the assumptions underlying Macgregor's Theory X have some validity. In other words, it can be argued that some staff in certain organisations and at certain times are essentially uncommitted to their work and liable to minimise the amount of effort they expend in performing it. These employees come to work because they need to and not because they want to. They are thus often unresponsive to positive, coaching-based techniques of performance management and respond only when faced either with the threat of punitive action or some form of pecuniary incentive. Where the latter cannot be afforded, employers are left with no choice but to employ disciplinary approaches.

For the benefits of such approaches to be maximised and the long-term motivational drawbacks minimised, there is a need to ensure that disciplinary measures are applied in a fair and reasonable manner. Arbitrary punishment and perceived unfairness in the way different groups of employees are treated has the effect only of reducing staff morale and hence the general level of commitment.

Furthermore, where there is no clear link between poor performance and the taking of specific disciplinary action, any deterrent effect is greatly reduced. It is therefore wise to heed the principles discussed below in managing disciplinary policies and practices.

Established procedures should be followed

Procedural issues are covered in greater detail in Chapter 14 in the context of dismissal. It is thus necessary simply to state here that an organisation's disciplinary procedure should always be followed to ensure that all employees are treated consistently. Disciplinary procedures should be explained to new employees and be available in written form for them to see so that no one can claim to be ignorant of their contents at a later stage. Moreover, in the context of performance standards, procedures should always make provision for employees to improve by requiring a number of warning stages before dismissal is considered.

Disciplinary sanctions should be appropriate

In choosing the penalty or punishment to be administered, it is important to ensure that it is neither too harsh nor too lenient. The former risks engendering feelings of injustice or even victimisation, while the latter reduces the power of any subsequent deterrent effect.

It should be remembered that a wide range of possible disciplinary sanctions are available to employers aside from threatening, or carrying out, dismissal. Others include demotion, withholding promotion, changes in responsibilities, the removal of perks or privileges, reductions in bonus or incentive payments and delaying access to training courses. Furthermore, in all cases it is always open to employers either to impose a temporary sanction or simply to warn the employee concerned that a failure to improve standards of performance may lead to taking one or more of the actions mentioned above.

Discipline should be constructive in intent

It is important to remember that the purpose of disciplinary action is corrective and not simply punitive. The aim of any formal disciplinary hearing or informal meeting to discuss poor performance should thus not just be to listen to the two sides of an argument before reaching a decision about the sanctions that will be applied. Instead a good deal of attention has to be given to counselling and to agreeing measures designed to ensure that standards improve in the future. It is also important that the whole tone of disciplinary actions is constructive. Carrell *et al* (1995: 704) put the case for positive approaches very succinctly:

> Positive discipline corrects unsatisfactory employee behaviour through support, respect and people-oriented leadership. The purpose of positive discipline is to help rather than harass the employee. Positive discipline is not an attempt to soft-pedal or sidestep an employee problem. Rather, it is a management philosophy that assumes that improved employee behaviour is most likely to be long lived when discipline is administered without revenge, abuse or vindictiveness.

For this reason, as Alan Fowler (1996b: 42) points out, it is important for P&D specialists to learn the skills associated with the effective handling of disciplinary matters. In particular, there is a need to develop the ability to control formal disciplinary interviews so as to ensure that they do not simply become occasions for supervisors and subordinates to trade mutual recriminations. Above all, any formal disciplinary hearing must end with an agreed framework for the acceptance by all concerned of future action. It is not only important in itself that disciplinary measures are constructive; it is also important in case the matter ultimately leads to dismissal, because the nature of the discipline sanctioned will be considered by an industrial tribunal in its evaluation of an employer's actions.

> In your view, for which forms of poor individual performance are disciplinary approaches most suitable? For which are they most poorly suited?

IMPROVING PERFORMANCE THROUGH REWARD

The use of financial incentives and bonuses of one sort or another for raising performance levels of individual employees and teams has a long history. Interest has grown in recent years with the development of profit-related pay schemes and the extension of individual performance-related incentives to a larger number of employees. The use of payment to raise performance standards has already been discussed in the context of negotiated settlements. Moreover, the whole issue is covered in far greater detail in other books in this series (see Marchington and Wilkinson 1996, Armstrong 1996). The aim here is therefore to draw readers' attention to the availability of the approach and to the possibility of using non-monetary rewards as part of a strategy to improve performance.

Strategies that make use of reward systems to raise standards of performance are based on the kind of assumptions of human motivation described by Vroom (1964) in his expectancy-valence theory. Quite simply, the theory suggests that people take rational decisions when choosing which course of action they will follow, and that their decision is influenced primarily by their perception of which course will deliver most by way of reward. In the field of performance management the relevant decisions include the following:

- the decision to come to work in the morning
- the decision to come into work on time
- the decision to put in extra effort
- the decision to complete work that is dull rather than moving on to more interesting activities
- the decision to stay late at work to complete a project
- the decision to persevere in building effective working relationships with difficult colleagues.

It follows that employers can influence decisions of this kind by manipulating their remuneration systems. Hence we see examples of all manner of bonus systems that tie salary levels and incentive payments to the achievement of performance outcomes and forms of employee behaviour.

Careful design of payment systems has an important role to play in managing performance through reward, but it is not the only method that can be adopted. Indeed, in some areas (as is shown in Chapter 11, in which the problem of absence is considered), rewarding good performance with cash appears to have only a limited chance of success. It is therefore wise to consider other forms of reward too.

Psychologists traditionally categorise work-based rewards as either 'extrinsic' or 'intrinsic'. Extrinsic rewards are external to the job and tend to be tangible. They therefore include various forms of payment, along with fringe benefits, promotion and the various trappings that tend to accompany advancement up organisational hierarchies (bigger offices and cars, newer computers, larger expense accounts etc). All of these have a potential role in influencing employees to improve performance levels and to increase the amount of effort they expend at work. Intrinsic rewards, by contrast, are fundamentally inherent to the job and thus tend to be less tangible. Intrinsic motivation is also more difficult to define than extrinsic, with the result that different writers conceive of it in slightly different ways. However, according to Shamir (1991: 152), there are two basic underlying concepts that are generally accepted:

- intrinsic motivation stems from the expected pleasure of the activity rather than from the results

- intrinsic motivation is based on self-administered rewards rather than on rewards administered by an external agent.

He goes on to argue that intrinsic rewards are fundamentally concerned with the enhancement of self-esteem and self-worth. They thus involve the development of feelings of influence, purpose, achievement and competence – all of which are brought about through different experiences and behaviours in different people. What leads to increased self-esteem in one person may have little or no effect on another. It follows that managers can do no more than encourage the achievement of intrinsic rewards. By their very nature, they cannot be administered to someone by someone else (as is, by contrast, the case with extrinsic motivation). However, that does not mean that specific actions cannot be taken, because it is possible for employees to be 'rewarded' with opportunities to gain intrinsic rewards. Examples would include giving an employee greater responsibility or a higher level of control over his or her own work. Alternatively, developmental opportunities can be conferred in the form of access to training or through involvement with new projects.

It can also be argued that some forms of extrinsic reward have in fact a positive effect on intrinsic motivation. This is particularly true of praise, which is administered extrinsically but which can have its greatest impact in increasing people's feelings of self-worth. Similar claims can be made on behalf of formal schemes run by employers to recognise exceptional individual performance. In such cases, as with all actions designed to enhance intrinsic motivation, it must be remembered that the nature of the impact varies from individual to individual. It thus follows that managers seeking to improve performance through intrinsic rewards will be successful only if their action is appropriate for the particular employee concerned. Heaping praise on individuals, however genuine the sentiment, will motivate some to strive for even greater improvements in performance, while others may regard it as either patronising or inadequate. Similarly, some of those chosen as 'employee of the month' and rewarded by having their photograph displayed in a public place will enjoy increased feelings of self-esteem, while others will find the experience embarrassing and ultimately demotivating. Similar judgements have to be made when deciding how to balance recognition of effective team performance with recognition of specific employees who form part of the team. Some individuals will resent having their own achievements reflected in a team-based reward, while others will prefer that to being singled out for special recognition.

However, there are clear difficulties associated with rewarding different employees in different ways for good performance. These result from the possibility that one individual or group may perceive the action as inequitable and thus demotivating. Hence, formally recognising outstanding performance by one employee – by, for example, mentioning it in a corporate newsletter or team brief – while not giving the same reward to another, equally good, performer may very well lead to feelings of unfairness on this other team member's part. There are thus limits to how far it is possible to reward different personality types in different ways. The sensible approach is to take a very pragmatic, common-sense line in such situations by making sure that all good performance is recognised, even though in some cases it is done more publicly than in others. Perhaps the best way forward in such situations is simply to ask the employee concerned whether he or she wishes to have outstanding achievements made public or not.

In what ways does your organisation formally reward staff who perform exceptionally well? Which of these would you define as extrinsic and which as intrinsic?

IMPROVING PERFORMANCE THROUGH WORK DESIGN

Another approach that draws on notions of intrinsic motivation involves improving performance through the judicious design and redesign of jobs. It is based on the idea that employees achieve higher levels of motivation, satisfaction and performance if the jobs they do are made more interesting and challenging. The approach thus goes a great deal further than simply seeking to reward people for performing well: it involves finding ways of adjusting the whole working environment so as to make all jobs in an organisation as intrinsically motivating as possible.

In practical terms, the main vehicles for achieving this are job rotation, job enlargement and job enrichment. In each case, jobs are redesigned so as to make them less monotonous. Job rotation, for example, involves training employees to undertake a variety of jobs in an organisation so that different groups of tasks are performed on different days, weeks or months. In a manufacturing plant the rotation is likely to be daily or weekly, so that each employee works on different pieces of machinery and takes responsibility for different parts of the production process at different times. In other environments, perhaps where jobs take somewhat longer to learn, the rotation may be organised on a six-monthly or yearly basis. In each case the aim is to reduce the likelihood that people undertaking routine tasks become bored and uninterested in their work.

The use of job enlargement and job enrichment to improve workforce motivation are chiefly associated with the work of Frederick Herzberg (1966, 1968). Both approaches were defined as ones by which employees were given a wider variety of tasks to undertake, but in the case of job enrichment these required the acquisition of a higher level of skill. Hence, in addition to making jobs more interesting, enrichment also opens up wider developmental and career opportunities. Further, work carried out by Eric Trist and others (eg Trist *et al* 1963) led to the evolution of the socio-technical systems perspective on job enrichment, which sought to identify the key features needed in a job if it is to be motivating. In addition to a requirement for interesting work with opportunities for development and advancement, they stressed the importance of decision-making autonomy and discretion over the way the work is organised. The implication is that the less overt control is exercised over employees at work, the more motivated they will be and the higher their standard of performance will be.

According to Buchanan (1982), job enrichment had something of an 'unhappy history' in the 1960s and 1970s, with far more interest shown in its possibilities by academic researchers than by managers in organisations. However, in recent years interest has grown substantially, so that it is now very common to hear managers talking about empowering employees, developing new work roles, multi-skilling their workforces and refashioning reporting structures. Total Quality Management (TQM), a fashionable management philosophy of the 1980s and 1990s, also draws on many of these assumptions with its emphasis on self-supervision and the 'flattening' of management hierarchies. It is probably still the case that the rhetoric is more common than the reality, but the ideas that underpin job enrichment theories are now accepted with a great deal less scepticism than was the case 15 or 20 years ago.

In what ways could your job be enlarged or enriched? How far would this increase your level of motivation, and why?

Improving the performance of P&D managers

In May 1997, *People Management* magazine distributed a questionnaire for readers to fill in and return entitled 'What makes people work harder?' The questions asked readers about their working environment and, more specifically, about the intensity and time commitment required in their jobs. Over 3,000 people responded, and preliminary results were published in July 1997. Among the conclusions reached by the team analysing the responses was that P&D specialists are motivated most when they perceive that their role is meaningful. In this they differ from other groups who have been studied, notably salespeople, who have been found to have a strong need for 'psychological safety' in the form of support, clarity of objectives and recognition from managers. The survey findings suggest that these features do not have to be created by managers in order to motivate P&D people, because they emerge naturally from the work itself. Clear direction from senior managers, praise and backing for the decisions they take are thus not likely to improve P&D performance to any great extent. Instead the emphasis should be on enhancing the perception that the role is meaningful by ensuring that P&D job-holders feel that they are key members of the organisation and that they are not taken for granted. A perception that the work is demanding also appears to be important in enhancing motivation.

Source: McHenry (1997)

One method of altering work arrangements to improve efficiency and quality that has of late received a great deal of attention is team-working. The approach is derived from Japanese management practices and involves giving autonomous or semi-autonomous groups of employees responsibility for carrying out a particular task or group of tasks. How different elements of work are divided among them is a matter for the groups themselves to determine, so it is for them to decide how best to maintain high levels of motivation and performance. Job enrichment thus goes beyond the development of challenging roles and the reduction of direct management control to include systems of social support and interdependence among members of each team. Not only is the job itself made intrinsically more pleasurable to undertake, it also provides a basis for the development of valued social relationships.

However, it is not always necessary to alter working arrangements quite so radically to generate performance improvements. Rather, it is quite possible to move down this kind of route a short step at a time by adjusting the content of jobs, the level of autonomy or the amount of teamworking as opportunities to do so arrive.

IMPROVING PERFORMANCE THROUGH COUNSELLING

Whereas job design and redesign focus on improving aspects of the way work is organised, the use of counselling approaches aims to help employees solve any personal problems, whether related to home or work life, that are affecting motivation and performance on the job. Aside from informal counselling sessions, the two principal, formal vehicles used by employers to address such issues are Occupational Health Services and Employee Assistance Programmes (EAPs). The former are primarily involved in dealing with medical problems and the prevention of illness and injury, but they also often provide counselling services – particularly where employees are suffering as a result of drug addiction, alcoholism or eating disorders. EAPs can help in these fields, but also have a wider remit. EAPs employ trained counsellors as well as people with practical expertise in dealing with issues such as debt, divorce, bereavement, domestic violence and a wide range of legal questions.

In both cases, the rationale is broadly the same, namely that it is in the employer's interest for employees to be both healthy and content with their lives. It follows that where counselling services are capable of having a positive effect, and where they can be afforded, they are a worthwhile investment as part of a programme to raise standards of performance. That said, even where such services are not provided, it is necessary, when one is faced with a performance problem, to ask how far it might be explained by personal difficulties of the sort described above. It is particularly likely in the cases of individuals whose personal level of performance drops after a prolonged period of highly satisfactory working. Where such is believed to be the case a counselling approach should probably be used in the first instance.

FURTHER READING

- A number of books cover several of the topics covered in this chapter. Of the text books, *Human Resource Management* by Michael Carrell, Norbert Elbert and Robert Hatfield (1995) gives the most comprehensive treatment. Two books of articles edited by Richard Steers and his colleagues are also very useful. These are *Motivation and Work Behavior* (1991) and *Motivation and Leadership at Work* (1996). A number of the *Harvard Business Review* articles gathered together in *Manage People, Not Personnel* (1990) also cover general issues of performance management.
- The CIPD publishes several books covering the practical aspects of managing performance. Those that specifically cover the subjects included in this chapter are *Coaching* by Paul Kalinauckas and Helen King (1994) (now out of print but available from libraries), *Positive Influencing Skills* by Terry Gillen (1995) (ditto), *Negotiation: Skills and strategies* by Alan Fowler (1996) and *Performance Management: The new realities* by Michael Armstrong and Angela Baron (1998)
- The debate about how best to obtain information on individual performance and how it can be measured is covered comprehensively by Kevin Murphy and Jeanette Cleveland in *Understanding Performance Appraisal* (1995).

10 Judgement Day

Performance appraisal can be seen, at least in theory, as a process that brings together and permits managers to exercise all the different approaches to the management of performance identified in Chapter 9. It is thus a procedure that can both reward and discipline, a means by which employees can be coached and counselled, and a vehicle through which negotiated improvements to performance levels can be agreed. It also often provides an opportunity for discussion about ways in which the working environment can be improved so as to facilitate better performance on the part of individuals and groups of staff. Moreover, it has the potential to fulfil a range of other organisational objectives in addition to the improvement of performance. It can raise morale, help clarify expectations and duties, improve upward and downward communication, reinforce management control, help validate selection decisions, provide information to support HR planning activities, identify developmental opportunities and improve workforce perception of organisational goals. What is more, it provides information on which to base the selection of individuals for promotion and redundancy, not to mention its potential role as the foundation of incentive reward systems. In theory, it can be portrayed as something of a panacea, so it is no surprise to find that it has generated a vast literature over the years.

Unfortunately, the practice rarely lives up to these high theoretical expectations. Research into the outcomes of performance appraisal systems shows that, far from improving motivation and performance, they can in fact very easily have the opposite effect – particularly when they form the basis for decisions about an individual's remuneration. Indeed, reading the results of some studies, it can easily be concluded that performance appraisal is in practice more of an organisational curse than a panacea.

Opinion differs as to why this is the case, some writers on the subject questioning the system itself and its underlying philosophy and others blaming the manner in which it is actually carried out in organisations. Undoubtedly, part of the problem is quite simply that appraising people is fiendishly difficult to do well. Its formality, in so far as it reminds the participants that their working relationships are hierarchical, can serve to set back or even destroy the development of genuine and fruitful relationships between supervisors and subordinates. Furthermore, the frankness and openness that the parties have to show during

ormance appraisals are a feature of the process with which many
understandably uneasy. Berkley Rice (1985) quotes an
aintance as saying that appraising a work colleague is 'the
valent of walking up to a person and saying "Here's what I think
of you, baby"' – an uncomfortable activity that most would avoid if
they could.

This chapter looks at a number of features of performance appraisal,
both in theory and practice. Attention is given to criticisms of the
approach and to some of the ethical issues to be considered in
introducing and running an appraisal system. Finally, the question of
cultural differences is assessed, both among occupational groups and
between people of different nationality.

By the end of this chapter readers should be able to:

- distinguish between evaluative and developmental aspects of
  performance appraisal

- make recommendations on the design and installation of appraisal
  systems appropriate for staff of different cultural backgrounds

- provide advice on the legal and ethical aspects of performance
  appraisal

In addition, readers should be able to understand and explain the:

- advantages and disadvantages of behavioural and output-based
  approaches to appraisal

- criticisms made of both the theory and practice of performance
  appraisal

- principles underpinning effective 360-degree appraisal

- potential implications of the growth in atypical working for performance appraisal.

VARIETIES OF PERFORMANCE APPRAISAL

Although performance appraisal comes in a number of shapes and
forms, in its most typical incarnation it involves the formal appraisal
of an employee's work performance over a set period of time (usually
six months or a year) by his or her immediate line manager. In most
organisations it has an official character, with some form of report
submitted by the line manager which is then placed on the employee's
file. As a result, appraisal interviews are acknowledged by all concerned to be significant occasions which require considerable preparation.
In many cases, standard forms are provided by P&D departments to
help line managers reach judgements about the main aspects of
employee performance. The interviews themselves typically last an
hour or more to allow proper discussion to take place concerning past
performance and the best way to maintain or improve its standard in
the future.

In Chapter 9, a divergence of view was identified between those who
advocate the measurement of performance on the basis of results or
outputs and those who believe it is more effective to focus on

behaviours or the way that results are achieved. This dichotomy is also reflected in the literature on performance appraisal, two basic alternative approaches being put forward: behavioural assessments and output-based assessments.

Behavioural assessments

Here the supervisor reaches a judgement about overall performance on the basis of his or her evaluation of the employee's general conduct during the assessment period. Although specific outputs may come into the calculation, they are subordinate to a consideration of behaviour, and are used principally to provide evidence of its effective and ineffective aspects. Hence, the appraiser may decide that an appraisee has performed particularly well in the field of customer care, and will justify this judgement with reference to evidence from a number of sources. Some of these will relate to observation of the employee at work, while others will be derived from formal output measures such as the number of customers who stated that they were very satisfied with the service they received from the employee concerned.

The behavioural approach is often associated with a requirement on managers to consider performance against certain criteria already defined and determined elsewhere in the organisation. Typically, this will require a standard form to be completed which obliges the appraiser to comment on, or score, different aspects of performance. Although the use of such forms can be helpful in guiding managers to those aspects of individual performance that they should consider, they can also be very inflexible, because they do not focus on the specific requirements of individual jobs.

A more sophisticated approach, which is also a good deal more time-consuming, involves first identifying which particular behaviours or 'competencies' are most important for employees in particular jobs or departments to display. In other words, the starting-point is the individual job description and person specification. In selection processes these documents are used as the basis for reaching judgements about likely *future* performance; by contrast, their use in this context involves assessing *past* performance. Employees are thus appraised according to how far, in the judgement of their immediate supervisor, they are actually meeting or exceeding the basic requirements of the job in question. Hence, if the person specification states that conversational French, good interpersonal skills, the ability to work under pressure and an interest in law are essential or desirable characteristics for successful performance, then it is against these criteria that the appraisee's actual performance is judged.

Output-based assessments

In the case of some kinds of job it is possible to appraise people on the basis of quantifiable data. The most common examples are those in which employees repeat the same procedure or activity continually, allowing clear measures of their efficiency or effectiveness to be obtained. Such an approach is thus possible in the case of groups such as fruit-pickers, some manufacturing employees, clerical workers who process paperwork, and a wide variety of salespeople. Often such employees will be set some form of target to work towards and against which they are later formally appraised.

The other form of output-based appraisal seeks to apply the target-setting principle to a far wider range of jobs. Under such schemes, specific performance objectives or goals that the employee agrees to complete are set at the start of the appraisal cycle. At the end, the employee's performance is then appraised according to how many or how fully these objectives have in fact been achieved. At each annual or six-monthly meeting, the manager reviews past achievements with the employee and then moves on to determine the objectives for the next appraisal period. The level of employee involvement in the determination of objectives varies from organisation to organisation. In some, they are basically set by supervisors, and clearly reflect organ-isational needs, whereas in others the responsibility is placed on employees to devise their own objectives and to state what action they intend to take to ensure that these are fulfilled. In most cases, a mixture of these two approaches is used, supervisors and subordinates agreeing a set of appraisal objectives which satisfies both the oper-ational needs of the employer and the personal goals of each individual employee concerned. As is shown by the General Electric study described below, employee involvement in the setting of objectives is an important feature of successful output-based appraisal systems.

The debate about which of these two broad approaches is most effective has been a consistent theme of writing about performance appraisal for decades. As long ago as 1957, Douglas Macgregor was questioning the objectivity and motivational qualities of behavioural approaches, and advocating the use of approaches drawing on the 'promising' notion of Management by Objectives or MbO (Macgregor 1957: 159). Since then, the debate has continued through a period in which goal-setting approaches have become increasingly common. In more recent years, attention has turned to the wisdom and practic-alities of their use in appraising professional and technical employees, manual staff and public-sector workers (IDS 1993, IRS 1994a, 1994c, Elliott and Murlis 1996, Fletcher 1997). Since the late 1970s, objective-setting has itself come in for a great deal of criticism, writers again advocating more general behavioural approaches and making use of the 'competency frameworks' that have been established in many organisations (Beer and Ruh 1976, Fletcher 1997: 26–33).

Vigorous debate over these issues is possible because both the above approaches have distinct advantages and disadvantages. Goal-setting appraisal systems have the virtue of being the more objective of the two, because the overall assessment of performance is based on specific achievements. Behavioural approaches, by contrast, are by their nature far more subjective, however fairly they are actually carried out. It is far easier for supervisors to reflect any liking or dislike that they may have for an individual appraisee in a behavioural assessment than in an assessment based on the achievement (or non-achievement) of specific objectives. Such assessments are made all the more unfair because they are not necessarily job-related, but can be heavily influenced by a manager's general view of someone's personality or lifestyle. In addition to objectivity, output-based systems have the advantage of clarity. In other words, they leave each employee in no doubt as to what they need to do over the coming months to secure a favourable appraisal review. Moreover, systems in which individuals are able to participate in the goal-setting process have been found to have significant motivational qualities (Fletcher 1997: 21).

However, there are also drawbacks with results-based approaches that are not present in the behavioural systems. First and foremost, it is often argued that objective-setting is wholly unsuitable for many jobs, because there are so few clear goals to achieve. This is particularly true of those jobs the main function of which is the maintenance of an operation or body of work to a set standard. In such cases there are no specific new objectives to be achieved, let alone goals that are appropriate for individuals to be set. This is true of many unskilled and semi-skilled jobs, but is also the case in a number of professional occupations. Examples include medicine and teaching, where the effectiveness of job-holders' performance is based on the skill with which they carry out day-to-day tasks. Such people's contributions to the achievement of specific initiatives may be important, but none may happen to form an especially significant part of their working lives. It is therefore both unnecessary and unfair, so the argument runs, to judge their performance on the basis of such crude results.

Appraising appraisal at General Electric

A classic research study into the effectiveness of different approaches to performance appraisal was reported in the *Harvard Business Review* in 1965. This occurred in the General Electric Company in the USA and involved looking in detail at the appraisal experience of 92 male employees. At that time, the company had an established appraisal system in operation that was used to identify developmental opportunities, and also as the basis for setting salary levels.

In order to study employee reactions to different approaches, the managers were divided into two groups. The first group was instructed to use a high-participation approach, whereby the appraisee was asked to set his own goals for achieving improved job performance. By contrast, the second group was asked to take a low-participation approach, in which goals were set by the manager and then presented to the employee for comment.

Interviews after the appraisal process, together with an analysis of the number of personal goals achieved, suggested that the high-participation approach was more successful in general terms. It tended to lead to higher levels of motivation and to positive attitudes towards the appraisal system, in addition to the completion of more of the objectives set in the appraisal. However, an interesting finding was that employees who were judged to be performing relatively poorly, and who had thus been criticised in the interviews, appeared to do better under the low-participation regime.

Source: Meyer *et al* (1965)

Because they involve judging different employees on the basis of different criteria, goal-setting methods of appraisal also make it very difficult to compare one employee's performance with another's. Although this could be done crudely on the basis of the number of objectives achieved or exceeded, it would be most unfair, given how greatly the nature of objectives varies. Where appraisal results are used to determine promotion, pay and redundancy decisions, it is thus necessary to include behavioural approaches, so as to allow employees to be judged against the same basic criteria.

> Which jobs in your organisation would be impossible to measure on the basis of objectives met? Would other results-based approaches be more acceptable in these cases?

AIMS OF APPRAISAL

As was indicated in the opening paragraph to this chapter, performance appraisal is potentially useful for managers in many ways. At base, however, there are two fundamental reasons for developing such systems: assessing past and improving future performance. These are also often referred to as the *evaluative* and *developmental* objectives of appraisal systems. Although each in itself can be met using either of the basic formats outlined above, research suggests that problems arise from trying to carry out both aims at the same time. In other words, the extent to which it is possible effectively to evaluate and develop an employee using the same appraisal procedure is questionable.

The incompatibility arises from the different ways in which employees perceive each of these objectives. When the purpose appears to be evaluative, there is naturally a tendency for appraisees to talk up the good aspects of their performance and perhaps to be less forthcoming about the poorer ones. As a result, they tend not to open up about their developmental needs. This is no great problem if the objective of the exercise is indeed evaluative. Managers know that employees are unlikely to tell the whole truth, and can make allowances for this in reaching judgements about each individual's performance. However, it is clearly a problem when there is a wish also to focus on future performance and on any need employees may have for additional training or experience in order to achieve future goals. In order to persuade subordinates to give a wholly frank picture of their own performance, it is necessary not only to stress the developmental aspects of appraisal but also to make quite sure that information gained is not used for evaluative purposes. As soon as employees suspect that their appraisal results are informing decisions about pay, promotion or redundancy the likelihood of an open and honest exchange of information diminishes considerably. For this reason a number of writers have suggested that organisations should make a choice about whether their appraisal system is to be principally used for evaluation or developmental purposes, on the grounds that it is not possible to achieve both effectively (eg Frechette and Wertheim 1985: 225, Anderson 1992: 188–89, Randell 1994: 237, Murphy and Cleveland 1995: 107–09).

Others such as Beer and Ruh (1976) have argued that both can indeed be achieved, but that a clear distinction has to be made between the two objectives nonetheless. Their approach involves setting up two wholly distinct organisational procedures with different names, one of which focuses on performance evaluation and the other on development. Meetings associated with the two procedures are then held at different times of the year to reinforce the separation. Fletcher (1997: 33) suggests a different solution involving a single procedure, but one that is both 'results-oriented' and 'competency-based'. Such a system would require supervisors and subordinates to agree objectives at the start of the appraisal cycle, thus permitting performance evaluation to occur at a later date, but would also require the objectives to be developmental in character. So, instead of setting someone performance objectives linked directly to current organis-ational needs (eg the development of a new appraisal training pro-gramme), the goals to be achieved would all relate to the development of an individual's own skills and knowledge (eg the development of competence in the field of employee appraisal).

> To what extent do you agree with the suggestion that appraisals cannot achieve both developmental and evaluative aims together?

PROBLEMS WITH PERFORMANCE APPRAISAL

Academic research into performance appraisal has rarely focused on its effectiveness in general terms. Instead, the literature consists on the one hand of general surveys establishing which approaches are being used, and for what purposes, and on the other of case-studies that describe the problems encountered with typical schemes. It is therefore difficult, as yet, to come to any firm and defensible conclusion about their overall effectiveness in different situations. Instead, it is necessary to focus on potential effectiveness with reference to research that draws attention to faults in the workings of performance appraisal, with a view to suggesting improvements.

Broadly speaking, critiques of performance appraisal come in three distinct forms: criticisms of the way that managers carry them out in practice; criticisms from a practical point of view of the appraisal in general; and theoretical criticisms from those who advocate wholly different approaches to performance management. Each of these is summarised below.

Specific practical problems
A number of research studies have drawn attention to the way in which appraisal is carried out in organisations and, in particular, to unfair bias in managerial assessments of performance. Rowe (1986) identified the following problems with rating systems:

- the tendency to give a good overall assessment on the basis that one particular aspect has been accomplished well

- a tendency to avoid giving low ratings, even when deserved, for fear of angering or upsetting a weak performer

- the tendency to give a poor overall assessment on the basis of particularly poor performance in one area

- the tendency to rate employee performance as 'average' or 'good' rather than to use the end-points of rating scales

- the tendency to give particular weight to recent occurrences in reaching judgements about individual performance

- the tendency to give high ratings to people who have performed well historically, whatever their performance over the previous year

- a tendency to refrain, on principle, from giving particularly high ratings

- a tendency to rate subordinates at a lower level than the appraiser achieved when in their position.

Michael Beer (1985) draws attention to problems that can occur in the interview itself. In particular, he criticises the tendency for managers to do all or most of the talking, leaving insufficient opportunity for appraisees to respond or to participate in addressing future objectives. According to Philp (1990), other common problems that can reduce the effectiveness of appraisal interviews result from poor management preparation, leaving insufficient time for a proper discussion to take place, and allowing interruptions to occur during the interview.

General practical problems

The specific problems described above can in many instances be reduced, or even eliminated, with effective appraisal training and regular evaluation of how appraisal interviewing is working in practice. By contrast, the more general practical problems are rather harder to put right. The first of these was alluded to in the introductory paragraphs: the reluctance of managers to carry out appraisals. A number of reasons have been put forward to explain this phenomenon, ranging from a general dislike of passing judgement on others to an inability to handle the emotional responses that often arise when appraisal ratings are less impressive than employees expected. The appraisal interview, as an activity, does not often fit in very well with individual management styles, and this too may explain some managerial reluctance. Where a supervisor has a close and open relationship with his or her subordinates, the formality implicit in appraisal interviewing may well serve to create greater distance between appraiser and appraisee. In such situations, especially ones in which an individual's performance is substandard, supervisors may well feel that a formal appraisal interview is an inappropriate forum in which to discuss performance issues. Instead, subtler approaches are preferred. By contrast, where a supervisor prefers to manage employees from a distance, eschewing close personal contacts, appraisal interviews can reduce distance by providing employees with the opportunity to force a frank and open exchange of views.

Another practical criticism relates to the inevitably political nature of some appraisal decisions. In their research into US executives' perceptions, Longenecker *et al* (1987) found that such political considerations very often led to the 'generation of appraisal ratings that were less than accurate'. What is so interesting about their findings is that this did not arise because of ignorance or carelessness on the part of appraisers, but was carried out quite deliberately after careful consideration. In other words, it appears to be a problem inherent to the appraisal process and thus not easily solved by the provision of better training or standardised paperwork. The general message is neatly summed up by one of their interviewers:

> There is really no getting around the fact that whenever I evaluate one of my people, I stop and think about the impact – the ramifications of my decisions on my relationship with the guy and his future here. I'd be stupid not to. Call it being politically minded, or using managerial discretion, or fine tuning the guy's ratings, but in the end I've got to live with him, and I'm not going to rate a guy without thinking about the fallout. There are a lot of games played in the rating process and whether we admit it or not we are all guilty of playing them at our discretion.

This research brings strongly into question the extent to which appraisal can ever be carried out in anything approaching an objective manner. The implication is that it is therefore bound, as sure as night follows day, to result in a degree of demotivation and dissatisfaction on the part of some employees.

Theoretical criticisms
A third critique challenges the assumption that has been accepted so far in this chapter that performance appraisal is great in theory but difficult to carry out well in practice. The view is thus expressed that performance appraisal is wrong in principle and represents an ineffective philosophy of management. The most celebrated critic to put forward this kind of view is W. Edwards Deming, the leading advocate of 'Total Quality Management' (TQM) approaches. His views have been echoed in the work of other gurus too, such as Tom Peters (1989: 495), who described objective-setting approaches to performance appraisal as 'downright dangerous'.

The essence of the case can be summed up in Deming's exhortation to 'replace supervision with leadership'. In short, it is argued that supervision, particularly when it involves the inspection of subordinates' work as a means of achieving quality, is a barrier to the achievement of long-term competitive advantage. Performance appraisal, in reinforcing the significance of the supervisor-subordinate relationship, is therefore exactly the opposite of what is actually required. According to Deming, it creates fear, encourages the development of adversarial relationships and 'robs' people of their 'right to pride of workmanship'. By its very nature, he argues, appraisal reduces motivation, makes less likely the achievement of genuinely shared objectives throughout the organisation, and so wastes organisational resources.

Other principled criticisms of appraisal are based on the notion that, whereas such approaches to the management of employees were generally appropriate for much of the past 200 years, this is no longer the case. This view is eloquently put forward by Fletcher (1997:

163–64), who argues that traditional approaches to appraisal are inappropriate for organisations that are knowledge-based, have flatter hierarchies, and need to maximise flexibility in order to compete effectively. Annual performance appraisals, in which the year's achievements are evaluated and new goals set for the coming year, are thus by their nature too inflexible to be useful as tools of performance management. Instead, there is a need to focus wholly on today's business needs, and to recognise that these are likely to change considerably over the course of a year, as will the contribution that individual employees will be expected to make. Moreover, it is argued that because performance appraisal sits uneasily with the ethos that characterises the attitudes of most professional groups, it is an inappropriate approach to take if an organisation wishes to maximise its performance. According to Fletcher (1997: 149), the professional ethos is typified by:

- high levels of autonomy and independence of judgement

- self-discipline and adherence to professional standards

- the possession of specialised knowledge and skills

- power and status based on expertise

- operating, and being guided by, a code of ethics

- being answerable to the governing professional body.

By contrast, the principles of performance appraisal emphasise wholly conflicting characteristics:

- hierarchical authority and direction from superiors

- administrative rules and the following of procedures

- the definition by the organisation of standards and goals

- the demand that primary loyalty be given to the organisation

- the basing of power on one's legitimate organisational position.

It follows that the greater the extent to which professional and 'knowledge' workers are employed, the less appropriate traditional forms of top-down appraisal are for organisations.

> How far does Fletcher's view accord with your own experience? Is he right to suggest that appraisal by supervisors is inappropriate in the case of professionally qualified employees?

LEGAL AND ETHICAL ISSUES

In practice, the law does not intervene to any great extent in the performance appraisal process itself, but it can nevertheless have an indirect impact in that individual appraisal records inform decisions in the fields of promotion, payment, dismissal, access to benefits and access to training opportunities. There is, to date, a far less extensive body of case-law in the UK dealing with these issues than there is in the USA, where fairness in appraisal systems is now defined quite tightly by the requirements of the law (Carrell *et al* 1995: 354–55). Nevertheless, the legal principles are clear, and P&D professionals are thus well-advised to bear them in mind when basing important decisions on the results of performance appraisal procedures.

In selecting employees for redundancy, it is quite lawful to use appraisal ratings as one of several selection methods. Indeed, according to Lewis (1993: 101), special appraisal exercises can be carried out specifically as part of a redundancy selection programme. Where such an approach is contemplated, there is clearly a need to ensure that the performance criteria used are fair, objective and verifiable by reference to documentary evidence. Performance appraisal ratings and reports can also have a role to play in other forms of dismissal, particularly where employees are dismissed on grounds of poor performance. The appraisals themselves, of course, often form part of the procedure used, whereby employees are formally warned that their performance is unacceptable, given time and assistance to help it to improve, and then dismissed should insufficient improvement have occurred. Employers must always remember in such situations that, were their decision to dismiss to be challenged in court, the fairness and objectivity of formal appraisals would form part of the evidence on which their case would be decided. Paradoxically, performance appraisal results are often produced by dismissed employees as part of their own cases against dismissal. This occurs when supervisors, lacking a knowledge of the potential legal consequences, refrain from giving low ratings to their subordinates or choose to give positive performance feedback only. Of course there may be good motivational reasons for taking this approach in the case of poor performers, but it can easily come back to haunt the appraiser if the employee concerned is subsequently dismissed on account of poor performance.

Performance appraisals can also have legal consequences in the fields of discrimination on grounds of sex, race and disability. This occurs when they are used as the basis of or justification for promoting employees, increasing or decreasing individual pay levels, or selecting employees for new opportunities in the organisation. Here it is necessary to be able to show that the decision was taken objectively and that no unlawful discrimination occurred. Performance ratings that appear to be subjective or arbitrary are therefore unlikely to help in the defence of such cases. Where P&D managers are unhappy about the way that an appraisal has been carried out, or are uncertain whether the criteria used were fair, they are wise to ensure that decisions in these fields are not taken on those grounds alone.

Where appraisal involves explicit scoring of an individual's perfor-mance, there is also a need to monitor the results, or at least to keep an eye out for any general biases against particular racial groups and for patterns that show one sex to be achieving higher ratings than the other. Where such biases do appear to be occurring, it is wise to investigate the reasons and to take remedial action through training interventions or by talking to individual managers. If this is not done, the organisation could be open to challenge on the grounds that it is indirectly discriminating against one or other protected group.

Similar considerations apply where pay rates are determined as a result of performance ratings. Here it is equal value law that provides the basis for a legal challenge, for example where an employee believes his or her pay to be unjustifiably lower than that of a comparator of the opposite sex. Where it has been established that the two jobs in question are 'of equal value', it is for the employer to show that any difference in pay is due to 'a genuine material factor, not of sex'. Where the difference arises as a result of disparate appraisal ratings, the employer is likely to lose the case if he or she cannot satisfy the tribunal that the appraisal procedure operates objectively, ie without unfair discrimination.

Leaving aside the possibility of legal action, P&D professionals should in any case seek to ensure that principles of natural justice are always applied in the field of performance appraisal to everyone, whatever their sex or race. It is very easy to devise schemes that permit supervisors who are so minded to justify unfair decisions or to use them as a means of advancing the careers of particularly favoured individuals. Apart from being unethical, such activities can have adverse effects for the organisation, in so far as they demotivate employees and contribute towards a poor reputation in key labour markets. Care has to be taken in drawing up policy in this field, in setting up appraisal systems and in training appraisers, in order to minimise the occurrence of such injustices. Where it is suspected that managers are abusing their positions in this regard, there may be a case for disciplinary action; but where that is considered unnecessary, a possible way forward is to ensure that two or more managers rate each employee's performance separately. A further possible solution is to include consideration of the ability to appraise effectively in managers' own performance appraisals.

> What examples of unethical practice have you observed or suspected are occurring in the field of performance appraisal in your organisation? What would be the most appropriate remedial action to take in such cases?

INTERNATIONAL DIFFERENCES

The type of appraisal system described in this chapter is very much the creation of Anglo-Saxon business cultures. In its formality, its requirement for active employee participation and its reliance on frank and open discussion of individual achievement, it fits by and large with the established cultural norms in US and UK organisations. Appraisal systems of this kind are less well established elsewhere, and will not necessarily be processes to which employees with different cultural backgrounds and assumptions will adapt very easily. For this reason, in international organisations it is often difficult and unwise to introduce a single, global approach to employee appraisal. Instead, there is a need to be sensitive to local traditions and to permit managers in each country to operate the performance-management systems most appropriate to their populations. The following examples come from diverse sources published over the past few years:

- According to Ling Sing Chee (1994: 154), Singapore Airlines found that they had to adapt their worldwide appraisal system for employees based in Thailand. This arose because it was found that Thais had particular difficulty in highlighting the bad points in an appraisee's performance. The reluctance derives from the Buddhist belief in reincarnation and consequently in the role that 'good and bad deeds' in one's present life plays in determining how one will be reincarnated.

- Fletcher (1997: 97), drawing on the work of Hofstede (see Chapter 2), suggests that many people of Chinese origin are likely to feel uncomfortable when appraised under a system based on Anglo-Saxon assumptions. This is because of their reluctance to assert their own views directly to a superior. As a result, it is argued, appraisers need to be trained to anticipate such a response and to accept that they will have to adapt their appraisal style if they are to achieve a positive outcome.

- Prokopenko (1994: 154) states that in Eastern European countries, although changes are occurring, many of the norms and expectations of the Communist era still influence P&D practice. An example of this is the continued diffidence towards performance appraisal that is associated with the bureaucracy characteristic of State-managed organisations before 1990. Because promotion and reward were rarely based on merit or performance, but instead on loyalty and political status, people have been understandably slow to adjust to a situation in which performance appraisal has a constructive role to play in management and motivation.

- Sparrow and Hiltrop (1994: 558–560) note that performance management operates very differently in France from the way that it does in most UK organisations. Linking this suggestion to Hofstede's (1980) finding that French management culture was characterised by 'high power-distance' and 'high uncertainty-avoidance', they suggest that the Anglo-Saxon model of performance management is ill-suited to French organisations. In particular, the French are uneasy with the notion that subordinates should be involved in objective-setting, being used to more autocratic forms of management and a situation in which decision-making is carried out at the highest levels within organisational hierarchies.

It is thus clear that in this field, as in so many in P&D, it is not possible simply to take a model or approach off the shelf and install it in a subsidiary or branch office anywhere in the world. Care has to be taken, training has to be given and thorough research has to be carried out before it is safe to install such systems or procedures. The more innovative the approach, the more necessary it is to adapt its use in different countries. A good example is 360-degree appraisal of the kind described below. It is hard enough to gain acceptance for its use in countries that Hofstede characterised as having low power-distance work cultures; it would be tougher still in the Latin countries, where high power-distance assumptions prevail.

360-degree appraisal

A method of appraising managerial employees that has received a great deal of attention in recent years is 360-degree appraisal, whereby ratings are given not just by the next manager up in the organisational hierarchy, but also by peers and subordinates. Appropriate customer ratings are also included, along with an element of self-appraisal. Once gathered in, the assessments from the various quarters are compared with one another and the results communicated to the manager concerned. The idea itself is nothing new. Management writers, particularly in the USA, have long advocated the use of upward and peer appraisal as a means of evaluating management performance, but such views have taken a good deal of time to become generally acceptable. In theory, it is, like many innovations, very attractive. Who better to provide constructive feedback on a manager's performance than his or her own staff? What better source could there be for suggestions about personal developmental needs? What better criteria for promotion to a senior management role than proof of the respect and admiration of peers and subordinates?

In practice it is, of course, far harder to achieve well. First and foremost, there is the problem of objectivity. How is it possible to ensure that peers and subordinates are not rating someone in such a way as to promote their own interests? It would be very tempting to take the opportunity to exercise personal vindictiveness against a manager whom one personally disliked rather than to give a balanced account of their work performance. Similarly, where two peers are competing for one promotional opportunity, it is inevitable that they will be tempted into rating each other poorly, however little justification there is for doing so. Secondly, there is the potential for managerial reprisals against subordinates perceived to have rated them (the managers) poorly and thus set back their careers. Thirdly, there is a range of problems that can arise when managers, in a bid to gain high ratings, are tempted to take action that is popular but not necessarily right for the organisation.

It is impossible to remove all these practical problems from the process but, with careful thought and planning, progress can be made. Two conditions in particular stand out as necessary if any such initiative is to be successful:

- It must be stressed that the appraisal process is entirely to be used for developmental purposes. In other words, a situation must be engineered in which no one perceives that promotion or pay are directly linked to the outcome of the process. Although it is true that the result of the developmental process might be better performance, and thus promotion, the link should be no more direct than this.

- It is necessary to ensure complete confidentiality, so that employees are left in no fear whatsoever that their manager will be able to victimise them on account of the ratings they give or remarks they make. For this reason, the only realistic approach is to produce standard appraisal forms to be used across the whole organisation and returned, once completed, to a central office.

APPRAISING A FLEXIBLE WORKFORCE

In their comprehensive review of recent US research into performance appraisal, Murphy and Cleveland (1995) consider possible consequences of increased flexible working practices such as those described in Chapter 2. Although some of their arguments are rather speculative, they make an interesting contribution to wider debates about the most effective approaches to the appraisal of employees. Two conclusions stand out as being particularly interesting.

A predicted increase in the use of output-based systems

Murphy and Cleveland argue that a number of trends designed to increase operational flexibility are greatly reducing the amount of day-to-day contact between employees and their line managers. This arises from increased homeworking, greater flexibility in terms of precisely when and where individuals work, and a tendency for organisations to develop matrix structures, in which people report to different managers about different areas of their work. In each case, the result is much less opportunity than has traditionally been the case for supervisors to observe their subordinates actually performing their jobs. In such situations it is natural for appraisers to focus more on results in compiling their evaluations than on employee behaviour.

A general reduction in the significance of appraisal as a management tool

It is also argued that the growth in part-time employment, temporary working and subcontracting will have the effect of downgrading the significance of much traditional appraisal activity. This occurs because of the lack of internal career progression opportunities for most employees in these peripheral categories. Because two of the main aims of performance appraisal are the identification of candidates for promotion and the determination of long-term individual development needs, it follows that appraisal, as traditionally practised, is less significant in the case of such employees. The result is a need to find other motivational mechanisms and to focus attention on the achievement of short-term performance objectives.

> How far do you agree with Murphy and Cleveland's conclusions? To what extent do they reflect your experience of managing staff employed on atypical contracts?

A DEFENCE OF PERFORMANCE APPRAISAL

It is clear from reading the literature on performance appraisal that it is far from a perfect management technique. As has been shown, traditional top-down approaches that focus as much on evaluation as development have been widely criticised from a number of angles. Some people find fault in the way that the schemes operate, others dislike the principles on which they are based, while a third group sees them as outdated and inappropriate for today's corporate environment. Although these arguments have some validity, a strong counter-argument can also be put in favour of traditional performance appraisal.

The defence is based on the notion that performance appraisal need not, and indeed should not, be seen as the principal tool for managing performance in organisations. Instead, it should be used in a relatively minor way to achieve only those objectives for which it is best suited. The arguments of its critics all share a common assumption: that performance appraisal should be judged on its ability demonstrably to motivate employees and to enhance their overall performance. This is a tough test to set any single P&D intervention, and performance appraisal is not exceptional in failing to pass. However, that does not mean that it has no role to play at all, or that it cannot be used in tandem with other approaches to performance management.

In the author's view, performance appraisal continues to be used widely not because it has a great contribution to make to enhancing individual motivation at work but because it is an effective tool of management control. At the end of the day, whatever criticisms are made, it retains this key attraction – a feature that becomes more powerful when decisions relating to individual remuneration and promotion are clearly tied to appraisal results. In short, it remains the case that formally setting someone an objective or goal to achieve, and stating that recognition, pay and career opportunities will *in part* be influenced by that person's ability to achieve it, greatly increases the chances that it will get done. In this way, appraisal contributes to organisational performance and the achievement of corporate goals in a steady and unostentatious way. It follows that the main problem with performance appraisal is not its actual effectiveness but the inflated expectations that people have of its ability to achieve far more grandiose organisational outcomes.

The key to using appraisal systems effectively is thus to recognise their limitations. It is true that, for certain groups of employees, it is difficult to formulate clear objectives on which to base performance appraisals, but that does not mean that the approach has no role whatever to play in their management. The problem arises when it is the *only* tool used to judge their performance. For example, it can be employed usefully and effectively in a relatively modest way as a means of ensuring that medical staff spend sufficient time during the course of a year making a contribution to specific projects, or that technical employees complete important but less interesting tasks that are nevertheless significant for their organisation. In this way it forms a small yet effective part of a wider performance-management system. It will demotivate and have damaging consequences only if it is used either ineptly or as the only vehicle by which the organisation communicates its evaluation of an individual's contribution. It can thus be concluded that, with adequate training and experience, performance appraisal remains an important skill for managers to master.

PRACTICAL MATTERS

The day-to-day practice of performance appraisal is not an area of management work that P&D specialists spend a great deal of time undertaking. By its nature, this is primarily a job for line managers and first line supervisors. With the obvious exception of the appraisal of their own staff, the P&D specialist's role is largely restricted to policy-making and the giving of advice. However, there are two areas in which the P&D function often takes a more hands-on role: in the design of standardised appraisal documentation and in training other managers to carry out effective appraisals. It is to these two areas of activity that we now turn.

Documentation

The extent to which there is a need for standard documentation clearly varies, depending on the type of performance-appraisal system operated. The more individual the appraisal criteria, the less role there is for any standard form for appraisers to complete. Where appraisal is based on specific objectives or goals set for each employee, the need for documentation is limited to some mechanism whereby managers confirm that they have carried out each appraisal interview. A good deal more is usually required where behavioural approaches are being used, particularly when employees across the organisation are appraised against similar generic criteria.

Those who have sought to identify best practice in the field of appraisal, such as P.B. Beaumont (1993: 81–2) and Clive Fletcher (1997: 56–9), argue that a strong element of self-appraisal should be a feature of any well-designed system. Standard documentation has an important role to play here, as it gives employees a clear framework within which to assess their own performance. Typically, the self-appraisal form will be sent to employees at the same time as their supervisors are sent theirs. Both parties then complete these before comparing the content of each other's forms at the appraisal interview itself. Some organisations issue identical forms to appraiser and appraisee, but because the purpose of the self-appraisal is different from that of the employer appraisal, it is probably better if rather different forms are designed. Self-appraisal forms have two main purposes. The first is to provide a means for employees to communicate their own perception of the job and what they believe their strengths and weaknesses to be. The second is to provide an opportunity for appraisees to look forward and state how they would like their career to progress, were they to be given the right training and experience over the coming months. The kind of questions that are included are as follows:

- What parts of your job give you most satisfaction?

- What parts of your job give you least satisfaction?

- How would you assess your technical skills?

- How would you assess your ability to communicate with your colleagues?

- How would you describe your working relationships?

- What do you feel are your main achievements over the past year?

- What did you fail to achieve? Why?

- In what areas do you believe you have the ability to improve?

- What training courses would you like to attend in the coming year?

- What are your career objectives for the coming year?

- What suggestions do you have for ways in which the organisation of work in your department could be improved?

- How might communication in the organisation be improved?

The list is not exhaustive and can clearly be added to and made specifically relevant to particular employee groups, but these questions illustrate the type of approach that is generally taken to self-appraisal forms. The questions are open-ended and thus cannot simply be answered with a simple yes or no. Once completed, therefore, the form provides the basis for constructive discussion in the appraisal interview itself.

Standard forms for appraisers to complete cover similar areas, but also usually include some sections that require formal scoring or rating of performance to be recorded. Hence, while appraisees are asked simply to comment at some length on their communication skills, supervisors will both comment and score them – often using a Likert scale such as that illustrated in Table 9 (see page 170). In addition, other sections require objectives or targets agreed with the appraisees to be recorded, along with developmental initiatives that are to be taken to assist in their achievement. Typically, appraiser forms also require specific mention to be made of areas that need attention (ie those in which performance is weaker than it should be) and room for the supervisor to write a general summary at the end. The advantage of this last part is the chance it gives to finish on a high note. In other words, where faults or poor performance have been noted early in the form, there is an opportunity for a more general positive statement to be made in order that morale is not too badly damaged.

Appraiser training

If there is one issue that all writers on appraisal agree about, it is the vital importance of effective training for the people who are going to be carrying out appraisal interviews. The general message is that a badly done appraisal is worse than no appraisal at all in terms of the adverse effect that it has on motivation, job satisfaction, commitment and trust between managers and subordinates. Furthermore, as has been made clear, getting it right is no easy matter. It is not, as some managers like to believe, something that cannot be taught. Just as it is necessary to learn how to interview candidates for new positions effectively, managers also have to learn basic appraisal skills. Aside from the particular features of the scheme in operation, including the use of standard documentation, the following points need to be included in training courses designed to help supervisors develop appraisal interviewing skills:

- the importance of objectivity and consistency

- the need to avoid passing judgement on any aspect of an employee's personality or attitudes that does not relate 100 per cent to his or her performance at work

- the need to prepare thoroughly for all appraisal interviews

- the need to be able to justify with factual evidence any negative comments that are made

- the importance of putting employees at ease and encouraging them to do most of the talking

- the need to stress good aspects of performance as much, or more than, poorer aspects

- the need to take a constructive approach to weaknesses in the employee's performance and to make positive suggestions as to how matters may be improved

- the need to end appraisal interviews on a forward-looking, positive and constructive note.

Appraisal training sessions themselves tend to be highly participatory, exercises of one kind or another being undertaken as a means of developing the key skills of active listening, the giving of constructive feedback and effective counselling. These take a number of forms. First, there is the kind that involves showing a video to course members in which a particular set of tasks is performed (some well and some badly) by an actor. The group then works out how it would be best to handle an appraisal interview with that individual. Secondly, there are exercises in which course members or leaders undertake some task in front of a group of others, such as making a short presentation, and are then formally appraised on their performance. Thirdly, there are role-playing exercises in which course members appraise each other according to the contents of briefs provided by the course leader. In this case, participants can also be asked to give feedback to the appraisers on their performance. In each of these exercises there is scope for introducing unusual or particularly difficult scenarios that appraisers have to tackle. Wherever possible, this should include the appraisal of an employee with a particularly poor performance record, caused in part by emotional or personal difficulties. The importance of developing effective counselling skills is thus emphasised.

FURTHER READING

- There is a vast literature covering different aspects of performance appraisal. Two books that cover a great deal of the ground and draw on years of academic research are *Understanding Performance Appraisal* by Kevin Murphy and Jeanette Cleveland (1995) and *Appraisal: Routes to improved performance* by Clive Fletcher (1997).

- IDS and IRS regularly publish the results of case-studies and surveys of employer practice in this field. Recent IDS studies include *Performance Management* (1992), *Performance Appraisal for Manual Workers* (1993), *Appraisal Systems* (1995) and *Performance Management* (1997). IRS published the results of a survey looking at appraisal arrangements in UK firms in the March and May editions of *Employment Trends* in 1994. The results of a wider research programme sponsored by the (former) IPD were published in 1992 in *Performance Management in the UK: An analysis of the issues*.

- Evidence of the way in which debates about performance appraisal have veered this way and that over the years is provided by Gerry Randell (1994) in his contribution to *Personnel Management: A comprehensive guide to theory and practice in Britain* edited by Keith Sisson, and in the book of short articles on the subject published by the *Harvard Business Review* in 1990 under the title *Manage People, Not Personnel.*

- The topic of 360-degree appraisal is covered by Fletcher (1997) in the book recommended above, by Peter Ward (1997) in *360-Degree Feedback*, and by Robert McGarvey and Scott Smith (1993) in their article entitled 'When workers rate the boss', which is included in *Human Resources Management: Perspectives, context, functions and outcomes* edited by Gerald Ferris and Ronald Buckley (1996).

Part 6

ABSENCE AND TURNOVER

11 And what if they don't show up?

According to two recent and extensive employer surveys, the average annual absence rate in the UK is approximately 3.6 per cent (CBI 1997: 4, Industrial Society 1997: 11). This represents between eight and nine days per employee, and means that around 190 million working days are being 'lost' annually as a result of absenteeism. Government statistics published in the *Labour Force Survey* suggest that the figure is rather higher (between 4 and 6 per cent) and that consequently the UK occupies a position towards the bottom of international absence league tables (see IDS 1994: 2, Watkins 1994: 42).

The need to reduce absence has risen up the agendas of many P&D managers since April 1994, when the government ceased reimbursing all but the smallest employers the cost of administering and paying out Statutory Sick Pay (SSP). Henceforward, employers have had to shoulder the bulk of the bill generated as a result of absenteeism in the UK, estimated by the CBI (1997: 12) to be over £12 billion a year. One consequence has been the publication of a great deal more literature concerning the causes of absenteeism and the various approaches used to reduce the number of days on which employees fail to show up for work. Despite this, absence management remains an area of P&D activity about which commentators and researchers take widely differing positions. It is also a field characterised by the presence of apparently contradictory research evidence.

In this chapter the management of absence or attendance is viewed as a specialised subfield of performance management. We therefore continue with a number of the themes introduced in Chapters 9 and 10, while also introducing new material that relates specifically to the improvement of absence rates. We first discuss methods used for measuring and costing absence before moving on to focus on its possible causes and the various approaches that have been taken in search of long-lasting remedies. In the main, we are not concerned here with the management of issues arising from chronic illness on the part of employees. Situations in which people have genuine, long-term illnesses that prevent them either from coming to work or performing effectively when present are distinct P&D activities that are in practice governed by the requirements of the law. These will be dealt with in Chapter 14 in the context of dismissal on grounds of incapability. The focus in this chapter is absence of a different kind: situations in which individuals who could come into work choose not to. This may be on account of a relatively insignificant illness such as a mild headache, stomach upset or cold, or it may be for other reasons.

By the end of this chapter readers should be able to:

• set up systems to monitor absence rates

• estimate the costs of absence and the savings generated by its reduction

• develop and undertake a programme to reduce absence levels.

In addition, readers should be able to understand and explain the:

• causes of absenteeism

• implications of absenteeism for employers and employees

• potential benefits and shortcomings of alternative approaches to the management of absence.

MEASURING ABSENCE

Monitoring absence levels is, by all accounts, a prerequisite for the development of policies and practices aimed at their reduction. Without a system for calculating current rates of absence it is not possible to set targets for its reduction, or even to track the direction of trends across different divisions or among different groups of employees. Measurement must also form the basis of any analysis of the causes of absence and thus of programmes of remedial action.

The standard and most widely used measure is the crude absence rate expressed as a percentage of 'working days lost'. This is simply calculated by working out the total number of days that employees are contracted to work and dividing it into the number of days on which employees failed to come to work over a given period of time. Multiplying the total by 100 gives the percentage figure. General absence rates of this kind can be calculated for the organisation as a whole, particular departments or staff groupings, or for individual employees. Without taking the same approach to measurement and monitoring across the whole organisation, it is impossible to compare department with department. Furthermore, inconsistencies are likely to develop in the approach taken to the management of absence, which can lead to unfairness in the way individual employees are treated.

Absence data can be collected in a variety of ways. Many organisations still rely on time-sheets filled in by each line manager and copied weekly or monthly to the pay-roll department. Others employ systems of self-certification, whereby individuals are required to notify the personnel department of their absence when they return. Larger organisations, and those with integrated computerised personnel systems, will ask line managers to record absences against each employee's record on the database. Reports can then be generated centrally showing how many days have been lost in each department. Perhaps the most technically sophisticated approach is the use of a clock-in/clock-out system, which records hours worked as well as instances of absence. Each of these methods has advantages and disadvantages in particular situations. The clock-in system, for example, is of little use where employees work away from the employer's premises for a substantial proportion of their time. Organisations also frequently experience difficulties in ensuring that line managers do actually record absence on computerised systems.

Presenteeism

The opposite of absenteeism is 'presenteeism' – a phenomenon that has received attention in the P&D press recently. The term refers to situations in which employees spend a good deal more time at work than is necessary for them to complete their job tasks. Typically, it involves people arriving very early in the morning and leaving very late at night. They may also come in at the weekend or decline to take their full holiday entitlement. Often it is done in an effort to impress superiors, and can become engrained in the culture of certain work groups. A limited amount of presenteeism is no big problem; indeed, it is useful when the workload is high to have people willing to work extra hours. However, when it is excessive, it can have negative effects. For example, it can make people overtired and bad-tempered, leading to a deterioration in workplace relationships. People who come in too much also tend to become narrow-minded, as they lack sufficient stimulation from outside the workplace. According to Balcombe (1997), this reduces their capability 'to contribute fresh ideas and different perspectives' or to bring to their work 'a sense of proportion and humour'.

Managers should therefore be open to the possibility that individuals or groups of employees are turning into 'presentees', and take steps to discourage such behaviour. This can be done by making clear to them that they are not impressing anyone by their actions and that their careers will not be enhanced as a result. It is also possible for managers actively to set an example by leaving on time themselves.

Source: Industrial Society (1997: 58)

The measurement process is invariably more complicated than it looks. First, there is a need to establish a clear policy for including the absence of part-time workers – particularly those who have irregular hours of work. Which system should be used to record a part-timer's failure to turn up to work three hours over a busy lunch-time period? This cannot be recorded as a day lost, so it should be recorded as a portion of a day (eg 37 per cent), as a half day, or as a percentage of that individual's contracted hours in the week in question. Where there are large numbers of part-time employees, organisations can use 'hours lost' rather than 'days lost' as the basic unit of absence for monitoring purposes.

There is also a need to consider what counts as absence and what does not. For example, a decision has to be taken whether holidays or days taken in lieu of overtime payments are included in the calculation. What should be recorded when someone comes into work a few hours late? What about days lost, or partially so, as a result of industrial action or by employees looking for work when under notice of redundancy? What is recorded when someone is absent because he or she has a dental appointment or is required to do jury service? What about maternity leave?

Once decisions have been made on these points, it is possible to calculate a standard absence rate for the organisation, or a part of the organisation, in any given period, and to undertake a meaningful analysis of trends over time. A great advantage of the more sophisticated computerised systems is their capacity for recording and subsequently reporting causes of absence, as well as the ball-park rate. Such systems contain a set of codes or a menu of options listing the whole range of possible reasons for absence that have to be chosen by the person feeding in the statistics. It is then possible to generate overall reports that include or exclude particular causes.

Many have also argued that the crude absence rate expressed as a percentage of time lost is too all-encompassing to be of any great use in analysing absence and planning courses of action aimed at its reduction. In particular, it is said that there is a need to record the number of distinct spells of absence (ie its frequency) as well as the total number of days. This is because one long spell of absence lasting 10 days is considerably less disruptive for the organisation than several short spells that total 10 days. Making such a distinction also allows an employer, in developing strategies to reduce absence, to differentiate between absence that results from a genuine illness and that due to other, less acceptable, causes. According to IDS (1994a: 6), a useful approach is 'The Bradford Factor', which was devised by a team of researchers at Bradford University.

Here, a points system is used, rather than 'days lost', as the unit of analysis. The formula used to calculate the number of points is $S \times S \times D$, where S is the number of separate spells of absence taken in a year and D is the number of days taken. Hence, someone absent for a total of 10 days in a year taken in a single spell would be recorded as having 10 points ($1 \times 1 \times 10$), whereas someone absent for 10 days in five two-day spells would be given 250 points ($5 \times 5 \times 10$). Such figures are easily calculated by a computerised system and can then be used as a basis for determining at what point individuals are formally interviewed on the subject of their absence record. It also provides a more useful basis for comparing levels across different departments, for setting absence reduction targets, and for tracking progress over time.

It is because of these complexities that benchmarking performance in terms of absence levels against those of competitor organisations becomes an intricate process. Unless everyone applies the same assumptions and rules, meaningful comparisons are difficult. A figure of 1 or 10 per cent means little unless you know what types of absence are included and on what basis the calculation has been made. That is not to say that there is no use at all in comparing figures with those of other employers operating in the same industrial sector, but that great caution should be taken when doing so, and that it should be recognised that figures can be calculated in markedly different ways. In particular, it is important to qualify comparisons made with industry-sector averages or 'norms' published in commercial surveys and in government publications. Data from the 1997 CBI survey is shown in Table 10.

Table 10 **CBI absenteeism survey data**

Sector	Average no. days taken by each employee in a year	Percentage
Government agencies	10.6	4.6
Education and training	10.4	4.6
NHS Trusts	9.9	6.7
Local government	9.2	6.0
Food and drink	7.9	3.5
Chemical	7.8	3.4
Utilities	7.7	3.4
Media and broadcasting*	7.5	3.2
Other services	7.4	3.2
Professional services	7.3	3.2
Retail and wholesale	6.8	3.0
Transport and distribution	6.8	3.0
General manufacturing	6.7	2.9
Financial services	6.3	2.8
Paper and packaging	6.0	2.6
Publishing*	6.0	2.6
Hi-tech	5.8	2.5
Pharmaceuticals*	5.7	2.5
Hotels and leisure*	4.6	2.0
Construction	4.2	1.8
Oil and mining*	3.3	1.4
(* sample size fewer than 10)		

Source: CBI (1997: 10)

Huczynski and Fitzpatrick (1989: 158–160) argue that comparing performance against average absence rates for the industry is a fatuous exercise even when it can be done accurately, because the variations within each industry are so great as to make the average figure meaningless. Instead, they suggest that all organisations should set a figure of 3 per cent as their aim, on the grounds that it has been shown to be achievable in all industrial sectors. Taking comfort from the fact that a 5 per cent absence rate is good by industry standards is thus seen as unnecessarily complacent.

> What is the current absence rate in your organisation? What methods are used to collect the data?

COSTING ABSENCE

The process of putting a cost on absence and thus calculating the value to the organisation of initiatives that aid its reduction is a complex and controversial field. According to an Industrial Society survey (1997: 11), it is attempted by only 54 per cent of organisations – for the most part, larger employers with the resources to invest in a well-thought-out costing system. A variety of reasons for not undertaking costing exercises was given. Some believed the process to be of little value or did not perceive that absence was a priority for them, while others believed such exercises to be too time-consuming. A further group stressed their inability to cost absence accurately because they lacked accurate attendance records or a computerised personnel system.

For those who do attempt to calculate the cost, there is a range of approaches available. The simplest is to calculate it in terms of the earnings paid to absent employees. Where pay is not deducted when people are absent, calculating the overall cost of absence is straightforward. An organisation simply works out the average daily earnings of its employees and multiplies this figure by the number of days on which employees were absent. Figures can also be worked out for subgroups and for particular departments. Hence, if average individual daily earnings in a clerical division employing 20 people are £50 and absence levels average 10 days a year, the total cost would be calculated at £10,000 (20 × 50 × 10). It is this approach that is used by the Industrial Society (1997: 11) to estimate the total annual cost of absence in the UK:

Average daily earnings per employee:	£70.34
Average number of absences per employee:	8.26 days
Total number of employees in the UK:	22.3 million

Total cost = (£70.34 × 8.26) × 22.3 million = £12.956 billion

However, such crude figures can act as only rough guides to the actual overall cost. In some ways it overestimates the total cost, because few employers pay their employees full earnings for days that they are away. Some pay only the rate of SSP, while others reduce the level during long periods of sickness. In the public sector, it is common for people who are sick for a long period to be put onto half-pay after six months. However, such an approach also underestimates costs in a variety of other ways. First, in basing the calculation on average earnings, it fails to take into account employment on-costs such as employers' National Insurance contributions, pension scheme contributions and the cost of any other benefits provided. Secondly, it does not include other direct and indirect costs incurred by the employer as a result of the absence. These include:

- temporary staff to cover for absent staff
- overtime paid to existing staff who cover
- reduced quality of work or productivity
- disruption to smooth running of systems
- management time spent managing the consequences of individual absences
- low morale or dissatisfaction on the part of colleagues left to cover the work.

Clearly, some of these are indirect and very difficult to quantify in practice; it is nonetheless possible to make estimates and to add these to the direct costs that are straightforward to calculate. A number of approaches used in individual industries to estimate indirect costs is given by Huczynski and Fitzpatrick (1989: 15–21). Arguably, because greater costs are incurred by frequent, short-term absences than by the more manageable long-term variety, these should be reflected in any assumptions used to calculate organisation-wide costs. Perhaps the most substantial costs of all are those associated with a continual need to overstaff the organisation so that absence can be covered. If the absence rate is running at 5 per cent a year, it is necessary to employ 5 per cent more staff than would otherwise be the case in order to allow the organisation to function. In a large organisation employing thousands of people, the total cost is therefore very considerable indeed.

However, it is also important to recognise that a certain amount of absence is unavoidable, because employees inevitably fall ill from time to time. Assumptions of this kind also have to be built in to estimates of the overall costs incurred. Employers can either look at their absence records to work out what proportion of sickness is definitely unavoidable or make a general assumption about its likely level based on published data. It seems to this author that a figure of 1.5 per cent, or approximately four days a year per employee, is reasonable, since this represents the lowest levels of absence achieved by organisations taking part in the most recent surveys. Subtracting this figure from the total cost will thus give a more useful estimate of the total avoidable cost.

THE CAUSES OF ABSENCE

It is not easy to identify with confidence what the main reasons for absence are, either in general terms or in particular organisations, because research findings on the issue have tended to differ. Undoubtedly, the uncertainty stems in part from the fact that employees are often unwilling to admit that they have been absent for reasons other than serious illness. However, it is also the case that there are no simple answers to the question, and that there is a variety of reasons that may contribute to an individual employee's being absent from work on a particular day. Moreover, the same reason can often be seen as being more or less justifiable depending on your point of view – a truism neatly summed up by Johns and Nicholson (1982) in their suggested conjugation of the verb 'to be absent':

> I am sometimes prevented from attending work through no fault of my own. You lack motivation to attend work regularly. They are lazy malingerers, wilfully milking the system.

The 1997 Industrial Society survey suggests that managers are often unconvinced by the excuses given by employees to explain their absence. This is illustrated by the differences that exist between what managers believe the major reasons for short-term absence to be and what employees state their reasons are when completing self-certification forms (see Table 11).

Table 11 **Five main causes of absence**

A	As recorded on certification forms	B	In managers' opinions
1	Colds and flu	1	Colds and flu
2	Stomach upsets and food poisoning	2	Stress and personal problems
3	Headaches and migraines	3	Sickness of other family member and childcare problems
4	Back problems	4	Low morale/boring job
5	Stress and personal	5	Monday morning blues

Source: Industrial Society 1997:10

However, Huczynski and Fitzpatrick warn against taking a simplistic view of the reasons for absence, and argue that, in doing so, managers invariably fail in their efforts to improve attendance levels. It therefore follows that there is a need to recognise that a variety of different factors may influence absence levels and that, in most cases, this calls for the development of a range of remedial tools.

> Our argument is that much of what is done by managers to combat absence in their organisations is taken in total ignorance of the causes of absence. Most managers neither understand, nor have investigated the causes of their absence problem. Instead, personal hunches, prejudices and rules of thumb represent the basis on which corrective action is decided. The failure of managers to deal effectively with their absence problem derives, to a large extent, from a lack of proper understanding.
>
> (Huczynski and Fitzpatrick, 1989: 32)

In an influential and often-quoted article published in 1978, Steers and Rhodes developed a process model to illustrate the different influences that determine attendance levels. Their work broke new ground in so far as it recognised first that dissatisfaction with work was not necessarily the most important explanation for absence and, secondly, that there might be situations in which employees were prevented from attending by 'situational constraints' that included factors other than poor health. They therefore divided the reasons into two broad categories: those concerned with the ability of employees to attend work, and those concerned with their willingness to do so. Their model is useful in that it makes a distinction between first-order or immediate causes of absence and the underlying influences that lead to poor attendance. The model is presented in Figure 4.

Figure 4 **Diagnostic model of employee attendance**

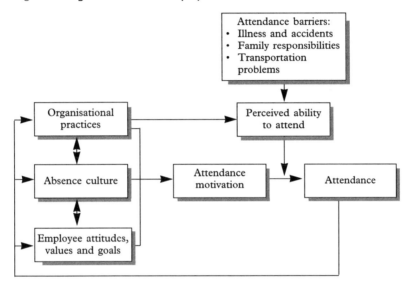

With reference to the work of Steers and Rhodes, as well as that of other writers who have researched employee attitudes and perceptions, it is possible to divide into five broad categories the various factors, aside from genuine illness, that may explain why one employee opts not to come to work when a colleague employed to do the same job chooses to attend. However, it is important to recognise that these are not distinct categories and that, in many cases, one factor influences another. For example, high absence could be due to boredom at work, which might in turn result from poor supervision and the orientation of the individual's personality. It may also reflect apathy towards life in general, which may in turn be related to home circumstances. Alternatively, the extent to which individuals have a strong social attachment to colleagues may well also derive from a mixture of factors relating to personality, home circumstances and the way the organisation is managed.

Employee attitudes
A number of authors have cited research that suggests some people are more prone to absence than others throughout their working lives. The presence of a poor history of attendance was one of the few

factors that Keller (1983: 536) found could be used to predict future absence rates with any confidence. Huczynski and Fitzpatrick (1989: 61) go further in suggesting that between 5 per cent and 10 per cent of individuals in any work group usually account for around 50 per cent of all absence. They go on to point out that studies have consistently shown particular personality types to be more absence-prone than others. It would seem that there is more likelihood that individuals who are tense, anxious and emotionally less stable will be absent more often than colleagues who exhibit traits of introversion and stability. However, research has also suggested that proneness to absence declines as people age. While older workers tend to have longer periods of illness, they tend to take less absence of the short, unauthorised variety than younger employees (Huczynski and Fitzpatrick 1989: 56).

Others have found evidence that attitudes and orientation towards work are correlated with social class and family background. Those who have had instilled in them a strong work ethic tend also to have a pronounced sense of family responsibility and a desire to do their jobs well. Such people tend to have excellent attendance rates and often come into work when, in truth, they are too ill to do so (Steers and Rhodes 1978: 369, Huczynski and Fitzpatrick 1989: 75). Personal attitudes towards work and absence are also shaped by the prevailing values and norms of the work group. Those who have hitherto been absent relatively seldom may become poor attenders if they join a group of employees who share an 'absence culture' (Nicholson and Johns 1985: 378). Conversely, in groups that display a strong work ethic colleagues are less likely to be absent, for fear of letting down fellow employees or attracting their disapproval (Steers and Rhodes 1978: 368).

Home circumstances
A number of authors have argued that family responsibilities are an important 'hidden' cause of absence. According to Sargent (1989: 16), such obligations often produce split loyalties for employees who otherwise exhibit a robust attachment to their jobs or possess a strong work ethic. This is the main reason cited in the literature for the tendency for younger women to have relatively high absence rates, because it is they who are most likely to take time off to care for sick children or elderly relatives. Huczynski and Fitzpatrick (1989: 80) have found from their research that rates of female absenteeism increase as those women's families become larger. In the case of women who employ child-minders, there may also be an economic incentive to take a day off occasionally, as long as no loss of pay is involved (Harvey and Nicholson 1993: 845).

Transportation difficulties can also affect the propensity to take days off work. The implication is that people who live some distance from their place of work, or have to undertake a difficult journey every morning, are more likely to opt for a day away from work than those whose travel-to-work arrangements are less disagreeable. In such cases it is not dislike of the job that deters people from making the effort to come to work, but the unpleasantness of commuting. Studies have found that it is not just the length of the journey that is off-putting, but that its complexity and cost are also important factors (Huczynski and Fitzpatrick 1989: 79).

In addition, home circumstances may also determine the importance of the economic incentive to come to work. It is often the case that one member of a household earns a great deal more than the others. The second or third income, while useful, is not therefore as essential, and reduces the importance of their work to the members concerned. Because there is less incentive for employees in these categories to earn more, they are less likely to be deterred from being absent by the prospect of losing pay or promotion opportunities. In their research, Huczynski and Fitzpatrick (1989: 53) found instances of employees who wanted part-time work but had to take full-time jobs because that was all that was available; so there was no incentive or even desire to attend for more than two or three days a week.

The economic climate
A key factor identified in the literature is prevailing economic conditions and, in particular, employee's perceptions of their own job security. Several studies have shown that at times of relatively high unemployment, or when there is fear of an economic downturn, people tend to be more diligent in attending work. It is assumed by Steers and Rhodes (1978: 366) that this occurs because employees fear for their jobs and do not wish to jeopardise their positions at work. Alternatively, as Huczynski and Fitzpatrick (1989: 65) suggest, the correlation could reflect a tendency on the part of managers to clamp down on absence when profit margins are particularly tight. Unsurprisingly, by contrast, absence appears to rise during economic recession among individuals under formal notice of redundancy.

Dissatisfaction with work
The question of a link between job satisfaction and a propensity to be absent is one the most controversial issues in this field. Its importance, when compared to other factors, is downplayed by Nicholson (1976: 734), Steers and Rhodes (1978: 362) and Edwards and Scullion (1984: 566), but is recognised as having potential significance by Huczynski and Fitzpatrick (1989: 38–40) and Sargent (1989: 12–13). Steers and Rhodes accept that satisfaction has a part to play, but stress that it is individual expectations and attitudes that determine satisfaction to a great degree.

Despite the conflicting opinions, it is clear from surveys of management perceptions that dissatisfaction with elements of the job and the work environment are believed to have a role to play in explaining absence patterns. In their review of the literature in this field, Huczynski and Fitzpatrick (1989: 38–51) cite evidence of the significance of the following factors in some cases (the extent to which findings can be generalised remains an open question):

• general boredom with the job

• lack of responsibility and challenge

• forms of work-related stress

• poor working conditions

- work overload
- lack of a defined workplace role
- poor relationships with colleagues
- poor supervision
- frequent internal job moves.

Interestingly, shift-working, although found to increase stress, does not appear to lead to increased absence. On the contrary, research suggests that people working variable shift-patterns have a lower level of absence than those employed on fixed shifts. There is also evidence to suggest that absence decreases as employees become more satisfied with their jobs and, in particular, form strong relationships with colleagues or attachments to a work group or team of which they form a part. This perception is used to explain why absence increases when individuals move from department to department within an organisation and why attendance tends to deteriorate as an organisation becomes larger (Huczynski and Fitzpatrick 1989: 46 and 51).

Control systems

There is a body of literature that examines absence from work not from the perspective of managers but as a social phenomenon in its own right. Here it is seen less as a managerial problem with the potential to be 'solved' and more as a natural state of affairs arising from the way work is organised in capitalist societies. Nevertheless, there are findings in this literature with important implications for those viewing absence through managerial eyes.

Those writing within sociological frames of reference (notably Paul Edwards and his colleagues) have tended to see absence as a form of unorganised or individual industrial conflict, which they accept as an inherent feature of manager-worker relationships. Seen in this light, absence is not a reaction to dissatisfaction with a particular job at a particular time, but one of a range of means used by employees in resisting management control of the labour process. In discussing their research, Edwards and Scullion (1984: 562) state that 'absenteeism was neither a response by individuals to the physical work environment nor a simple reflection of protest against management control ... it was the product of the control system'.

Seen in this way, the key variable is the extent and nature of the management control systems in operation. Edwards and Scullion (1984: 560–564) illustrate this point by contrasting absence rates in two factories. The first, in which there were high rates of absence, was characterised by the presence of intensive control systems and did not allow workers a means of 'challenging' the effort levels and quality standards demanded by managers. The second factory was organised very differently and as a result, in the view of the researchers, had a lower absence level. Here, although the work tasks were unpleasant and mundane, 'workers had sufficiently generous manning levels to enable them to perform their work comfortably, to enjoy a period of leisure at the end of the day and to move around and chat to their mates'. This occurred because of the degree of control that employees exercised over the way they organised their own work. Edwards and Scullion thus concluded that low rates of absence in their case-study companies arose from situations in which managers did not retain 'tight control over the work process', but where an environment had been created 'in which workers accepted managerial requirements as legitimate'.

> Think about recent occasions when you have been absent. Which of the above causes played a role in your case?

REDUCING ABSENCE LEVELS

A great deal has been written about the methods available to P&D practitioners in trying to reduce absence levels. However, no consensus has emerged as to what might constitute best practice in this field, with the result that this, like the debate about the causes of poor attendance, is a controversial area. Broadly speaking, the different approaches advanced fall into three categories: punitive measures, the use of incentives, and action that addresses the causes of absence with a view to preventing its occurrence. None of these three basic approaches, nor the various techniques they encompass, are mutually exclusive. It is therefore possible to argue that absence can be addressed from a number of different angles at the same time.

Punitive approaches

The most commonly used approach is the use of punitive or disciplinary sanctions, or the threat of so doing. According to an IRS survey (1994a), the majority of organisations monitor absence levels centrally, formally interview people about their absence when they return to work, and review absence records when the number of days taken by an individual reaches a predetermined trigger-point. Often these policies are couched in positive terms, the aim in the early stages being to offer help to individuals who may be experiencing some of the problems identified and discussed above in the section on causes of absence. However, they also serve as a means by which employees are informed that their absence has been noted and are warned that, except in cases of serious illness, they are expected to attend. As such, they effectively form the start of a formal disciplinary procedure which will be geared fully into action if the absence becomes persistent.

A variation on this approach is to require all employees returning from a period of absence to complete a sickness form. Such forms usually contain the same kind of questions that would be asked at a return to work interview, but have the appearance of being 'official' and state that they will be kept on an employee's personal file. Again, the aim is to underline the fact that the employer has noticed the absence, and that such conduct will be permitted only in cases of genuine illness. Forms typically ask for quite detailed information, such as that requested below, and require employees to sign a declaration stating that the information given is true:

• On which day did you fall sick?

- When and how did you notify your manager?
- On which day did your sickness end?
- Please specify the symptoms of your sickness.
- Please specify the actions you took to aid your recovery.

The law effectively defines the shape and broad approach that employers take in treating absence as a disciplinary matter. It is quite legal to dismiss people whose absence records are deemed too high, provided the employer acts reasonably and operates an acceptable procedure. The fact that the sickness is genuine or that medical certificates are presented does not stop an employer from legally dismissing someone whose attendance record is persistently poor. Often in these cases employees complain of back pain, minor emotional stress or other conditions which are not, in truth, sufficient to stop them coming to work if they wish to. According to Sargent (1989: 68–69), these are the important steps to take:

- Investigate the facts to establish how much absence has been taken and whether there are any patterns to suggest that it might not be due to genuine sickness (eg not returning after a holiday, skipping Mondays and Fridays or the day after a staff night out etc).
- Give employees every opportunity to explain their absence record.
- Give formal written warnings explaining that an improvement is required and that dismissal will result if this does not occur.

Many organisations also, in their formal warnings, set employees specific targets to aim at, so that they know exactly what is expected over a review period. There is no hard-and-fast rule about what the target should be, but a common approach is to use the average rate for the individual's department or work group. A period of six months is considered a reasonable length of time between formal review meetings, although it may be shorter where the record is particularly poor.

In practice, these cases are very much more difficult to deal with than it appears on paper – especially when warnings fail to have the desired effect and dismissal is imminent. Where there is a genuine problem, eg relating to sickness in a child or parent, handling these matters sensitively but firmly is one of the most unenviable tasks that a P&D manager has to perform. It nevertheless remains important that all cases are handled consistently and in accordance with an agreed procedure or formal absence policy. Otherwise, were a legal case to be brought, the employer would be unable to show that he or she had acted with sufficient reasonableness to satisfy an industrial tribunal.

Another commonly used application of punitive sanctions involves reducing or docking pay for days or hours not worked. In this field the employer has considerable if limited discretion. At the time of writing (late 1997), organisations are obliged to pay SSP to employees earning over £61.00 a week when they are absent for more than three days. It is only reasonable to refuse this payment where employees fail to notify their employer that they are sick. Self-certification is acceptable to cover the first seven days of absence; thereafter a medical certificate is required if the employer is to continue paying SSP. At present, the weekly rate of SSP set by the government is £54.55.

However, there is a great deal more flexibility for employers seeking to reduce other payments or withdraw payment altogether. Provided employees are made aware of the position through a written statement of terms and conditions of employment, it is permissible for an employer to pay no money at all to employees who are absent, over and above their obligation to pay SSP. A number of employers take this approach in the first weeks of employment if they find that absence rates among new starters are particularly high. Others take a less severe view but nonetheless reduce pay by a proportion for all sickness not covered by a medical certificate. Effectively, such approaches involve fining employees as a deterrent against unauthorised absence.

A further set of punitive methods are somewhat longer-term in their effect. These involve taking attendance records into account when making fundamental decisions about individuals' future employment. The most common examples are in:

- selecting candidates for redundancy

- deciding when or whether to promote someone

- determining pay increases or increments

- determining performance-related payments or bonuses

- the allocation of interesting work or new projects.

All or some of these may be a deterrent, provided people know in advance that their absence may count against them in these ways. That said, it is vital that people suffering from serious illness are not included – to do so would be iniquitous and inevitably prompt strong feelings of injustice, low morale and low trust among employees generally.

Despite their apparent proliferation, punitive approaches such as these have attracted a great deal of criticism. First, it is argued that they have little effect in reducing absence levels except in the short term (Harvey and Nicholson 1993: 843) – a trend confirmed in a number of published case-studies. Allen and Torrington (1996: 101), remarking on absence patterns in a case-study company, conclude that it is not the punitive measures themselves that cause a reduction in absence, but the signalling by management that they intend to make absence an issue. The result is a temporary, if substantial, reduction in absence while the 'purge' is on, followed by a return to previous levels – or, in this case, higher levels than before. By contrast, Nicholson (1976) found in a similar study that absence did not decline following a management clampdown but that employees simply started producing medical notes so as to ensure that their absence was classified as authorised rather than unauthorised.

Others criticise the use of punitive measures in absence control on the grounds that they often operate unfairly. In particular, they make no distinction between absence that, from the perspective of an employee, could be classed as avoidable, and that which is not. Hence, people who take days off to care for a sick relative or because they themselves are genuinely suffering from a minor ailment are treated in the same way as those who simply opt for more leisure time by feigning sickness. True, the effect from the employer's perspective is the same, but if the workforce perceives the approach to be unjust it will lead to other problems – such as low morale, higher staff-turnover and reduced work effort (Harvey and Nicholson 1993: 843).

Edwards and Whitston (1993: 31) go further, arguing that the introduction of stricter absence-control mechanisms of this kind may actually be counter-productive, because employees resent such initiatives and are inclined to react against them by 'withdrawing the day to day commitment to the enterprise on which (management) had hitherto been able to rely'. In an earlier article, Edwards and Scullion reported an example of such considerations' being taken on board by an employer:

> In one company this was explicitly recognised, with an internal report on absenteeism and its relationship to the company's sick pay scheme arguing that tolerating a certain level of absence could be in the company's interests because other more disruptive expressions of discontent were rendered less likely: absence could be an important safety valve.
>
> (Edwards and Scullion, 1984: 555)

Despite these formidable criticisms, all the survey evidence indicates that most employers continue to operate some punitive techniques, and that they believe them to have a degree of effectiveness (CBI 1997: 17, IRS 1994a, 1994b, IDS 1994a). Furthermore, Harvey and Nicholson's (1993) survey of opinion in the Civil Service strongly suggests that most employees also support the use of penalties to discourage absence, provided they are applied fairly. It would thus appear that many either remain sceptical about the merits of alternative approaches or are unwilling to view unauthorised absence as anything other than a disciplinary matter.

How far does your organisation rely on punitive measures to control absence? Have other approaches ever seriously been considered?

Attendance incentives

Taking active steps to reward good attendance is a controversial approach to the reduction of absence. Many managers are unwilling to consider such practices because they involve rewarding employees merely for fulfilling a basic term of their contracts. Some argue that this amounts to paying people twice. Others feel that attendance bonuses are unfair because they effectively punish people who, if they are genuinely ill, lose out through no fault of their own. A third set of criticisms relates to the apparent ineffectiveness of incentive approaches when applied in practice.

A number of different methods by which employees can be rewarded for attending every day over a defined period are identified in the literature. Huczynski and Fitzpatrick (1989: 118) provide a long list, which includes the following possibilities:

- *Attendance bonuses*
  The payment of additional cash to employees with a perfect or near-perfect attendance record. This can be done on a weekly, monthly, quarterly or annual basis.

- *Lotteries*
  All employees with a perfect attendance record over a week or a month are entered into a prize draw. Winners are then publicly recognised and rewarded with a cash sum or some other prize.

- *Adjustments to profit-sharing*
  Where some form of profit-related pay scheme is in use, the proportion of bonus allotted to individuals is increased if their attendance record is good.

- *Well-pay plans*
  No payments are made over and above SSP for days absent, but extra payments are made for months where attendance is perfect.

- *Group-based approaches*
  Bonuses are paid to every member of a team or department, provided absence levels on average reach set targets.

Incentive schemes of one kind or another appear to be used by a substantial minority of employing organisations. Edwards and Whitston (1989: 10) state that they are operated in around 10 per cent of organisations, while more recent surveys (Industrial Society 1997: 13, CBI 1997: 17) put the figure somewhat higher. In the case of the CBI survey, 34 per cent of respondents claimed to have implemented some kind of attendance-reward system – a figure double that of their 1994 survey. However, according to the Industrial Society, around half of these schemes are non-monetary. That is to say, prizes are offered rather than bonus payments.

Attendance incentives at Victoria Station

At the Victoria Coach Station in London managers claim to have had considerable success in reducing absence levels by using both attendance bonuses and return-to-work interviews. Between 1987, when the scheme started operating, and 1991, absence levels fell from 16.3 days per year per employee to 9 days.

The incentive scheme was based on a points system calculated using 'The Bradford Factor' described above. It is paid quarterly, but relates to attendance records over the previous 12-month period. Each employee with fewer than 200 points at each review date receives a bonus payment equal to one day's pay. The result is that staff who are off work with genuine illnesses qualify even if they are absent for 200 working days in a single spell. Those who take more than five single days of absence over a year do not qualify, because six spells multiplied by six spells multiplied by six days equals 216 points. After a few years of operation, over three-quarters of the staff were found to be qualifying for the bonus payments.

Source: IDS (1992: 4)

Opinion is divided as to how successful these approaches are in the reduction of absence. Cherrington (1989: 316) found evidence of absence rates declining by 40 per cent in a manufacturing company following the introduction of rewards for good attendance, and others also quote examples of individual schemes that appear to have had a positive effect (Steers and Rhodes, 1978: 367). However, by and large the literature comes down against such approaches. Huczynski and Fitzpatrick (1989: 115) describe a series of studies that suggest either that these approaches are unsuccessful in reducing absence or that, where there is an improvement in attendance, they prove not to be cost-effective. The same broad conclusion is reached by the CBI (1997: 17) and the Industrial Society (1997: 13), who suggest that these are ranked among the least effective approaches by managers, and that they are associated with organisations that have higher-than-average absence levels.

However, it can be argued that it is unwise to treat all reward plans as being alike, because in reality they differ greatly one from another in terms of their design and value. What is important is to pick out those features of incentive plans that appear to give them the best chance of success. A number of conclusions can be made in this regard. In particular, there is evidence that attendance bonus systems work most effectively when the employees themselves are involved in the design of the scheme (Steers and Rhodes 1978: 367, Huczynski and Fitzpatrick 1989: 121). Another conclusion is that incentive schemes are more appealing to employees who are paid relatively little. Harvey and Nicholson (1993) found that lower-grade Civil Servants were far more attracted to the prospect than colleagues who earned higher salaries. It can therefore be assumed that such schemes work best where people come to work primarily for money, and are keen to increase their take-home pay in whatever way possible.

The central problem in designing schemes is setting the right level of bonus. On the one hand, the payment or prize must be of sufficient value to act as an incentive, while on the other, if it is too high, the scheme will be too costly. A bonus of 10 per cent may be effective as a means of discouraging absence, but it will end up costing the employer a great deal more than was being lost as a result of poor absence levels in the first place. There is also the problem of employees' losing all incentive to attend once they have taken time off in any one review period. In such circumstances, seeing their colleagues collecting the bonus can act only as a disincentive.

An interesting conclusion reached by several authors is that non-monetary or intrinsic rewards are both a relatively effective means of reducing absence and cost very little. Essentially, these involve publicly recognising good attendance. A number of such schemes is described by Huczynski and Fitzpatrick (1989: 120–121), including one operated at Rank Xerox that involved granting employees who completed a year without any absence a 'perfect attendance award', consisting of a small gift and a certificate. The result was successful, 31 per cent of the workforce qualifying for the award in 1986. A three-year certificate was then introduced, which 12 per cent of the workforce received. The great potential of such approaches is summed up by Harvey and Nicholson (1993: 854):

> Many respondents with little or no absence for long periods expressed much pride in the fact, but at the same time many commented on lack of recognition for their attendance. These two responses strongly suggest that reinforcing pride in attendance by explicit recognition of good attendance is likely to be one of the most cost-effective management actions.

It can thus be concluded, first, that there are great practical problems associated with the introduction and maintenance of monetary-reward systems that pay extra cash to employees who have good attendance records, and, secondly, that they appear to have only limited success in practice. That said, it is clearly not impossible to make them work well when the circumstances are right and when the main pitfalls associated with their introduction are avoided. On the other hand, there is a strong body of evidence suggesting that non-monetary forms of reward are effective and cost considerably less than the first kind. As so often in personnel management, it is important to avoid being swift to criticise and slow to praise – a general rule of particular relevance to absence management.

Preventative measures

The third set of approaches open to employers wishing to reduce absence levels involves tackling the root causes rather than using penalties and incentives to encourage better attendance. The aim is to assess what factors are motivating employees to stay away from work when they could come in, and to strive for the elimination of such factors. It is suggested above that the main causes of absence could broadly be divided into five distinct categories. We now look again at these, reflecting on which preventative measures might have most effect.

The first category of causes was employee attitudes, both those that people bring to their employment and those developed in response to prevailing organisational norms. In the case of the former, little can be done short of seeking to influence people's views through effective leadership. Perhaps the most effective action that employers can take is to give consideration to absence records at the selection stage. References from former employers may have something to offer here, because the information requested is essentially factual and thus does not rely on someone's opinion of an employee. However, great care must be taken in assessing past absence records, for they can be highly misleading. High absence over the previous 12 months might very well have resulted from a one-off illness, and so should not be used as evidence of a general proneness to absence. It is necessary to probe beneath the 'headline figure' by asking the candidate to explain why he or she was absent on so many days. The use of personality questionnaires can also help to screen out people likely to be more prone to absence than others. It is also possible to include some form of attitude survey in selection procedures which could include questions on perceptions of absence from work. The aim here is not simply to weed out those likely to be absent most often, but also to make sure that the right people are appointed to the right jobs, thus reducing the likelihood of absence occurring as a result of dissatisfaction.

Addressing the problems that stem from a prevalent absence culture is a harder task. There are no simple solutions here, but the use of some of the incentive and punitive techniques outlined above, when applied over a sustained period, may have a positive effect. Alternatively, efforts can be made to probe a little more deeply in order to discover the main reasons for the existence of such cultural norms in a particular department. The work of Nicholson and Johns (1985) is useful here, in that it identifies four distinct types of absence culture and suggests different means by which each might be tackled to best effect. For example, they distinguish between situations in which some unauthorised absence is perceived by employees to be an entitlement and those in which employees calculate and then balance the costs and benefits accruing to them when they take a day off. In each case, different managerial actions are needed if employee attitudes are to be changed and the absence culture weakened.

In situations where it is not attitudes that are the problem, but home circumstances, different preventative measures are clearly justified. The aim here should be to give practical help so that employees are able to come to work more easily. It may be possible to allow people to work from home from time to time, or to work more flexible hours so as to allow them to juggle home and work responsibilities more easily. Larger organisations may devise systems whereby people can apply to take unpaid leave in addition to their annual holiday entitlement, or longer career breaks or sabbaticals. It may also be possible to take a more flexible attitude to start and finish times, to enable those with further to travel to cut their journey time by avoiding rush-hour traffic or to use different buses. All these measures cost very little, but may have the effect not only of cutting avoidable absence but also of increasing morale and commitment. Other more costly developments, such as the introduction of childcare facilities, can probably be justified only in terms of other benefits, but are likely to have a positive effect on attendance records.

Other areas of activity that have received a good deal of attention in recent years are occupational health services, counselling sessions and more general forms of employee assistance programmes (EAPs) which aim, amongst other things, to assist employees improve their situations both at home and at work. Occupational health services clearly have a direct role to play as far as absence is concerned, because they can help employees to avoid contracting medical complaints. There are also situations in which interventions by an occupational health department can ease the strain of coming to work and thus minimise the occasions on which employees stay at home on account of relatively minor medical conditions. Back pain is one example, as are a whole range of mental and emotional illnesses.

In the case of absence rooted in employee dissatisfaction at work or resistance to overbearing control on the part of managers, there is a wide range of preventative actions open to employers. Many are discussed elsewhere in this book – several in the following chapter in the context of staff turnover – so there is no need to cover them in detail here. The following are identified by Huczynski and Fitzpatrick (1989: 123–127, 144–145) as particularly significant:

- job enrichment
- work rotation
- teamworking
- employee participation
- improving the work environment
- better training in supervision
- improved communication
- improved developmental opportunities.

The benefits of initiatives in these areas are, of course, not restricted to improving attendance. They should also have a general effect on

---

ALIEDIM

At the end of their book on absence management, Huczynski and Fitzpatrick (1989) conclude by presenting a 'seven-step approach to absence control' which draws together their main themes. It is given the acronym ALIEDIM, which represents the following steps: Assess, Locate, Identify, Evaluate, Design, Implement and Monitor. They also provide very informative and useful check-lists and activity briefs to assist managers in completing each step, along with a case-study illustrating the model's use in practice.

The first step involves assessing the size of the absence problem and estimating what it is costing the organisation. They suggest that indirect long-term costs be included in the assessment, as well as the obvious and easily quantifiable direct costs. The second step involves locating where in the organisation (ie among which groups of employee) the problem is worst – inevitably, this requires the assembly of comparative statistical data. The third step entails investigating the causes of absence among the groups identified in step 2. Step 4 necessitates evaluating the effectiveness of existing absence-control techniques and deciding how appropriate they are in the light of the investigation undertaken in step 3. That is followed by the design stage (step 5), in which new and more appropriate remedial plans are decided upon, due consideration being given to the range of available options. They are then implemented at step 6. The final stage involves monitoring the results of the initiative against pre-defined criteria.

---

trust, commitment and morale, with positive consequences for staff turnover, employee relations, employee development and, ultimately, competitiveness. However, their effect on absence, in so far as it can be costed, may be used to form part of a business case for their introduction.

FURTHER READING

- Good general books on absence written from a management perspective are few and far between. The best is undoubtedly *Managing Employee Absence for a Competitive Edge* by Andrzej Huczynski and Michael Fitzpatrick (1989), which provides plenty of ideas together with a summary of research evidence. A shorter book covering practical issues and containing a number of helpful suggestions is *The Missing Workforce: Managing absenteeism* by Andrew Sargent (1989).

- Updates on developments in the field of absence management, together with case-studies illustrating initiatives undertaken by employers, are covered in the IDS Studies and Industrial Society publications. Both produce a major new study of the topic every two years or so.

- The topic is well covered in *Motivation and Work Behaviour*, edited by Steers and Porter (1978). The book includes the articles by Steers and Rhodes and Nicholson and Johns referred to in this chapter.

- A thought-provoking and critical view of practice in the field of absence management, based on interviews with employees about their perceptions, is *Attending To Work: The management of attendance and shopfloor order* by Paul Edwards and Colin Whitston (1993).

12 Reluctantly saying farewell

It is common to hear employers characterise difficulties in staffing their organisations as 'recruitment problems', often summed up in the familiar phrase, 'You just can't get good staff these days.' In fact, many such predicaments are due more to the existence of problems in retaining people. If good staff chose not to resign in the first place there would be no need to stumble across such difficulties in recruiting their successors! However, managers are often reluctant to concede this truism, because it may mean implicitly admitting that a frustrating situation is, at least in part, of their own making.

Employees leave organisations for many reasons. While some depart involuntarily as a result of dismissal, redundancy or forced retirement, the vast majority resign of their own volition – some to take up new jobs, others to take either a temporary or a permanent break from the workforce. This chapter focuses on the implications for personnel specialists of voluntary turnover and its cost to organisations; it starts by looking at recent turnover trends and the extent to which increases in the number of voluntary resignations can be seen as either positive or negative for employers. The methods used to monitor staff turnover, to calculate its costs and to benchmark results against those of other employers are then examined. This is followed by an analysis of various explanations for voluntary resignations, and consideration of the plans of action that can be adopted to reduce their number. Finally, attention is given to the legal and ethical issues of voluntary release.

By the end of this chapter, readers should be able to:

- distinguish between voluntary and involuntary release from organisations
- monitor and analyse staff turnover
- conduct effective exit interviews and staff attitude surveys
- develop plans aimed at reducing turnover levels.

In addition, readers should be able to understand and explain:

- theories explaining staff turnover
- legal requirements in respect of contractual notice periods and restraint-of-trade clauses
- ethical considerations relating to the management of voluntary release.

DEFINING VOLUNTARY RELEASE

Distinguishing between departures from employment initiated by employees and those initiated by the employer is not straightforward. While some cases are clear-cut (eg dismissal for gross misconduct or resignation to take up a job with a competitor), many others result from a mixture of factors. A common example is the resignation of an employee on grounds of serious ill-health, when dismissal would have resulted in any event. Another situation arises with retirement, when it is not always easy to tell how keen individual employees are to quit at a predetermined retirement age. It is also difficult to say with any degree of certainty whether someone 'was pushed' or 'jumped' when he or she resigns when redundancies are threatened.

However, it is important to reach some kind of accepted judgement as to what is defined as voluntary termination if any meaningful comparative analysis is to be undertaken as regards turnover rates in different departments or among other employers. Perhaps the simplest approach is to use the very broad definition that includes all resignations not formally initiated by the employer. Data of this kind is straightforward to collect and is thus unlikely to take up a great deal of management time. Results can then be adjusted or re-interpreted at the analysis stage to take account of any grey areas such as those identified above.

A further distinction to be made in deciding how to manage turnover levels is that between resignations that might have been avoided and those that would have occurred anyway, irrespective of employer actions. These are often referred to as, respectively, 'controllable' and 'uncontrollable' reasons. The former category includes employees who quit primarily because of dissatisfaction with some aspect of their job or the organisation in comparison with perceived alternative employment opportunities, while the latter encompasses resignations that result from factors such as ill-health, the relocation of spouses and other domestic responsibilities. Naturally, it is the controllable resignations to which is given most attention when organisations seek to reduce turnover levels.

The distinction between voluntary and involuntary turnover is becoming increasingly significant with the rising number of employees on fixed-term contracts working on specific projects. In organisations where flexible working of this kind has become common, the proportion of resignations categorised as 'involuntary' will also have grown. Whereas previously a situation in which someone left at a time of the organisation's choosing was relatively rare, it is now an accepted part of organisational life. As a result, organisations seeking to monitor voluntary turnover can no longer rely on crude general turnover rates as their main tool of measurement.

What factors explained your decision to resign from positions you have held? To what extent are these readily categorised as voluntary/ involuntary or controllable/uncontrollable?

TURNOVER TRENDS

A number of surveys are undertaken each year in the UK to establish overall turnover rates. The largest is provided by *Skill Needs in Britain,* funded by the Department for Education and Employment (DfEE). This contains the results of a large-scale annual telephone survey of approximately 4,000 employers. Because it covers organisations in both the public and private sectors and across a whole range of industries, it can claim to encompass the majority of employees in the UK. Details of recent findings have been published in *Employment Review* (see *Employee Development Bulletins 75* and *87,* 1996, 1997), revealing considerable fluctuations in national turnover rates over time. In particular, the survey shows the extent to which people are less inclined to move jobs in a recession. The UK rate fell substantially after 1991, only to rise again in 1995 and 1996 (see Table 12). Another survey, *Employment in Europe,* confirms this broad pattern for the UK. It also shows that turnover rates here have tended to be higher than in other European countries, averaging 16 per cent between 1984 and 1992.

Table 12 UK national turnover rates

Year	Rate (per cent)
1991	15.5
1992	10.0
1993	11.0
1994	11.5
1995	21.0
1996	14.0

The sudden leap in the rate in *Skills Needs in Britain* data for 1995 may result from sampling error or may reflect the tendency for large numbers of people who want to leave their employers to wait until a recession is over before seeking new jobs. Writers have referred to this phenomenon as 'pent-up turnover', and have suggested that employers are wise to plan for its likely impact (IDS 1995e: 13).

Of more interest to employers seeking to benchmark their turnover rates against appropriate comparators are the figures that these and other smaller surveys generate for specific industrial sectors, regions and occupational groups. These show considerable variations. For example, in 1995, while the average UK turnover was 21 per cent, it was as high as 26 per cent in East Anglia but only 15 per cent in Greater Manchester. There is also a tendency for larger employers to have markedly lower turnover rates than smaller competitors. In 1995, the average rate for organisations employing over 500 people was just 11 per cent.

For data on variations between specific industrial sectors it is necessary to rely on smaller-scale surveys such as that carried out each year by the CIPD. One should not read too much into these results, because of the very small sample sizes used and the inclusion of involuntary as well as voluntary turnover. They do, however, give a *general* indication of substantial variations between industries (see Table 13).

Table 13 Turnover rates, various industries

Industry	Average turnover, 1994–95 (%)
Retailing	36.13
Hotels and catering	35.93
Professional services	2.75
Construction	1.42
Financial services	17.30
Transport and distribution	7.28
NHS Trusts	16.85
Other public sector	1.96
General manufacturing	11.87

Source: IPD Labour Turnover Surveys (1995, 1996)

Turnover among personnel specialists

According to the *Remuneration Economics Survey*, the overall voluntary turnover rate for personnel specialists in the UK in 1996 was 7.1 per cent – pretty low when compared with other occupational groups, but high when compared with previous years. The more senior the position, the lower the turnover (it was 8.5 per cent among junior personnel specialists but only 4.4 per cent among senior colleagues). As with other occupational groups, there is a marked inclination for older personnel people to remain in their jobs longer than their younger counterparts when given the choice. Turnover was 8.7 per cent for the under-30s in 1996 but only 1.7 per cent for over-50s.

Data from these and other surveys published in *Employment Review* (1996, 1997) suggest that turnover figures also vary quite considerably between people in different occupations. Perhaps unsurprisingly, it appears to be highest among sales staff and those employed to do routine, unskilled work (20–25 per cent in 1994 and 1995), and lowest among management and craft workers (10–14 per cent). In other words, turnover rates are highest among those who possess fewest industry-specific skills. By contrast, there is less movement where individuals are more restricted in their choice of alternative jobs because their skills and experience are less readily transferable.

DOES TURNOVER MATTER?

There is some debate in the literature about how far employers should be concerned about turnover levels. Some writers have emphasised the potentially positive effects of a continuous transfusion of fresh blood into the organisation. Carrell *et al* (1995: 777) distinguish between 'functional' and 'dysfunctional' turnover, and suggest that the former serves to promote innovative ideas and methods and can thus 'renew a stagnating organisation'. Hom and Griffeth (1995: 27–30) also draw attention to research that has shown functional turnover to be commoner than the dysfunctional form. The net result is an improvement in productivity as poorer employees quit, leaving a higher proportion of good performers to enhance organisational effectiveness. They also note that high turnover gives employers more opportunity to promote and develop valued staff and reduces the need to make costly redundancies when there is a downturn in business.

High turnover is probably least worrying in industries employing people in relatively low-skilled occupations that nevertheless require high levels of customer service (eg fast-food restaurants and telesales operations). According to Kearns (1994: 11), this is because the employer wishes to harness what is, in all likelihood, a short-term burst of enthusiasm on the part of the employee. Such a situation has allowed the various brands of burger restaurant to expand rapidly across the world while coping with annual turnover rates averaging 300 per cent (Ritzer 1996: 130).

Despite these points, it is safe to conclude that, for most organisations, turnover in excess of 5–10 per cent has more negative than positive consequences. The more valuable the employees in question, the more damaging the resignation – particularly when they move on to work for a competitor. According to Hom and Griffeth (1995: 13–27), there are various reasons, aside from the costs directly associated with the resignation, for employers to minimise the numbers of employees leaving. These include productivity losses, impaired quality of service, lost business opportunities, an increased administrative burden and employee demoralisation.

However, it is the direct costs associated with turnover that have received the most attention from writers on this topic, and that provide the meat of the business case for seeking to reduce the frequency of voluntary resignations. The following is a list of potential costs associated with employee attrition, incorporating material from a variety of sources (IDS 1989, Fair 1992, IDS 1995e, Hom and Griffeth 1995, *Employee Development Bulletin 75* 1996, and *Employee Development Bulletin 87* 1997). It is clear that some are more readily quantifiable than others:

- direct recruitment costs (advertising, use of agents etc)

- recruitment administration (responding to enquiries and sending out application forms, equal opportunities monitoring)

- selection costs (travelling expenses for candidates, psychometric testing, staff time in interviewing or running assessment centres, checking references)

- development costs (training the new employee using formal and informal development methods, induction training)

- administrative costs associated with resignations (pay-roll arrangements, calculation of holiday entitlements, pension transfers, conducting exit interviews)

- administrative costs associated with new starters (contract writing, medicals, sending out documentation, issuing uniforms, parking permits, identity badges, company cars etc, relocation expenses for new starter)

- inefficiency in production or service provision (resulting from slackness on the part of the resigner, inexperience of the replacement employee and inefficiencies resulting from a period in which the vacancy is unfilled)

- overtime and costs of hiring temporary workers (during the period between resignation and the hiring of a new member of staff).

Although not all of the above cost implications will apply in any one case of voluntary resignation, several are likely to feature in some way. Each element will not in itself necessarily result in a great deal of expenditure, but it is the cumulative effect that gives the business case for attacking turnover its potency.

Estimates of the actual cost of turnover vary considerably depending on which of the factors listed above are included in the calculation. The level of the final figure also varies with the nature and content of the job under consideration. Ball-park figures are thus of only limited use to personnel specialists seeking to compare the performance of their organisations with others. However, they do give a useful indication of the potential scale of cost implications associated with high turnover.

Fair (1992) suggests that replacement costs equate, on average, to six months' salary of the post in question, rising to two years' salary in the case of very senior posts. J. Douglas Phillips (1990) goes further, suggesting that the total figure averages 1.5 times the annual starting salary (see IDS 1995: 11). Surveys of employers indicate that while costs are not generally perceived to be this high, they are nevertheless very significant. According to the 1996 IPD survey on labour turnover, one in six employers estimates costs associated with turnover to be £12,000 per employee (IRS 1997a: 15), while a recent exercise undertaken by the TSB gave a figure of £6,500 for each clerk who left within six months of taking up his or her position (IDS 1995e: 11). The overall figures from the 1996 IPD survey reveal a considerable variation between the costs associated with turnover among different occupational groups, managers topping the table and unskilled workers bringing up the rear (see Table 14).

Using the figures in Table 14 and those for turnover rates in 1995, it is possible to calculate the total cost of turnover for a fictional company employing a total of 400 people (50 in each of the occupations listed in Table 14):

Total number of staff resigning: 63

Total replacement cost: £134,545

Table 14 Turnover rates by occupational group, 1995

Occupational group	estimated cost per person (£)	average turnover (%)
Management/administration	4,295	11
Professional	4,140	13
Technical	2,925	13
Sales	2,551	22
Craft/skilled	1,402	12
Clerical/secretarial	1,335	17
Operatives/assembly	1,001	15
Routine unskilled	841	23

A simple exercise of this kind gives an indication of how great the potential savings would be if turnover were reduced, however modestly. For large organisations, particularly those operating in high-attrition sectors such as retailing and catering, the annual 'turnover bill' can easily run into many millions of pounds. An example is W.H. Smith, who calculated in 1993 that, for each percentage point they reduced their staff turnover rate, they would save £250,000 (IDS 1994d: 25).

While these figures seem to give incontrovertible justification for attacking turnover and setting out plans for its reduction, it must be remembered that such strategies themselves can cost a great deal of money. There is therefore also a good case for judicious consideration of appropriate courses of action in terms of their likely long-term costs and benefits to the employer.

> Does your organisation measure its turnover rates? How varied are the figures for different occupational groups?

MEASUREMENT AND BENCHMARKING

Generating meaningful turnover statistics that form a robust basis for the development of remedial plans is a very inexact science. It is easy to misinterpret figures, which can lead to problems in multi-divisional organisations where one unit's turnover rates are compared with others'. A classic example arises from the tendency for turnover to be at its highest in the first months of an individual's employment. For this reason, units that are performing well (and are thus expanding) are very likely to have higher figures than those in relative decline. So great care has to be taken in analysing raw turnover statistics and in using them as a means of formally assessing the performance of particular personnel functions or line managers.

The two most commonly used measures of turnover were discussed in some detail in the context of human resource planning (see Chapter 6). They are the 'wastage index' and the 'stability index'. The former measures crude turnover rates by dividing the number of voluntary resignations over the course of a year by the average number of staff employed in the organisation over the same period. This is then multiplied by 100 to give a percentage figure. Wastage indices of one form or another are those used by the various government and commercial surveys of turnover described above. By contrast, stability indices effectively discount high turnover in the first months of employment by focusing only on the number of individuals employed for a prolonged period – usually a year – rather than on the number who actually leave. This index is also expressed as a percentage figure, but is calculated by dividing the number of staff with more than one year's service by the total number of employees in post a year ago.

It would be quite possible for an organisation to have a very high wastage rate and, at the same time, a high stability rate – reflecting particularly high turnover in the first year of employment. Alternatively, an employer could have a relatively healthy overall wastage rate but a worryingly low stability rate, reflecting a tendency for individuals to leave once they had completed some years of service. In each case, the most appropriate P&D response as a means of reducing turnover will be rather different. However, the figures themselves are often meaningless until they are put in context by comparing them with those of other departments, divisions and organisations, or with those computed for previous years. As we have seen, substantial turnover levels are part-and-parcel of life in certain industries at particular times and in particular regions. What is significant, in business terms, is how the results compare with those of key competitors. It is only when figures are benchmarked that they can inform personnel priorities and policies.

Within a single company or conglomerate, in theory, it is relatively straightforward to obtain benchmarking information. An example might be a chain of restaurants or shops, where each unit is very similar to the others. In theory, it would be possible to set up a monitoring system that compared turnover in each unit on the same basis over time, and many such organisations have attempted to do so. However, problems can arise when turnover statistics are used to compare individual managers' performance and not primarily to identify promising methods by which the level of voluntary resignations can be reduced.

Wherever managers feel that they are in any way being judged on the basis of their turnover there will be a strong temptation to 'massage' figures so as to impress their superiors, or at least to avoid their disapproval. This can very easily be done, even where the pay-roll function is managed centrally, by wrongly recording voluntary resignations that fall into the 'controllable' category as 'involuntary' or 'uncontrollable'. Ways in which such activity can be discouraged include downplaying the extent to which turnover is taken into account in judging management performance, and giving the central personnel function responsibility for undertaking exit interviews and surveys of ex-employees.

Benchmarking against competitors is a less exact activity, but one that can be effectively undertaken using one of two methods. First, managers can compare their own performance against the figures included in the published government- and industry-sponsored surveys of turnover in the UK. We made reference above to the regular CIPD and DfEE studies, but there are many others, too – by industry federations (such as the Institute of Management, the British Retail Consortium and the Engineering Council) and by commercial research organisations (see IRS 1996a: 8–11, for details of 20 published surveys). The alternative approach is to set up or join an informal association of similar employers to enable mutual exchange of information. Such arrangements resemble the long-established 'salary clubs' in their nature and methods.

BP Chemicals

Since 1992, BP chemicals division has been benefiting from benchmarking its HR operation against those of similar companies. In the absence of sufficiently detailed published data, they decided to set up their own benchmarking club. They started by cold-calling their opposite numbers in other large manufacturing firms to enquire whether or not they would be interested in sharing data, but were rejected by many 'for reasons ranging from pressure of work to suspicion of the process and plain secretiveness'.

Eventually they set up arrangements with 10 companies, and began exchanging data on a wide variety of HR practices, including voluntary and involuntary turnover. The process then continued with visits to other companies so that judgements could be made about best practice and how policy could be improved in the future. Qualitative research therefore followed on from the initial quantitative benchmarking exercise.

Source: Holt (1994)

Does your organisation exchange data of this kind with other employers? What do you think are the main disadvantages of such associations?

EXPLAINING TURNOVER

There is a very wide variety of possible explanations for voluntary resignations. People become dissatisfied with their jobs for a range of reasons; they may become bored with the content, frustrated by lack of promotion, fed up with their supervisors or irritated by changes in their working environment. In some cases the job may simply fall short of their expectations at the time of appointment. However, such phenomena are only half the story – in most cases, for a resignation to occur, the individual concerned must first perceive that there are better opportunities elsewhere and then secure another position. The complexities of this process were effectively illustrated by William Mobley (1977) in the following 10-stage model of 'the employee turnover decision process':

a) Evaluate existing job.

b) Experience job dissatisfaction.

c) Think of quitting.

d) Evaluate expected utility of search for a new job and the cost of quitting.

e) Decide to search for alternatives.

f) Search for alternatives.

g) Evaluate alternatives.

h) Compare best alternative with present job.

i) Decide whether to stay or quit.

j) Quit.

It is therefore important, when assessing the reasons for turnover and devising remedial plans, to take account not just of employee dissatisfaction, but also of the possible alternatives open to employees, as well as the relative ease with which any such opportunities can be taken up.

Several different methods are available to employers seeking to investigate why employees choose to leave. Here we consider four contrasting approaches: exit interviews, surveys of ex-employees, attitude surveys, and quantitative approaches.

Exit interviews
Undertaking formal interviews with employees before they leave the organisation is a common method used to develop an understanding of their motivation for resigning. The most straightforward approach is to take the resigner through a questionnaire of direct questions concerning his or her satisfaction with pay, supervisor, development opportunities, relationships with colleagues and job content. There is, however, a number of problems with such approaches that can serve to reduce their effectiveness. First, there is the tendency for employees to develop a far more optimistic outlook after they have secured a new job and resigned. Their original reasons for seeking alternative employment often get forgotten as they move towards their last day. Such feelings are compounded if counter-offers are made to encourage them to stay, and may disappear completely in the last days as cards are signed, leaving presents bought, affectionate speeches given and farewell parties held. This is often not, therefore, the best time to ask them for an honest and well-balanced assessment of their reasons for quitting.

A further problem arises when supervisors or department heads undertake exit interviews, because leavers will often baulk at implying any criticism of them – particularly if they believe that they will require positive job references in the future. The reason given for leaving may thus conceal the whole truth or may even be entirely false. It is far easier to say that you are leaving because you were offered more money elsewhere or because your spouse is moving, than to state openly that you disapprove of your new manager's style or feel that you have been treated unfairly in some way. According to ACAS (1985: 7), employees often 'simply quote some small incident which proved the last straw' as a means of avoiding the admission of deeper or less tangible factors.

It can thus be argued that exit interviews, if used at all, should be undertaken very soon after the resignation has been confirmed, and that they should be carried out by an individual who will not have any role in writing future job references. A personnel officer is very well placed to carry out such work. According to Carrell et al (1995: 770), another way of encouraging candour is to explain to the leaver that the aim of the interview is to gather information for improving work conditions. In other words, the individual should be asked directly for his or her opinion on how things can be improved and only indirectly about any personal reasons for resigning.

> Have you been responsible for conducting exit interviews? If you have, to what extent have you experienced the problems identified above?

Surveys of ex-employees

A more promising, if less straightforward, approach is to contact former employees some months after they have left in order to ask them for a considered view of their reasons for resigning. While the use of this method is relatively rare, there has been a number of cases covered recently in the personnel journals that indicate some large organisations are experimenting with it (see Hobby 1995: 31, IDS 1995e: 9 and the boxed text below). Candour is further encouraged if the surveys are carried out by independent bodies and are clearly labelled 'Private and confidential'.

> **Exploring reasons for turnover among nurses**
>
> In 1996, a large NHS Trust hospital in the north of England undertook a detailed investigation of the high turnover rates among junior qualified nurses, which was running at 23 per cent. An independent researcher was brought in to conduct a questionnaire survey of 193 nurses who had left voluntarily over the previous two years and to undertake interviews with nurse managers about the causes of turnover in their departments. Over 70 per cent of the nurses who had left were still employed in the NHS, and all but 5 per cent had remained in nursing or nursing-related careers.
>
> The questionnaire results showed that 63 per cent had left for reasons that could be categorised as 'controllable'. While a number of reasons for turnover were established, three were particularly significant. These were: a poor working relationship with the supervisor; failure to secure promotion; and general dissatisfaction with aspects of the working environment (including low staffing levels). Of particular interest was the identification of departments in which there was a pattern of poor

supervisor-subordinate relationships. It became very clear from the questionnaire that some nurse managers were far more effective motivators than others, and that developing their supervisory skills would lead to improved retention of nurses in their departments.

Source: Burton (1996)

Attitude surveys

A third approach is to seek the views of employees before they leave and so provide a basis for the development of policies and practices that will deter them from so doing. These too are truly effective only if confidential – so as to maximise the chance of employees' stating honestly how they feel about their jobs, their perceived opportunities, their bosses, colleagues and the organisation as a whole. Questions can also be asked about their current intentions as regards the future and about their perceptions of alternative career paths open to them. Such approaches enable employers to anticipate in which areas future turnover is most likely to occur, and to gain an insight into the main causes.

Quantitative approaches

An alternative method to the use of surveys is to make use of employee records to compare the data or characteristics of those who leave with those who stay. Although quantitative approaches are unlikely in themselves to give a particularly clear picture of reasons for turnover, they may reveal some interesting general trends, and can usefully supplement information gathered using the three other methods outlined above.

Any number of ratios can be investigated using quantitative analyses. Examples might include comparing leavers with stayers in terms of their age, the distance they travel to work, their shift-patterns, pay levels, performance record or length of service. It is also possible to use these techniques to identify the extent to which turnover varies with the type of job undertaken or with the supervision of different managers. As with all quantitative analyses, the data is really useful only when there are large sample sizes available. Such approaches are thus inappropriate for smaller organisations.

REDUCING TURNOVER

Once the reasons for resignations have been established and analysed, the next step is to formulate plans to reduce them. Clearly, it is impossible to generalise about the form such plans will take, because they will vary dramatically depending on the causes of turnover in specific organisations. Employers may often find that very different factors explain resignations in each department or business unit. However, there are several possible courses of remedial action that can usefully be considered and which have been shown by researchers to have a positive effect in some circumstances. Hom and Griffeth (1995), in their comprehensive review of recent US research into the management of turnover, describe nine areas for employers to consider. The first six are described as 'robust' methods of controlling turnover, for which there is strong research evidence, and the final three as 'promising' methods:

- realistic job previews

- job enrichment

- workspace characteristics

- induction practices

- leader-member exchange

- employee selection

- reward practices

- demographic diversity

- managing interrole conflict.

Several of these areas are investigated elsewhere in this book and in others in the series (eg realistic job previews, selection, induction and reward). In the following paragraphs, we therefore focus on the other areas identified by Hom and Griffeth as worthy of consideration.

Job enrichment

Psychological research has strongly suggested that employees are far less likely to consider looking for new jobs when they feel fulfilled in their existing roles. According to Hom and Griffeth (1995: 203), the following perceptions of jobs by job-holders are particularly significant:

- There are opportunities for self- and career development.

- The job is meaningful or significant.

- A variety of skills is used.

- There is a high degree of personal responsibility.

- There is the ability to work with a degree of autonomy.

- Positive feedback on performance is given.

Increasing the extent to which these features are present in a job leads to its 'enrichment'. There is thus a good case, where retention rates need to be improved, for looking at ways in which job content can be refined in some or all of these directions. In many cases the costs associated with such actions will not be particularly high.

Workspace characteristics

In a series of research papers G.R. Oldham and his colleagues have reported research findings on working environments and their effect on employee satisfaction (see Hom and Griffeth 1995: 203–205). Their experiments have involved providing similar groups of employees working for the same organisation with radically different office designs, which has led to interesting results. While they have found various factors to be significant, particular attention has been paid to Hom and Griffeth's discovery that large open-plan offices with few dividing walls or partitions tend to reduce employees' feelings of autonomy and significance, and therefore increase dissatisfaction significantly. Overcrowding and darkness make matters worse. It can thus be argued that, except where it clearly matches the established workplace culture, the idea of doing away with partitions to decrease feelings of isolation and to encourage people to identify and socialise with other group members may be mistaken.

Leader-member exchange

The suggestion here is that turnover is reduced, particularly in the first months of appointment, if managers have been trained to develop high 'leader-member exchanges' with their subordinates. This term is defined as paying new starters particular attention and actively trying to develop high-trust relationships with them from the start. This involves taking special care to ask employees their opinion about operational matters, giving them influence in decision-making processes and allowing them as much latitude as possible to undertake their job roles in the way they prefer. Essentially it means resisting the display of any feelings of suspicion managers may have, and relying on 'social exchange' rather than 'formal authority' to ensure that work gets done.

Such techniques might be regarded as simply attributes of effective supervisors. The point made by researchers working in the field is that they do not necessarily come naturally to managers and that it is possible to develop appropriate characteristics with formal training.

Demographic diversity

Research in the USA reported by Hom and Griffeth (1995: 239–252) has indicated that, on average, women and members of ethnic minorities are more likely than white males to leave jobs voluntarily. Furthermore, studies have shown that this is partly explained by perceptions on the part of these groups that they have been unfairly discriminated against while in their jobs. The point is made that it is irrelevant from a management perspective whether the discrimination is 'imagined' or 'real': it is the perception of inequality that is significant, and that needs to tackled if turnover is to be reduced. The US research has found that perceptions of supervisor bias, inequality in pay awards, unsupportive colleagues and blocked careers all contribute towards high turnover among women and ethnic minorities. Others identified extra pressure to perform well, and a tendency for the most interesting and highly visible tasks or projects to be given to whites and males as factors in their decision to resign voluntarily.

Such problems are familiar in the UK but, as yet, little formal research appears to have been undertaken here as regards their specific effect on employee turnover. However, it is reasonable to assume that, at least in some cases, involuntary resignations could be explained by perceptions of unfair discrimination. Clearly the way to tackle this is to introduce and communicate effective equal opportunities policies that managers at all levels are obliged to accept. There is a need not just to monitor the pay and job progression among members of the relevant groups but also to communicate results and plans of action to employees. Problems with particular supervisors or departments could be effectively identified using the survey techniques described above. A good start would be for questions relating to unfair discrimination to be included in exit interview questionnaires.

Managing interrole conflict

Another reason for turnover identified by Hom and Griffeth (1995: 252–255) relates to conflicts between the demands of work and family – a problem made worse with recent increases in the number of single-parent families. Research into turnover in the USA suggests that whereas 33 per cent of women cite such conflicts as contributing to their reasons for quitting a job, it was significant for only 1 per cent of men.

Such findings may back a business case for employers to go further than the minimum standard required by the law in the provision of maternity leave (paid or unpaid), career breaks, childcare, day-care for elderly dependants, flexible work schedules and forms of home-working. Although some of these may be expensive for employers to introduce (particularly in small organisations), they are at least worthy of consideration where the costs do not outweigh those associated with high levels of staff turnover.

In addition to organisation-wide policy initiatives such as those outlined above, employers can also improve staff retention rates simply by giving the issue a far higher profile in the organisation than is often the case. This involves securing senior management commitment by developing a robust business case and then giving responsibility for turnover reduction to individual line managers. It is possible to go as far as to incorporate departmental turnover records into performance appraisal criteria for supervisors, so that career progression or bonus levels are determined in part by success in this area.

Turnover reduction at W.H. Smith

A great deal of work has been undertaken in recent years by the retail and distribution group W.H. Smith to reduce turnover levels. Of particular concern was turnover in high-street stores, which ranged from 34 per cent to 60 per cent in the early 1990s. Statistical analysis showed that turnover was far higher among younger staff, and that females were harder to retain than males of the same age. Voluntary resignations were particularly high among employees with less than one year's service, nearly 50 per cent of new starters leaving within their first year. This last statistic was seen as especially costly because, in the judgement of the company, it takes 13 weeks for a new shop assistant to become 'fully productive'.

A number of elements made up the company's action plan to reduce turnover. These included:

* improved recruitment procedures
* improved induction programmes
* employing a greater number of older workers
* the development of a schools liaison programme
* opening up internal promotion channels
* measures to attract women returners
* the introduction of long-service awards.

Source: IDS (1994a)

LEGAL ISSUES

As a general rule, employers do not have the protection of the law in preventing or discouraging employees from leaving their employment – even when they quit in order to join a competitor or set up in a similar business themselves. However, there are two important exceptions of which personnel professionals should be aware so that they can give general advice to line managers in specific cases. These are the implied duty of fidelity in all contracts of employment and specific restraint-of-trade clauses. Another legal issue relevant to voluntary resignations is the right of the employer to be given reasonable notice of the employee's intention to leave.

Duty of fidelity

All contracts of employment, however informal, are accepted by the courts to contain an implied duty on the part of employees to act in good faith towards their employer. This means that even if no such agreement has been made between the two parties it is nevertheless deemed to exist in law. Rulings in this area are complex and depend very much on the individual circumstances of each case, so personnel specialists are well advised to seek advice from legal experts if at all unsure of their position.

First, contract law prevents employees who are planning to resign in order to set up in direct competition to their employer or to work for a competitor from unfairly using their current employer's resources to help them do so. Hence, test cases have found that a milkman about to set up his own delivery business was wrong to have solicited for customers while still employed by a large dairy (*Wessex Dairies* v *Smith* 1935), and that employees are liable to pay compensation if they copy lists of customers prior to joining a competitor company (*Robb* v *Green* 1895). In both these cases, the individuals were found to have breached their duty of fidelity while employed by their original organisations. However, the courts have made it quite clear that this duty does not prevent ex-employees in the service of a competitor from making use of skills and non-confidential knowledge acquired while working for their previous employer.

In practice, it is sometimes difficult to draw a clear distinction between what is and what is not permitted. The extent of the grey area is illustrated by the example of a driving instructor planning to set up his own business in competition with an existing employer. What is he supposed to say to his existing pupils? Is it a breach of duty to inform them that he is leaving to set up an independent driving school? What if he gives them a business card or home telephone number to enable pupils to make contact with a view to arranging lessons? What if he telephones existing pupils to invite them to continue their instruction with him? At what stage the breach of contract occurs is difficult to state – particularly when pupils have had contact with the individual instructor only and believe it to be in their interests to continue being taught by him.

The duty of fidelity has also been found to extend to the use of 'confidential information' by an ex-employee who has taken up employment with a competitor. Here, too, the case-law is far from clear as to what exactly can be defined as being confidential. A recent case, *Faccenda Chicken* v *Fowler* 1986, stated clearly that the answer to this question will vary from situation to situation depending on the circumstances. These will include the extent to which a piece of information has been labelled confidential in some way, or the number of individuals in the organisation who have knowledge of it. It is therefore possible to conclude that, except in very clear-cut cases, where an employee has clearly abused his or her position prior to resigning, employers are unlikely to be able to rely on implied contractual terms to stop information, skills or knowledge being used in the service of a competitor.

Restrictive covenants

Where trade secrets do exist but do not fall within the limited legal definition of the term 'confidential' described above, employers can, and probably should, seek to protect themselves by inserting an express restraint-of-trade clause into contracts of employment. This would clearly be appropriate where an employer wished to keep a particular manufacturing process secret from competitors, or where information about new products being developed or advertising campaigns might be bought by a rival company via an employee who was in the know. Employees would then have to sign contracts on taking up their employment that clearly stated they were not permitted to work for a competitor within a defined timescale (eg a year) after resigning.

In companies where such circumstances are prevalent, restrictive covenants of this kind can act very effectively to deter employees from resigning voluntarily. Restraining clauses are also common in contracts of employment issued to solicitors, accountants and doctors, where customer connections might permit them to set up in competition in the same area. They are also used by all kinds of other employers whose business might be severely threatened by direct competition from ex-employees.

However, in interpreting restrictive covenants, the courts have tended to uphold the rights of ex-employees to work where and for whom they please, except where the clause is clearly 'in the legitimate interests of the employer' (see IDS 1994b). In other words, if the intention of the clause is simply to restrict the ability of employees to resign, it would be declared to be void by a court. To be enforceable, the restraint-of-trade clause must refer specifically to the passing-on of trade secrets or trade connections to another organisation.

A well-known case that illustrates these principles was *Greer* v *Sketchley* 1979. Here, a senior manager in a dry-cleaning business decided to resign in order to take up employment with a rival company. However, he was constrained from so doing because of a restraint-of-trade clause in his contract of employment that forbade him associating 'with any other person, firm or company' engaged in any similar business in the UK for a period of 12 months. Believing the clause to be overly restrictive, Mr Greer took his employer to court and succeeded in persuading the court to declare it invalid on the grounds that it was not reasonable to seek to restrict an employee from working anywhere in the country.

According to IDS, in drawing up 'reasonable' restrictive covenants, employers should focus on four areas:

- the nature of the employees' activities (ie restrict ex-employees only in fields directly related to their work, not the business of the organisation as a whole)

- geographical area (ie include in the clause only those geographical areas in which the company has significant business interests)

- duration (ie put only the minimum necessary time-limit on the clause – 12 months is usually sufficient to deter employees from resigning to pass on trade secrets or details of customers)

- employee rank (ie treat senior employees with access to a range of confidential information differently from relatively junior staff with limited knowledge).

There are two broad conclusions that can be made regarding the use of restraint-of-trade covenants. First, it is clearly unreasonable in law to use them as a matter of course in seeking to deter employees from leaving. They have to be specific and restricted to the protection of genuinely confidential information if they are to be upheld by the courts. Secondly, it is apparent that the more restrictive the clause, the harder it will be to defend in court. Employers are thus wise to restrict the scope of their clauses only to areas in which they clearly have legitimate commercial interests to protect.

Notice periods

Employers are strongly advised to include in their contracts of employment specific reference to the amount of notice an employee must give when deciding to leave. Where this is not the case, according to the Employment Rights Act 1996, the employee is entitled to give just one week's notice. Traditionally, most employers have declared the notice period to be the same as the payment period, so that weekly paid staff are required to give a week's notice, whereas their monthly paid colleagues are required to work for a full four or five weeks after handing in their notice. For senior managers it is reasonable to ask for more notice to reflect the need for a more involved procedure in the selection of a replacement. Three months is common for such jobs.

In practice, of course, there is little employers can do to force the employee to work out the full period of notice. Technically they could sue the employee for breach of contract, but the damages that would be awarded would rarely be sufficient to justify the legal expenses incurred. Instead, employers tend to rely on the goodwill of employees and on the fact that they often have an incentive to stay on – if required to do so – to ensure good references in the future. It is also possible for an employer to decline to pay the final pay-packet in circumstances where an employee leaves without giving the notice required in his or her contract.

ETHICAL ISSUES

There are various practices that are, apparently, commonly used by employers when managing voluntary resignations that could be seen as unethical. One familiar to many employees of smaller businesses is the use of explicit or implied threats to deter employees from seeking alternative employment. These take the form of the manager's informally disciplining or punishing employees discovered to have applied for new jobs. The punishment can take a number of forms, ranging from verbal castigation and the withdrawal of perks to exclusion from decision-making and the blocking of pay-rises. It is for such reasons that employees often feel that they must keep their job searches secret and conceal from their colleagues the fact that they have visited job centres or attended interviews.

Another heavy-handed practice occurs when resigners are told to leave with immediate effect, and may even be escorted from the premises. Although the practice is most commonly used in cases of dismissal, there have been instances of its use with voluntary releases, when individuals have announced their intention to take up a position with a competitor. The aim is to protect confidential information of the kinds referred to above. However, the extent to which the interests of the employer are really served by immediate departures of this kind is highly questionable. As soon as employees realise that it is likely to occur, they will take steps to prepare for it – including taking home any information they believe will be helpful to them in the future.

It can thus be argued that both of these practices are unprofessional and not conducive to the development of healthy, high-trust relationships with employees. Effectively, they amount to a deliberate attempt to restrict employees from seeking to develop their own careers and, as such, are likely to generate dissatisfaction and so encourage more staff to seek alternative employment. In the long term they are liable to increase rather than decrease staff turnover, and to make it harder for employers to recruit and motivate the best people.

> What other practices that might be described as 'unethical' have you come across in the field of voluntary release? How convincing a business case could you make in arguing for their cessation?

FURTHER READING

- *Employee Turnover* by Peter Hom and Rodger Griffeth (1995) is by far the most comprehensive publication on the topic. All aspects are explored and all the most up-to-date research reviewed.

- The best source of data on turnover levels in different regions, industries and occupational groups is the journal *Employment Review*, which regularly publishes statistics and useful articles on the subject in its *Employee Development Bulletin*. The most recent detailed reports appeared in the issues published in February 1996 and March 1997.

- Some of the best general guides to managing turnover are now rather old, but still contain thoughtful and useful advice. These include *Labour Turnover: Towards a solution* by P.J. Samuel (1969) and a book of articles on turnover edited by Barrie Pettman (1975) entitled *Labour Turnover and Retention*.

- Incomes Data Services have also produced a number of useful publications on the management of turnover. General issues are dealt with in *IDS Focus 51* (June 1989) and *IDS Study 577* (May 1995). Relevant legal matters are dealt with comprehensively in *IDS Employment Law Supplements 62* and *72* (1994) on notice rights and employee confidentiality.

- Information about initiatives taken by particular employers is often featured in articles published in the CIPD's twice-monthly journal, *People Management*.

Part 7

RELEASE

13 The two big Rs

After voluntary resignations, the next most common reasons that people leave employment are retirement or redundancy. In some cases, where the figures add up, people opt to take early retirement or willingly accept an offer of redundancy. In others they are made compulsorily redundant or are forcibly retired by employers once they have reached a certain age. Both events thus occupy something of a grey area between terminations that have an essentially voluntary character and those that are involuntary. Indeed, a voluntary retirement is often a means to avoid making someone compulsorily redundant.

Retirement and redundancy are both covered by an extensive body of law yet, unlike other forms of dismissal, legislation does little more than set a basic minimum standard of employer conduct. Whereas in the case of a termination on account of poor performance, misconduct or ill-health 'best practice' has effectively been determined by Parliament and the courts, in the case of the management of redundancies and retirements most employers prefer to offer far more generous terms than are strictly required by law. This is particularly so in the field of redundancy payments where, according to a recent IRS survey, 90 per cent of employers offer severance payments beyond the statutory minimum.

In this chapter, a number of aspects of these two specific forms of release from employment are explored. The main legal requirements in each case are summarised, and some of the approaches that can be used to minimise the distress and disruption associated with involuntary redundancy and forced retirement are assessed. The methods that employers can use to avoid making compulsory redundancies, or at least to reduce their number, are also described.

By the end of this chapter readers should be able to:

• define the term 'redundancy'

- calculate redundancy payments

- organise job-search and pre-retirement courses

- run or commission the provision of outplacement services

- draw up policies on the management of retirement and redundancy

- determine fair criteria for selecting employees to be made compulsorily redundant.

In addition, readers should be able to understand and explain:

- the main legal issues relating to the management of redundancy and retirement

- best-practice approaches to handling redundancy and retirement over and above what is required by law.

DEFINING REDUNDANCY

In the UK, the term 'redundancy' is defined by law as a situation in which, for economic reasons, there is no longer a need for the job in question to be carried out in the place where it is currently carried out. Although the selection of employees to be made redundant can take into account the ability to perform the job, individual failings are *not* the main reason that a job is being lost. The Employment Protection (Consolidation) Act 1978 states that redundancy occurs only when a dismissal arises either mainly or wholly for one of the following reasons:

- where the employer has ceased, or intends to cease, carrying on the business in which the employee is or was employed

- where the employer ceases, or intends to cease, carrying out this business at the place where the employee is or was employed

- where the requirements for employees to carry out work of a particular kind have ceased or diminished (or are expected to), and where the employee is employed to carry that work out

- where the requirements to carry out work of a particular kind have ceased or diminished at the place where the employee is employed.

The starting-point is, therefore, a reduction in the need for employees either in general or at a particular location. If such is not the case, whatever the dismissal might be called by those involved, it is not considered a 'redundancy' in legal terms. Although a reduction in the requirement for employees usually results from a reduction in the volume of work, that is not a necessary condition for a legal redundancy to occur. It is quite possible for an expanding business to make redundancies, provided certain types of work are becoming less necessary and the employees concerned are unable to transfer to other jobs. A common example would be a situation in which new technology is introduced to meet increased demand, leading to a requirement for fewer low-skilled employees.

It is important to grasp the legal definition, because it sets out the circumstances in which employees are entitled, as of right, to a redundancy payment. Where the dismissal is mainly for other reasons, such as misconduct or incapability, the employer is not obliged to pay compensation, except in cases where individual contracts of employment require it. Redundancies also require a wholly different procedural approach if they are to be judged to have been carried out reasonably by industrial tribunals. Moreover, the distinction between true redundancies and other dismissals is also a matter of interest to the Inland Revenue, because redundancy payments below £30,000 are tax-free. The practice of making someone redundant and paying a redundancy payment when the above definitions do not in fact apply can thus lead to as much difficulty as situations in which payments are not made to dismissed employees who are truly redundant.

Redundancies fall into the category of 'potentially fair dismissals' as far as industrial tribunals are concerned. Like the other kinds of dismissal discussed in the next chapter, employers are therefore legally able to dismiss employees on account of redundancy provided they meet the tribunal's standards of 'reasonableness'. In other words, a redundancy will be judged fair as long as the correct procedures are followed and the appropriate redundancy payments made. As is the case with all kinds of dismissal, industrial tribunals can hear only cases brought by employees with over two years' continuous service after the age of 18.

AVOIDING REDUNDANCIES

One of the issues that tribunals look at in judging the reasonableness with which a redundancy programme has been carried out is the extent and nature of the steps taken either to minimise the number of redundancies or to avoid them altogether. A variety of management actions can be taken to avoid making people compulsorily redundant, some of a general nature that help prevent redundancy situations' arising in the first place and others that come into play once it becomes apparent that redundancies are likely or necessary.

Long-term approaches
In his book on redundancy, Fowler (1993: 18–34) gives considerable attention to the approaches that managers can take to prevent, or reduce the likelihood of, redundancies. Each involves planning in order to avoid as far as possible scenarios in which the employer has no alternative but to dismiss employees whose jobs have become redundant. The approaches fall into three broad but distinct categories: effective human resource planning, flexible working practices, and the sponsorship of early retirement incentives.

The arguments for and against human resource planning were explored at length in Chapters 3 and 4 of this book. One strong argument in favour of carrying out formal forecasting of staffing needs is the assistance that the development of human resource plans give in avoiding redundancy. If one can foresee months or even years ahead a downturn in business levels or a change in business processes likely to reduce an organisation's need to employ people or to undertake work of a particular kind, then one can take steps to reduce the number of compulsory redundancies that will have to be made. For example, an organisation can reduce the number of new employees taken on and focus its attention on retraining and developing existing employees for new roles that they may have to undertake in the future. Such a course of action also permits natural wastage to occur, so that over time the size of the workforce diminishes as people leave voluntarily and are not replaced.

The second long-term activity is the maximisation of flexibility in an organisation, so that where work of a particular kind is expected to grow less, the employees engaged in that work are able to develop new job roles. Fowler (1993: 24–26) distinguishes between 'organisational flexibility', which involves both reducing the number of steps in organisational hierarchies and also organising employees into multi-functional teams, and 'job flexibility', which requires enlarging and enriching individual jobs so that each employee becomes multiskilled. Such courses of action make modern organisations more efficient and the employees working within them more adaptable to changing circumstances. Each of these consequences contributes to the avoidance of redundancies.

Other kinds of flexibility with a role to play are the employment of subcontractors to carry out peripheral tasks and the development of flexible contractual terms. Because subcontractors are hired on a temporary or fixed-term basis, it is clearly less expensive to dispense with their services or to renegotiate new terms than is the case with established employees. However, the introduction of such outsourcing may itself reduce job security and increase the likelihood that individual employees will be made redundant. Over time, though, it can be accomplished without harming the prospects of current employees, as long as retraining opportunities are offered to those affected. In smaller, growing organisations such forms of flexibility can be developed as the business expands. Contractual flexibility also contributes by ensuring that an organisation is able to maximise its efficiency through reducing its inherent rigidity. Wherever possible, therefore, staff can be employed on contracts that do not define job content or hours of work too narrowly.

Early retirement is often an attractive way of reducing the extent to which compulsory redundancies are necessary. The Inland Revenue permits organisations to release people after the age of 50 with enhanced pensions, so in most cases such schemes apply only to employees who have reached that age. Many employees find it an attractive option, because it permits them to draw their occupational pensions early (if at a reduced rate) but also permits them to continue working elsewhere either as a full-time employee or on a part-time basis. In practice, they are made voluntarily redundant, but are better off financially than they would have been with a straightforward redundancy payment. In most cases the costs are met by using pension fund assets, and so do not have to be drawn from current organisational budgets. In theory, therefore, everyone benefits: the employer loses employees amicably and at low cost, the retiree leaves on acceptable financial terms, and fewer compulsory redundancies are needed from the ranks of other employees. Early retirement is, of course, an option only for organisations with an established occupational pension fund that has successfully attracted members from among its employees. For this reason, it is best categorised as a long-term activity that can help reduce the need to make compulsory redundancies.

Short-term approaches

The above preventative measures will not always have been introduced and will, in any case, often fail to prevent the need for compulsory redundancies. In these circumstances the 'reasonable' employer will seek to minimise their number by using a range of other established tools and practices. The most common of these is to ask formally for volunteers – to give long-serving employees in line to receive substantial redundancy payments the opportunity to claim them. However, there are problems. First, this is often more expensive for the employer than a situation in which the employees to be made redundant are not volunteers but are identified by management. Secondly, it often allows the most employable and valuable staff to depart, leaving less effective employees in place after the programme of redundancies has been completed.

In practice, the process of seeking volunteers is fraught with difficulty and has to be managed with great care if the many pitfalls are to be avoided. A common problem arises when too many people volunteer for redundancy, leading to a situation in which weaker performers appear to have been rewarded with redundancy while more valued volunteers are left to soldier on until they reach 65 (or whatever the contractual retirement age is). Such situations are common where redundancy terms are excessively enhanced in order to attract a pool of candidates. The result is demotivation among those required to stay on. Another problem relates to people's fear that their careers may suffer or that their relationships with line managers may deteriorate if they are known to have applied unsuccessfully for voluntary redundancy. This may deter people from applying in the first place, but can also lead to further problems of morale if the employee is kept on.

According to Lewis (1993: 28–32), these and other problems can be overcome provided the volunteering process is carefully controlled and planned. The first decision to make involves establishing the coverage of the voluntary scheme. To whom is voluntary redundancy to be offered? Should it be to everyone in the organisation or just to selected grades or departments? Some organisations, particularly those having to effect large numbers of redundancies in a short period of time, will make a blanket offer to all employees, or may exclude only a few groups – such as people in jobs that are to remain and into which others could not be redeployed. By contrast, where the redundancies are restricted to limited areas of the organisation it makes sense to target these alone so as to avoid raising expectations among those working in other areas.

It is also possible to target offers on individuals who are performing poorly and who have built up a number of years' service. This can be done by developing a package specifically designed to appeal to them, perhaps including early retirement options. Offers can then be made individually ahead of any general announcement, with a view to developing tailored settlements to suit those whom the organisation most wants to lose. Flexibility over the timing can also be discussed to increase the incentive to volunteer. The other approach is to use the stick as well as the carrot, by indicating that the people concerned are likely to find their jobs disappearing in the post-redundancy structure anyway.

The next step is to establish the criteria for selecting candidates for redundancy from among those who volunteer. It is important that these are drawn up *before* the offer is made, in order to avoid raising the hopes of people whom the organisation has no intention of selecting. It can, for example, be made clear that those with good performance and attendance records, long service and valuable skills are unlikely to be selected. A general offer can then be made to all staff within affected departments, which will nevertheless deter from applying those who are still very much wanted.

Other approaches to avoid or minimise redundancies are rather more straightforward. Where there exists several months' warning, it is possible to institute a general restriction on all recruitment of new employees. A post that becomes vacant that will continue after the redundancy programme has been completed may only be advertised internally and be filled by someone at risk of redundancy. Another

---

Avoiding redundancies at Volkswagen

In 1993, despite a 9 per cent reduction in the size of its workforce, the Volkswagen Group reported a fall in annual sales of over 25 per cent. Relatively inefficient systems of production, combined with high labour costs, had led to a situation in which the company was struggling to compete in international markets. At the start of 1994 it was calculated that, to rectify the situation, DM 2 billion had to be saved from production costs over a two-year period – the equivalent of making 30,000 employees redundant.

In the event, the company managed, by using other approaches, to achieve its cost savings without redundancies. The strategy was to lower production costs for two years while simultaneously introducing innovations in work organisation and production-planning. The aim was to have the new production methods in place by the start of 1996, thus improving productivity without needing to make redundancies.

The two-year cost-reduction programme had three elements:

- a temporary reduction in the working week to 29 hours, leading to a 10–12 per cent reduction in salaries
- giving younger workers part-time contracts for two years after they had completed their apprenticeships, and offering similar terms to all employees over the age of 55
- offering career breaks to employees to take up places in government-sponsored training establishments.

The trade union agreed to the terms within a month of the publication of the annual results in 1993. The size of the crisis facing the company meant that the workforce accepted the sacrifices as a means of avoiding mass redundancies.

Source: Garnjost and Blettner (1996)

approach is to fill vacancies externally but to do so only on a fixed-term basis. If it is known that redundancies are likely in six months' time, new starters are hired on six-month contracts which can later be extended but which are occupied by people with no expectation of longer-term employment. Where the period is shorter than six months it is better to bring in agency staff or subcontractors.

A recruitment freeze effectively allows the organisation to minimise the number of redundancies it will have to make in that it allows the size of the permanent workforce to diminish by natural wastage. When redundancies are expected, individual employees will often take steps to look for other work in any case, and many will thus resign of their own accord rather than wait to see whether their job will survive the programme of staff reduction. This has cost-advantages for employers, in so far as it reduces the number of redundancy payments, but it can be risky if more valuable employees resign, leaving the poorer performers in place.

A further means of reducing redundancies is to cut staff costs in general. The commonest approach is to cut or radically reduce overtime. The result is less pay for employees in return for greater job security. Other approaches include pay-freezes and the abandonment of profit-based bonus schemes. Where negotiated with staff represent-atives, such methods of redundancy avoidance can be the most satisfactory. The reduction of non-pay costs can also be considered: for example, the amount of office space occupied can be reduced or less expensive premises rented.

SELECTING PEOPLE FOR REDUNDANCY

The body of case-law on the selection of employees for redundancy is now substantial but remains based on straightforward principles: that the employer, in choosing which staff to make redundant, must use criteria that are fair and objective. If this is judged not to be the case, the test of 'reasonableness' will have been failed and the dismissals will be declared unfair by an industrial tribunal. Some selection criteria fall into the 'automatically unfair category'. If these are found to have been used, the tribunal will not even get as far as debating the issue of reasonableness. Automatically unfair criteria, as in all cases of unfair dismissal, include the following:

• a trade union reason (ie selection either because a member is or is not a member of a trade union, or took part in trade-union activities or refused to take part)

• pregnancy

• sex, marital status, race or disability

• breach of a collective agreement

• acting not in accordance with custom and practice.

This last point requires some explanation. It arises in cases where trade unions are recognised, but where there is no agreed redundancy procedure or written agreement as to the selection criteria to be used. In such cases, the courts have decided that managers are not free to develop new sets of criteria wholly different from those used customarily in the organisation. Hence, if staff have always been selected before on the basis of last-in-first-out (LIFO), managers cannot suddenly change tack without first gaining the agreement of recognised trade unions.

Aside from the automatically unfair selection methods, many others are acceptable provided they are fair and objective. While LIFO has traditionally been the most common approach, and is accepted as fair by tribunals, in recent years it has been used less frequently, because managers have sought to use criteria that better distinguish staff with ability and potential. Other commonly used methods include the following:

- skill or competence

- performance records

- attendance records

- record of conduct

- health

- qualifications

- age

- attitude.

While some of the above, such as attendance, are easy to verify objectively, others are not. How, for example, is it possible to judge an employee's attitude or commitment in an objective fashion? The answer, according to Fowler (1993: 108), is to ensure that there is evidence to back the decision and that the latter is not based on a subjective judgement and does not arise from a personality clash. He suggests that where a choice has to be made between two employees, and only one has volunteered for unpleasant tasks in the past or taken the initiative in a specific case, it will be reasonable to take that into account when deciding which person is to be made redundant. What is important is the presence of some kind of evidence (letters, reports, mentions in performance-appraisal records etc) that could be used to show a tribunal that the selection was based on *objective* criteria.

The same care must be taken when using other methods. Health, for example, is a potentially fair criteria. Where there are grounds for believing that an employee's state of health is likely to lead to poor attendance in the future, it is reasonable to take that into account. What is important is that the judgement is made on objective grounds and can be justified if necessary at a tribunal. What is not acceptable is to single out one employee for redundancy on health grounds while failing to apply the same criteria to others. Moreover, it would be unfair to base a redundancy on a poor health record in past years where there was evidence that a full recovery had been made.

At present, in the absence of legislation outlawing age discrimination, it is still possible to use age as a criterion in determining redundancy. Indeed, in some ways it is encouraged by the law in so far as redundancy payments can be reduced when someone is aged 64. Furthermore, unfair dismissal cases cannot be brought by people over the age of 65. However, it should be noted that the use of such factors, while legal, is not recommended by the CIPD and is not one of the criteria listed in its guidance documentation.

According to the (former) IPD's *Guide on Redundancy*, published in 1996, tribunals are increasingly looking with favour on points systems as a means of selection when redundancies are made. Such an approach involves taking into account a number of criteria from among those listed above and weighting them according to the perceived future needs of the organisation. Each employee within the group to be considered for redundancy is then scored against the others, and the employees with the lowest tallies are then selected. An example of a points system operated by a vehicle manufacturer was given in a recent IDS study covering redundancy (IDS 1995f: 11). Here seven criteria were included:

- length of service
- qualifications
- attendance
- skills
- flexibility
- quantity of work
- quality of work.

Length of service was weighted higher than the other factors, with 11 points given to employees with 11 years' service, rising on a sliding scale to 58 points for 40 years' service. With the exception of attendance, the other factors were scored with a maximum of 18 points. In each case there were four-point scales awarding 0, 6, 12 and 18 points respectively. The scale for quantity of work was devised as follows:

Struggles to meet minimum workload: 0

Usually meets workload requirements: 6

Generally exceeds workload requirements: 12

Consistently exceeds workload requirements: 18.

Attendance was weighted less heavily, and was adjusted where recent absence statistics were shown to be untypical of an employee's long-term record.

A wholly different approach to the selection of staff for redundancy is to start by developing a new organisational structure, identifying which jobs will be present in the organisation, undertaking which roles or duties, after the redundancy programme has been completed. This is the kind of approach used by organisations undergoing a planned downsizing operation, and has been used extensively in public-sector organisations, as well as those that have been privatised. In such situations, the new structure is agreed and job descriptions or person specifications drawn up for the jobs that remain. Where a job remains essentially unchanged and is currently undertaken by a single person, that person is then 'slotted in' and told that he or she will not be made redundant. Others then apply for the jobs in the new structure and, if necessary, undergo a competitive selection process. Where two or three jobs of a particular type are disappearing, to be replaced by a single job, the application procedure is 'ring-fenced' so that only those currently employed to undertake the roles in question compete for the new position. Those that are unsuccessful are then selected for redundancy. The advantage of this arrangement is the control that it gives managers over the selection process. Its great disadvantage is its effect on morale and teamworking, as employees compete with one another for positions in their own organisations. Of course, it remains the case that the selection criteria have to be both fair and objective, and capable of being justified in court if necessary.

Which of these approaches to the management of redundancy have you experienced or observed? In your view, which is least distressing for the individuals involved, and why?

PROVIDING HELP FOR REDUNDANT EMPLOYEES

One area of redundancy management in which the law does not intervene to any great extent is the provision of counselling and assistance to employees who are under notice of redundancy. All that the law requires is that such employees should be given reasonable time off work to look for a new position or to undergo job-search training. However, because few cases have been brought, it remains unclear what exactly 'reasonable time off' means. At present, it depends on the facts in particular cases (eg the nature of the job, the extent of expected difficulties in finding comparable work and the need for retraining). That said, according to recent surveys (IDS 1995f, IRS 1995b), most large employers offer further practical assistance to employees who are going to be dismissed on account of redundancy, and many also provide counselling where necessary.

According to Fowler (1993: 181–184), there are two broad stages in counselling redundant employees. The first is helping them to come to terms with their fate and to understand the reasons. The second is future-oriented, and involves assisting them to see the future as an opportunity to make new plans for their careers. Although in practice both issues are dealt with together, the first is a prerequisite for the second. It is only when people have successfully 'put initial feelings of resentment, anger and fear behind them' that they are psychologically able to face the future constructively. For this reason, Fowler argues strongly that professional, trained counsellors should be employed to carry out this work. Where well-meaning but untrained people attempt to carry out counselling the result is often counter-productive. If there are no trained counsellors in-house there is, therefore, a good case for hiring external specialists. The other great advantage of bringing in outsiders is the experience they have of dealing specifically with redundancy situations. Moreover, employees are more likely to open up and talk freely to outsiders than they are to colleagues who will be remaining with the organisation. Established Employee Assistance Programmes (EAPs), should an organisation have them in operation, can obviously be used as providers of counselling services.

A number of firms also offer to provide services of a more practical kind for employees under notice of redundancy. These are usually known as outplacement or career consultants, who specialise, on the one hand, in the provision of advice to individuals and, on the other, in running job-search courses or workshops for groups of employees. In both cases, the content of outplacement programmes covers similar grounds. The following is a typical list:

- sources of further employment
- options concerning part-time and self-employed work
- analysis of skills
- application forms or CV preparation
- interviewee skills
- advice about retraining
- salary negotiation.

Some outplacement consultants also operate as headhunters and are thus in a position to give more assistance than simply advice. This raises a potential conflict of interest, which may mean that the advice given is not sufficiently unbiased. The CIPD *Code of Conduct for Career and Outplacement Consultants* deals with this issue, along with others concerning the appropriate system of payment and the question of proper qualifications. Managers considering employing consultants should thus take note of the Code and make sure that potential providers adhere to its contents and are CIPD members.

Aside from formal outplacement and counselling, there are many other ways in which employers can give helpful and practical assistance to employees seeking new positions. First and foremost, they can offer more than just time off to look for a job by permitting the use of company facilities as well. Secretarial assistance can be given in the preparation of CVs and in other aspects of the job-search process; company cars can be used; and employers can waive any routine restraint-of-trade clauses that might otherwise prevent employees from working for competitors. Larger companies can also offer retraining courses or pay for redundant employees to attend training events elsewhere. Managers can also get in touch with professional contacts and other employers in the area to see whether opportunities exist for those whose jobs are going.

Another option is redeployment to another location within the same organisation, if necessary with further training provided. Although no employee can be obliged to relocate, some may show interest in such opportunities if allowances are paid to assist with removal expenses and if the career prospects are perceived as good. Employers also sometimes negotiate rehire agreements, whereby ex-employees are employed as subcontractors or consultants after they have been made redundant. Again, such arrangements are unlikely to be attractive or feasible for most, but may prove satisfactory for some redundant employees. Another approach is the establishment of a recall arrangement, whereby employees are given advance notice of any jobs advertised at their old place of work following their redundancy.

The final area of support that employers often choose to give reflects the possibility that ex-employees will spend a period without work following their redundancies. For some, this will mean applying for state benefits and surviving with a greatly reduced standard of living. For others, such as those leaving with substantial redundancy payments, a period out of the workforce may be more welcome. In either situation, there is a need for psychological preparation and sound financial advice. Some organisations make funds available to employees to organise their own counselling or training in these areas. They might, for example, add a sum of a few hundred pounds to the final redundancy payment to fund individual financial advice. Others take a more pro-active role, laying on courses covering benefit entitlements and investment for employees who are leaving without a job to go to.

> If you were to be made redundant, what other forms of help and support would you like to have? Which of those described here would be of most use to you?

REDUNDANCY PAYMENTS

Since 1965, the law has set out minimum levels of compensation to which redundant employees are entitled. In most cases, the rules are straightforward and have remained unchanged for 30 years. The main features are as follows:

- The amount due to redundant employees depends on their length of service with the employer.

- The calculation is based on the number of continuous years' service and the employee's weekly salary at the time the notice period expires.

- If the weekly salary varies, the average figure for the 12 weeks preceding termination is taken into account.

- Only completed years count.

- The maximum weekly salary that can be used as the basis for the calculation is determined by the government. At the time of writing (late 1997) it is £210.

- The maximum number of years' service that can be used as the basis of the calculation is 20.

- Only employees with more than two years' continuous service are entitled to redundancy payments.

- The formula for the calculation is as follows:

  For every completed year between the ages of 41 and 65 = 1.5 weeks' pay

  For every completed year between the ages of 22 and 41 = 1 week's pay

  For every completed year between the ages of 18 and 22 = 0.5 week's pay

- No one under the age of 20 can claim a redundancy payment.

- Employees who are 64 years old and older have their redundancy payment reduced by one-twelfth for each completed calendar month over the age of 64.

- Employers with pension schemes can reduce the redundancy payments due to employees within 90 weeks of the retirement age.

However, the statutory scheme is widely recognised as very much a minimum standard. The (former) IPD's guide on redundancy (1996b: 6) recommends that higher redundancy payments are made 'if at all possible, as the statutory sums are often too small to adequately compensate for the loss of a job'. The 20-year rule, combined with the £210 earnings limit, mean that the largest payment that employers are currently obliged to make is £6,300 – not a great deal for someone in his or her sixties with over 20 years' service. As a result, many have introduced more generous arrangements to ensure that those leaving are treated fairly. According to IRS (1995b: 12–15), the ways in which improvements to the statutory package are made vary from organisation to organisation. Examples from their survey include the following:

- doubling the statutory minimum

- increasing the number of weeks' pay used in the calculation (often to one month per year of service)

- making additional *ex gratia* payments for each completed year of service (eg 5 per cent of salary per year)

- disregarding the statutory earnings limit.

There are rarely any problems in calculating and communicating the entitlements due to full-time employees with unbroken periods of service. However, difficulties often arise where work patterns take a less standard form and where periods of employment have been temporarily broken. Cases have also been brought over the question of what figure represents a week's pay. Is it just base pay, or are overtime payments and bonuses to be considered too? The law states that all contractual payments should be included but is silent on the question of what figure should be used as the basis of calculations where weekly earnings fluctuate from one month to the next. In such cases, tribunals are forced to look at the facts in each individual case with a view to establishing what is 'reasonable'. Another common problem occurs in the case of employees who have completed a number of years' service as full-timers but have then opted for part-time work.

Unjust though it may be, at present employers are permitted to calculate redundancy compensation on the basis of the current part-time salary, thus disregarding however many years have been completed as a full-time employee. In all such cases it must be stressed that employers have the discretion to award more generous terms, and they often choose to do so as a means of avoiding additional unpleasantness and bad feeling.

> What level of redundancy payments does your organisation pay? What are the reasons for calculating them in the way that it does?

MANAGING THE SURVIVORS

An important feature of the successful management of a redundancy programme is the attention given to those who remain employed in the organisation after the dismissals have taken place. Ultimately, the long-term success or failure of the redundancy programme depends on these people's ability to come to terms with new structures and working practices. In practice, as anyone who has experienced such a situation can verify, it is not always easy to bring about a soft landing. Like soldiers who have survived a bloody battle, employees left to run organisations in the absence of colleagues can suffer from strong feelings of guilt and shell-shock. Added to this, it is likely that there will be some who would have preferred to take voluntary redundancy had they been given the chance, and who experience demotivation as a result.

The *IPD Guide on Redundancy* (1996b: 11–12) provides sound advice on approaches to managing these issues and reducing the likelihood that survivors will lack 'commitment, enthusiasm and initiative'. First and foremost, the guide stresses the need to manage the redundancy process in a fair and open way. Survivors are more likely to recover and look forward if they are satisfied that the dismissal of colleagues was truly unavoidable in the circumstances and was handled professionally. There is thus a need not only to select redundant employees fairly, to provide fair levels of compensation and to offer practical assistance, but also to make sure that these matters are communicated effectively to all employees, whether or not they are individually affected by the redundancy programme. Secondly, it is important that communication with staff is two-way and that managers respond to suggestions and criticisms from employees at different stages throughout the process.

The other emotion that survivors often display is fear arising from concern that further redundancies will follow and that they may be next in line. If this is not dealt with, organisations will find that they have difficulty retaining the very individuals they most need to ensure future prosperity. Extra attention has to be given to reassuring employees of their value and continued employment prospects. The IPD guide suggests that this is best achieved by line managers' putting time aside to meet employees individually both to reassure and to listen. Once more, two-way communication is vital to success.

OTHER LEGAL ISSUES

As in many areas of employee-resourcing practice, in the field of redundancy there is a great deal of relevant employment law which it is beyond the scope of this book to explore in detail. Readers are thus recommended to turn to specialised texts, such as those identified at the end of this chapter, for more detail on these topics. Here, therefore, we simply give a short description of a number of significant legal issues that P&D managers should be aware of when approaching the management of a redundancy programme.

Trade unions

The law now requires employers to undertake meaningful consultation exercises with trade unions in situations where they are recognised and where members are under threat of redundancy. To that end employers have to disclose in writing to relevant trade union representatives the number of employees likely to be dismissed and details of the groups of employees at risk. Moreover, the proposed selection criteria must be outlined, together with the method that will be used in selection and the proposed redundancy payments.

The time-scale for consultation is 30 days where between 10 and 99 employees are to be made redundant, and 90 days if more than 100 are affected. Where fewer than 10 redundancies are proposed there is still a requirement to consult, but not to any predetermined time-scale. The consultation process has to be more than a formality. In other words, employers are required to seek agreement with trade union representatives on such issues as ways of minimising numbers and of mitigating the consequences.

Notification

Whether or not a trade union is recognised, employers proposing to make 10 or more employees redundant are obliged to notify the Department for Education and Employment (DfEE) in writing. Standard forms are produced for this purpose and the time-scales are the same as those for trade union consultation. The DfEE also has to be informed which trade unions, if any, are involved.

The need to dismiss

An important legal technicality is the requirement that employees have to be formally dismissed in order to qualify for the receipt of a tax-free redundancy payment. Employees who volunteer for redundancy must, therefore, not resign. Instead they have to express an interest in being made redundant and then must wait to be dismissed by the employer.

'Bumping'

'Bumped' or transferred redundancies occur when an employee whose job is to be made redundant is given a position elsewhere in the organisation, leading to the dismissal of someone else. In other words, an occupant of a position whose own job is not being made redundant is dismissed in order to retain the services of an employee whose job *is* being removed.

The courts have ruled that such manoeuvres are potentially 'reasonable' where it can be shown that the business clearly benefits as a result. It is thus unacceptable to bump simply in order to find a job for a particularly liked person who would otherwise be redundant; it has to be shown that there are sound operational reasons to justify the action. Where that is the case, it is acceptable to pay a redundancy payment to the bumped individual, despite the fact that his or her job is not itself affected.

Offers of alternative work

Where employees under threat of redundancy are offered suitable alternative work by their employer before they are dismissed and refuse to take the offer up, the employer is under no obligation to pay them a redundancy payment. Where redundancy payments are substantial, the suitability of the new job offer is often a contentious issue. Tribunals have tended to avoid applying general principles in cases of this kind, preferring to look at the facts and take into consideration the employee's reasons for rejecting the offer. Where the job is in the same location, pays the same salary, is of a similar status and is within the capability of the employee concerned, it is likely that a refusal to accept would be found unreasonable by a tribunal.

The law also provides for four-week trial periods to be offered to employees where new jobs are offered on terms different from those on which the previous contract was based. At the end the employee has to decide whether or not the work is suitable. Again, where an employee who has been given every assistance to settle into the new position resigns for trivial reasons, the employer is entitled to refuse the redundancy payment. Here, too, tribunals judge reasonableness by looking at the particular facts in each case rather than setting down hard-and-fast principles.

Waiver clauses

Where staff are employed on a fixed-term basis for one year or more, employers are entitled to include 'waiver clauses' in written contracts of employment. These then form the basis of an agreement between employer and employee that there will be no liability for redundancy payments, or indeed any other form of unfair dismissal, on the expiry of the contract. This is a standard and straightforward matter in most cases but can become complicated when individuals are employed over a period of time on a succession of separate fixed-term contracts. In such cases it has now been established that each new contract is treated separately, and that if an employee has his or her contract renewed with any new terms, any previous waiver clause is void. Employers therefore need to ensure that new waiver clauses are incorporated each time a fixed-term contract is renewed if they wish to avoid redundancy costs.

INDIVIDUAL CASES

So far in this chapter the topic of redundancy has been examined from a collective perspective. The topic has therefore been seen from the perspective of managers faced with decisions involving groups of employees. However, there are also occasions when individuals are dismissed for reasons of redundancy – situations that tend to be handled rather differently. Although the basic legal principles remain the same, there is no requirement to inform the Secretary of State, and the process may be managed in a less formal and standardised fashion.

The kind of situation under consideration here arises when, for example, one member of a team has to be dismissed. Examples might be losing one teacher from a school when the number of pupils declines, or needing to dismiss one of a pool of clerical workers following the introduction of new technology. In such circumstances, the use of impersonal approaches, such as putting people under formal notice that they are at risk of redundancy and making them undergo highly formalised selection procedures is too brutal. What is needed is a great deal more sensitivity and confidentiality.

First, where they are not already laid down in a redundancy policy, it is necessary to agree the selection criteria that will be used in choosing the individual to be dismissed. Instead of asking generally for volunteers, the next step involves privately approaching individuals who might be interested in taking voluntary redundancy and establishing whether or not this is the case. If no one expresses an interest in leaving, the individual to be compulsorily dismissed should then be informed and discussions carried out with him or her personally to explore alternative opportunities and the extent to which practical assistance can be given to help him or her find a new position. The principles of reasonableness are thus adhered to, just as in the case of collective redundancies, but the manner in which the process is managed is made more appropriate to the case of the individual concerned.

THE LAW ON RETIREMENT

As has already been stated, in the UK at present there is no legislation outlawing discrimination on grounds of age. Moreover, existing employment law, far from advancing the rights of employees considered to be past the age of retirement, specifically precludes them from bringing cases of unfair dismissal against their employers. However, because there is no set retirement age, employers are free to determine what it should be for their organisations. The current legal situation is put concisely by IDS (1992b: 2):

> An employer may specify in employees' contracts of employment any retirement age so long as that age is the same for men and women. Employees may of course leave employment when they please, subject to whatever period of notice is required. But if they stay on until the retirement age specified in the contract of employment, the contract will automatically end as agreed at that point without a termination by either party. There will be no need for notice on the part of either employer or employee.

In practice this means that an employer, provided all are treated in the same way, can set a retirement age of 60 and effectively dismiss all employees at that age, irrespective of whether they are entitled to a state or occupational pension. Because the employees' contracts are deemed in law to have ended, there is no technical dismissal, and no right to a redundancy payment. In cases where the contract does not specify a set retirement age, the courts have judged that the age of 65 should apply, unless it is common practice in the organisation concerned to retire people at an earlier date. Indeed, common practice is now considered to override the contract where the two are in conflict. So, if the contract specifies a normal retirement age of 60, but in practice most staff remain in post until 65, then all employees are deemed to be reasonable in thinking that they too can remain until 65. The test in cases of uncertainty, according to the House of Lords judgment in *Waite* v *Government Communications Headquarters* [1991], should be 'the reasonable expectation or understanding of an employee holding that position at the relevant time'.

The state thus offers only minimum protection to retired people in the form of a state pension. Should they choose to work beyond 65, they are given no legal protection over and above what is agreed in their contracts of employment. Furthermore, where they are legally forced to retire before 65 (or 60 for women born before April 1950), they will not be entitled to a State pension until they have reached that age. As with redundancy, therefore, there are many opportunities for good employers to improve on the deal that the law offers by affording employees a degree of flexibility in choosing their own dates of retirement and in assisting them to adjust to the years that follow their departure from the workforce.

EARLY RETIREMENT

The first area in which most larger employers now improve on the legal requirement is to offer employees the opportunity, if they so wish, to retire early. A recent survey undertaken by the Institute for Employment Studies (IRS 1996b: 3) indicates that a clear majority welcomes the opportunity to take early retirement, and that only 14 per cent regret doing so after the event.

Although people with private savings or personal pensions that have performed particularly well may be able to retire before their contractual dates, the term 'early retirement' is more commonly associated with membership of the employer's occupational pension scheme. Precise terms and methods of calculation vary from organis-ation to organisation, but most employers (72 per cent, according to IRS 1995b: 15) agree to pay a reduced pension to retirees who leave before the contractual retirement age. Where employees have accrued sufficient pension rights to provide a satisfactory income, such offers are very tempting – especially if there is a possibility of continuing to work on a part-time or consultancy basis.

However, in order to prevent a general exodus of highly valued employees, most employers also reserve the right to refuse requests for early retirement. Where the financial liability for the pension fund is increased by such arrangements, scheme trustees also have a right of veto. Where redundancies are in the offing, managers often improve the early retirement provisions somewhat in order to provide an incen-tive for older employees to take up the opportunity. In so doing, they reduce the number of compulsory redundancies, while much of the cost is shouldered by pension scheme funds.

XR Associates

In 1991, in order to sweeten the incentive to take early retirement at a time when large numbers of redundancies were being made, Ford UK set up a consultancy company called XR Associates. It was unusual in that it was staffed entirely by ex-Ford employees over the age of 50 who had accepted offers of early retirement. In return, they were guaranteed 90 days' work a year on a consultancy basis with either Ford or one of its suppliers. After two years of operation, it was reported that XR employed 400 people, including a third of the managers who had left Ford in that period. By 1996 there were 600 consultants.

XR people work on one-off projects on behalf of the company, rather than simply working in their pre-retirement roles again. They are paid daily rates at a level commensurate with the type of work undertaken. They can take as much or as little work as they please, some opting to work three or four days a week and others reducing their commitment to one day. The advantage for the company is the ability that it gives to call on experienced people with a knowledge of the business to undertake project work. This leaves full-time managers free to carry out day-to-day duties.

Source: IDS (1996: 17)

PREPARING EMPLOYEES FOR RETIREMENT

In her book on retirement, Phil Long (1981: 38–50) puts a very good case for the provision by employers of effective pre-retirement training. Without it, she claims, employees often experience shock and prolonged depression when they suddenly find that they no longer have jobs to go to. The sense of loss and lack of purpose in life leads many to deteriorate mentally and physically:

> The emergence from the world of work is as much a culture shock as the entry, yet in neither situation is there much preparation. The young school leaver, entering his or her first job, usually finds a supportive environment, however informal this might be. By contrast, the newly retired have to adjust to an equally novel situation unaided and for many the transition can be a difficult one ... Three score years of being indoctrinated in the Protestant work ethic, which stresses the virtues and values of work, is no preparation for what should be a period in which to do one's own thing. Unfortunately few have been educated to use their leisure in a creative way.

In France and in the Scandinavian countries governments are actively involved either in providing or promoting pre-retirement training courses. In the UK, although some local authorities operate events of this kind, it is mainly up to employers to do so.

The contents of pre-retirement training courses appear to be fairly standard. In practice, there is usually a need to blend group-based training with individual counselling and advisory sessions. Wherever possible, spouses should be invited to attend along with the prospective retirees. According to Long (1981: 49), the following are typical issues to be covered:

• understanding pension provision

- taxation of savings

- investment of lump sums and annuities

- social security entitlements

- health and nutrition

- safety in the home

- developing leisure activities

- re-employment and part-time working

- moving house

- drawing up wills.

In addition, courses include sessions designed to help people to adjust psychologically to the idea of retiring. These involve explaining what difficulties might be encountered and suggesting approaches to managing the transition. Reynolds and Bailey (1993), in their book on pre-retirement training, give a good deal of attention to this topic and offer helpful advice for those delivering training of this kind. Drawing on their experience, they provide a depressing description of the emotional problems that people suffer when they are required to retire. However, they also show how it is possible to work through the initial feelings of shock, denial and depression in order to adjust and accept retirement as the new, normal state of affairs. Unsurprisingly, a major part of this process is the development of new interests and the revival of those left dormant during busy working lives. The taking-up of voluntary work or part-time paid work is also a possibility. By all accounts, one method of avoiding the psychological problems associated with retirement is to find ways of phasing it in over a period of a year or two. A number of larger organisations have well-established schemes of this kind which permit employees gradually to reduce their working hours as they approach the date of retirement. Ideally, in order to attract employees, such schemes should not involve too great a loss in income.

POST-RETIREMENT CONTACT

The final area of activity that contributes to the smooth transition into retirement is the maintenance of formal contacts with the organisation. These can take a wide variety of forms. At one extreme, there is the continuation of an economic relationship, whereby the retiree is hired again, but on a casual or part-time basis, and thus continues to come in to work from time to time. For professional and managerial staff, an option is to work on a consultancy basis. In such cases the employee is freed from having to come into work at set times, but is still required to provide advice or to undertake specific projects.

At the other end of the scale is the organisation of social events. Where organisations operate social clubs or provide weekend trips, Christmas parties and evening functions for staff, it is possible to invite retired employees, too. The larger, more paternalistic organisations go further, setting up benevolent funds for retirees in order to provide, or assist in the provision of, private health care, sheltered housing and holidays.

> What formal contact does your organisation maintain with retirees? To what extent could greater use be made of retirees' skills and expertise?

FURTHER READING

- Two excellent general texts covering all aspects of redundancy management were published in 1993. These are *Redundancy* by Alan Fowler and *The Successful Management of Redundancy* by Paul Lewis.

- Legal aspects are well covered in employment law handbooks and textbooks. The most up-to-date case-law is described in the various loose-leaf subscription services covering legal issues. IDS also regularly publish employment law supplements on redundancy.

- Surveys and case-studies looking at redundancy and retirement practices are published from time to time by IRS in *Employment Review* and by the IDS Studies. Recent issues that cover these topics are *Study 511 (Managing Redundancy)* (1992b), *Study 586 (Redundancy Terms)* (1995f) and *Study 595 (Older Workers)* (1996). The results of two extensive surveys covering redundancy and early retirement were published in the March and April editions of *Employment Review* in 1995.

- Best practice in redundancy is set out by the IPD in its *Guide on Redundancy* (1996b) and in its *Key Facts* publication on the topic published in February 1997.

- Two invaluable publications on the preparation of employees for retirement are *How to Design and Deliver Retirement Training* by Peter Reynolds and Marcella Bailey (1993) and *Retirement: Planned liberation?* by Phil Long (1981).

14 The end of the line

Dismissing individual employees, however strong the justification, is undoubtedly the most difficult task that P&D practitioners are required to undertake. Since 1971, as the law of unfair dismissal has developed, it has become a task that can very easily lead to costly and time-consuming legal actions when carried out poorly. For both these reasons it tends to be an area of work that other managers have little inclination to take over. When carried out effectively, it enhances the reputation and authority of P&D practitioners in the organisation, raising their profile and giving them greater influence. By contrast, when carried out sloppily, the result is tribunal actions, bad publicity, ill-feeling and even industrial action. It is thus a key skill for any aspiring P&D specialist to learn.

The unpleasantness of dismissal and the risks associated with carrying it out poorly mean that there is always a temptation to put it off or avoid taking action wherever possible. Yet this can often lead to greater problems at a later date. It is thus an area of P&D work requiring the exercise of considerable skill and judgement, as well as being a significant means by which P&D practitioners justify their role. Furthermore, dismissal and the disciplinary procedures associated with its management typically consume a great deal of time.

Inevitably, given its centrality to the topic, the law occupies much of this chapter – in particular, its requirements as to the handling of dismissals. In this field, recourse to legal action is very common indeed. According to the most recent IRS survey (1995a: 5), 64 per cent of employers reported being involved in unfair dismissal tribunal cases over a five-year period, and 26 per cent admitted to having been on the losing side.

By the end of this chapter, readers should be able to:

- manage the process for dismissing employees on grounds of ill-health and misconduct
- compile the documentation required in the dismissal process
- advise line managers and other colleagues about the major requirements of the law as it relates to dismissal
- distinguish between gross and 'ordinary' misconduct
- distinguish between unfair and wrongful dismissal.

In addition, readers should be able to understand and explain:

- the legal concept of 'reasonableness'

- automatically fair, automatically unfair and potentially fair reasons for dismissal

- the importance of following correct procedures when dismissing employees

- the role of the ACAS code of practice and the role that can be played by ACAS itself.

INTRODUCTION TO THE LAW OF UNFAIR DISMISSAL

The law of unfair dismissal in the UK dates from 1971, when it was included among a host of other measures in the Industrial Relations Act of that year. Although much of this legislation was later repealed, the measures relating to dismissal and the industrial tribunal system have remained on the statute book and have developed over time as new regulations have been introduced and legal precedents set. For some time, the basic principles have been well established, and now form the basis of the manner in which dismissals are carried out by most employers. To an extent, therefore, it is possible to argue that best practice in this field is synonymous with the principles of the law. The only substantial way in which best practice and legislation part company arises from current regulations that exclude certain groups of employees from protection. By far the largest of these is employees who have completed less than two years' continuous service.

For these reasons, it is essential for anybody with responsibility for the dismissal process to gain a sound basic knowledge of unfair dismissal law. The best way of avoiding the time, expense and inconvenience of appearing in court to justify one's action in dismissing someone is to anticipate the consequences of that action and to make sure that there is no case to answer. This is why even though only a minority of P&D managers are ever called to give evidence to a tribunal, they should all be familiar with the relevant law and legal processes, and allow this knowledge to guide their actions.

When an industrial tribunal is faced with a claim of unfair dismissal, and when it is satisfied that a dismissal has actually taken place, it is required to ask two questions:

- Is the reason for the dismissal one of the potentially fair reasons identified in law?

- Did the employer act reasonably in treating the reason as sufficient to justify the dismissal?

Only if the answer to the first question is yes will the second even be considered. In other words, if it cannot be established at the outset that the dismissal has actually occurred for a *bona fide* reason, the employer's case will fail, and the tribunal will not get round to considering the issue of the employer's 'reasonableness'.

When reaching a judgment about the first question, the burden of proof is on the employer. The tribunal thus expects the employer's representatives to show that they dismissed the individual for one of the reasons laid down as fair or potentially fair in the relevant statutes. For the second question, the burden of proof shifts and becomes neutral, so that the tribunal considers the facts and makes its decision without requiring either side to prove its case. In industrial tribunals, as in all civil courts, the standard of proof is 'on the balance of probabilities' and not, as in criminal courts, 'beyond reasonable doubt'.

FAIR AND UNFAIR REASONS

In considering the reason for dismissal, the tribunal has to decide into which of three categories a particular case can be classified. These are: automatically unfair, automatically fair and potentially fair. Only if they decide that the reason is 'potentially fair' will the second question (ie reasonableness) be considered. If they find the reason to be either automatically fair or unfair they will reach an immediate judgment.

The list of automatically unfair reasons has grown over the years. It now includes the following:

- asserting the right to trade union membership or stating an intention to join a trade union

- taking part, or intending to take part, in lawful trade union activities

- asserting the right not to join a trade union

- pregnancy, childbirth or any related reason

- refusal to carry out instructions that jeopardise health and safety at work

- carrying out actions intended to protect people from danger

- refusing to work on Sundays (in the case of retail workers)

- having a criminal record where the conviction is spent

- for a reason relating to an employee's status as a pension fund trustee

- as a result of a transfer of undertaking

- asserting a statutory right.

These last two require further explanation. A transfer of an undertaking occurs where control of an organisation or part of an organisation transfers from one body to another, leading to a change of employer. There is a series of regulations that apply in such situations, one of which gives protection to employees who might otherwise be dismissed as a direct result of a business take-over, merger or change of employing authority. There are, however, important exceptions where an employer can show that, while occurring as a result of a transfer of undertaking, the dismissal occurred for 'an economic, technical or organisational reason entailing changes in the workforce'. In other words, it is generally possible to dismiss someone before or after a transfer occurs, provided a good business reason for doing so can be established.

Statutory rights include several conferred on employees in recent Acts of Parliament. Examples are: the right to minimum periods of notice, the right not to have union dues deducted from pay without consent, the right to time off to carry out legitimate trade union duties, and the right not to be subjected to any disciplinary action on account of trade union activity or a refusal to take part in such activity. It is now automatically unfair to dismiss employees who demand these rights or who begin legal proceedings in order to enforce them.

There are far fewer automatically fair reasons for dismissing employees; most of them relate to industrial action. Effectively, employers have immunity from liability where a dismissal occurs directly as a result of unofficial industrial action (ie strikes or other forms of collective action that do not satisfy the definition of 'official' as laid down in industrial relations law). They are also entitled to dismiss employees taking official action, provided all those involved are treated alike. It is thus unfair to dismiss one of a group of strikers, but automatically fair to dismiss all of them. The other category of dismissals over which employers enjoy immunity are those that relate to safeguarding national security. In most cases, this will apply only to certain government employees working in the intelligence services or armed forces, but may also conceivably be relevant to some private-sector employers, such as those engaged in weapons production.

The vast majority of cases falls into the third category of potentially fair dismissals, and it is in these that the issue of the employer's reasonableness and the circumstances of individual cases become relevant issues. The law states that there are five potentially fair reasons: capability, conduct, redundancy, statutory restrictions, and 'some other substantial reason'.

Capability
This term is defined broadly as encompassing skill, aptitude, health or 'any other mental or physical quality'. In other words, it is potentially fair to dismiss someone who, in the judgement of the employer, is incapable of carrying out their work because they are ill-qualified, incompetent or too sick to do so.

Conduct
Poor conduct or misconduct on the part of an employee is also deemed to be a potentially fair reason for dismissal. The most common instances involve absenteeism, lateness, disloyalty, refusal to carry out reasonable instructions, dishonesty, fighting, harassment, drunkenness and swearing.

Redundancy
This term relates to economic dismissals that meet the definitions laid down. They are discussed at length in Chapter 13.

Statutory restrictions
This category is intended to cover situations in which employers cannot continue to employ particular individuals in a job because they are legally barred from doing so. The two examples most frequently given relate to foreign nationals who do not have work permits (or whose permits have run out) and drivers who lose their licenses.

'Some other substantial reason'

The final category has attracted criticism in so far as it is seen as being something of a 'catch-all', permitting employers to dismiss on a variety of grounds not covered by the other fair or potentially fair reasons. The question of how substantial the reason is in practice is a matter for the courts. Over the years the following reasons for dismissal have been included:

- business re-organisations that do not result in redundancies

- pressure from customers

- termination of temporary contracts

- staff mutinies

- misrepresentation of qualifications at interview.

The law is very clear, however, that no employee can be dismissed as a result of threatened or actual industrial action on the part of other employees. Where a tribunal has reason to believe that this is the real reason for the dismissal, they will find it automatically unfair.

> What other cases have you come across that could be classed as 'some other substantial reason'?

REASONABLENESS

Having established that the reason for the dismissal is indeed one of the above 'potentially fair' ones, industrial tribunals go on next to judge how reasonable the employer has been, given the circumstances of the case, in deciding to dismiss the employee concerned. It is thus on the issue of 'reasonableness' that most unfair dismissal cases hang. The following quotation from the Employment Protection (Consolidation) Act 1978 sets out the approach that is taken:

> The determination of the question of whether a dismissal was fair or unfair, having regard to the reasons shown by the employer, shall depend on whether in the circumstances (including the size and administrative resources of the employer's undertaking) the employer acted reasonably or unreasonably in treating it as a sufficient reason for dismissing the employee; and that question shall be determined in accordance with equity and the substantial merits of the case.

For a number of years tribunals interpreted these words in different ways, but since the judgment in the case of *Iceland Foods* v *Jones* [1983] a new standard test has operated. Since that time, members of tribunals have not simply asked whether, in their view, the course of action taken by the employer was what they themselves would have done in the circumstances, but whether or not it fell within a band of reasonable responses. It is thus quite possible that a decision to dismiss might not be what the members of the tribunal believe should have occurred, given the facts of the case, but will nevertheless be found fair because the employer's action was one that fell within a range of approaches that could be considered reasonable.

In judging reasonableness, tribunals look at a number of factors relating to the individual and the organisation concerned. They will, for example, wish to satisfy themselves that the employer treats all staff alike in deciding to dismiss. Where it is shown that, in similar circumstances, an employer has acted inconsistently in dismissing one employee while retaining the services of another, it is likely that the dismissal will not be found to have been 'reasonable'. However, tribunals also like to see account taken of an employee's past record, especially in questions of conduct. This means that staff who have been employed for a good number of years and have impeccable disciplinary records are expected to be treated rather more leniently than colleagues with less service and records of poor conduct. Where relevant, tribunals will also investigate how far employers have sought to avoid the dismissal. Such matters are particularly associated with dismissals due to ill-health, where there may be alternative jobs or duties that employees can carry out, even though they are no longer fit to undertake their existing job.

The size and relative resources of the employer concerned are also issues considered when judging 'reasonableness'. A large organisation employing hundreds of people will thus be judged against different standards from those expected of a small business employing half a dozen. In the former case, it would probably be unreasonable to dismiss someone who was sick but expected to return to work in five or six months' time. For a small business, by contrast, such an action might be necessary to permit it to continue in operation. Similarly, a large employer will have more opportunities than a small counterpart to find alternative work for an employee struck down with a serious illness such as multiple sclerosis or a severe neck injury.

The other major issue that tribunals are required to look at in judging 'reasonableness' is the procedure used. Since the landmark case of *Polkey* v *Deyton Services Ltd* [1987], the question of the procedure used to carry out the dismissal has become central to tribunal decision-making. Prior to that date, there were cases of tribunals' disregarding procedural deficiencies on the grounds that it made no difference to the final outcome – namely the decision to dismiss. This is no longer acceptable, and tribunals are now required to find dismissals unfair where they consider the procedure used to have been unreasonable. In practice, this means that, in dealing with employees in matters of ill-health, misconduct or poor performance, as well as redundancy and the other potentially fair reasons, employers are obliged to adopt the procedures recommended by ACAS in its advisory handbooks. Although these are not prescribed by law, they are still the yardstick by which tribunals now judge reasonableness, and so have formed the approach used by most employers.

The most widely used ACAS code is that concerned with discipline. It dates from 1977 and forms the model that employers are expected to follow when dealing with poor conduct, work performance and poor attendance. Based on the principles of natural justice, it includes the following basic features:

- Organisations should have written disciplinary procedures, and not handle cases on an *ad hoc* basis.

- There is a need to state who has the authority to take what action at each stage of the procedure.

- The procedure should clearly specify what employee action or lack of action will be treated as sufficiently serious for formal procedures to be invoked.

- Provision must be made for employees to be informed of the complaint against them and to have every opportunity to state their case.

- Employees should have the opportunity to be accompanied at any formal hearing by a trade union representative or work colleague of their choice.

- A fair-warnings system must be in place to ensure that employees are given at least two warnings and thus the opportunity to improve before being dismissed.

- Provision should be made for a right to appeal, and an individual or committee should be specified to whom appeal may be made.

In recommending its procedure, ACAS suggests that provision is made for three formal warnings to be given before dismissal is considered (formal oral warning, first written warning, final written warning). The aim is to ensure that all issues are investigated promptly and objectively, that employees are fully aware of any complaints against them, that they have every opportunity to state mitigating factors, and that they have an opportunity to put matters right and are not dismissed on the whim of an overpowerful manager or for spurious reasons.

The disciplinary conundrum

A problem for P&D practitioners managing disciplinary issues is how to resolve the tensions inherent in procedures such as those recommended by ACAS – tensions that pull in two very different directions. The problem arises from a situation in which the procedure is at once supposed to be both corrective in intent and also the mechanism by which lawful dismissals take place. Often the two aims conflict.

The problem is best illustrated with an example. A common situation is that of an employee who has become seriously demotivated (for whatever reason) and whose standard of performance drops. He or she starts arriving late, phones in sick on Mondays, ceases to complete work tasks on time and becomes a disruptive influence on other members of the department. In theory, such a situation needs action to be taken that addresses the employee's lack of motivation and seeks to provide new challenges and incentives. Giving a formal oral warning and setting attendance and performance targets is thus an inappropriate course of action, because it is likely to demotivate further. It may also lead to a breakdown in trust between the employee concerned and his or her line manager.

Yet any P&D manager who has seen many such situations in the past knows that, in all likelihood, there is no practical means by which the employee's level of motivation can be lifted. He or she is unsuitable for promotion, has already alienated work colleagues and has formed an apathetic attitude towards training and development opportunities. There is thus a strong probability that this situation will lead to dismissal if the employee concerned does not voluntarily resign first. In order for the dismissal to be fair, and to protect the organisation from possible legal challenge, the P&D response is to start the disciplinary procedure.

Therein lies the problem. There are two conflicting requirements. First there is a need to meet with the employee formally, to inform him or her that he or she can be represented or accompanied by a colleague or union official, to warn that his or her performance is unsatisfactory, to give an opportunity to state his or her own case, and then to send a letter that confirms the outcome and informs the employee of the right to appeal.

Secondly, there is a need to find ways of looking forward positively, of offering opportunities, and of seeking to remotivate the employee concerned. In practice, this is fiendishly hard to achieve. The very act of setting up a formal hearing, particularly in the case of relatively senior staff, signals a breakdown in trust. However positive and helpful the managers present at the hearing try to be, invariably the fact that the procedure has started at all will have the opposite effect.

GROSS MISCONDUCT

A common misconception is that an employer must always start disciplinary proceedings at the start of the ACAS-recommended procedure with an oral warning. In most cases, such as those involving poor attendance, persistent lateness, minor mistakes or instances of negligence, or failure to carry out legitimate instructions, stage 1 (oral warning) is indeed the appropriate approach to take. However, where more serious instances of poor performance or breaches of discipline occur, it is well within the definition of 'reasonableness' to start the procedure with a first written warning, final written warning or even summary dismissal (ie dismissal without notice), when the circumstances are apt.

The ACAS handbook gives no guidance on what issues might require written warnings to be issued, except in the case of repetition of an offence by an individual who has already received formal warnings. It does, however, define situations in which employers would be justified, after full and fair investigation, in summarily dismissing employees – provided, of course, that all employees are treated alike. These offences, described as acts of 'gross misconduct', are the following:

- theft, fraud or deliberate falsification of records

- fighting or assault on another person

- deliberate damage to company property

- serious incapability through alcohol or drug use

- serious negligence causing unacceptable loss, damage or injury

- serious acts of insubordination.

This list is meant to provide examples, and is therefore not definitive or exhaustive. It does, however, indicate the degree of seriousness that an incident must reach if it is to justify summary dismissal. Whether or not misconduct is to be construed as 'gross' inevitably depends on particular circumstances. Drinking three pints of beer at lunch-time may not even qualify as any kind of misconduct in many jobs, but where someone works as a driver, dispensing chemist, or operator of dangerous machinery, it would in all likelihood justify summary dismissal. Similarly, depending on the job and organisation, careless breaches of confidentiality can either be irrelevant or highly damaging. Provided employees are made well aware of what is and what is not acceptable, it is thus possible for employers to determine for themselves what they class as gross misconduct.

In practice, managers do not often find themselves debating whether or not an act of gross misconduct has occurred. That much is usually pretty clear. The problem is deciding whether the organisation's response should be to dismiss the individual or individuals concerned (which it would be within its rights to do) or to give either a first or final written warning. Factors to take into account include whether it is a first breach of discipline, the nature of any mitigating circum- stances, the extent to which the employee shows remorse, and their persuasiveness in stating that the offence will not be committed again. It is inevitable that subjective judgements come into play here, with employees who have potential, who are hard to replace or whose work is generally valued, treated more leniently than less-favoured colleagues. Provided there are genuine, defensible reasons for this, some inconsistency will be justifiable should the matter be raised in a tribunal. What is important is that these judgements be not clouded by personal likes and dislikes or grudges.

Procedure also plays a significant role in tribunal decisions concerning the reasonableness of dismissals for gross misconduct. It is not acceptable to fire someone in a fit of temper on the spot (however tempting that course of action can be on occasions). If the dismissal is to meet the legal definition of 'fairness', the following eight steps need to be taken:

- Inform the employee or employees concerned that they are under suspicion of committing an act of gross misconduct.

- State that a full and fair investigation will now take place to establish exactly what has occurred.

- State that the individuals will be suspended on full pay while the investigation proceeds.

- Inform them that a formal hearing will be held when the investigation has been completed at which they have the right to be represented and will have every opportunity to state their case.

- Formally investigate the issue, taking formal statements from any witnesses and keeping a written record of all relevant evidence.

- Hold a hearing within five working days.

- Put the case to the employee or employees and allow them to respond.

- Make a decision either to dismiss or to take other action short of dismissal.

In addition to the above, larger organisations are expected to make provision for dismissed employees to appeal to a more senior manager, and to inform them of this right at the time of their dismissal.

It is important to give serious consideration to taking disciplinary action short of dismissal. This is particularly so where cases are not clear-cut and where there is some doubt as to whether dismissal is the only practicable outcome. It is important even where dismissal does occur, so that it can be used as evidence of reasonableness in the event of the case coming to court. Apart from the giving of a final written warning, actions short of dismissal include suspension without pay or at a lower rate, demotion, moving employees to another job or to different duties, requiring them to pay for damage done, withholding bonus payments or withholding promotions. These measures can be either permanent or temporary, depending on the circumstances.

ILL-HEALTH DISMISSALS

Of all the tasks that P&D professionals have to undertake, by far the most unpleasant is to dismiss employees because they are no longer fit to work. It is particularly hard when the individuals involved are supporting other family members and when there is no possibility of providing financial assistance through a pension or other insurance scheme. Where it is believed that the illness is terminal, the process becomes even more difficult. However, that said, it remains a task that has to be carried out from time to time, and one that has to be done lawfully as well as sensitively.

It is very difficult to give any kind of general definition of 'reason-ableness' in such cases, because the law requires above all that each individual case is treated on its own merits. However, the basic considerations are the following:

- Long-term illness is a potentially fair reason for dismissal.

- The decision to dismiss need not be taken on medical grounds alone. It is at root a management issue, which has to be determined against the background of the available medical evidence.

- Jobs should be kept open for sick individuals for as long as is practically possible wherever there is a reasonable expectation that they will be able to return to work in the foreseeable future.

- Sick-pay arrangements are wholly distinct. There is no right for an employee to have his or her job held open until sick pay ends, nor are employers permitted to dismiss at this point for no other reason than that no further payments are being made.

The decision to dismiss has thus to be taken in the light of individual circumstances and so cannot be determined by written policy. Where the employee's duties cannot practicably be covered by others, the employer will be justified in dismissing the sick employee in order to hire a replacement after a relatively short period of time. By contrast, where covering through the use of temporary employees, overtime or departmental reorganisation is possible, and where the employee's illness is believed to be long-term and yet temporary, the 'reasonable' employer is expected to keep the job open, and not to dismiss.

Such judgements are impossible without medical evidence, so tribunals expect employers to take all possible steps to obtain it. In most cases this is no problem, because employees have no objection to a letter of enquiry's being sent to their GP or specialist. Indeed, they themselves will often provide copies of medical reports to their employers. However, employees are not obliged to do so, and are legally entitled to refuse their employer access to a report once it has been written. There are also situations in which doctors refuse to send reports to employers because they believe that to do so would be potentially damaging to the employee's health and or chances of speedy recovery. Often these arise when doctors do not wish their patients to see the full content of such reports. Employees who are sick can also be invited to see a company doctor or medical practitioner employed by an employer's occupational health service. Here too, though, they are under no obligation to attend.

From the P&D manager's perspective, the more information that is provided the better, but the law only requires that serious efforts be made to obtain that evidence. Often this will include formally warning employees concerned that their job is at risk if they do not co-operate. Where no medical evidence is forthcoming despite taking all reasonable steps to obtain it, and the employer has good reason to believe the illness to be sufficiently serious to justify dismissal, the decision to dismiss will generally be held to be fair by a tribunal. Where it is written into contracts of employment that employees are obliged to submit to a medical examination when they are sick for a prolonged period, the issuing of formal warnings is more easily accomplished.

As in other cases of unfair dismissal, tribunals also pay attention to the procedural arrangements when judging the employer's reasonableness. In ill-health cases, they will look at how far the employer has kept in touch with employees during their illness, how far they have been consulted and informed about the possible consequences of their continued ill-health, and whether or not colleagues or trade union representatives have been present at meetings. Here too there is a need, wherever possible, to give formal consideration to taking action short of dismissal. Among the questions that ACAS suggests should be asked are these:

• Could the employee return to work if some assistance were provided?

• Could some re-organisation or re-design of the job speed up a return to work?

• Is alternative, lighter or less stressful work available, with retraining if necessary?

- Could re-organisation of the work group produce a more suitable job?

- Could early retirement be considered, perhaps with an enhanced pension or an *ex gratia* payment?

- Have all possibilities been discussed with the employee and his or her representative?

To these could be added the possibility that a temporary replacement could be appointed on a fixed-term basis, or the suggestion that the employee works part-time or from home during his or her recovery. It may also be possible to offer help in bringing the employee in to work and taking him or her back home at the end of the day.

In some respects, greater difficulties are caused in situations where employees who are sick continue to come into work despite the fact that they are incapable of adequately performing their jobs. The problem is made worse when such staff have to take time off to undergo medical examinations or to be treated in hospital. In the case of a long-term sickness that results in poor performance and intermittent periods of absence, it is not always easy to judge under which procedure (misconduct, performance or ill-health) it should be managed. It is made all the harder when employees are unwilling to admit that they are seriously ill, for fear of losing their jobs. In such situations, the principles set out above are the same. There is a need to reassure the employees concerned and to deal with the situation as sensitively as possible but, ultimately, if no recovery materialises, there is a need to take all reasonable steps to obtain medical evidence and to consider dismissing on grounds of ill-health. Again, provided the above procedural steps have been followed, the dismissal would be defensible at a tribunal, and a legal challenge would therefore be unlikely.

How far does your organisation follow the above principles in handling ill-health dismissals? In what ways could your procedures be improved?

Offences committed outside work

An interesting area of employment law concerns the response that employers should make when employees commit criminal offences of no direct bearing on their work. As a general rule, the courts take the view that convictions of this kind should have no lasting effect on the individual's employment, and it is unfair to dismiss someone on those grounds alone.

However, exceptions have been made where courts have judged that the offence effectively breaches an employer's trust, or where potential harm might be done to the business if the employment was to continue. Examples have included acts of dishonesty, indecency and violence committed outside working hours and away from the premises. Dismissal may also be fair, provided no industrial action is threatened, where other employees find the individual's continued employment to be unacceptable.

Nor should imprisonment necessarily lead to dismissal, although in many cases it would amount to a breach of trust and confidence. Where terms of imprisonment are short (eg for non-payment of a fine), where the disciplinary record of the individual concerned has been good and where the business can function without appointing a permanent replacement, there is a case for arguing that summary dismissal is unfair, both legally and ethically. In such cases, because the employee is known to be returning to work in a few weeks' time, the case should be treated as would an absence due to ill-health.

Longer terms of imprisonment are different. In most instances, even where there is no clear loss of trust and confidence, the contract of employment can be judged to have been frustrated by the inability of the employee to attend. Dismissal is an option in such circumstances but unnecessary, as frustration of a contract renders the formal act of dismissal unnecessary. The law of unfair dismissal will thus not apply and the only legal challenge possible would be in the civil courts on the rather spurious basis that the contract had not in fact been frustrated.

DOCUMENTATION

As has already been made clear, it is necessary, in managing and carrying out individual dismissals, to bear in mind the possibility that a tribunal case might be brought. It is therefore important that affairs are dealt with in such a way as to ensure that, if the dismissed employee decides to launch a legal action, the organisation is well placed to defend it. In any event, where the dismissal has been carried out lawfully and the procedure used has been fair, the aggrieved employee will be less likely to take the organisation to court. Making sure that the documentation associated with the dismissal is in order has a significant role to play in the deterrence process, because documentary evidence is crucial for a tribunal seeking to judge how reasonable the procedural aspects of the dismissal were. There is no point in undertaking all the necessary procedural steps if, at the end of the day, it cannot be shown that this actually occurred. Documentary evidence, as well as that given by witnesses, is the only means open to a tribunal to make such judgements, and documents tend to be rather more reliable.

Perhaps the most important document of all is the organisation's disciplinary procedure. Since 1993 all employers with more than 20 staff have been obliged to have a written disciplinary procedure, and to make it available to staff through incorporation in an employee handbook or inclusion among the various pieces of information that now have to be given to all new starters within two months of the beginning of their employment (see Chapter 5). If no such document exists, or if a dismissal has been carried out without adopting these procedures, the organisation will lose credibility in the eyes of a tribunal, and may not be seen to have acted 'reasonably'. Ex-employees could also quite honestly claim that they did not know what the procedure was and were put at a disadvantage as a result.

In practice, most organisations base their written procedures on that outlined in the ACAS advisory handbook entitled *Discipline at Work*, although they may adapt it to meet local needs. In particular, the list of offences considered to be acts of 'gross misconduct' may be extended to cover the particular circumstances of the organisation concerned.

Other documents that it is important to draw up correctly are any letters sent to the employee prior to his or her dismissal. Here again there is a need to be able to demonstrate that the employee was made fully aware of his or her rights and of the consequences of future actions, and had been issued with clear warnings. The same is true in cases of ill-health and in many of the occurrences that fall under the heading 'some other substantial reason'. It is necessary not only to keep employees informed of their rights and obligations, but to be able to prove that this occurred and thus that any dismissal was carried out with procedural fairness. To that end, employers are well advised to write to employees after any meeting or formal hearing, stating the outcome and the reasons for any decisions taken. Above all, there is a need for clarity so that there is no room for debate later about what was said. If the warning is final, it is vital that the letter confirming the outcome of the hearing states that such is the case.

In the ACAS handbook covering discipline there is an appendix that contains a number of example letters on which it is suggested employers base correspondence with employees who either are under threat of dismissal or have been dismissed. In each case the right to appeal is stressed and explained, as is the right to representation at any formal hearing. A suggested letter to be sent to doctors is also included for adaptation in cases of ill-health. In the case of formal letters to employees, it is good practice to send two copies and to ask the member of staff concerned to sign one, stating that they have received it and understood its contents, before returning it. There is then no possibility of an employee's claiming later that no correspondence was received.

A further consideration to bear in mind is the right of tribunal applicants to 'discovery and inspection' of documentary evidence. This means that, in preparing their case, they have a right not only to ask only what documents exist but also to see any that are relevant, and to take copies. Where confidential matters are included, the tribunal chairman is given the disputed papers and makes a judgment as to whether or not they should be made available to the applicant. For this reason, care must be taken in compiling minutes of any meetings or hearings that took place, to ensure that their content is clear and not readily misinterpreted.

NOTICE PERIODS

One of the classes of information that has to be provided for all employees within two months of their start-date is the period of notice that they have to give their employer when they resign and which they can expect to receive if dismissed. This is not simply a matter for the contract of employment, because there are also minimum notice periods required by statute (Employment Rights Act 1996) linked to an employee's length of service:

- Continuous service of between four weeks and two years entitles the employee to a minimum of one week's notice.

- Continuous service of between two and 12 years entitles the employee to one week's notice for each completed year.

- After 12 years' continuous service the minimum notice period remains 12 weeks.

These limits apply wherever no specific mention of notice periods is made in contracts of employment. However, if the contract specifies longer (eg 12 weeks for everyone), then that overrides the statutory minimum and must be given, whatever the circumstances of the case. It is interesting to note that employees voluntarily resigning are required to give only a week's notice where no separate contractual agreement has been made.

There are two situations in which an employer can summarily dismiss an employee without notice. The first is where the dismissal results from gross misconduct of the kind discussed above. The second is where the employee has acted in such a way as to have effectively 'repudiated' the contract of employment. In most cases, these two categories overlap, but there are situations in which courts have found repudiation to have occurred even though it could not be said that the employee concerned had committed an act of gross misconduct. Examples include a sportswriter who publicly criticised his employers at a press conference, and a shop steward who made unauthorised use of a password to enter a colleague's computer.

In practice of course, with the exception of redundancies, most dismissals are intended to take immediate effect. Employees are thus not required to work the notice to which they are entitled. What usually happens is that employees are offered 'pay in lieu of notice', a lump sum covering the number of weeks to which they are entitled. The law accepts such payments as marking the end of the contractual employment relationship, and judges their receipt by employees as marking the effective date of termination.

In the case of more senior jobs, perhaps where the individuals employed have access to sensitive or confidential commercial inform-ation, it is not in the employer's interest to dismiss with pay in lieu of notice. To do so would immediately free the individual concerned of all contractual obligation and permit him or her to take up a post with a competitor within a few days or weeks of the dismissal. For jobs where this situation could arise, employers insert into the original contract of employment a clause that gives them the option of requiring the dismissed employee to take 'garden leave'. In practice this means that the employee, once dismissed, remains on the pay-roll during the period of notice but is not required to undertake any work. Instead he or she is expected to stay at home (gardening or undertaking some other pastime – hence the above expression) until the period of notice has been completed. Often this occurs where the employees concerned have held very senior positions and have been entitled to six or 12 months' notice.

UNFAIR DISMISSAL CLAIMS

As was mentioned in the introduction to this chapter, it is not at all unusual for organisations to have unfair dismissal cases launched against them by aggrieved ex-employees. The cost to the individuals concerned is very low, so they may feel that they have nothing to lose and everything to gain by bringing an action. At the very least, many hope to receive something by way of an out-of-court settlement, even where their case is comparatively weak.

Dismissed employees are required to make a claim in writing to the secretary of tribunals via their regional tribunal office. In cases of alleged unfair dismissal, the application must be received by the office within three months of the effective date of termination, and in most cases a standard form – IT1 – is used to launch a claim. The tribunal officer then sends a copy of this form to the employer, who is required to issue a 'notice of appearance' within 14 days. Although a further form is provided for this purpose – IT3 – the employer is free to reply by letter. A notice of appearance states whether the claim is to be contested, and, if so, on what grounds. At this stage, all that is required is a brief statement of which statutory provisions form the basis of the defence, and not a detailed statement describing events surrounding the dismissal. That said, the notice of application is significant because, once completed, the grounds of any defence cannot easily be changed.

The next stage involves the setting of a date for the hearing and the preparation of cases. In many circumstances this will be preceded by 'pleadings' in which the two parties exchange documents and submit written evidence to the tribunal. The purpose is to clarify beforehand the issues about which there is a dispute, so as to reduce the length of time the hearing actually takes. Where the crux of the matter is clear and the issues in dispute straightforward, tribunals will proceed to a hearing without need for lengthy pleadings.

In practice, most cases brought never get so far as a hearing, either because they are withdrawn or because they are settled out of court beforehand. Intervention from officers employed by ACAS facilitates most withdrawals and settlements, making their role crucial to the way the system operates. The conciliation arm of ACAS becomes involved as a result of its statutory duty to seek settlements between parties before cases are formally presented before a tribunal. All IT1 applications and 'notices of appearance' are copied to ACAS, together with other relevant documents, to allow officers to judge the prospects of reaching such a settlement. Where they decide to proceed, they contact the parties, review the strength of the respective cases, and then either advise one party to withdraw or seek to negotiate a financial settlement. Of the cases received by ACAS for conciliation, fewer than a third actually go on to a full tribunal hearing. Where agreement between the parties is reached in this way, it is deemed binding in law only where it has been confirmed in writing. ACAS provide a COT3 form for this purpose.

QUALIFICATIONS AND REMEDIES

All those who have been employed by the organisation from which they are dismissed for a period of two years or more have the right not to be unfairly dismissed, and are therefore able to bring a tribunal case against their former employers. There are a few exceptions (eg people over the normal retiring age, crown employees, some domestic servants) but, in most cases, provided the individual is an employee and not a self-employed contractor, the same statutory rights apply. There is also a need to have been employed continuously for two years without contractual breaks. However, where the reason for dismissal is one of those classed as 'automatically unfair', there is usually no two-year qualifying period.

In cases of unfair dismissal, where a tribunal finds in favour of an employee, a number of options is open to it by way of remedy. First, it can require that the applicant is re-employed either in the same position (re-instatement) or in a comparable one (re-engagement). However, in practice, this occurs in only a handful of cases, because the vast majority seek compensation. In determining the sum the applicant is to receive, tribunals make two distinct calculations: the basic award and the compensatory award. The first is calculated in the same way as a redundancy payment (see Chapter 13), taking into account the salary level and the length of service of the individual concerned. To this is added the compensatory award, which seeks to take account of losses sustained by the employee as a result of the dismissal. At present there is a ceiling of £6,300 on basic awards and £11,300 on compensatory awards, meaning that in straightforward cases of unfair dismissal the maximum that a tribunal can award is £17,600, taking both awards together.

The two-year qualifying period, together with the statutory maximum payments, has been criticised on the grounds that it tips the balance of justice heavily in favour of the employer. Prior to the Employment Act 1980, the qualifying period was only six months. Thereafter it was increased, first, to one year and then to two. However, the reasons for these measures were (and remain) controversial. Aside from a general attachment to deregulation and to the idea that employment contracts should be freely and individually negotiated, the two main reasons given were as follows:

- the belief that less than two years was too short a period of time for employers to determine whether they wished to employ someone over the long term

- the belief that employment protection legislation increased unemployment by acting as a deterrent to employers' considering the employment of new staff.

In both cases, it was concern for the needs of small and growing businesses that most appears to have influenced government thinking (Davies and Friedland 1993: 561).

Despite these arguments, many disagree with the qualifying period and maximum penalties. It can thus be expected that campaigns to change the law in these areas will continue to be run.

What is your view about these issues? What effect would a return to the pre-1980 regulations have for your organisation?

The act of dismissal

There is no definite right or wrong way to inform people that they are being dismissed, because the circumstances of each case are very different. In cases of gross misconduct, the news may well come as a shock to some employees whereas, in other cases, where a lengthy procedure has been followed, the response is more likely to be anguish. Employees may become abusive, but such cases are relatively rare.

Whatever the circumstances, this is a difficult and cheerless task. Some of the general rules to follow are these:

• Prepare for the meeting at which the dismissal is to take place very thoroughly.

• Be certain of the facts of the case and the precise reasons the decision to dismiss has been arrived at.

• Organise practical matters such as pay in lieu of notice before the meeting takes place.

• Consider in advance the likely reaction of the individual and prepare an appropriate response.

• Talk to employees concerned firmly but sympathetically. It is important that they understand that the decision is final, but they should be given as much practical assistance in planning for their future as is possible. Where the services of outplacement specialists would be helpful, consider offering these.

• Wherever possible, avoid the need for employees to leave immediately. There is nothing more humiliating and liable to cause ill-feeling than being frog-marched off the premises like a criminal when there is no intention on employees' part of causing damage or removing company property.

WRONGFUL DISMISSAL

In some situations employees who do not qualify for unfair dismissal rights or who believe they should receive more by way of compensation than is permitted under unfair dismissal law can choose instead to sue their ex-employers for damages under the law of wrongful dismissal. Until 1994 such cases could be heard in the civil courts only, requiring considerable expenditure on the part of the applicant. However, since then jurisdiction over claims worth up to £25,000 has passed to industrial tribunals, making the wrongful dismissal route more attractive.

Cases of wrongful dismissal differ from those of unfair dismissal in that they do not rely on statute. The question of how reasonably an employer has acted is thus not at issue. What matters is whether or not the dismissal contravened the terms of the employee's contract of employment. The court is thus asked to rule whether the employer was entitled to dismiss the employee for a particular reason in the way that occurred, given the nature of the particular contractual terms agreed.

There are two situations in which someone who has been dismissed might choose to sue for wrongful rather than unfair dismissal. The first is where the employee, for whatever reason, does not have the protection of unfair dismissal law. This might apply to people with less than two year's service, people whose continuity of employment has been temporarily broken and people over the age of 65. Secondly, it might apply in cases where the damages that could be gained might reasonably be expected to exceed those likely to be offered as an unfair dismissal award. An example would be a highly paid person who was summarily dismissed and whose contract entitles him or her to three months' notice.

However, no claim of wrongful dismissal can be successful unless the terms of the contract of employment have been breached by the employer. In practice, this can happen very easily, because many employers explicitly incorporate disciplinary procedures into all contracts. In some cases, it is the contents of an employee rulebook or staff handbook that are incorporated, in others it is the terms of collective agreements with trade unions. Often these documents include lists of offences that may be considered to constitute gross misconduct, rules for selecting people for redundancy and details of ACAS-type disciplinary procedures. Where that is the case, any employee, whether or not he or she has two years' continuous service between the ages of 20 and 64, can expect the terms of the contract to be honoured. If he or she is then dismissed in contravention of those terms, there is a possibility that there will be a sound case under wrongful dismissal law.

BEST PRACTICE

As has been shown, in most situations best practice in the field of dismissal is effectively defined by law. It is thus only at the margins that employers seeking to implement 'best practice' approaches across all fields of employee-resourcing activity can improve on the legal requirements as far as procedure is concerned. Perhaps the only major area where improvement can be made is in applying the same principles to all employees regardless of length of service or age. In making it clear that *everyone* will be treated according to the ACAS code from the very start of their employment, an employer extends the principles of natural justice to all, and could claim to be going as far as it is possible to go in treating employees fairly when conduct or capability are in need of improvement.

That said, best practice in dismissal should not be concerned just with procedural matters – the manner in which the procedures are operated is also important. Employers could therefore look at improving the training of managers in these fields, at the clarity of documentation and at ways of improving the investigation stage of any enquiry.

Moreover, in the field of dismissals on account of ill health there is a number of improvements that can be made on the statutory requirements. Here it is a question of handling matters sensitively and seeking to give as much practical and financial assistance as is possible. No employer who terminates contracts in these circumstances without making appropriate and adequate provision for a sick employee's future, either through a pension scheme or other funds, can reasonably claim to be operating 'best practice'.

FURTHER READING

- The starting-point for any further reading on the topics covered in this chapter are the relevant ACAS advisory handbooks *Discipline at Work* (1987) and *Absence* (1988).

- There are many books on the market that offer a layman's guide to unfair dismissal law. A good starting-point is *Employment Law* by Deborah Lockton (1997). Lynda Macdonald's *Hired, Fired or Sick and Tired* (1995), though intended for employees, is a useful guide for managers, too. It contains hundreds of examples of cases that have come to court, to illustrate key legal principles.

- The following CIPD books should be consulted: *The Disciplinary Interview* by Alan Fowler (1998), *Dismissal* by Hammond Suddards Edge (1999) and *Managing Redundancy* by Alan Fowler (1999).

- *Principles of Employment Law* by Michael Jefferson (1997) is more technical but also very comprehensive in its treatment of dismissal issues.

- The law in this field develops at a fair pace, often rendering books more than year or two old out of date. Readers are therefore advised to turn also to journals for details of new legislation and case-law. *IDS Brief* and *IRS Industrial Relations Law Bulletin* regularly include guidance-notes focusing on key legal issues geared for practitioners rather than lawyers. Recent examples relevant to this chapter include the following:

IDS Brief 593 (1997a):	*Disloyalty Dismissals*
IDS Brief 594 (1997b):	*Gross Misconduct*
IRS IR Law Bulletin 530 (1995c):	*Sickness Absence*
IRS IR Law Bulletin 549 (1996c):	*Wrongful Dismissal*
IRS IR Law Bulletin 570 (1997c):	*Misconduct Dismissals*

- *IRS Employment Trends* contained in issues 591 and 592 (1995) the results of an interesting and informative survey of disciplinary practices in 50 UK organisations.

References

ACAS (1985) *Labour Turnover.* London. ACAS.

ACAS (1987) *Discipline at Work: The ACAS advisory handbook.* London. ACAS.

ACAS (1988) *Absence.* London. ACAS.

AIKIN, O (1997) *Contracts.* London. IPD.

ALLEN, C *and* TORRINGTON, D (1996) 'It all depends on your frame of reference: a study of absence', in A McGoldrick (ed.): *Cases in Human Resource Management.* London. Pitman.

ANDERSON, G (1992) 'Performance appraisal', in B Towers (ed.): *The Handbook of Human Resource Management.* Oxford. Blackwell.

ANDERSON, N *and* SHACKLETON, V (1993) *Successful Selection Interviewing.* Oxford. Blackwell.

ANDERSON, N *and* SHACKLETON, V (1994) 'Informed choices'. *Personnel Today* (8 November).

ARMSTRONG, M (1995) *A Handbook of Personnel Management Practice.* Fifth Edition. London. Kogan Page.

ARMSTRONG, M (1996) *Employee Reward.* London. IPD.

ARMSTRONG, M and BARON, A (1998) *Performance Management: The new realities.* London, IPD.

ATKINSON, J (1984) 'Manpower strategies for the flexible organisation'. *Personnel Management* (August).

ATWATER, L, PENN, R *and* RUCKER (1991) 'Personal qualities of charismatic leaders'. *Leadership and Organisation Development Journal* (12 December).

BADARACCO, J *and* WEBB, A (1995) 'Business ethics: a view from the trenches'. *California Management Review* (Winter).

BALCOMBE, J (1997) Quoted in Industrial Society (1997).

BARBAGELATA, H (1985) 'Different categories of workers and labour contracts', in R Blanpain (ed.): *Comparative Labour Law and Industrial Relations.* London. Kluwer.

BARTHOLOMEW, D J (ed.) (1971) *Manpower Planning: Selected readings.* London. Penguin.

BASS, B M (1990) 'From transactional to transformational leadership: learning to share the vision'. *Organizational Dynamics* (Winter). Also reprinted in R M Steers, L W Porter and G A Bigley (eds): *Motivation and Leadership at Work* (1996). Sixth Edition. Singapore. McGraw-Hill.

BEAUMONT, P B (1993) *Human Resource Management: Key concepts and skills.* London. Sage.

BEER, M (1985) 'Note on performance appraisal', in M Beer and B

Spector (eds): *Readings in Human Resource Management.* New York. Free Press.

BEER, M *and* RUH, R (1976) 'Employee growth through performance management'. *Harvard Business Review* (July/August).

BRAMHAM, J (1987) 'Manpower planning', in S Harper (ed.): *Personnel Management Handbook.* London. Gower.

BRAMHAM, J (1988) *Practical Manpower Planning.* Fourth Edition. London. IPM.

BRAMHAM, J (1994) *Human Resource Planning.* Second edition. London. IPD.

BREWSTER, C, HEGEWISCH, A, LOCKHART, T *and* MAYNE, L (1993) *Flexible Working Patterns in Europe.* London. IPM.

BRIDGES, W (1995) *Jobshift: How to prosper in a workplace without jobs.* London. Nicholas Brealey.

BROWN, G (1993) 'Finding new employees for high reliability operations', in D Gowler, K Legge and C Clegg (eds): *Case Studies in Organisational Behaviour and Human Resource Management.* London. Paul Chapman.

BUCHANAN, D (1982) 'High performance: new boundaries of acceptability in worker control', in J Hurrell and C Cooper (eds): *Job Control and Worker Health.* Chichester. John Wiley.

BURTON, N (1996) *The Retention and Turnover of D-Grade Nurses.* Unpublished MSc Dissertation. Manchester. UMIST.

BYRON, M *and* MODHA, S (1991) *How to Pass Selection Tests.* London. Kogan Page.

BYRON, M *and* MODHA, S (1993) *Technical Selection Tests and How to Pass Them.* London. Kogan Page.

CARRELL, M R, ELBERT, N F *and* HATFIELD, R D (1995) *Human Resource Management: Global strategies for managing a diverse workforce.* Fifth Edition. New Jersey. Prentice Hall.

CERIELLO, V *with* FREEMAN, C (1991) *Human Resource Management Systems: Strategies, tactics and techniques.* New York. Lexington.

CHERRINGTON, D J (1989) *Organisational Behaviour: The management of individual and organisational performance.* Boston and London. Allyn and Bacon.

CONFEDERATION OF BRITISH INDUSTRY (1997) *Managing Absence in Sickness and in Health.* London. CBI.

COOK, M (1993) *Personnel Selection and Productivity.* Second Edition. Chichester. John Wiley.

COOPER, D *and* ROBERTSON, I (1995) *The Psychology of Personnel Selection.* London. Routledge.

COURTIS, J (1985) *The IPM Guide to Cost-Effective Recruiting.* London. IPM.

COURTIS, J (1989) *Recruiting for Profit.* London. IPM.

COURTIS, J (1994) *Recruitment Advertising: Right first time.* London. IPD.

COWLING, A *and* WALTERS, M (1990) 'Manpower planning: where are we today?' *Personnel Review* (19 March).

DALY, N (1996) 'Staff sit in on top job interviews'. *Personnel Today* (16 July).

DAVIES, P *and* FRIEDLAND, M (1993) *Labour Legislation and Public Policy.* Oxford. Clarendon Press.

DAVISON, J *and* REES MOGG, W (1997) *The Sovereign Individual: The coming revolution, how to survive and prosper in it.* London. Macmillan.

DE WITTE, K (1989) 'Recruiting and advertising', in P Herriot (ed.): *Assessment and Selection in Organisations.* Chichester. John Wiley.

DEPARTMENT OF EMPLOYMENT (1971) *Company Manpower Planning.* London. HMSO.

DEPARTMENT OF EMPLOYMENT (1987) *Employer's Labour Use Survey.* London. HMSO.

DICKEN, P (1992) *Global Shift: The internationalisation of economic activity.* Second Edition. London. Paul Chapman.

DOBSON, P (1989) 'Reference reports', in P Herriot (ed.): *Handbook of Assessment in Organisations.* Chichester. John Wiley.

DONALDSON, L (1995) 'A criminal waste'. *Personnel Today* (February). p 45.

DONKIN, R (1997) 'Self employment: predictions of the portfolio career are wide of the mark'. *Financial Times* (8 October).

DOUGLAS PHILLIPS, J (1990) 'The price-tag on turnover'. *Personnel Journal.* (December).

DOWNS, S (1989) 'Job sample and trainability tests', in P Herriot (ed.): *Handbook of Assessment in Organisations.* Chichester. John Wiley.

DRAKELEY, R (1989) 'Biographical data', in P Herriot (ed.): *Handbook of Assessment in Organisations.* Chichester. John Wiley.

EDER, R and FERRIS, G (eds) (1989) *The Employment Interview: Theory, research and practice.* Newbury Park, California. Sage.

EDWARDS, J (1983) 'Models of manpower stocks and flows', in J Edwards *et al* (eds): *Manpower Planning: Strategy and techniques in an organisational context.* Chichester. John Wiley.

EDWARDS P and SCULLION, H (1984) 'Absenteeism and the control of work'. *Sociological Review* (31 March).

EDWARDS, P and WHITSTON, C (1989) *The Control of Absenteeism: An interim report.* Warwick Papers in Industrial Relations (23).

EDWARDS P and WHITSTON, C (1993) *Attending to Work: The management of attendance and shopfloor order.* Oxford. Blackwell.

ELLIOTT, R and MURLIS, H (1996) 'The state of the art in the public sector', in H Murlis (ed.): *Pay at the Crossroads.* London. IPD.

EQUAL OPPORTUNITIES COMMISSION (1986) *Fair and Efficient: Guidance on equal opportunities policies in recruitment and selection procedures.* Manchester. EOC.

FAIR, H (1992) *Personnel and Profit: The pay-off from people.* London. IPM.

FARNHAM, D (1995) *The Corporate Environment.* Second Edition. London. IPD.

FINE, S and GETKATE, M (1995) *Benchmark Tasks for Job Analysis.* New Jersey. Lawrence Erlbaum.

FLETCHER, C (1991) 'Personality tests: the great debate'. *Personnel Management* (September).

FLETCHER, C (1997) *Appraisal: Routes to improved performance.* Second Edition. London. IPD.

FLOOD, P, GANNON, M and PAAUWE, J (1995) *Managing without*

Traditional Methods: International innovations in human resource management. Wokingham. Addison Wesley.

FOWLER, A (1993) *Redundancy.* London. IPM.

FOWLER, A (1996a) *Employee Induction: A good start.* Third Edition. London. IPD.

FOWLER, A (1996b) 'How to conduct disciplinary interviews'. *People Management* (November).

FOWLER, A (1996c) *Negotiation: Skills and strategies.* Second Edition. London. IPD.

FOWLER, A (1998) *The Disciplinary Interview.* London, IPD.

FOWLER, A (1999) *Managing Redundancy.* London, IPD.

FRECHETTE, H *and* WERTHEIM, E G (1985) 'Performance appraisal', in W R Tracey (ed.): *Human Resources Management and Development Handbook.* New York. Amacom.

GARNJOST, P *and* BLETTNER, K (1996) 'Cutting labour costs without redundancies', in J Storey (ed.): *Blackwell Cases in Human Resource and Change Management.* Oxford. Blackwell.

GENNARD, J (1992) 'Industrial relations and technological change', in B Towers (ed.): *A Handbook of Industrial Relations Practice.* Third Edition. London. Kogan Page.

GENNARD, J *and* JUDGE, G (1997) *Employee Relations.* London. IPD.

GILLEN, T (1995) *Positive Influencing Skills.* London. IPD.

GOODWORTH, C (1979) *Effective Interviewing for Employment Selection.* London. Hutchinson.

GREENHALGH, R (1995) *Industrial Tribunals.* Second Edition. London. IPD.

HACKETT, P (1995) *The Selection Interview.* London. IPD.

HADDOCK, C *and* SOUTH, B (1994) 'How Shell's organisation and HR practices help it be both global and local', in D Torrington (ed.): *International Human Resource Management: Think globally, act locally.* London. Prentice Hall.

HAKIM, C (1990) 'Core and periphery in employers' workforce strategies: evidence from the 1987 E.L.U.S. survey'. *Work, Employment and Society* (4 February).

HAMMOND SUDDARDS EDGE (1999) *Dismissal.* London, IPD.

HANDY, C (1989) *The Age of Unreason.* London. Business Books.

HANDY, C (1994) *The Empty Raincoat: Making sense of the future.* London. Hutchinson.

HARRISON, R (1997) *Employee Development.* London. IPD.

HARVARD BUSINESS REVIEW (1990) *Manage People, Not Personnel.* Boston, Massachusetts. Harvard Business School.

HARVEY, J *and* NICHOLSON, N (1993) 'Incentives and penalties as a means of influencing attendance: a study in the UK public sector'. *International Journal of Human Resource Management* (4 April).

HENDRY, C (1994) *Human Resource Strategies for International Growth.* London. Routledge.

HERCUS, T (1992) 'Human resource planning in eight British organisations: a Canadian perspective', in B Towers (ed.): *The Handbook of Human Resource Management.* Oxford. Blackwell.

HERRIOT, P (ed.) (1989) *A Handbook of Assessment in Organisations.* Chichester. John Wiley.

HERZBERG, F (1966) *Work and the Nature of Man.* Cleveland. World Publishing.

HERZBERG, F (1968) 'One more time: how do you motivate employees?' *Harvard Business Review* (January-February).

HOBBY, J (1995) 'Farewell notes'. *Personnel Today* (July).

HOFSTEDE, G (1980) *Culture's Consequences: International differences in work-related values.* Beverley Hills, California. Sage.

HOFSTEDE, G (1991) *Cultures and Organisations: Software of the mind.* London. McGraw-Hill.

HOLT, B (1994) 'Benchmarking comes to HR'. *Personnel Management* (June).

HOM, P *and* GRIFFETH, R (1995) *Employee Turnover.* Cincinnati. South Western.

HUCZYNSKI, A *and* FITZPATRICK, M (1989) *Managing Employee Absence for a Competitive Edge.* London. Pitman.

HUDDART, G (1995) 'A whole new ball game'. *Personnel Today* (January).

INCOMES DATA SERVICES (1989) 'Labour turnover'. *IDS Focus 51* (June). London. IDS.

ILES, P *and* SALAMAN, G (1995) 'Recruitment, selection and assessment', in J Storey (ed.): *Human Resource Management: A critical text.* London. Routledge.

INCOMES DATA SERVICES (1990) 'Industry links with schools'. *IDS Study 456* (April). London. IDS.

INCOMES DATA SERVICES (1991) *Retirement: Employment Law Supplement 61.* London. IDS.

INCOMES DATA SERVICES (1992a) 'Controlling absence'. *IDS Study 498* (January). London. IDS.

INCOMES DATA SERVICES (1992b) 'Managing redundancy'. *IDS Study 511* (August). London. IDS.

INCOMES DATA SERVICES (1992c) 'Performance management'. *IDS Study 518* (November). London. IDS.

INCOMES DATA SERVICES (1992d) *Recruitment: Employment Law Supplement 64.* London. IDS.

INCOMES DATA SERVICES (1993) 'Performance appraisal for manual workers'. *IDS Study 543* (December). London. IDS.

INCOMES DATA SERVICES (1994a) 'Absence and sick pay policies'. *IDS Study 556* (June). London. IDS.

INCOMES DATA SERVICES (1994b) 'Employee competition and confidentiality'. *Employment Law Supplement 72.* London. IDS.

INCOMES DATA SERVICES (1994c) 'Graduates'. *IDS Focus 71* (August). London. IDS.

INCOMES DATA SERVICES (1994d) 'Staff turnover'. *IDS Report 661* (March). London. IDS.

INCOMES DATA SERVICES (1995a) 'Appraisal systems'. *IDS Study 576* (April). London. IDS.

INCOMES DATA SERVICES (1995b) 'Assessment centres'. *IDS Study 569* (January). London. IDS.

INCOMES DATA SERVICES (1995c) 'The jobs mythology'. *IDS Focus 74* (March). London. IDS.

INCOMES DATA SERVICES (1995d) 'Large scale recruitment'. *IDS Study*

581 (July). London. IDS.

INCOMES DATA SERVICES (1995e) 'Managing labour turnover'. *IDS Study 577* (May). London. IDS.

INCOMES DATA SERVICES (1995f) 'Redundancy terms'. *IDS Study 586* (September). London. IDS.

INCOMES DATA SERVICES (1996) 'Older workers'. *IDS Study 595* (February). London. IDS.

INCOMES DATA SERVICES (1997a) 'Disloyalty dismissals'. *IDS Brief 593* (July). London. IDS.

INCOMES DATA SERVICES (1997b) 'Gross misconduct'. *IDS Brief 594* (August). London. IDS.

INCOMES DATA SERVICES (1997c) 'Performance management'. *IDS Study 626* (May). London. IDS.

INCOMES DATA SERVICES/INSTITUTE OF PERSONNEL AND DEVELOPMENT (1995) *Contracts and Terms and Conditions of Employment.* London. IPD.

INDUSTRIAL RELATIONS SERVICES (1990) 'Succession planning'. *Recruitment and Development Report* (2) (February).

INDUSTRIAL RELATIONS SERVICES (1994a) 'Improving performance? A survey of appraisal arrangements'. *Employment Trends 556* (March).

INDUSTRIAL RELATIONS SERVICES (1994b) 'Non-standard working under review'. *Employment Trends 565* (August).

INDUSTRIAL RELATIONS SERVICES (1994c) 'Performance appraisal assessed'. *Employment Trends 559* (May).

INDUSTRIAL RELATIONS SERVICES (1994d) 'Sick pay trends, absence control developments and the impact of SSP changes'. *Employment Trends 569* (October).

INDUSTRIAL RELATIONS SERVICES (1994c) 'Sickness absence monitoring and control: a survey of practice'. *Employment Trends 568* (September).

INDUSTRIAL RELATIONS SERVICES (1995a) 'Discipline at work – the practice'. *Employment Trends 591* (September).

INDUSTRIAL RELATIONS SERVICES (1995b) 'Early retirement survey 2: redundancy and employee's request'. *Employment Trends 582* (April).

INDUSTRIAL RELATIONS SERVICES (1995c) 'Sickness absence'. *IRS Industrial Relations Law Bulletin 530* (October).

INDUSTRIAL RELATIONS SERVICES (1996a) 'Benchmarking and managing labour turnover'. *Employee Development Bulletin* (March).

INDUSTRIAL RELATIONS SERVICES (1996b) 'Early retirement'. *Employment Trends 622* (December).

INDUSTRIAL RELATIONS SERVICES (1996c) 'Wrongful dismissal'. *IRS Industrial Relations Law Bulletin 549* (July).

INDUSTRIAL RELATIONS SERVICES (1997a) 'Benchmarking labour turnover: an update'. *Employee Development Bulletin* (March),

INDUSTRIAL RELATIONS SERVICES (1997b) 'The changing nature of the employment contract'. *Employment Trends 635* (July).

INDUSTRIAL RELATIONS SERVICES (1997c) 'Misconduct dismissals'. *IRS Industrial Relations Law Bulletin 570* (June).

INDUSTRIAL RELATIONS SERVICES (1997d) 'The state of selection: an IRS survey'. *Employee Development Bulletin 85* (January).

INDUSTRIAL SOCIETY (1997) *Managing Best Practice: Maximising attendance*. London. Industrial Society.

INSTITUTE OF PERSONNEL AND DEVELOPMENT (1992) *Performance Management in the UK: An analysis of the issues*. London. IPD.

INSTITUTE OF PERSONNEL AND DEVELOPMENT (1996a) *Guide on Recruitment*. London. IPD.

INSTITUTE OF PERSONNEL AND DEVELOPMENT (1996b) *Guide on Redundancy*. London. IPD.

INSTITUTE OF PERSONNEL AND DEVELOPMENT (1997a) *Guide on Psychological Testing*. London. IPD.

INSTITUTE OF PERSONNEL AND DEVELOPMENT (1997b) 'Key facts: redundancy'. *People Management* (February).

INSTITUTE OF PERSONNEL MANAGEMENT (1992) *Statement on Human Resource Planning*. London. IPM.

INSTITUTE OF PERSONNEL MANAGEMENT (1993) *Flexible Working Patterns in Europe*. London. IPM.

JACKSON, C (1996) *Understanding Psychological Testing*. Leicester. British Psychological Society.

JACKSON, S E *and* SCHULER, R S (1990) 'Human resource planning: challenges for industrial/organisational psychologists'. *American Psychologist*. Vol. 45. Reprinted in G R Ferris and M R Buckley (eds): *Human Resources Management: Perspectives, Context, Functions and Outcomes*. 1996. Third Edition. Englewood Cliffs. New Jersey. Prentice Hall.

JAMES, P *and* LEWIS, D (1992) *Discipline*. London. IPM.

JANSEN, P *and* DE JONGH, F (1997) *Assessment Centres: A practical handbook*. Chichester. John Wiley.

JEFFERSON, M (1997) *Principles of Employment Law*. Third Edition. London. Cavendish.

JENKINS, J (1983) 'Management trainees in retailing', in B Ungerson (ed.): *Recruitment Handbook*. Aldershot. Gower.

JOHNS, G *and* NICHOLSON, N (1982) 'The meaning of absence: new strategies for theory and research', in B Straw and L Cummings (eds): *Research in Organisational Behaviour*. London. JAI Press.

KALINAUCKAS, P *and* KING, H (1994) *Coaching: Realising the potential*. London. IPD.

KEARNS, P (1994) 'Measuring the effectiveness of the personnel function'. *IRS Employment Trends 564*.

KELLER, R T (1983) 'Predicting absenteeism from prior absenteeism: attitudinal factors and non-attitudinal factors'. *Journal of Applied Psychology* (68.3).

KENT, S (1996) 'Ready to recruit?' *Personnel Today* (June).

KINNIE, N *and* ARTHURS, A (1993) 'Will personnel people ever learn to love the computer?' *Personnel Management* (June).

KIRNAN, J, FARLEY, J *and* GEISINGER, K (1989) 'The relationship between recruiting source, applicant quality and hire performance: an analysis by sex, ethnicity and age'. *Personnel Psychology*. Vol. 42.

LEAP, T *and* CRINO, M (1993) *Personnel/Human Resource Management.* Second Edition. New York. Macmillan.

LEGERE, C L J (1985) 'Occupational analysis', in W R Tracey (ed.): *Human Resources Management and Development Handbook.* New York. AMACOM.

LEVINSON, H (1973) 'Asinine attitudes toward motivation'. *Harvard Business Review* (January-February).

LEVINSON, H (1976) 'Appraisal of what performance?' *Harvard Business Review* (July/August).

LEWIS, P (1993) *The Successful Management of Redundancy.* Oxford. Blackwell.

LEWIS, R D (1996) *When Cultures Collide: Managing successfully across cultures.* London. Nicholas Brealey.

LING SING CHEE (1994) 'Singapore Airlines: strategic human resource initiatives', in D Torrington (ed.): *International Human Resource Management: Think globally, act locally.* London. Prentice Hall.

LIVY, B (1988) 'Personnel recruitment and selection methods', in B Livy (ed.): *Corporate Personnel Management.* London. Pitman.

LOCKTON, D (1997) *Employment Law.* Second Edition. London. Macmillan.

LONG, P (1981) *Retirement: Planned liberation?* London. IPM.

LONGENECKER, C O, SIMS, H P *and* GIOIA, D A (1987) 'Behind the mask: the politics of employee appraisal'. *American Academy of Management Executive.* Reprinted in G R Ferris and M R Buckley (eds): *Human Resources Management: Perspectives, context, functions and outcomes.* 1996. Third Edition. Englewood Cliffs. New Jersey. Prentice Hall.

LOVERIDGE, R *and* MOK, A (1979) *Theories of Labour Market Segmentation: A critique.* The Hague. Martinus Nijhoff.

MACDONALD, L (1995) *Hired Fired or Sick and Tired.* London. Nicholas Brealey.

MACGREGOR, D (1957) 'An uneasy look at performance appraisal'. *Harvard Business Review* (May-June).

MACGREGOR, D (1960) *The Human Side of Enterprise.* New York. McGraw-Hill.

MAKIN, P, COOPER, C *and* COX, C (1989) *Managing People at Work.* Leicester. British Psychological Society/Routledge.

MARCHINGTON, M *and* WILKINSON, A (1996) *Core Personnel and Development.* London. IPD.

MARSH, C (1991) *Hours of Work of Women and Men in Britain.* Manchester. Equal Opportunities Commission.

McGARVEY, R *and* SMITH, S (1993) 'When workers rate the boss'. *Training Magazine* (March). Reprinted in G R Ferris and M R Buckley (eds): *Human Resources Management: Perspectives, Context, Functions and Outcomes.* 1996. Third Edition. Englewood Cliffs. New Jersey. Prentice Hall.

McGREGOR, A *and* SPROULL, A (1992) 'Employers and the flexible workforce'. *Employment Gazette* (May).

McHENRY, R (1997) 'The secrets of making staff work harder'. *Personnel Management* (July).

MEYER, H H, KAY, E *and* FRENCH J R P (1965) 'Split roles in performance appraisal'. *Harvard Business Review* (January-February).

MICKLETHWAIT, J and WOOLDRIDGE, A (1996) *The Witch Doctors.* London. Heinemann.

MINTZBERG, H (1976) 'Planning on the left-side and managing on the right'. *Harvard Business Review* (July-August).

MINTZBERG, H (1994) *The Rise and Fall of Strategic Planning.* New York. Prentice Hall.

MOBLEY, W (1977) 'Intermediate linkages in the relationship between job satisfaction and employee turnover', in R Steers and L Porter (eds): *Motivation and Work Behaviour.* 1987. New York. McGraw-Hill.

MUNRO FRASER, J (1979) *Employment Interviewing.* Plymouth. Macdonald and Evans.

MURPHY, K R and CLEVELAND, J N (1995) *Understanding Performance Appraisal: Social, organisational and goal-based perspectives.* Thousand Oaks. California. Sage.

NICHOLSON, N (1976) 'Management sanctions and absence control'. *Human Relations* (29 February).

NICHOLSON, N and JOHNS, G (1985) 'The absence culture and the psychological contract – who's in control of absence?', in R Steers and L Porter (eds): *Motivation and Work Behavior.* 1987. New York. McGraw-Hill.

NORTH, S J (1994) 'Employers turn to handwriting tests'. *Personnel Today* (December).

O'DOHERTY, D (1994) 'Towards human resource planning?', in I Beardwell and L Holden (eds): *Human Resource Management: A contemporary perspective.* London. Pitman.

O'REILLY, N (1997) 'Promotion system too complex'. *Personnel Today* (March).

PEARN, M and KANDOLA, R (1993) *Job Analysis: A manager's guide.* Second Edition. London. IPM.

PERSONNEL TODAY (1995) 'Data projection'. September.

PETERS, T (1989) *Thriving on Chaos.* London. Pan.

PETTMAN, B (1975) *Labour Turnover and Retention.* Epping. Gower.

PHILP, T (1990) *Appraising Performance for Results.* Second Edition. London. McGraw-Hill.

POLLERT, A (1987) 'The flexible firm: a model in search of a reality (or a policy in search of a practice?)' *Warwick Papers in Industrial Relations* (19). University of Warwick.

POLLERT, A (1988) 'The flexible firm: fixation or fact?' *Work, Employment and Society* (2 March).

PROKOPENKO, J (1994) 'The transition to a market economy and its implications for HRM in Eastern Europe', in P Kirkbride (ed.): *Human Resource Management In Europe: Perspectives for the 1990s.* London. Routledge.

RANDELL, G (1994) 'Employee appraisal', in K Sisson (ed.): *Personnel Management: A comprehensive guide to theory and practice in Britain.* Second Edition. Oxford. Blackwell.

REYNOLDS, P and BAILEY, M (1993) *How to Design and Deliver Retirement Training.* London. Kogan Page.

RICE, B (1985) 'Performance review: the job nobody likes'. *Psychology*

Today. Reprinted in G R Ferris and M R Buckley (eds): *Human Resources Management: Perspectives, context, functions and outcomes.* 1996. Third Edition. Englewood Cliffs. New Jersey. Prentice Hall.

RIFKIN, J (1995) *The End of Work: The decline of the global labour force and the dawn of the post-market era.* New York. Puttnam.

RITZER (1996) *The McDonaldization of society: an investigation into the changing character of contemporary social life.* Revised Edition. Thousand Oaks, California. Pine Forge.

ROBERTSON, I and MAKIN, P (1986) 'Management selection in Britain: a survey and critique'. *Journal of Occupational Psychology.* Vol. 61.

ROTHWELL, S (1995) 'Human resource planning', in J Storey (ed.): *Human Resource Management: A critical text.* London. Routledge.

ROWE, T (1986) 'Eight ways to ruin a performance review'. *Personnel Journal* (January).

SAMUEL, P J (1969) *Labour Turnover: Towards a solution.* London. IPM.

SARGENT, A (1989) *The Missing Workforce: Managing absenteeism.* London. IPM.

SHACKLETON, V and NEWELL, S (1989) 'Selection procedures in practice', in P Herriot (ed.): *Handbook of Assessment in Organisations.* Chichester. John Wiley.

SHAMIR, B (1991) 'Meaning, self and motivation in organisations'. *Organisation Studies* (12 March).

SHEA, G F (1985) 'Induction and orientation', in W R Tracey (ed.): *Human Resources Management and Development Handbook.* New York. AMACOM.

SILVER, M (1983) 'Forecasting demand for labour using labour productivity trends', in J Edwards *et al* (eds): *Manpower Planning: Strategy and techniques in an organisational context.* London. John Wiley.

SISSON, K and TIMPERLEY, S (1994) 'From manpower planning to strategic human resource management?', in K Sisson (ed.): *Personnel Management: A comprehensive guide to theory and practice in Britain.* Second Edition. Oxford. Blackwell.

SKEATS, J (1991) *Successful Induction: How to get the most from your new employees.* London. Kogan Page.

SMITH, A R (1976) 'The philosophy of manpower planning', in D J Bartholomew (ed.): *Manpower Planning.* London. Penguin.

SMITH, A R (ed.) (1980) *Corporate Manpower Planning.* London. Gower.

SMITH, K (1996) 'Managing without traditional strategic planning: the evolving role of top management teams', in P Flood *et al* (eds): *Managing without Traditional Methods: International innovations in human resource management.* Wokingham. Addison Wesley.

SMITH, M and ROBERTSON, I (1993) *The Theory and Practice of Systematic Personnel Selection.* London. Macmillan.

SMITH, M and SUTHERLAND, V (1993) *Professional Issues in Selection and Assessment.* (Vol. 1) Chichester. John Wiley.

SMITH M, GREGG M and ANDREWS D (1989) *Selection and Assessment: A new appraisal.* London. Pitman.

SPARROW, P and HILTROP, J M (1994) *European Human Resource Management in Transition.* London. Prentice Hall.

SPEECHLY, N (1994) 'Uncertainty principles'. *Personnel Today* (May).

STAINER, G (1971) *Manpower Planning*. London. Heinemann.

STEERS, R M and RHODES, S (1978) 'Major influences on employee attendance: a process model', in R Steers and L Porter (eds): *Motivation and Work Behavior*. 1987. Fourth Edition. New York. McGraw-Hill.

STEERS, R M, PORTER, L W and BIGLEY, G M (1996) *Motivation and Leadership at Work*. Sixth Edition. Singapore. McGraw-Hill.

TOPLIS, J, DULEWICZ, V and FLETCHER, C (1991) *Psychological Testing: A manager's guide*. London. IPM.

TOPLIS, J, DULEWICZ, V and FLETCHER, C (1997) *Psychological Testing: A manager's guide*. Third edition. London. IPD.

TORRINGTON, D (1994) *International Human Resource Management: Think globally, act locally*. London. Prentice Hall.

TORRINGTON, D and HALL, L (1995) *Personnel Management: HRM in action*. Third Edition. London. Prentice Hall.

TRIST, E L, HIGGIN, G W, MURRAY, H and POLLOCK, A B (1963) *Organisational Choice: Capabilities of groups at the coal face under changing technologies*. London. Tavistock.

ULRICH, D, LOSEY, M and LAKE G (eds) (1997) *Tomorrow's HR Management*. New York. John Wiley.

VAN DER MARSEN DE SOMBRIEFF, P and HOFSTEDE, W (1989) 'Personality questionnaires and inventories', in P Herriot (ed.): *A Handbook of Assessment in Organisations*. Chichester. John Wiley.

VROOM, V (1964) *Work and Motivation*. New York. John Wiley.

WALKER, L (1996) 'Instant staff for a temporary future'. *People Management* (January).

WANOUS, J P (1992) *Organizational Entry*. Reading, Massachusetts. Addison Wesley.

WARD, P (1997) *360-Degree Feedback*. London. IPD.

WATKINS, I (1994) 'Sick excuses for swanning around'. *Personnel Management* (April).

WATSON, T (1994) 'Recruitment and selection', in K Sisson (ed.): *Personnel Management: A comprehensive guide to theory and practice in Britain*. Second Edition. Oxford. Blackwell.

WES, M (1996) *Globalisation: Winners and losers*. London. Institute for Public Policy Research.

WILLS, J (1997) 'Can do better'. *Personnel Today* (June).

WOODRUFFE, C (1993) *Assessment Centres: Identifying and developing competence*. Second Edition. London. IPD.

WRIGHT, M and STOREY J (1994) 'Recruitment', in I Beardwell and L Holden (eds): *Human Resource Management: A contemporary perspective*. London. Pitman.

Index